A s i a

Shan

▲ ▲ *Bhutan*

a

DISTANT
A MOUNTAINEER'S
SNOWS
ODYSSEY

Australia

Stirlings ▲

Southern
Alps

New
Zealand

▲ *Tasmania*

DISTANT
SNOWS

DISTANT
A MOUNTAINEER'S
SNOWS
ODYSSEY

FOREWORD BY
ROBIN HANBURY-TENISON OBE

**bâton
wicks**

Published by Bâton Wicks, Sheffield.
www.v-publishing.co.uk/batonwicks

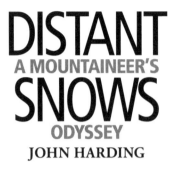

DISTANT
A MOUNTAINEER'S
SNOWS
ODYSSEY
JOHN HARDING

First published in 2016 by Bâton Wicks.

 Bâton Wicks
Crescent House, 228 Psalter Lane, Sheffield S11 8UT, UK.
www.v-publishing.co.uk/batonwicks

This book is a work of non-fiction based on the life, experiences and recollections of John Harding. In some limited cases the names of people, places, dates and sequences or the detail of events have been changed solely to protect the privacy of others. The author has stated to the publishers that, except in such minor respects not affecting the substantial accuracy of the work, the contents of the book are true.

A CIP catalogue record for this book is available from the British Library.

ISBN: 978-1-898573-78-4 (Hardback)
ISBN: 978-1-898573-79-1 (Ebook)

 Design and production by Nathan Ryder.
Vertebrate Publishing – www.v-publishing.co.uk

Bâton Wicks is committed to printing on paper from sustainable sources.

 MIX
Paper from
responsible sources
FSC® C013056

Printed and bound in the UK by T. J. International Ltd, Padstow, Cornwall.

CONTENTS

*In memory of my companions
past and present*

FOREWORD BY
ROBIN HANBURY-TENISON OBE

Certain literary prerequisites are essential for any good adventure book. Pre-eminently, it must have a proper character at its heart who can express his or her experiences with a clarity and euphony that transports the reader into a vivid external world. Once upon a time, the mountain literature of mountain-lovers was considered finer than that of mountaineers largely because the mountaineers tended to be over-modest in recording their experiences; were uncomfortable in expressing their more intimate emotions, thoughts and fears and disinclined to admit their true feelings towards their companions. Contemporary mountaineering writers have tended to shed such inhibitions, though professional mountaineers and guides will usually bear their clientele in mind before expressing themselves unreservedly.

John Harding's evocative and atmospheric mountaineering autobiography, covering a period of over sixty years, fulfils my prescribed literary criteria as he steers a deft course between candour and sensitivity without pulling his punches and mercifully eschewing political correctness. His powerful narrative not only celebrates the grandeur and spirit of the mountains, but also imparts a lyrical feeling for landscape interwoven with acute historical insights. His many expeditions on foot and ski have covered unusual ranges such as Turkish Hakkiari and the Yemen which are now virtually inaccessible, while some of the more familiar in Europe and East Africa have changed dramatically in character during his lifetime. Others, though easily accessible, remain relatively unknown to the commonalty of British mountaineers.

Given my own passion for championing tribal peoples' rights through Survival International, I read with particular interest John's experiences with and sympathies for the tribal and mountain peoples of Iran, Turkey and Central Asia who, despite innumerable buffetings, still survive and broadly maintain their traditional way of life.

By his own admission, John is essentially a mountain wanderer who has sought out distant horizons. This book reflects his enthusiasms; recreates the challenges of mountaineering and describes with discernment and good humour the complexities and characters of the many companions who accompanied him on his odyssey. Many fine photographs complement the text and John's delicate hand-drawn maps add freshness and individuality to the whole. This impelling story, modestly told, proclaims the spirit of adventure and deserves to become a classic of its kind.

PREFACE

The frontispiece photograph of Sir Julian Huxley's famous book *From an Antique Land* depicts the crumbling pillars of Palmyra's Grand Colonnade, still upstanding seventeen centuries after the desert city's glory days as capital of Queen Zenobia's caravan empire. Huxley's seminal account of his 1948 visit to the Middle East had served as a companion guide to the Cambridge North Persian Expedition 1956 and had prompted our 200 miles diversionary drive across the Syrian desert to witness for ourselves this magnificent site of antiquity. As a twenty-one year old, that first expedition remains etched on memory as was the admonition that closes Huxley's book, 'It is one of the duties and privileges of man to testify to his experience'. I took this to heart by maintaining the diaries that underpin my story of sixty years of mountaineering as recorded in this book.

Whether these personal experiences justify publication is another matter particularly when compared with the feats of skill, daring and endurance that are the stuff of modern mountaineering sagas. I might have survived the odd scrape, but have touched no voids nor ventured into the thinnest air. Yet mountaineering embraces a broad church and what scarcely raises the pulse of one, stretches the limits of another. Happily, the quest for adventure is common to all at whatever level of achievement.

My fascination with mountains goes back to early boyhood when, as a five-year old, my school was evacuated in 1940 to Dolaucothi, a Georgian mansion set deep in the wilds of Carmarthenshire. This sowed a seed that prompted my adolescent winter excursions into the hills of south Wales, then virtually deserted save for the occasional mounted shepherd rounding up his flocks. The passing of time may add perspective for when I came to climbing in the early 1950s, the Alpine Climbing Group had only just been formed to bring British alpine standards into line with those of Europe and match the exploits of such as Cassin, Gervasutti, Rébuffat and Buhl. My mountaineering bible was then Winthrop Young's *Mountaincraft*; my hyper-expensive Robert Lawrie climbing boots were nailed with clinkers rather than rubber-soled 'Vibrams', and 'Viking' nylon climbing ropes were only just coming on to the market. Improvements in equipment and technique, training, skills and attitude have since revolutionised mountaineering.

Almost a third of this book is about ski mountaineering, that combination of skiing and mountaineering that John Hunt once described as producing 'the complete mountaineer', but which still remains the Cinderella of British mountaineering. As a latecomer to the sport, I came to realise that it offered scope for exploratory winter mountain travel in the little-frequented ranges of Turkey, Greece and Spain despite the restraints of employment, limited holidays and family responsibilities. Ski mountaineering was to become my main mountaineering focus so I make no apology for touching on some of the contentious issues to which it gave rise when I became involved in its promotion as president of the Alpine Ski Club and Eagle Ski Club and a vice-president of the Alpine Club.

Mountaineering at whatever level has peaks and troughs, successes and setbacks, triumphs and tragedies. Over a wide canvas, I have tried to convey something of the grandeur of the mountain world and the diversity of its peoples as well as paying tribute to less familiar names such as Sidney Nowill who fostered my love for Turkey's ranges; Robin Fedden in whose steps I often seemed destined to follow, and Colin Wyatt, a forgotten pioneer ski mountaineer. I have also recounted some family excursions that gave more pleasure than any others, as well as a selection of treks in the Himalaya and Central Asia. Above all, I aim to commemorate the memory of friends past and present whose support and *camaraderie* made these adventures worthwhile.

I owe sincere thanks to Robin Hanbury-Tenison, a peerless explorer and conservationist, for writing the foreword; to Johanna Merz, editor of the *Alpine Journal* from 1992-1998, for her wise counsel; to Tim Fearnside, formerly lecturer in cartography, Swansea University for his technical assistance in the reproduction of my hand-drawn maps; to Bill Norton, Julian Mustoe, Keith MacDougall for authorising the publication of their Cambridge North Persian Expedition photographs and to David Williams for his (No. 123); to Colliers of Swansea for photographic reproduction; to Martin Shoesmith of No Duff Stuff for scanning my slides and prints, and to my publisher Jon Barton of Vertebrate for his advice and encouragement. Finally, to my daughters Emma, Victoria and Joanna for their literary criticism and particularly to my wife Georgina for her companionship in the hills and her forbearance at the hearth.

1

THE PERSIAN EXPEDITION

CAMBRIDGE VENTURERS

'So may we assume, Mr Norton, that you and your companions have come here properly equipped with boots and ropes to climb our mountains?'

Colonel Kachpiss of the Royal Iranian Army was still smiling, but now only half-joking. At this critical stage of what had become an increasingly embarrassing interview, he gave the impression that we might be wasting his time.

On that sultry evening of 16 July 1956, His Imperial Majesty, Mohammad Reza Pahlavi, the Shahanshah of Iran and 'Light of the Aryans', was firmly ensconced on the Peacock Throne. Six of us Cambridge undergraduates were seated less comfortably on hard, wooden chairs in a windowless basement room in a grey, concrete building in the heart of Tehran. Only three days before, we had arrived in Iran's capital having driven 4,500 miles overland from Cambridge. Barely recovered from an epic twenty-two-day journey bedevilled by punctures, written-off tyres, overturns, arrests and incident, we had been summoned to appear before the Mountaineering Federation of Iran to explain why we wanted to climb in the country's highest mountain range, the Elburz.

Led by a mute guard through labyrinthine corridors whose white-washed walls were lined with sepia photographs of beefy Iranian weightlifters, the building seemed deserted save for one room in which a group of heavily bearded men were playing chess. Was this some sort of Savak interrogation centre? Hopefully not, for the room in which we sat nervously awaiting the Colonel's arrival sipping tepid Pepsi-colas, was dominated by an aerial photograph of

Mount Demavend, which filled an entire wall. At last, the double doors burst open and the man himself strode in followed by a phalanx of uniformed officers to break the tension.

'Good evening gentlemen', said the Colonel in clipped English.

'My name is Colonel Kachpiss. You are welcome guests of the Iranian Mountaineering Federation. Let our meeting begin!'

With that, he sat down and opened proceedings by banging his fist down on the table.

1956 was the year in which Khrushchev publicly denounced Stalin; when President Nasser seized the Suez Canal; and when the Red Army invaded Hungary. It was also the year of the Cambridge North Persian Expedition when British atlases and Winston Churchill still referred to Iran as 'Persia', the land of Cyrus, Darius and Xerxes against whom the Greeks had fought their historic battles at Marathon, Plataea, and Salamis. And had I not met Bill Norton the previous year on that Cambridge University Mountaineering Club's (CUMC) Easter meet at the Steall Hut in the shadow of Ben Nevis, I might never have gone to Persia.

Most of those attending that meet were mountaineering novices making do with ex-army battledress trousers, anoraks and ice axes. But one immensely tall man dressed in pukka climbing kit looked every inch the part. Back in the hut after our third and final attempt to bag a blizzard-swept Ben Nevis I ventured, 'That's a mighty fine anorak you're wearing Bill. Looks as if it must have seen some service.'

'Actually, it's a parka', he replied loftily, his nostrils twitching. 'It was my father's. He wore it on Everest.'

Everest! The very name resonated even more sonorously in 1955 than it does today for only two years before, John Hunt's successful coronation year Everest expedition had captured the world's imagination. Having only just met Bill, I had never before associated him with his famous father General E.F. Norton DSO, MC, the leader of the 1924 Everest expedition. Mallory and Irvine's fatal summit bid is the stuff of legend, but almost forgotten is Norton's feat of climbing to within a thousand feet of the summit, solo and without oxygen, a record unsurpassed for another fifty-four years. Bill was then aged twenty-one. I was a year younger. I didn't exactly doff my balaclava, but took respectful notice.

Early the following year, Bill invited me to his rooms in Magdalene. We hadn't seen much of each other since that fateful Steall meet, but over a customary glass of sherry, he came to the point.

'I'm organising a mountaineering expedition to the Elburz this summer. Just wondered whether you might you be interested in joining us. We've already got four starters, but need a couple more climbers to make the party up to six. Plans are pretty well advanced already.'

Nonplussed, I could think of nothing to say except: 'Who else is in the party, Bill?'

'Julian Mustoe who's here at Magdalene with me; Keith MacDougall and Bruce Anderson are both at Caius reading natural sciences and will add some scientific credibility. The fifth member is likely to be David Cook, a regular soldier reading engineering at St John's.'

'I don't know any of them but what's likely to be involved?'

At this, Bill came in as if briefing for a military operation.

'Our main objective is to undertake mountain exploration in two little-known areas of the Elburz. First, we'll tackle the Takht-i-Sulaiman group, some sixty miles northeast of Tehran, which has glaciers and alpine-style peaks. Secondly, we'll move across to the Orim Niswa massif, about 200 miles to the east which the latest Bartholomew map puts at 18,000 feet. That may be an exaggeration, but I'm assured on good authority that the area's virtually unexplored. A subsidiary aim is to do scientific and natural-history research. We'll be travelling out to Iran overland through Western Europe, the Balkans and Turkey and coming home via Iraq, Syria, Jordan and the Lebanon. The return journey's a bit of a cultural swan, but definitely worth the effort. We're aiming to leave Cambridge on 21 June and be back in time for the autumn term. Does this appeal?'

It certainly did and I was flattered to be asked. But puzzled too. Why me? My own climbing experience was very limited whereas Bill was the scion of a distinguished climbing family. Apart from his illustrious father, his grandfather had been Alfred Wills, President of the Alpine Club when Whymper first climbed the Matterhorn in 1865. Bill himself had already climbed in the Alps and had another 150 members of the CUMC to choose from at a time when Cambridge climbers took themselves very seriously. Modern alpine routes were no longer regarded with awe and although the *CUMC Journal's* Climbing Notes grading of Everest's South-West Ridge as 'Difficult (Hard) with Hillary and Tenzing leading through and the rest of the party unable to follow' was preposterous, the spirit of adventure was genuine. This was not the moment to admit to Bill that I had very little mountaineering experience, so I asked him to give me a few days to think it over.

My father had captained both Cambridge and Wales at Rugby, but had no real interest in mountaineering and although my mother's family were hearty, outdoor types used to tramping about the Welsh hills and had some acquaintance with the Swiss Alps, none of them had *climbed* a serious mountain. Even so, mountains had always held a fascination for me from early childhood. To avoid the blitz, my primary school had been evacuated from Swansea in 1939 to Dolaucothi, a Georgian mansion in deepest Carmarthenshire which had its own Roman gold mine. Almost my first six-year-old memories were of those wild games of Fox and Geese we played in the surrounding hills. A year later, when confined to my TB sick bed at my grandparents' house near Hirwaun, I would gaze across the Cynon Valley to Talcyn y Byd, 'The World's Forehead', crowning the scarp of the Glamorgan Uplands which, in my mind's eye, was always dusted with snow.

As a teenager, I had made winter excursions into the hills of South Wales imagining myself as an embryonic mountaineer. But my first proper climbing experience was during National Service with the Welsh Guards at the Guards Training Battalion. The padre, the Reverend Fred Jenkins, was known to be a mountaineer so I persuaded him to take me for a week's climbing in the Cairngorms. Like General Charles Bruce, leader of the 1922 Everest expedition, Fred was a native of Aberdare. He never spoke about his native hearth, but was a member of the Alpine Club and seemed to have climbed everywhere. Although Fred had served with the 6th Airborne Division as a parachutist, I didn't doubt that I was more than fit to accompany this forty-year-old, undemonstrative cleric into the hills. As a nineteen-year-old busily training guardsmen for battle and captaining both the Battalion's rugby and athletics teams, I thought myself a very fine fellow. The quartermaster issued me with a parachutist's parka and I got the camp's cobbler to hobnail a pair of standard-issue boots around both its soles and welts. Fred almost had a fit when he saw what had been done to the boots. Nonetheless in early March 1954, we caught the overnight sleeper from Euston to Aviemore.

I have never forgotten my excitement on first seeing snowdrifts piled twenty-feet high on either side of the Drumochter Pass and my first view of the Cairngorms. At that time, there was no proper road access into the range from Aviemore and merely to reach the Lairig Ghru, the great pass that splits the Cairngorms in two, involved an eight-mile hike. Throughout that week, we never once saw the sun and while climbing Einich Cairn, Cairn Toul, Braeriach and Ben Macdui, blizzards often forced us to crawl to avoid being blown away.

The experience left me with an abiding respect for Highland winter conditions and for Fred's fitness, mountain craft and navigational skills. His effortless stride left me struggling in his wake and, at the end of each day, I had to haul myself hand over hand up the Aviemore Hotel's banisters to get myself to bed. I owe a lot to the unflappable, good-humoured Fred who embodied the wisdom of an Old Testament prophet without the homilies. Though for many years our paths diverged, they came together again when he was still the Alpine Ski Club's longest serving honorary secretary when I became its president.

That autumn, I went up to Trinity College, Cambridge and joined the CUMC. The novices meet in North Wales that December was undertaken in dreadful weather and climbing slippery granite in nailed boots did not inspire mountain fervour. However, I had already met a fellow spirit at Trinity called Neil Macpherson who had learned to climb and ski during his National Service in Austria. We agreed to join the CUMC's forthcoming Easter meet at the Steall Hut after first getting fit on his father Ian's 30,000-acre Attadale estate in the western Highlands. This conveniently had two of its own 'Munros' (Scottish peaks of over 3,000 feet as catalogued by the nineteenth century baronet Sir Hugh Munro) on which Neil had stalked deer since boyhood.

We practised crevasse-rescue techniques hanging from the boughs of a large Scots pine and tested the efficacy of the new-fangled Tarbuck knot by hurling ourselves off a near-vertical slope within rescue distance of the house. After climbing a brace of snow couloirs in the nearby Applecross Hills, we joined the Steall Meet and notched up An Garbanach, Stob Ban and a blizzard-swept Ben Nevis. Back at Attadale, we decided to make a four-day circuit of the clutch of remote Munros that surround Loch Monar. It was so cold that winter, that Loch Calavie was frozen solid enough for us to take a shortcut across the ice before traversing the five-mile ridge of An Riabhachan to the summit of Sgurr na Lapaich, one of the most inaccessible Munros. Stumbling into Braulen Lodge long after dark to pick up the key for a night in the deserted Braulen Bothy, the weathered resident stalker grasped Neil's hand, 'Ah, Mr Neil, now it's good to see ye now! And how might ye be keeping?'

As we moved off into the night, Neil whispered to me, 'It must be ten years since I last stalked with that man.'

The Sgurr na Lapaich traverse had left our feet so blistered that we forwent the planned west Monar circuit and limped back to Attadale.

Neil was my first and last climbing companion. Our friendship has lasted to this day.

Those Scottish winter sorties gave me the confidence to apply to Professor

A.C. Pigou for the annual mountain travel grant he generously offered needy Cambridge undergraduates. Pigou, who had held the chair of political economy at Cambridge for thirty-five years, had successively taught, opposed and eventually come round to supporting Keynes and his economic theories. As the 'patron saint of Kings' climbers', he had encouraged and promoted Wilfred Noyce's climbing career and it was his grant that enabled me to finish off my 1955 long vacation in Scandinavia with a week's wanderlust in Norway's Jotunheim Mountains with two very sporting Norwegian girls. Skinny dips in icy fiords and saunters up Norway's two highest peaks, Galdhopiggen and Glittertind, hardly qualified me for Bill's Elburz expedition, but whatever doubts I had about my climbing credentials, a more serious hurdle was money.

When Bill first invited me to join his expedition, I had hesitantly raised this delicate subject.

'Naturally, an expedition like this is bound to be expensive,' said Bill airily.

'But we've already got promises of generous financial support from the Mount Everest Foundation, the Royal Geographical Society, the Royal Central Asian Society and the British Museum of Natural History, as well as from Magdalene and Caius. Julian's been negotiating free petrol throughout the journey with major oil companies and I'm banking on British firms to supply most of the medical equipment and food.'

'But surely, this can't be a free ride?'

'No, of course not. Let me show you the most recent estimates to put you in the picture.'

With that he produced a four-page, typescript memorandum headed *Cambridge North Persian Expedition* detailing the expedition's expenses 'before' and 'after' including the cost of two jeeps and trailers; hire of War Office camping and surveying equipment; food and petrol; transport, mule hire and insurance. The total came to exactly £1,222 19s 6d.

'But what about assets?'

'It's all in there,' he replied with a slight sniff. 'Apart from contributions from mountaineering and scientific funds, there'll be plenty of cash when we get back from the resale of vehicles and other equipment as well as fees from newspaper and magazine articles. Naturally, we'll each have to chip in with personal contributions which I've set at £75 a head. This brings total assets up to £1,071 leaving a £153 14s 6d deficit which I'm confident that we can make up in due time.'

I made a quick calculation that my overall contribution was going to be at least £100 (£2,000 in today's money) and could see no way of finding this before 21st June.

'Let's go through the detail Bill. Can't we cut down on some of these costs. For example, why are the jeeps seen as a *"danger factor"*?'

'Obviously, we've had to economise somewhere along the line. We can't possibly afford new vehicles, so Julian's buying two ex-US Air Force jeeps with trailers to carry our equipment, spare petrol and the free food, which should reduce expenses en route. Anyway, if push comes to shove, we can always cut down on food and with careful driving will avoid breakdowns.'

'I don't quite see how we can necessarily avoid breakdowns with second-hand jeeps. And what's this item, *'Eighty donkey days'*?'

'Oh that!' chortled Bill. 'When Julian and I went before the MEF Board last November, John Hunt asked pointedly whether we were satisfied with our porterage estimates. I almost died of embarrassment when Julian piped up with: 'But Sir John, this isn't a Himalayan expedition!''

'However, no harm done apparently. Even so, I've bumped up donkey-days just in case. At the end of the day, everything depends on the MEF grant. Luckily, we've got at least one influential friend in court, Sir Claremont Skrine, who's agreed to be the expedition's patron along with an eminent Cambridge Persian scholar, Dr Laurence Lockhart.'

'But who *is* Sir Claremont Skrine?'

'An old friend of my father's actually, and very well respected by the MEF people. Knows Persia like the back of his hand and all the Persian VIPs who really matter. As a matter of fact, it's Sir Claremont we've got to thank for the original Elburz idea.'

'Give me more time to think about it, Bill. Money's my problem.'

Money was indeed my problem. Nonetheless, I was determined to get to Persia some way or another. To bone up on the Elburz, I read Freya Stark's *The Valleys of the Assassins* describing her 1930 and 1931 Elburz journeys. Although she never got closer than five miles of Takht-i-Sulaiman, her fuzzy sepia photograph of the mountain (which she compared to Switzerland's Weisshorn) taken from the Salambar Pass, and her retelling of the legend of how King Solomon lured the Queen of Sheba to its icy summit to share his bed rather than freeze to death, lent enchantment to the peak that is still called 'Solomon's Throne' to this day.

But it wasn't just for the sake of a mountain that I wanted to join Bill's expedition. Social mythology has it that the 1950s were a dreary prelude to the swinging 1960s. We didn't see it that way. Money was tight, food rationing had only just ended and the future was clouded by the threat of nuclear annihilation. Yet these were our salad days. Cambridge's hallowed traditions and conventions were generally respected and petty restrictions, unimaginable today, cheerfully accepted, at least in principle. Work was also taken less seriously than today because postgraduate employment was almost guaranteed. Self-confidence, imbued by a school regime of prefect rule and fierce competition, had been bolstered by two years of national, and sometimes active, service. The moving spirit of the time was adventure and a form of collective 'expeditionitis' had seized Cambridge. I was determined not to be left out, so when my father generously stumped up £75 and an MEF cheque for £400 came through the post, I signed on and took over from Bill the medical officer and treasurer slots.

Today, £400 is equivalent to £6,000. The Mount Everest Foundation had only been established the previous year from the successful 1953 Everest Expedition's surplus funds '*to encourage, or support … expeditions for the exploration of the mountain regions of the earth*'. In 1955–1956, twenty-four other expeditions had applied for grants including Charles Evans' 1955 Kangchenjunga expedition and Vivian Fuchs' Trans-Antarctic expedition. The Cambridge North Persian expedition (or 'CNPE' as we now called ourselves) was a sprat, yet we got as much as several other more worthy expeditions thanks to the MEF's absurdly generous policy of paying out twenty-five per cent of its accumulated fund that year.

I was anxious to prove my worth as treasurer, but Bill's meticulous estimates already bore the stamp of a future treasury mandarin. The medical officer slot offered more scope because generous donations from drug companies had created a medicine mountain sufficient to equip a dozen high-altitude expeditions. Sir Alan Rook, the senior health officer at Cambridge, helped reduce this to a manageable first aid kit and advised that our only serious health problems were likely to be dysentery and malaria. Bill's antidote to dysentery, by digging holes in the ground as a form of 'cat sanitation', did nothing to prevent my having to make several post-expedition visits to the London School of Hygiene and Tropical Medicine to cure amoebic dysentery. Of greater personal concern was a persistent pain in my right hip. When I consulted Professor Trueta, the Nuffield Professor of Orthopaedic Surgery at Oxford about it, his prognosis was that the hip was deteriorating as a result of my childhood TB. His last words were, 'You must get this seen to as soon as possible. I strongly advise you *not* to embark on this expedition.'

Eric Shipton, Britain's most famous inter-war Himalayan mountaineer, reckoned that any expedition worth doing could be planned on the back of an envelope. Ours occupied a fat file with Bill issuing a stream of lists and directives that covered everything from stores, cooking kit, personal equipment reminders, visas, passports and vaccinations. His *Suggested Budget for Bulk Food* detailing all foodstuffs required throughout included a sixty-five word English/Turkish *Culinary Extract* supplement. His *Contacts and Addresses List* named twenty-five British consulates likely to be useful en route and over twenty of Tehran's most prominent VIPs including HE Husain Ala, Iran's prime minister, and HE Amir Assadollah Alam, the minister of the interior and the Shah's closest confidante.

The principal source of this private and confidential Persian information was Sir Claremont Skrine who, spurred on by his father's reproof that 'I would rather you dead than undistinguished' followed the old man into the Indian Civil Service, once described by Lord Curzon as that run by men 'whose hands uphold the noblest fabric yet reared by the genius of a conquering nation.' The very embodiment of empire, Skrine's distinguished career had included military and political service in both India and Persia with a spell in Baluchistan where he had particularly relished the task of 'raider chasing'. In 1922, accompanied by his dauntless wife Doris, his forty-nine-day crossing of the Pamirs to take up his appointment as British consul-general in Kashgar had earned him the Royal Geographical Society's prestigious Gill Memorial Medal. Without Sir Claremont's patronage, the CNPE might never have got off the ground, so it was not without justification that he had written to the British Ambassador in Tehran, Sir Roger Stevens, to say that he had 'more or less sponsored the Cambridge University Expedition to the Elburz ... (and that) if a diplomatic disaster ensues, the fault will be mine.'

Skrine's anticipation of 'a diplomatic disaster' was prescient. He might well have known more about Iran than any other living Englishman, but his role in escorting the pro-Nazi Reza Shah, founder of the Pahlavi dynasty, into exile to Mauritius in 1941 after the allies had forced his abdication, had made him a bitter enemy of Reza's son Shah Mohammad, Iran's reigning monarch. And as one of that generation of British diplomats held responsible by the Iranians for engineering the fall of the country's radical Prime Minister Dr Mossadeq after his nationalisation of the Anglo-Iranian Oil Company in 1951, Skrine was deeply mistrusted by the current Iranian establishment.

Anglo-Iranian relations had been so badly fractured by the Mossadeq affair that the Shah had insisted that the diplomatic *status quo ante* would only be restored on condition that none of the old-guard British diplomats would ever serve in Iran again. As a result, when diplomatic relations were eventually resumed in late 1953, Sir Roger Stevens, previously Britain's ambassador to Sweden, was appointed as a new-broom British ambassador to Iran in February 1954 uncontaminated by any previous Middle Eastern experience.

For undisclosed reasons, Skrine had, in his own words, 'blotted his copy-book' the previous year and caused Stevens 'no little embarrassment.' To compound this, he had assured Bill, without first seeking Stevens's permission, that the CNPE was at liberty to camp in the grounds of the British Embassy's summer residence at Gulhak. When Stevens got wind of this, he wrote to Skrine 'that although an exception would be made in this case, in future years ... it will be impossible to provide such facilities ... a point of which you would perhaps wish to be aware.'

Stevens' rebuff only reached Skrine three days before our departure for Iran. By then, Skrine had already written to Stevens asking him to instruct the Iranian minister of the interior, 'To have explicit instructions sent to the customs authorities at Maku and the Police at Tabriz to let through the equipment in question ... (and) check up nearer the time on what has actually been done.' The equipment in question included expensive Ministry of Defence surveying equipment, Keith's rifle and ammunition, and a Contax camera lent by the War Office for David to photograph strategic bridges en route. It is not known whether Sir Roger ever replied.

Despite his long-time membership of the Alpine Club and service on the 1952 Himalayan committee, Sir Claremont had little direct experience of climbing in the Elburz. There was, however, another Englishman eminently qualified to advise, namely Douglas Busk, an experienced mountaineer, who was currently serving as British ambassador to Ethiopia. During the 1930s, while posted to the Tehran Embassy, Busk had twice reached the summit of Takht-i-Sulaiman's higher neighbour Alam Kuh (4,826 metres), only to find his way to Takht-i-Sulaiman itself barred by Alam Kuh's seemingly impassable, two-mile-long north face.

Busk had written up his Elburz adventures in three pre-war *Alpine Journals* and in his book *The Delectable Mountains*, published in 1946. This included an account of Dr Hans Bobek's 1936 German expedition and their pioneer ascents of both Takht-i-Sulaiman and Alam Kuh's North-East Buttress. Busk had concluded that 'the exploration of this group may now be considered completed.'

However, by the time we had taken the import of this on board, the MEF grant had already come through and it was far too late to change course. As if to rub it in, only three weeks before our departure, the May 1956 issue of the *Alpine Journal* published an account of the French Himalayan explorer Bernard Pierre's 1954 Franco-Iranian Elburz expedition which had repeated the 1936 German routes and added a serious new ice climb. Pierre's crumbs of comfort were that Takht-i-Sulaiman's little-known western link had 'three or four summits of interest' and that the Elburz 'offered mountaineers a unique opportunity to travel and return enriched.' If Bill's hopes had been dashed, he didn't show it. And no one, it seemed, had ever set foot on the 18,000-foot Orim Nizwa, fully 2,000-feet higher than Mont Blanc and surely ours for the taking.

OUTWARD BOUND

On 14 April 1956, Julian took delivery of two 'hard-hat' ex-US Airforce jeeps, registration numbers SXB 205 and SXB 206, thus swallowing up in a single gulp the whole of the MEF's £400 grant. The original jeep, or 'general purpose vehicle', was first launched in 1940 in response to the US Army's wake-up call for a robust, lightweight, all-purpose vehicle that 'does everything, goes every-where, is as faithful as a dog, as strong as a mule, and as agile as a goat'. Unloaded, ours went like bombs, but seating was cramped, especially for Bill's six foot five inches, and as the foot brake had no servo-assistance, strong quadriceps were essential when the handbrakes failed, as they usually did. Designed to run at low speeds without overheating, two types of radiator were available. One for cold weather conditions and the other for hot. Deep into Turkey, we discovered that ours were fitted with the cold-weather version.

At 6 a.m. on 21 June 1956 in Magdalene College's tiny riverside car park, Bill and David were still arguing the toss whether there was enough room to take the twenty-eight pound barrel of honey kindly donated by a Cambridgeshire farmer. Over the past three weeks, SXB 205 and SXB 206 had been repaired, modified, re-fitted, wire-brushed, sand-papered, under-coated inside, outside and underneath, and painted Cambridge Blue over all with the insignia 'CNPE 1956' inscribed in black lettering on each door. An hour later, as the sun rode high above the spires of St Johns' College, SXB's crew, Julian, Bruce and I led off with me waving a choked goodbye to Hanne, my Danish girlfriend of the past year and my first true love. Keith, standing expectantly on the parapet of Magdalene Bridge, had to wait awhile to film the expedition's departure because 205's load was so heavy that it needed first gear and low ratio to surmount its barely perceptible humpback.

Due to early hiccups en route, the Lord Mayor of London's mansion house farewell reception for the CNPE that morning was a close-run thing. Sir Roger Ackroyd showed no visible surprise when Bill presented himself in a tropical jacket, tweed breeches and thick woollen stockings. A flight from Lydd Airport deposited us at Le Touquet where Purfina's Boulogne depot provided the CNPE's first free petrol and second champagne reception of the day. While press photographers busily snapped away, Purfina stickers were plastered over both vehicles. Later, on that balmy mid-summer evening, our tents were pitched in the fair fields of Picardy. It was almost the only day for the next four months when travel arrangements went more or less according to plan.

In 1956, the 4,500-mile overland journey to Tehran was no longer a novelty. But visa formalities had taken months to sort out and there was endless scope for trouble along the way. Yugoslavia was a bleak, unfriendly communist state while travel through Turkey, NATO's eastern bulwark against Russia, had required a sheaf of military permits. But as forewarned by the Foreign Office, the most serious troubles spots were likely to be Greece and the Arab countries of Iraq, Jordan, Lebanon and Syria. In Greece, anti-British feeling was running high on account of Britain's intention to move its Middle East land forces HQ from the Suez Canal to Cyprus whose predominantly Greek population was clamouring for *Enosis*, 'union with Greece'. The signing of the Baghdad Pact to maintain Britain's authority in the area in March 1955 with Britain and Turkey (Greece's historical enemy) its main signatories, had lent popular Greek support to EOKA, a guerrilla campaign in Cyprus which led to Field Marshall Harding's appointment to stifle the rebellion. By the summer of 1956 EOKA terrorist activity against both Turkish Cypriots and British Cyprus based forces was rife. Potentially more serious was the virulent anti-British campaign that had been stoked up by the Egyptian hero and British bogeyman General Nasser whose highly effective brand of revolutionary pan-Arab nationalism and avowed intention of purging Arab countries from imperialist, and particularly British, influence, was reaching fever pitch in the Arab world. In April 1956, the Jeddah Military Pact between Egypt, Saudi-Arabia and Yemen was designed to consolidate Nasser's political and military position and those with the vision to see, anticipated that the nationalisation of the Suez Canal would be an inevitable progression.

These potential pitfalls apart, the necessity to economise had created a 'Catch 22' situation. Thanks to the generosity of ninety-two British firms, we had over-burdened the trailers with freebies and tinned food when eating-out for a pittance would have wasted less cooking-time; cut down weight; and ultimately been cheaper. The boon of free petrol along the route also had its drawbacks, as the business of having to re-fuel at specified stations on set dates and times restricted freedom of movement. Once beyond Western Europe the ruts, potholes and corrugations of the unsurfaced roads that stretched from Yugoslavia to Tehran and back made for a deafeningly rough-ride. Yet the most serious problems that were to bug the expedition through-out were broken trailer towing hooks, degraded tyres and, above all, the wrong type of radiators.

Our troubles began on the second day out when 206 narrowly avoided a head-on crash when its trailer began to wobble uncontrollably before over-turning in the middle of the road just short of Nancy. A friendly garage man patched it up, but the following day, Bill noticed this same trailer passing him on the outside having slipped its towing hook. Repairs to the first of thirty-nine punctures revealed that years spent in an army surplus dump had perished the rubber and in some cases glued the tyres on to the wheel rims. The consequences of having cold-weather radiators first became apparent on crossing the Austrian Alps by the Potzen Pass when steam began to billow out from both of them. From then on, the endless stoppages caused by over-boiling completely threw Bill's schedule and made both the outward and inward journeys chapters of incident, accident and exhausting night drives.

The driving routine was two hours on, followed by two in the front passenger seat acting as navigator and two at the back for a quick kip – if you were lucky. The incessant din made normal conversation impossible and the evening ritual of finding a suitable camp site became a source of friction, Bill's 206 insisted on keeping to a prescribed daily mileage even if this meant camping after dark whereas 205 preferred early morning starts and camping by daylight. The compromise usually adopted produced the worst of all worlds. Throughout the 700-mile journey through Yugoslavia, fresh food was only available in local markets and was then sold out by dawn. The wads of devalued Yugoslav dinars I had smuggled inside my climbing boots, fearful of imprisonment or worse on discovery, only once came in useful at Skopje's solitary garage when Julian made the mistake of disputing the extortionate price demanded for a new battery. He smartly changed his mind when the garage gates were slammed shut and a posse of burly mechanics threatened him.

Greece had food in plenty, but EOKA-inspired anti-British terrorist violence had spilt over to the mainland. On entering Salonika, the patrons of a roadside cafe leapt to their feet shouting and fist-waving on seeing our GB number plates.

While shopping in the town's market, a rabble of jeering children followed at heel chanting 'Inglisi, Inglisi'. At Alexandroupolis, a politically sensitive town bordering Turkey, Bill drove 206 straight into a police speed trap. A hostile crowd jostled us at the Purfina filling station and daubed EOKA slogans in white paint over both jeeps.

The Greco/Turkish frontier marked the boundary between two profoundly different worlds. On the Greek side, men and women were still dancing and laughing at midnight in a brightly lit roadside cafe to the strains of a zither. At the Turkish passport control office, located in the faded *fin de siècle* waiting room of Edirne's railway station still decorated with dust-encased palm trees and aspidistra, a full-length portrait of Mustapha Kemal Ataturk in tailcoat and white tie glared balefully down on Turkey's newest arrivals. Old-style Ottoman bureaucratic obstruction ensured that we only got two hours' sleep that night.

Modern Turkey has the fastest growing economy in Europe, but in 1956 it was a mere shell of the once-great Ottoman empire whose frontiers had stretched from the Indian Ocean to the Atlantic. Then as now, it was NATO's front line against Soviet Union, but tourism was an alien concept and for much of the 140-mile-long drive to Istanbul, a succession of military camps, tank concentrations, and artillery installations lined the road. For the next ten days, the most familiar sight was that of frozen-faced, shaven-headed Turkish soldiers manning sentry posts at the entrance to every town and on every bridge.

In 1956 Istanbul's population stood at 1,500,000 with its great mosques more like run-down museums. Today, its population is estimated at 26,000,000 and this former capital of Byzantium and the Eastern Roman empire has once again become the 'City of the World's Desire'. That night, our concern was not sightseeing, but to find a campsite. In doing so, we inadvertently strayed into a military zone far up the Bosphorus. We were arrested at gunpoint and were lucky to get away with nothing more than an hour-long interrogation before a Turkish army tribunal and another sleepless night.

Ten days after leaving Cambridge, the CNPE's two jeeps and trailers boarded the Bosphorus ferry to Asia and began a week-long journey across the Anatolian sub-continent. Along the way, a foot-long centipede found its way into Bill's sleeping bag; poisonous steppe spiders interrupted supper as they crashed around in the crockery; and a half-crazed shepherd boy threatened me with his knife. On the road to Kayseri, which follows the course of the Persian Royal Road built 2,500 years ago to link Susa to Sardis, 205 went 100 miles off course imagining that the great salt lake of Tuz Golu was a mirage.

Forced to make a night-drive to reconnect with 206, our trailer overturned at the edge of a steep embankment smashing two of the precious British Museum collecting boxes and leaving in its wake a trail of dented kettles, punctured petrol stoves and burst cartons of porridge oats, flour and rice. Julian welded back the trailer's broken towing hook over one of the damaged petrol stoves and as dawn was breaking, we at last caught up with 206 for the first time in twenty-four hours. Parked near a cluster of low-slung, mud houses surrounded by a swarm of light-fingered ragamuffin children, their trailer had also over-turned and blown two tyres in the process. They had been unable to move because 205 had Julian, the expedition's mechanic, and the full repair tool kit.

Past the snow-capped volcanic cone of Ergiyas Dag floating phantom-like above the Cappadocian Plain, two days of roller coaster drives along gravelled roads that teetered above fathomless gorges led to the tranquil valleys that once belonged to the Christian kingdom of Armenia. On entering Erzurum, HQ of Turkey's eastern army, Bill repeated his trick of driving straight through a police checkpoint. Inevitably, this prompted another arrest and military interrogation. The armed guard that escorted the CNPE out of town was only too glad to see the back of us.

A first sub-zero night was spent on the bleak steppe lands of Dugubayazit in sight of Mount Ararat's 5,165-metre ice cap raised to the sky on massive snow-seamed shoulders which remained visible for the rest of that day. Sacred to Armenians and reputedly inviolable, it was first climbed in 1829 by the German explorer-scientist Frederick von Parrot. The eminent jurist Lord Bryce made its first British ascent in 1876 and in his book *Transcaucasia and Ararat* (1877) comprehensively demolished Ararat's ark myth. Those of the deluge persuasion may yet find comfort in recent scientific research, which holds that after the last major glacial retreat a cataclysmic flood caused the Mediterranean to burst through the Bosphorus dam and flood the Black Sea basin.

On the 10 July, the CNPE's two jeeps and trailers drove triumphantly through a crude archway spanning the road that led into a cramped courtyard before crossing a line in the dust that marked the boundary between Turkey and Iran. On the Turkish side, impassive soldiers stood rigidly to attention. On the Iranian side, those not otherwise asleep, were lounging in the shade of a veranda smoking cigarettes. The ground outside the Iranian customs office was littered with rubbish and the office itself deserted save for a dirty old man squatting in the doorway. He resolutely refused to let anyone across the thresh-old until Julian offered him a cigarette. He then helped himself to a handful.

An hour later, an unkempt man in pyjama trousers wandered across from the nearby *chaikhana* and spent the next two hours sealing every object in sight including the steering wheel, though not Keith's rifle. Evidently, Sir Claremont Skrine's message to the minister of the interior had not been passed on to the customs authorities at Maku. Relaxing in an atmosphere altogether friendlier than that in Turkey, we drank sweet tea in the village *chaikhana* and watched women in brightly coloured dresses harvesting the wheat that lay in yellow heaps by the roadside. A tattered old man, his feet trailing in the dust, trotted by astride a scrawny donkey.

Tehran was still 520 miles away and it took another four days to get there. Still dogged by punctures, broken trailer-hooks, makeshift repairs, halts for over-heating and night drives, 206 had to abandon David at the roadside on the final lap to guard its stricken trailer. In the early hours of 14 July a battered and exhausted CNPE regrouped at the British Embassy compound at Gulhak. It had taken twenty-two days to get there.

Seven miles north of Tehran in the foothills of the Elburz, the haven of Gulhak had been the embassy's summer retreat ever since Nasr ed-Din Shah had presented it to the British in 1862. It was a veritable Persian garden, shaded by plane trees with its ice-cold swimming pool fed by the snows of the 13,000-foot Tochal, Tehran's sentinel peak. Today, it no longer exists. That same morning, while we were still asleep, His Excellency Sir Roger Stevens, accompanied by his embassy's entourage, paid the CNPE an official visit. When our flustered and unshaven leader crawled out of his tent in pyjamas mumbling apologies, his excellency graciously invited the expedition to luncheon the following day.

Early the following morning whilst we were still abed, another unexpected visitor arrived in the form of Miss Palmer Smith. An old friend of Sir Claremont Skrine, she had first come to Tehran in 1926 as a governess to the British Minister Sir Robert Clive before moving on to teach English to the children of eminent Iranians. A blustering, warm-hearted do-gooder who had once had influence in some quarters, she was anathema to Sir Roger Stevens as a relic of the *ancien régime*. Standing stiffly to attention at her side was a young Iranian officer wearing an immaculately creased uniform and sporting a close-cut military moustache.

'I'm very sorry, and certainly surprised, that you couldn't find time to attend the party I had organised for your arrival Mr Norton', began Miss Palmer Smith, giving Bill a withering glance.

'But never mind that. Let me introduce you to Captain Akbar Ghaffari of the Royal Iranian Army. He's been appointed as your guide and interpreter during your time in Iran.'

A stony-faced Captain Ghaffari solemnly shook everyone's hands and then, with an unwavering stare, reeled off his mountaineering qualifications in heavily inflected French. Apparently, he had just returned from a year with the *Chasseurs Alpines*, the French Army's crack mountain troops with whom he had climbed most of the Chamonix Aiguilles.

'And why,' demanded Captain Ghaffari, 'as the first British climbing team to visit Iran, have you not done us the courtesy of contacting the *Federation Iranienne de la Montagne* as have all other foreign mountaineering parties? Our Chairman, Colonel Kachpiss, is *very* disappointed.'

Oh dear! Bill's *Contacts List* had mentioned a couple of Iranian climbers, but none called Kachpiss. After Bill had offered more grovelling apologies, the captain bowed slightly and informed us that a meeting with the federation would be arranged for the following evening. He then saluted stiffly and marched off in the wake of Miss Palmer Smith.

'What the hell's all this about?' demanded Julian. ' I can't believe that anyone can really be called "Kachpiss". Anyway, what is this Mountaineering Federation and who is this Captain Ghaffari? We never asked for a liaison officer, least of all someone who's damned unfriendly and patently way above our climbing class. No doubt, he'll try to take the whole expedition over. And who is this Palmer Smith harridan?'

'Come off it Julian,' cut in Bill. 'I've already explained to you that she's an old friend of Sir Claremont's and knows everyone in Tehran. Just count ourselves lucky we've got her to smooth our path. We can't possibly refuse the federation's offer of a liaison officer, particularly one who speaks reasonable French and can help square officialdom. Anyway, it's traditional in this country to have an official 'greeter and meeter' so we'd better get used to him.' From then on, Captain Ghaffari was dubbed 'The Tiger of Tehran'.

The following day, we had our first decent meal for three weeks at the Ambassador's Gulhak residence with its polished dining-room table resplendent with gleaming silver and cut glass. Over coffee, Reggie Burrows, the embassy's first secretary, took Bill aside.

'A word in your ear, Norton. I have to tell you that the name you have chosen for your undergraduate adventure has already raised any number of diplomatic eyebrows and put some important Iranian backs up.'

'I'm very sorry to hear that, Sir,' replied Bill, 'But why so?'

'Then let me explain,' said Burrows sharply.

'In the first place, your reference to 'north Persia' is wholly inappropriate. Iran has been this country's official name since 1934. The prefix 'north' is doubly unfortunate. You must surely have known that the 1907 Anglo/Russia demarche effectively divided this country into two spheres of influence. Russia took over the north, and Britain the south. The Iranians have forever resented this blatant bit of imperialism.'

'Most unfortunate', agreed Bill. 'We did discuss matters of etiquette with our sponsor Sir Claremont Skrine. I'm afraid the issue of nomenclature was overlooked.'

'Damned certain it was,' growled Burrows. 'And I must advise you *not* to bandy Skrine's name around here, especially with His Excellency. You should also have made it clear that yours is a *Cambridge University* expedition. *Cambridge* on its own could be anywhere. We've really had no idea what sort of expedition yours is supposed to be and had you only consulted us at the outset, I'd have suggested you call yourselves the 'Cambridge University Mountaineering Expedition to Iran'. It would have saved us no end of embarrassment. At least, you've brought suits with you and are clean-shaven. Bearded expeditions are *never* asked to embassy functions.'

That same evening we reported to the Iranian Mountaineering Federation for the fateful interview with Colonel Kachpiss. Captain Ghaffari, one of several officers present, would already have reported to his boss unfavourable impressions of the scruffy, pyjama-clad shower he had met at Gulhak. The colonel was charming with an urbane sense of humour, but when Bill with typical Wykehamist self-deprecation gave a disconcertingly low-key account of our modest climbing credentials, the colonel's eyes narrowed. It was at this point that he made the patronising enquiry about our climbing equipment that now spurred Bill to come out fighting.

'Perhaps it might help, colonel, if I were to explain our precise mountaineering and scientific objectives. We would then welcome the federation's advice and comments. Initially, we intend to concentrate on the Takht–i-Sulaiman group by establishing a base camp in the Hazarchal from which to climb whatever mountains are immediately available. We will then cross over to the north side of the massif to establish a subsidiary camp from which to climb Takht-i-Sulaiman and other peaks. In addition, our two scientists will make botanical and zoological collections for the British Natural History Museum.'

This exposition changed the atmosphere perceptibly.

'Certainly, the Takht-i-Sulaiman group has the best mountaineering in Iran,' conceded Kachpiss. 'But why camp in Hazarchal?'

'Because Hazarchal is relatively easy to reach by mule,' replied Bill.

'Last year's Franco-Iranian team were unable to take mules any higher than the Sarchal glacier. They then had to carry ten-days' food and equipment another 1,200 metres higher over four kilometres of glacial moraine to establish their base camp.'

'But everyone camps on the Sarchal,' insisted Kachpiss. 'No one camps in Hazarchal.'

At this, a man with the gnarled face of a mountaineer broke in.

'Even if it were possible, it would take you at least three days to move a camp to the north side.'

Conversation then became fragmentary, so Bill asked for advice on the cost and availability of mules at Rudbarek. No one came up with any suggestions, so he turned the discussion round to the subject of Orim Niswa.

'Niswa!' spluttered the man who had been so dismissive about moving camp. 'Niswa is a molehill unworthy of mountaineers!'

With that, everyone went quiet until Bill broke the silence.

'Then perhaps you would be kind enough to suggest some suitable alternative area, colonel?'

After hurried discussion between the Iranians, the Orim expert pronounced 'You should go to Zardeh Kuh in the Zagros. They are like the French Alps.'

He might as well have suggested the Mountains of the Moon. The Zagros lay hundreds of miles west of Tehran and we knew nothing about them.

'Unfortunately, colonel, we have neither the time nor the resources to visit the Zagros' said Bill acidly. 'Surely there are other parts of the Elburz you can recommend.'

The colonel pursed his lips. The meeting seemed to have reached an impasse. But Bill was not defeated and now rolled out our crumpled, oil-stained set of Survey of India maps. The maze of ill-defined contours representing the Central Elburz looked as bewilderingly opaque as they had done in Cambridge. But Kachpiss was looking thoughtful as his eyes ran to and fro across the phantom ranges.

'Here you are', he said at last, stabbing his finger into a tangle of contours. 'This range to the north-west of Demavend – the mountains of Palur. Several of its peaks are unclimbed and you will certainly need your crampons to tackle their ice ridges. And then, further to the west, there is Azad Kuh, an inaccessible rock pyramid above Shemshak.'

Somewhere at the back of my mind I recalled that Bernard Pierre had mentioned something about Azad Kuh. What a coup if we could climb it!

At 10 p.m. the colonel was getting restive. Until now, Captain Ghaffari had remained stern-faced and silent throughout. Suddenly he melted and flashed us a charming smile.

'Please call me Aki', he said. 'It is short for Akbar.'

The interview was over. As we filed out, Colonel Kachpiss reiterated his advice about avoiding the Hazarchal, but promised that he would arrange a reception for us with the president of the Iranian Mountaineering Federation, His Royal Highness Prince Golum Reza Pahlavi, the Shah's younger brother.

Bill's original schedule had allowed only three days in Tehran. But the incidents of the drive from Cambridge had already lost five days and the jeeps had taken such a hammering that a complete overhaul was now necessary. Coupled with the frustrating business of getting additional travel permits and sorting out customs formalities, we remained grounded in Tehran for a week. Bill's meticulously calculated food budget of £87 1s 5d was also wildly out. Fifteen pounds avoirdupois of rancid goat's cheese stuffed into an old paraffin tin at the bazaar cost more than it would have done at Fortnum's.

And Tehran was proving no rest cure. The near-intolerable heat of high summer in that teeming city whose open-street water conduits were used for drinking, washing, refuse disposal and defecation discouraged sightseeing on foot. Nonetheless, both Miss Palmer Smith and Reggie Burrows generously threw us cocktail parties and we duly attended Prince Golum Reza Pahlavi's palace reception, besuited and with fresh haircuts. Surrounded by a posse of high-ranking generals, HRH (unkindly described as 'blubber lips' by some embassy wag) made an effusive speech of welcome 'to the first British mountaineering expedition to visit Iran'. He then pinned metallic Iranian flags on to our lapels as we stood smartly in line at attention. When a discomposed Colonel Kachpiss arrived a tad late, Aki whispered gleefully, 'This afternoon, colonel will be major!'

SOLOMON'S SNOWS

Zoroastrian cosmology placed the 600-mile-long Elburz Mountains at the heart of the Hara Beresaiti, the universal range then believed to encircle the earth where Ahura Mazda, the supreme deity of the Persian Achaemenians, revealed the truth to Zoroaster. The Central Elburz is a fifty-mile-wide band of parallel ranges averaging 3,500 metres in height constituting a formidable barrier between the Iranian Plateau and the Caspian provinces with few natural passes as both Alexander the Great and invading Arab armies discovered to their cost. Our own journey to our road head village of Rudbarek, a mere 100 miles north-east of Tehran, would have taken a week had it not been for Reza Shah's Trans-Elburz highway built at immense cost during the mid 1930s.

The advance party of Bill, David, Keith and Aki left Tehran in SXB 206 early on 19 July. Delayed by last-minute repairs, SXB 205 following late that evening and spent a miserable night in the open, caught out by an unexpected rain-storm. The road across the Elburz followed the general line of an ancient caravan track winding through eroded spurs of baked brown earth with tiny, green oases embedded into the hillside to mark the sites of hamlets hidden amidst thickets of plane, poplar and walnut. Higher up, it twisted through a labyrinth of jagged, desiccated ridges. Higher still, it hugged the edge of a dizzying gorge.

The temperature-gauge needle had long gone off the clock when, at 9,000 feet, the road appeared to vanish into a black hole set in the mountainside. This, the Kandevan Pass tunnel marking the Elburz watershed, was unlit with water bucketing-down from its arched roof. With barely enough room for a single vehicle to pass and with no operating signalling system, we took a chance that no one was coming the other way. Twenty breathless minutes later, we emerged like Alice at the other end of the tunnel to find ourselves in another world. Gone were the cloudless skies, the crystalline light, the searing heat, the parched earth, the dust devils, and boundless horizons of the Iranian Plateau. We had reached the ancient kingdom of Mazanderan where the Persian hero Rustum fought his epic battles; from whose forests Hyrcanian tigers were exported for gladiatorial combat in the circuses of Rome; and in whose mountain fastnesses Hasan-i Sabah, the 'Old Man of the Mountains', founded the notorious sect of the Assassins. Everything around was a luxuriant green and enveloped in mist. From far below came the deep boom-boom of a waterfall. Julian's brake-jamming, spiralling descent down the hairpin bends of a precipitous gorge to the swollen Chalus River was a white-knuckled ride with the din of the rain drumming down on the jeep's tin roof drowning out the roar of the torrent.

Forty kilometres on, a side road with a barely visible sign marked 'Kalardasht' led to a low pass overlooking a cloud-filled plain. Somewhere away in its south-west corner lay Rudbarek, the village which at Cambridge had seemed as remote as Shangri La. As the rain redoubled, the road deteriorated into a track of treacly mud flanked by deep, water-filled ditches.

'This can't possibly be right' protested Julian. 'We must have missed a turning some way back.'

After man-handling the trailer to face about, a sinister figure in a black skull-cap and felt coat with pointed shoulders bound up with string emerged from the gloom. Surveying us like a great bat with folded wings, we shouted out to him 'Rudbarek?' and pointed down the track. He shook his head vigorously and indicated that the correct way was where we had just come from.

Just outside Rudbarek, 205's engine stalled and for the next half hour blocked the road to prevent an Iranian Army lorry-load of good-natured huntsmen from passing. The village was like nineteenth century alpine Switzerland, with its deep-eaved chalets built of horizontally laid logs capped by pitched roofs tiled with limestone slabs. Beyond it, a boulder-strewn track ran for another mile beside a foaming river before terminating at a clearing backed by a wall of rock. From two familiar tents set in a quagmire, there emerged the bedraggled figures of Bill and David, reuniting the expedition's two halves for the first time in twenty-four hours.

'We got to Kalardasht okay last night', explained a weary-looking Bill.

'But we couldn't see a damned thing in the fog and after taking a wrong fork fetched up outside the Shah's hunting palace at midnight. And then, if you can believe it, His Excellency, Reggie Burrows and Co. arrived in a fleet of Land Rovers early this morning for the weekend. His Excellency had to wake me up once again in my pyjamas. It's never stopped raining since we got here. However, the good news is that Keith has raised our profile by winning a local shooting competition and Aki has arranged for a mule-train to be here at dawn tomorrow.'

When Aki arrived, two hours later than promised, it was still raining. In his wake came fifteen mules and a gang of muleteers dressed in patched-up Reza Shah 'western' suits and shoes soled with tyre-treads. Their shop steward, a dour, heavily built man who we dubbed 'Brown Hat', was already giving Aki trouble.

'Boll, this man says that the best mules have been taken by those soldiers', complained Aki. 'He says we will need more mules.'

'But surely, I thought that everything was agreed last night?'

'Yes Boll, but the muleteers are angry. You want to camp in Hazarchal, but no expedition ever camps there. The Sarchal Glacier camp is seventeen kilometres away and can be reached in two days. Hazarchal is twenty-seven kilometres away and will take three days. That is why they want more mules and more money.'

Bill was having none of it and after more argy-bargy the mule train was reduced from fifteen to ten and the muleteers to eight. Even so, John Hunt's strictures about porterage were proving correct.

While loading commenced, Aki and I went down to the village to buy vegetables, a sack of bread, dried beans and peas, and a box of dried trout. Also, at Aki's insistence, a dozen chickens. He detailed the Headman's youngest son to find them and within minutes the lad was back with a gang of scruffy urchins each carrying a squawking fowl tucked under the arm. Twelve were chosen and promptly beheaded. As their headless bodies careered around in a ghoulish death-dance, a crowd of onlookers howled with laughter.

The CNPE's advance party eventually got moving at mid-morning up the ancient trade route that had once linked Kalardasht to the Plateau. Since made obsolete by motor transport, it was fast being encroached on by rampant bracken and giant nettles. The trough of the valley was flanked by a dense deciduous forest of oak, ash, beech, walnut, elm, hornbeam and hawthorn growing to a prodigious size. Aki's stream of anecdotes about man-eating leopards and bears with a penchant for raping local women was only interrupted when two bearded men humping outsize rucksacks came bounding down the track. Grinding to a reluctant halt after Aki had hailed them, they were about to move off when, after a peremptory hand-pumping introduction, I ventured, 'Who are you; where are you based and what climbs have you done?'

'We're members of this year's Franco-Iranian expedition,' replied the younger man in English.

'We're camped on the Sarchal and we're about to climb the North Wall direct. It's never been done before, but blizzards have covered it in snow and ice. And this is Minassian,' he continued, turning deferentially towards his older companion. 'He has climbed the North Buttress!'

Minassian? I vaguely remembered the name as one of the Iranian climbers on Bernard Pierre's 1954 expedition and would have liked to have a chat. But the great man was gazing into the middle distance, self-absorbed and totally disinterested.

'Why are you going down?' I persisted. 'I hope no one's been injured.'

'No one injured, but we've got to get more mules and food from Rudbarek. We'll be staying on for another ten days, so we'll see you up there.'

'Maybe, but we're going to be based on Hazarchal.'

'Hazarchal!' he cried, throwing up his hands. 'You can't camp there. No one camps in the Hazarchal!'

I was about to ask him why, but Minassian had already recommenced his furious descent. His companion followed at his heels without another word.

The forest was fast giving way to scattered clumps of sycamore, dwarf oak and juniper. A griffon vulture perched on a rocky scarp not far above and my headache signalled that we were gaining height. At Vanderbon, a stone-built *chaikhana* sited on a grassy flat at the treeline, Aki, Bill and I waited for the rear guard to catch up over a bowl of curdled goats milk, or *mast*. Vanderbon marked the junction of the Sardab and Barir rivers where the paths divided. One went up the Barir Rud to the Sarchal Glacier and the other up the Khorrumdasht to Hazarchal.

'Those wretched mules kept throwing their loads, and that damned Brown Hat's been dragging his feet all the way', snorted Keith as the rear guard straggled in.

Brown Hat complained to Aki yet again about having to camp in the Hazarchal, but Bill swiftly closed the argument. The caravan had only made twelve kilometres, yet no one complained about camping early that day near the army party who were expecting a good bag of ibex and moufflon the following day. At 2,400 metres the air chilled quickly as evening drew in and suddenly, for the first time in four days, the mists began to clear. Impossibly high above, ragged streamers flew off the Elburz's soaring crests suffused with gold from the dying sun.

Next morning, the Sardab Rud was fringed with ice that soon melted as the sun dissipated the Caspian mist. The hunters were long gone by the time Aki got the mule-train moving. Bill, pale, pinch-faced and clearly unwell, had to ride mule-back with his legs brushing the ground. Five kilometres higher up, on the scree-strewn slopes of the Khorramdasht, an accident and emergency halt was called at the deserted caravanserai of Tanakrud. Bill insisted that his condition was the result of eating some exotic fruit that Aki had given him the previous day and rejected my pills. The muleteers were more easily impressed by the sight of the medicine chest and after dispensing placebos, I dressed a mule with an ugly chest-wound with disinfectant, boracic ointment, plaster and a flourish of the forceps.

It was clear that the wilting Brits were going no further that day so Aki took command: 'Tonight, I make you all supper. Iran has cuisine like France.'

Two hours later, he produced a stew of chicken, millet, split peas garnished with limes and swimming in vegetable ghee. Feeling altitude sick, I surreptitiously dumped mine on the scree. Others persisted and paid the price later on. That night, while we shivered in our down sleeping bags, the muleteers slept in nothing but their felt cloaks, or '*shaulars*'.

By the following morning, Bill was on the mend but Aki's stew had done for David who now took his turn mule-back. The sun was already high when we passed the soldier-hunters stretched out on a grassy knoll shouting encouragement as they breakfasted off fresh moufflon steak. As the valley narrowed and the track disappeared into a snow-filled gorge, the mules began to struggle and Brown Hat began to gesticulate wildly pointing to his eyes, head and legs. He must have done this journey a hundred times, so I ignored him. Glancing back for a last look down the Khorramdasht, the Sarbad Rud had become a twisting, silver ribbon fast disappearing beneath a wall of mist creeping up the valley.

I can never forget that first view of Hazarchal, the 'Place of a Thousand Hollows'. Its glittering snowfields and incipient alpine meadows encircled by spiky peaks and a clutch of tiny glaciers made that precious moment the realisation of a dream. The old trade route now continued southwards, snaking upwards before losing itself in a massive snowfield and then emerging at a notch on the skyline ridge that marked the 4,000-metre Hazarcham, the highest navigable pass between the Atlantic and the Hindu Kush. Our own route swung away to the north-west into the upper reaches of the Hazarchal where Bill had decided to establish base camp.

Heaving and panting, head throbbing and with a blinding headache, I sat down on the grass for a breather and glanced down the valley.

'Bloody hell Bill! D'you see what's going on down there? Those wretched muleteers are offloading the baggage!'

Together we raced down the ground so hardly won to find Aki arguing furiously with Brown Hat.

'Boll, this man says that his men have already done an extra day's work because you Ingliz were ill and had to stop at Tanakrud. He refuses to go on any further.'

'But we must get at least a thousand feet higher than this,' insisted Bill. 'We'd lose hours of climbing time every day if we have to camp down here.'

Brown Hat refused to budge. Some of the muleteers reloaded reluctantly, but then quit halfway leaving two plucky twelve-year-olds to hump the fifty-pound collecting boxes up the last stretch. After Aki had paid off Brown Hat with the threat of imprisonment if he wasn't back within sixteen days, the old rogue slumped off, complaining bitterly. Only one small, rather spindly muleteer elected to stay behind.

'What is your name?' asked Keith.

'Saphar Ali Negani,' he replied with a winning smile. We could not have done better.

Set on a green knoll amidst a pattern of snow-covered moraines at 4,064 metres, Base Camp Hazarchal seemed ideally sited. But the listless Ingliz were making heavy work of just erecting their tents and it was Aki, radiating energy, who knocked up supper for those who could face it. With the meal barely started, Saphar suddenly let out a shout and pointed excitedly to a moraine ridge fifty metres away. At first, I thought it must be a stray cow until Julian yelled out 'Christ, it's a bloody great bear!'

Silhouetted against the darkening sky, the great beast sniffed meaningfully in our direction. Everyone dropped to the ground infantry fashion as Keith scrabbled around for his rifle and Aki unholstered his revolver. The bear stared at us, no doubt as surprised as we were, and then moved off soundlessly. After a decent interval Aki, Keith and Safar gave chase, but it had already vanished leaving only the imprint of its saucer-sized paws in the snow. Teeth chattering in the unaccustomed cold, Bill's yarns of lammergeiers attacking Alpine shepherd boys were comprehensively capped by Aki's more graphic tales of his encounters with leopards, panthers and bears.

The first morning in camp brought some unwelcome surprises. The melt-streams that had flowed so freely yesterday had frozen solid overnight and the dried trout which had been buried deep in the snow were already rotting after the briefest exposure to the sun. One of the food boxes which had been 'repacked' by the muleteers at Rudbarek now contained nothing but salt and vegetable ghee. Aki's precious *alimentation pour les montagnes*, a mixture of raisins, sultanas, dried mulberries and a delicious confection of almonds, sugar and saffron, had vanished. We were left with a surfeit of tinned sardines, ship's biscuits and nuts: the last things you need to assuage a high mountain thirst.

Only Aki was up to climbing anything that day and after lunch pointed to a prominent rock peak overlooking the camp.

'Boll, that is Gardune Kuh, an aiguille like in Chamonix. No one has yet climbed it. I will be the first!'

With that, the Tiger of Tehran strode purposefully towards its scree-strewn base while Bill wandered off to do some sketching and I retired to the tent that he and I shared to nurse a headache. Soon after, I spotted a large bear moving purposefully in Bill's direction, so crawled out of the tent and began gesticulating frantically at Bill. He took not the blindest bit of notice as the bear ambled past him before loping effortlessly up the screes below Gardune Kuh like a huge dog.

Retreating to the tent, my reverie was again interrupted by a fusillade of shots. Minutes later, Aki came bounding down the screes before skidding to a halt still clutching his smoking revolver.

'What happened Aki?' we chorused.

'A very lucky escape' said our hero, breathing heavily. 'I was climbing that mountain – *trés difficile*. Vultures mobbed me, but I drove them off with my revolver. Only then did I see a great bear hiding in the shadows above me. Allah is merciful! Those birds were warning me of mortal danger. I climbed down at once, thankful to be alive. Allah be praised!'

We could only marvel at this superman who had effortlessly organised the food at Rudbarek; sorted out the bolshie muleteers; and done all the cooking to date. Now, he alone was pushing a new route and defying ferocious animals while we weedy Brits sat around in a stupor.

'Tomorrow,' declared Aki, his chest swelling visibly, 'we will all climb Alam Kuh! Yes, Keith and Bruce too. The whole expedition together!'

I was still feeling rotten, yet even a cursory look at Alam Kuh's whale-back ridge persuaded me that its ascent should not pose many problems. The mountain had already been climbed several times from this side ever since two Austrian botanists, the Bornmueller brothers, had made its first recorded ascent in 1902. Nonetheless, the prospect of bagging it clearly excited Bill as he gazed summitwards.

'It's supposed to be well over 16,000 feet high,' he enthused. 'Quite a bit higher than Mont Blanc. The 3,000-foot climb from here to the top should make a good acclimatisation exercise. What's more, from the Lana Col just below the summit ridge we should be able to see whether there's a feasible way down to the North-West Glacier.'

Next morning, Aki shot into the lead and was soon a distant black dot set against the glacier's dazzling-white backdrop. The obvious route to the Lana Col lay up a prominent snow couloir at the head of a narrow glacial cwm above the camp. Neither Keith nor Bruce had ice axes so elected to make their own way to Alam Kuh's summit up the immense screes that covered its southern flanks. Following in Aki's wake, I was puzzled when he struck out halfway up towards an ill-defined rock ridge. On reaching the Lana Col, he was nowhere in sight. Surely, I thought, not even the Tiger of Tehran could have reached the summit, over a thousand feet higher, that fast. I waited for Bill to join me.

'Whatever's happened to Aki, Bill?'

'He's coming up behind', he replied stiffly. 'Can't understand it. He somehow managed to get himself stuck on that rock ridge and I had to give him a top rope.'

Foregathered on the Lana Col, the North-West Glacier was clearly visible below as was the 'western extension' that Bernard Pierre had enthused about and which we now identified as the Haft Khan Ridge.

'But how the hell do we get down on to that glacier?' asked David. 'It's a good 1,500-feet below and I can't see any run-out. I reckon Busk was right. It looks damned-near impossible.'

'That simply has to be our route' said Bill. 'I can't see how there can be any other.'

The rest of the climb to Alam Kuh's summit was a mere scramble along a shattered ridge. Bruce and Keith had no trouble in joining us and at 2 p.m. on the 25 July the whole expedition posed for a group photograph perched on a jumble of precariously balanced granite blocks. It was to be the only time that we all stood on an Elburz summit together. Little of the Elburz was visible above the Caspian's all-enveloping cloud sea, save for the elusive Throne of Solomon which now lay at our feet. Triangular in shape with its scree-strewn flanks riven by snow couloirs, it didn't look that impressive. But to get there was going to be problematic because it was separated from Alam Kuh by a line of sheer granite cliffs and a five-kilometre-long glacier that snaked away before disappearing round its eastern spur.

Next day, despite the curious incident on Alam Kuh, Aki was the obvious man to spearhead the assault on Gardune Kuh seconded by Bill and David. Julian and I would follow behind on a separate rope while Keith filmed proceedings. Aki's furious attack on the first pitch, an awkward chimney, sent down a shower of rocks that scattered everyone below. An hour later, Julian and I were still waiting to get started at the bottom of the climb.

'What the hell's going on up there?' muttered Julian. 'David is wedged under an overhang, but what's happened to Aki and Bill?' We climbed up together to investigate.

Twenty metres above David, Aki and Bill were exchanging French unpleasantries in the narrow chimney.

'What's the score, David?' I shouted up to him.

'Aki and Bill are having problems,' he replied wearily. 'Aki refused to belay Bill after the first pitch. Apparently, he was never taught belaying techniques by his bloody Chasseurs Alpins, so Bill's been trying to teach him on the job. They've come to a grinding halt. Time is running out, so I suggest we waste no more time and all go down.'

As it was now too late for anyone else to press their suit we did just that.

Next morning, Julian and I were the only takers for a second attempt on Gardune Kuh's virgin couloir. Until now, my only real rock-climbing experience had been on a CUMC novices meet in north Wales wearing clumpy nailed boots. Our expedition boots were soled with the altogether more effective cleated-rubber 'Vibrams'. But climbing helmets were still a new-fangled luxury and modern aids such as nuts, bongs, bolts, wire slings, wedges and such like were strictly for the *avant garde*. Security techniques were also rudimentary. Waist-loops did for climbing harnesses and 'run-outs' (the distance between the leader and his second) could be the length of a 120-foot rope, or 240 foot at full stretch. Thus, if a leader 'came-off' on a long run-out then, even if his second was securely belayed and managed to hold the fall, the consequent physical damage could maim or even kill.

At least we'd brought along a couple of pitons, the iron pegs used for belays that Alpine Club traditionalists still frowned on as artificial, unethical and un-British. I had never used them before.

Beyond Bill's high point, the gulley steepened to the near vertical. I hadn't spotted a single rock belay on the way up on which to attach a rope sling for security. Now, at the business end of a 120-foot run-out with no stances on which to rest, I found myself off balance and in danger of swinging into space. Grabbing a piton, I hammered it into a crack. The rock promptly disintegrated on impact sending chunks of shale hurtling down the gulley. They would have decapitated Julian had he not wedged himself under a protruding rock lip and stuck his rucksack over his head. Somehow, I willed my body to adhere to the rock and, after frantic fumblings, banged in the second piton as my legs began to shake uncontrollably. This time, it went in with a reassuring crescendo of 'ping, pings'. I grabbed it desperately and then hung on until my breathing slowed to near normal. After securing myself with a karabiner and sling, I shouted down to Julian to start climbing. He led through without a word, clambered over my shoulders and showered down more rubbish in his wake. With my rucksack planted firmly over my head, I took a perverse pleasure listening to dull thud of rock impacting inches above my skull.

Four hours after starting the climb, Julian and I emerged at the top of the gulley quivering like jellies only to find David sunbathing on the summit.

'What took you two? Bill and I found an easy route up the mountain's backside. We've been hanging around for hours.'

'Then where's Bill got to?'

'Look down that ridge,' said David, pointing to a distant figure striding away into the middle distance.

'He's determined to bag that scrappy-looking peak, Gormara Kuh, to make it his second first ascent of the day.'

I gazed down the ridge and then to our camp, a cluster of grey specks set in a tiny patch of green surrounded by retreating snowfields. To the south lay an entirely different world of desiccated, skeletal ranges rising and falling like waves to a horizon blurred by heat haze.

Gardune Kuh had marked a watershed. I had always assumed that Julian and I would make a good climbing partnership, but somehow, we hadn't clicked and never climbed on the same rope again. For Aki, Gardune Kuh had exposed the limitations that his good-natured braggadocio had first concealed. Later that evening he confessed to Bill, '*Vraiment, je deteste les montagnes!*' Over the past two days, the swashbuckling 'Tiger of Tehran' had suffered a catastrophic loss of *amour propre*. We all shared the warmest feelings towards this sensitive and intelligent man who was to remain a stalwart companion for the rest of our time together. But never again did he climb with us. We had overestimated his ability and he, perhaps, had underestimated ours. Bill's self-effacing presentation at the Iranian Mountaineering Federation and our early feeble showing had taken him off guard and might have been interpreted as typical British perfidy. Our fault was a naive ignorance of the subtleties of the Persian character and its trait for embroidery and exaggeration. We'd have done a lot better to have read *Haji Baba of Isfahan* before coming out to Persia.

Next morning, the sound of gunfire roused me from our tent. A moufflon was careering down the mountainside with Keith and Safar in hot pursuit. The animal collapsed within a couple of hundred metres of the camp.

'A lucky long shot' said Keith modestly, as he and Safar hauled its carcass in. 'Safar and I were up at dawn and spotted a herd high on the hill.'

Safar cooked its liver for a breakfast that never tasted better. This also turned out to be our last decent meal together for the next fortnight as later that morning Keith, Bruce and Safar set off on a four-day naturalist safari south across the Hazarcham Pass. With them went something of the party's cohesion and fun. Their absence also complicated the logistics of establishing a subsidiary camp on the North-West Glacier and shortened the time we might have spent there.

It was decided to make this crucial crossing to the north side of the massif in two stages. First, by establishing an advance cache of food and equipment on the Lana Col and then, when Keith and Bruce returned, carrying the rest over the col and down to the glacier. David and I led the way up the now-familiar snow couloir to the Lana Col, while Bill and Julian decided to bag a couple of peaks en route by traversing the Lana Ridge. After dumping our loads, David and I peered down the ridge and were disconcerted to see Bill and Julian stuck fast on the top of a gendarme. Clearly, we were in for a long wait.

'As you might have guessed,' explained a morose-looking Bill two hours later, 'we had our problems. While trying to negotiate that wretched gendarme I fell twenty feet, luckily into soft snow. Julian followed me, but failed to secure his rucksack properly. It rolled all the way down to the Hazarchal glacier, so he's had to go down to retrieve it. He won't be coming up here again today.'

Back at base, Julian was all gloom and doom.

'The rock in these bloody mountains is absolutely lethal. If it's all like this, I can't see much point in staying on. Maybe we should cut our losses and leave a few days earlier to explore those mountains that Kachpiss was banging on about.'

'Come off it, Julian', retorted Bill. 'I'm sure we'll find plenty of decent rock once we get across to the north side.'

To fill in time while Keith and Bruce were away, all four of us climbed the long, indented ridge of Siah Sang Kuh to Siah Kaman Kuh's virgin summit. The naturalists returned a day early having journeyed south with a mule caravan laden with rice and salt and then spent two nights with black-tented semi-nomads collecting snakes, lizards, butterflies and flowers. Unfortunately, Keith had picked up a bug on the way, so Bill's load-carrying schedule had to be recast.

On 1st August, everyone save Keith left base camp together humping loads that included Bill's outsize bedding roll/sleeping bag and a couple of Keith's flower presses. On reaching the Lana Col, there was no sign of Julian or Aki.

'What the devil's happened to them?' I asked Bill.

'No idea. But Bruce and I can't hang around here. We'll dump our loads and get back to camp for my second carry. See you later.'

I stuck around for half an hour, but with still no sign of Julian and Aki decided to go it alone. Stuffing most of the cached tinned food into my rucksack, I then strapped my rope, spare clothing and Bill's bedding-roll on top of it. The only possible way down to the North-West Glacier was by the scree couloir we had inspected tentatively six days before. It had no visible run-out, but having got so far, I thought 'What the hell, let's give it a go!'

Once launched, there was no way back. The descent down unstable scree of varying sizes and consistency was like riding the surf. Sliding and slipping with the rucksack repeatedly throwing me off balance, I careered downwards wildly out of control to where the couloir narrowed into a gulch. Here, what looked like a solid boulder shot from under me and triggered a rock avalanche fore and aft. Clinging desperately to a protruding spike of rock, I watched helplessly as several-thousand tons of stone roared past within inches of my boots. As the avalanche gathered strength, it scoured its way down the couloir leaving in its wake clouds of dust and the acrid smell of brimstone.

It was either me or Bill's bedding role. I hurled the wretched thing down the couloir and yelled with delight as it took a small hop and a step before bouncing from side to side all the way to the bottom. Seventy-five minutes after leaving the Lana Col, I reached the North-West Glacier bruised, shaken and exhausted. Dumping my load on a level bit of moraine, I stared up at Alam Kuh's near-vertical west face. Had I really come down that way? It looked absolutely lethal.

I took a short rest and then steeled myself for a second carry. The ascent was harder than the descent. For every upward step, I seemed to slip two back. Halfway up, I passed Julian and Aki gingerly descending a parallel couloir.

'What the hell happened to you two?' I shouted across to them. 'I thought we were supposed to be doing this carry together?'

When Julian shouted back, 'We had to spend the morning trying to find my bloody rucksack!' I didn't bother to reply.

Back on the col, the sun was already sinking behind the Haft Khan ridge and a sharp wind had sprung up. Suddenly, I felt completely drained and began to shiver uncontrollably. It was too cold to hang around for Bill and David and so, after shovelling the last load into my rucksack, I began my second descent. It was even scarier than the first. Bill and David breezed in close on my heels at 7.30 p.m. unflurried and unconcerned.

'Glacier Camp' on the North-West Glacier's moraine consisted of the mess-tent's tarpaulin cover propped up by tent poles. Not wide enough to fit in all five of us, I bagged the annexe formed by a groundsheet. For the past six weeks, I had shared a tent with Bill. His camping manners were impeccable, but his size fourteen boots made for an uneasy relationship and were mainly responsible for the multiple punctures sustained by his air mattress. As darkness fell, a deadening chill descended. The pressure cooker had blown up in Austria and at over 4,000 metres the punctured Primus stove barely functioned. Even so, cold corned-beef hash and half-cooked macaroni never tasted better.

Next morning, 2 August 1956, while breakfasting on the corned-beef remnants and the standard ration of four ship's biscuits, Bill reminded us that on this very day we were scheduled to climb Solomon's Throne. Leaving Aki to guard the camp 'against bears', we trudged a kilometre down the glacier and rounded Alam Kuh's north-east spur. Dead ahead, Takht-i-Sulaiman rose stark from out of its glacial moat. Only the eye of faith could have compared this scree-scarred pyramid to the Weisshorn, yet its surroundings were grand and as we crept along the base of Alam Kuh's intimidating north face towards the indented ridge that linked it to Takht-i-Sulaiman, I felt a sense of awe.

The crest of this connecting ridge was broken by a shapely little peak, Chane Kuh, whose summit gendarme yielded the most enjoyable climb of the expedition. Wedged near the top of the crux crack was a weathered wooden peg: a relic perhaps of Bobek's 1936 German expedition? The rest was merely a scramble. The Germans had reached this elusive summit twenty years earlier, as doubtless had many inquisitive shepherds done before them, but ours was surely a British first. To the north, a green sea of undulating ridges drifted away to the Caspian. To the south, Alam Kuh's four-kilometres long, 800 metres-high north face was split by two predominant features: the great rock buttress first climbed by the Germans and the hanging glacier that Bernard Pierre had called 'The Ice Curtain'. It was a magnificent spectacle, but had our journey been worth it?

Ludwig Steinauer who had led the first ascent of this North-East Buttress typified the national socialist *sturm und drang* tradition having previously made a string of extreme 'firsts' including the north-west face of the Dent Blanche and the fourth ascent of the Central Spur of the Grandes Jorasses, then regarded as the 'last great problem of the Alps'. By naming Alam Kuh's buttress 'The Persian Jorasses', he had given his seventeen-hour climb an inflated reputation. Only the upper section looked really difficult and I pondered then, as I did for years to come, why we never quite had the bottle to attempt it. Yesterday's 'last great problems' become today's classic routes. In 1963, Richard Isherwood and Henry Day, members of another Cambridge expedition, climbed the buttress in five hours and gave most of it a IV grading. Leyla Pope, a former president of the Cambridge Mountaineering Club, has since rated it an easy day for 'veiled Iranian ladies'.

Back at Glacier Camp, Aki awaited our return with hot soup, biscuits and coffee. Now indispensable to team morale, his good-natured bewilderment at the antics of the Ingliz had defused the 'butter battle' triggered by Julian's insistence that his butter and biscuit ration should be given him as a lump allocation rather than have it rationed at each meal like the rest of us. Over supper, I belatedly remembered that this was my twenty-second birthday. Next day, the four of us set off to do the first traverse of Haft Khan's indented granite ridge. It flattered to deceive, for once past two modest gendarmes, only Julian bothered to complete it. Back in camp, I pressed some flowers before taking to my sleeping bag with shooting stomach pains. That night, I dreamed that we were climbing an Alam Kuh of Himalayan proportions. When I slipped off a knife-edge ice ridge, I woke up shouting and gasping for breath.

Time and food were now running out. On our last full day at Glacier Camp,

Julian and Bill climbed a fine granite buttress coming off the Haft Khan Ridge. I only felt well enough to write up my diary; ponder on what might have been, and watch a succession of avalanches thundering down the same couloirs we had descended only four days before. David and Aki had spent a more constructive day investigating a less hazardous route back to Hazarchal. As the sun sank behind the Haft Khan ridge, we squatted round the spluttering stove for our last supper at Glacier Camp. Away to the north, the fires of shepherds showed up as pin pricks of light against the darkening hills.

The journey back over the glacier's headwall was easy and would have saved us the double carries and the dangerous route by which we had come. Base Camp was now barely recognisable with banks of yellow flowers and white-blossomed thistles occupying what had been snowfields. Keith, Bruce and Safar had already left in search of Daku, the mysterious village inhabited by what Freya Stark had described as 'fierce and primitive Jungalis'. That afternoon, two shifty-looking shepherds armed with antique rifles dropped by and grudgingly accepted Nescafe, aspirin and Elastoplast in lieu of 'camping dues'. When Aki purposefully unholstered his revolver and told them to push-off, they sloped away like dogs denied their dinner.

Evenings were always best at Hazarchal for by then the Caspian mists had melted away and the sun lost its bite to shed a softer light on the pale, grey ridges that stretched away eastwards to the ghostly cone of Demavend. On our last evening, wisps of cloud appeared for the first time and a cold wind blew in from the east. At dusk, a lone muleteer arrived to say that the mules were waiting at Tanakrud. Next morning, it was entirely predictable that 'Brown Hat' should try to swing an additional 300 rials for his having to spend an 'extra' night there. When Aki beat him down to 100 rials, I asked him how he did it.

'Simple', replied our intrepid soldier. 'First, I will be offensive. If that doesn't work, I will strike the man down. Finally, I will threaten him with my revolver.'

As the mule train wended its way down Hazarchal, now bright with flowers and sparkling streams, I glanced back for one last look at what had once promised to be our delectable mountains. Deserted when we first arrived, the valley was now alive with shepherds, bleating flocks and ferocious guard dogs. When Aki picked up a young goat and cradled it in his arms, I took a quick photograph on impulse, overcome with nostalgia.

The naturalists' return to Rudbarek coincided with our own. They had had no trouble locating Daku and had been warmly received by the 'Jungalis', So far so good, but when Julian and David eventually located SXB 205, the battery was flat and both towropes had disappeared.

'More to the point' said David 'we weren't able to buy any food. All the village shops are shut because Kalardasht is under curfew and martial law.'

Aki's version of events was more colourful.

'There was a terrible massacre while we were away. The headmen of Rudbarek and Hasankeif had a quarrel and 400 men began a fight. Four have been killed. Now, anything might happen!'

Nothing did, but life at Kalardasht was not like that in the Swiss cantons. Its inhabitants, mainly of Kurdish stock, had been forcibly resettled from their northern Zagros homeland at the end of the eighteenth century by Agha Mohammad Khan to stabilise this unruly corner of his kingdom. Long since, they had abandoned their national tongue, but not their cultural identity, feudal way of life, or Sunni religious affiliations. Generally monogamous, their unveiled women played a prominent part in community life. Marriageable girls, traditionally dressed in white head scarves, pleated skirts with trousers, brightly-coloured smocks and gay waistcoats jingling with trinkets, were courted not allocated. Fighting and brigandage, once the principal male preoccupations, had given way to farming, logging, and hunting and much less fun.

The headman of Rudbarek was the village's main landowner and tribal chief. A patriarch of powerful personality and impressive girth, he boasted of his lands, forests and mines and introduced us to two of his five sons, dressed in dark double-breasted suits together with a selection of his daughters. No favours were offered, but when he complemented Bill for our not molesting the village women, our leader's normal sangfroid deserted him. When the word got around, my morning dispensary was overwhelmed. I dished out aspirin, placebos and Elastoplast to casualties of the Rudbarek/Hasankeif fracas, but was helpless in the face of the malignant growths, trachoma and the serious illnesses that were so common in these parts. When a young woman presented me with a tiny child covered in septic sores, I spent half-an-hour simply cleaning off ingrained grime before applying antiseptic dressings.

RECEDING HORIZONS

No one was more reluctant to leave the mountains of Takht-i-Sulaiman on 10 August than Keith and Bruce for they had collected a valuable range of unusual flora and fauna and forged a close friendship with Saphar. My own feelings on leaving this enchanted corner of Iran were mixed. Mazanderan's viridescent forests; the kilometres-long glaciers that some embassy wiseacre had dismissed as non-existent, and the villages that would not have been out of place in Switzerland had come as unexpected wonders. For all that, the mountaineering had been disappointing with only some minor first ascents and one testing crossing to show for it. Admittedly, the rock around Hazarchal was lethal, but we had baulked at the challenge of the Alam Kuh's buttress through lack of confidence and experience. Maybe Kachpiss's mountains of Shemshack and Palur would offer new fields to conquer, but somehow I doubted it. From Hazarchal, the only snow mountain visible to the east had been Demavend, over a hundred miles away.

And although we weren't to know it at the time, those days round and about Solomon's snows were to be the most memorable of our Persian Expedition. Other adventures lay ahead, but from now on events took a predominantly downhill trajectory. It was Aki who first signalled the decline at the Chalus/ Tehran turn-off.

'I'm sorry Boll, but I must leave you now. I'm hitching an army lorry to take me back to Tehran.'

'But Aki, you can't possibly be leaving us now,' spluttered Bill, for once losing his composure.

'I'm sorry Boll, but I must rejoin my regiment.'

The consequences of losing Aki, now an integral part of the team, seemed unimaginable. Bill reasoned and cajoled, but Aki would not be moved.

'*A bientôt*, Aki', we chorused as each of us pumped his hand. 'We'll all meet up again in Tehran once we get back.'

'Yes indeed my friends,' replied Aki. 'I promise to show you the sights of my city and you will be welcome at my house as honoured guests.'

That night, 205 and 206 rolled into the dimly lit streets of Chalus and after bumbling around, eventually found somewhere to camp beside a murky creek. The Caspian's hot and humid shore makes a perfect breeding ground for flies, giant earwigs, scorpions, leeches, snakes and every other kind of pest, as well as malaria and cholera. Plagued by mosquitoes at night, my morning wake-up plunge into its brackish waters left my feet lacerated by sharp rocks. And having assumed that we would be able to cash travellers cheques in Chalus, I now experienced a much sharper shock as expedition treasurer. After spending an entire morning negotiating exchange rates with the manager of the town's only bank, he eventually admitted that only in Tehran would this be possible.

Our cash was almost exhausted and although Tehran was only a hundred miles away, in no way would the jeeps have been able to recross the Kandevan pass from this steeper side of the range. After two days of vacuous potterings along the Caspian with little to show for it save for the capture of a rare tortoise in the pressure cooker, we took the much longer route back to Tehran over the Gaduk Pass. This frustrating three-day journey became another catalogue of boiling radiators, multiple punctures, written-off tyres and broken trailer-towing hooks which reached its climax twenty miles short of Tehran when 205 had to be abandoned at the roadside leaving 206 to make a solo dash to catch the Bank Melli fifteen minutes before it closed for the four-day religious holiday of Muharram.

The Caspian idyll had lost a week, leaving only a fortnight before the start of the 5,000-mile-long homeward journey – assuming always that the jeeps would last that long.

'I suppose we might as well take a serious look at Kachpiss's mountains in Shemshak and Palur,' said Bill, as we sat on the curb outside the British Embassy in Tehran disconsolately sipping tepid Pepsi-colas. 'We've really no other option.'

There was, in fact, another option staring us right in the face in the shape of the 5,670 metre near-extinct volcano Mount Demavend. However, as Bill had originally dismissed it as a mere 'tourist mountain' we hadn't considered it further.

'But where exactly are Kachpiss's mythical peaks?' asked David.

The tattered Survey of India map, rolled out yet again, clearly showed a village called Shemshak barely twenty miles due north of Tehran set in a valley surrounded by mountains.

'I don't think much of that as an area for exploration,' growled Julian.

'The map shows several mines in the area with a road leading up to them. The MEF would have a fit if we made that an objective. What about Palur? It's about fifty miles further east very near Demavend and surely more promising.'

We plumped for Palur with no set plan in mind and on 15 August camped at nearby Abigarm, a pretty village with flat-roofed, mud-walled houses set amidst poplars, orchards and tiny fields. Famous for its hot mineral springs, its single street was thronged with holidaymakers up from Tehran to celebrate Muharram, the sacred Shi'a festival that commemorates the death of the martyrs Hassan and Hussein. That evening, the atmosphere darkened as a chanting procession of men with black banners marched through the village beating their bare breasts, rending their hair, and flagellating their backs with chains.

No one really knew quite what to do next, but the following morning the sight of Demavend freshly covered in snow revived interest in climbing it.

'What about the east ridge that Bernard Pierre's party did a couple of years ago?' I suggested.

'Surely we've got to be a bit more original than that,' replied Keith.

'A week spent exploring the mountains of Palur would much better fulfil the expedition's scientific programme.'

The issue remained unresolved until we bumped into the member of the Franco-Iranian expedition that I had met above Rudbarek.

'How did it go?' I asked him. 'Did you climb the north wall?'

'Absolutely not!' he replied. 'Much too dangerous. We scarcely got off the ground.'

'What are you doing here then?' I persisted.

'We were hoping to climb Demavend's north-east face. But just to get anywhere near it involved a two-day approach march with mules. We then had to carry loads for another 4,000 metres higher to establish a base camp. The face is protected by 1,000-metre-high ice cliffs so we abandoned it.'

'What about the east ridge?'

'That's also a very serious climb which can't be done in under a week and you'll need good weather.'

Even allowing for Iranian hyperbole, that clinched it.

Before the Mongols laid waste these lands, the highlands of Palur had been a stronghold of Larijan's mountain warlords. Nearby, was the Lar Valley itself, once a highway for caravans that plied their trade across the mountains to the Caspian coast. According to the map, this ancient track passed by a place called Kushak, some thirty miles away, set plumb in the middle of the range and therefore a perfect base from which to explore the surrounding mountains. To ensure a seamless start, we made a preliminary recce that morning to identify the entrance to the Lar Valley. At the bridge that crosses its river, a familiar figure was standing besides an Embassy Land Rover with two others.

'Glad to see that you're still with us,' grinned Reggie Burrows after waving us down. 'Where've you been all this time?'

Bill gave him a résumé of our adventures.

'At least you've got this far,' smirked Burrows. 'News of your exploits has filtered back to the embassy. You know my wife Jenny of course, but you won't have met Hugh Carless. He's a *proper* mountaineer just back from climbing in Afghanistan.'

At this, a suntanned younger man, immaculate in a tailored bush-jacket, stepped forward to proffer the hand. Confident in the camaraderie of the hills, I asked him what he'd been climbing.

'Just a short walk in the Hindu Kush,' he replied dismissively without the glimmer of a smile. 'We were hoping to bag Mir Samir, but didn't quite make the summit.'

Two years later, Eric Newby's classic *A Short Walk in the Hindu Kush* described the brave attempt that he and Carless made to climb the virgin 19,880-foot peak of Mir Samir. Carless, the pukka, politically-correct Foreign Office sahib, is portrayed as Newby's foil and the book closes with Wilfred Thesiger's immortal put-down as he watches the intrepid pair blowing up their airbeds, 'God, you must be a couple of pansies!'

'We're nipping up Demavend tomorrow so we're here to arrange mule transport,' continued Burrows.

'Perhaps we might camp together tonight?' suggested Bill.

'No question of that I'm afraid,' replied Burrows. 'We're driving back to Tehran this afternoon and will be back tomorrow at the crack of dawn for an early start.'

For the rest of that day, we prepared ourselves for a ten-day trek into the remotest Elburz cutting rations down to the nearest lump of sugar.

'This time, we're going to make do with only two mules and one muleteer,' said Bill after he and Keith had returned from a lengthy muleteer-hunting quest in Abigarm.

'Luckily, we've found just the right man. He's called Hussain and has promised to be here tomorrow at 7 a.m. sharp.'

Hussain, heavily-moustachioed and gap-toothed, wore a shabby western suit with a brown skull-cap that disturbingly resembled Brown Hat's. He fetched-up an hour late and promptly took his lead from a rascally French-speaking shopkeeper who had already broken his earlier agreement to guard the jeeps for a fixed price, by doubling his. At this, Julian suddenly lost his cool.

'I'm damned if I'm going to be blackmailed by these rascals. We shouldn't pay them a rial more than what's already been agreed. And I'm all for scrapping mules altogether. We can surely carry our own kit and food for a few days.'

Left to himself, Julian would have done just that. Fifty years on, his determination, self-sufficiency and technical skills were exactly the qualities that enabled him to complete a twelve-year, round-the-world, single-handed odyssey in a tiny junk-rigged yacht tracking Darwin's original *Beagle* voyage. This time, Bill persuaded him to forego hair-shirt heroics.

After a bad-tempered loading session, Hussain led the way up a bleak valley enclosed by desiccated hills devoid of either shade or vegetation. The map didn't seem to tally with the ground, but far away to the north, a line of jagged peaks broke the familiar pattern of rolling ridges.

'Must be Kachpiss's mountains,' said the ever-optimistic Bruce.

Heading up a side valley, we came upon a black-tented encampment where a garrulous old man riding a donkey tagged along uninvited while his veiled wife trotted along besides. Our packs were heavy and no one complained when, towards evening, Hussain called a halt near a spring occupied by an Iranian Army party and several burly American officers. Ensconced in luxurious bell tents with six servants in attendance, they were mighty pleased with themselves for having bagged two ibex and a wild boar. Perfunctory greetings over, they ignored us and tucked into juicy, he-man-sized steaks. Hussain scorned our offering of corned-beef hash and slid off to feast on richer pickings.

Assured by the Yanks that there were no snow mountains at the head of this valley, we set a new course westwards the following morning. Hours later, on rounding a bend, a neat cluster of tents appeared on a greensward with a uniformed functionary standing nearby.

'What is this place?' Bill asked the man.

'This is Yurt-i-Khan,' he replied. 'The British Embassy's summer camp.'

'I just don't believe this,' spluttered Julian, chucking down his pack.

'We must have started up the wrong valley yesterday, doubled back on our tracks today and gone round in a circle. I could murder this bloody Hussain!'

The British Embassy's Lar Valley camp had been a summer haven for British diplomats even before Beresford Lovett had written in 1883, 'The Lar plains … have been so often described that it is unnecessary to say anything more about them.'

Hussain grumbled that there was nowhere else to camp higher up, but we pressed on regardless. Picking up pace through the narrowing valley, the river had to be forded several times before it widened out again into a broad plain dotted with black goatskin tents. Suddenly, without warning, the sky became overcast with dark, scudding clouds and within minutes a rainstorm had soaked us to the skin. The day dragged on until the sun began to sink behind a line of distant hills, which, in the faint afterglow, appeared as a snow-streaked range.

'At last!' exclaimed Bill triumphantly. 'Kachpiss's fabled mountains!'

It was long past dusk when Hussain turned off into another side valley near the ruins of an ancient *caravanserai*. Stopping at a level patch of grass, he peremptorily unloaded the mules indicating that in no way was he going a step further.

'What is this place?' asked Bill.

'It is called Saphid Arb,' he replied defiantly.

We paid him half his hire with the promise that he'd get the rest, provided he was back within seven days.

The camp at Saphid Arb, the Place of White Waters, was 10,000 feet high, surrounded by bleak mountains and consisted of six poncho capes tied together with string and guyed by ice axes. Within shouting distance lay the main encampment of the Shahsavan, 'Followers of the Shah', who like the Kurds of Kalardasht had been resettled by Agha Mohammad Khan in the nineteenth century from their homeland on the steppes around the great volcano of Kuh-i-Sabalan in Iranian Azerbaijan. Reza Shah had seen the tribes and their way of life as a threat to his power so used the army to bludgeon them into submission by forced resettlement and imprisonment, executing those chiefs who resisted. After his abdication many tribes resumed their semi-nomadic way of life, but with their cultural and political influence significantly weakened.

The hillsides around were dotted with flocks of sheep and goats shepherded by fearsome dogs whose masters controlled them with shouts, whistles and yodels. A young shepherd boy stopped by to play a merry tune on a pipe fashioned from a metal tube. The headman invited us to tea in his spacious, white bell tent, incongruous amidst the traditional goat-hair variety. Squatting awkwardly cross-legged on a splendid red and purple tribal carpet, we sipped tea through sugar lumps served in delicate glasses from an ornate samovar. Bill and Keith's attempts at conversation made me regret my failure to persevere with Mr Khan Shad's lessons in Farsi at Cambridge. It was left to the headman's son, sporting a Tony Curtis haircut, to keep the chat stuttering on in broken English.

This louche young man was spending his summer holidays here with the family, though he normally worked in Tehran as a cinema projectionist much preferring the city lights to a semi-nomadic existence. Motor transport had destroyed the modest prosperity that the lucrative caravan trade passing through Saphid Arb to the Caspian had previously provided them and the once extensive juniper forests that had formerly clothed these hills had long ago been cut down for charcoal. Tribal life followed a changeless pattern. The flocks were shepherded by day and then rounded up every evening before being driven into horseshoe-shaped, dry-stone-walled enclosures where the men sat astride low stools and grabbed each animal as it passed and milked it on the spot. The women, unveiled and wearing brightly-coloured tribal dress, poured the milk into animal skins attached to a triangle of upright poles to churn the curds that formed the tribe's staple diet. Another of their tasks was to gather the spiny, thorn bushes that were used for fuel both to cook and dye wool in huge, blackened cauldrons placed over shallow trenches filled with hot embers. This work and child rearing apart, theirs was an immutable round of wool washing, carding, dyeing and weaving to make clothing and tentage. The tribe's only source of income derived from the colourful tribal carpets woven on horizontal looms and sold to Tehran dealers for a pittance.

By now, it was clear that the expedition's exploratory progress was in danger of grinding to a halt. To regain momentum, Bill dispatched recce parties to fix the precise location of Kachpiss's mountains. By the evening of the second day, only he and Bruce had anything significant to report.

'Did anyone else notice that isolated peak at the western end of the ridge marked on the map as Bareseng Ashter?' said Bill. 'I reckon it must be over 14,000 feet and could well be our mystery mountain.'

When the map was produced, Julian remained unimpressed.

'I didn't know that we were looking for any *mystery* mountain in particular. Anyway, according to the map this one's a thousand feet lower and at least sixteen miles away. It's also almost due north of Shemshak, so what the hell are we doing here? To get there and back would involve a round-trek of over thirty miles and at least 4,500 feet of ascent and descent during the heat of the day!'

'We could always start at midnight,' suggested Bruce brightly.

'Good idea!' said Bill. 'We could be there and back within sixteen hours.'

After sleeping on it, the Baresang party narrowed down to Bill, Bruce, Keith and me. Four and a half hours on, we had reached the far end of the Lar Valley without seeing anything of interest save a herd of moufflon. Another two-hour slog up execrable scree took us on to Baraseng Ashter's ridge from where Bill's peak was faintly visible as an indistinct bump at its far end. The ridge's seemingly endless crests and troughs kept losing hard-won height and the sun radiating off the clinker-like shale scorched my eyes even through dark glasses. When Keith and Bruce sensibly packed it in at 1 p.m. I would happily have followed suit. But by now Bill was away on his own and out of earshot. I followed in his wake harbouring uncharitable thoughts.

At 3.15 p.m. nine hours after leaving Saphid Arb, a final scree scramble led to the heap of rubble that marked Baresang Kuh's summit. A moraine-strewn cwm occupying its north-east flank might once have housed a small glacier, but otherwise there was nothing to distinguish this shattered summit from a hundred and one others that capped the crumbling ridges of the Elburz.

A rough cairn with a weathered wooden plaque bearing an inscription in Cyrillic confirmed that its first ascent had already been made by the Russian cartographers who surveyed the Elburz earlier in the century. I discovered later from the authoritative Russian *Moscow Atlas* (1954) that Baresung Kuh's height is 4,363 metres, or 14,175 feet, so Bill's estimate was almost spot on, as had been his timing for the round-trek. When at 10.30 p.m. that night, we stumbled into Saphid Arb with blistered feet and bleeding toes, Bill didn't bother to answer Julian's question, 'Where on earth have you been Bill?'

With summer fast giving way to autumn, our time at Saphid Arb had run out as it had for the Shahsavan. Long before dawn, the advance guard of their extended caravan was making its way down the valley bound for their winter quarters on the plains south of Tehran. The heads of the lead camels were bedecked with red and yellow tassels and their necks were hung with jingling bells. The imperious young tribeswoman riding astride a cushioned saddle with a fine carpet trailing down her camel's flanks might have been a Tartar princess. It made a splendid spectacle, but the reality of these annual migrations is anything but romantic. Bound by the rhythm of the seasons and captive to extremes of weather, these hardy people's livelihood depended entirely on their flocks and scanty pastures. Save for carpet weaving, invention and art had no place. Raiding and brigandage, once a *raison d'être* for the younger bloods, were no longer options. Migration might be an adventure, but at the end of each journey, nothing remained except 'an immense, traditional resignation'.

Hussain had sworn to be early. In his place, a callow youth with a reluctant mule turned up three hours late. The boy was so clueless that David and I took over the loading, leaving the others to push on ahead. A mile down the track by the ruined Basteh *caravanserai*, the mule bucked and shed its load scattering pots, pans, cutlery, jerry cans, cookers, flower presses and ropes into the dust. A group of loafers lounging outside hooted with laughter but raised not a finger to help. Eight hours on, after three more load-sheddings and two river crossings, we called it a day at the British Embassy's camp. Here the muleteer ran off without a word and when he reappeared next morning, it was too late for the planned early start. He then lost the way, turned truculent and bolted towards a scruffy settlement. Braving a pack of dogs, we ran him to ground but he refused to budge. His chosen substitute was even more hopeless than he was so we summarily dismissed him after half an hour. At Palur, Hussain was anxiously awaiting our arrival. The reluctant muleteer turned out to be his son.

For the sake of the CNPE's credibility, it was now agreed that we should all climb Demavend. This, the highest mountain between the Atlantic and the Hindu Kush occupies a special place in Iranian legend as the site of Noah's Ark and the abode of the heroes Jamshid and Rustum. Here too, Yasid bin Jigad, the Persian Prometheus, was bound in chains to have his liver devoured daily by an eagle. Deep inside its volcanic crater, the giant Zohak, imprisoned by the hero Feridun, still exhales his noxious sulphur fumes.

The thirteenth century geographer Yakut had already recorded several local ascents before that of a twenty-four-year-old Scot, William Taylor Thomson, who reached its summit in 1837 when Demavend's height was estimated at over 21,000 feet. It has since been reduced to 18,597 feet. The normal route is no more than an exhausting slog, but the weather can be capricious and dangerous. Steinauer's 1936 German party was hit by three severe blizzards within the space of a week, one of which lasted for twenty hours.

On the strict time schedule we had set ourselves, the only way to climb Demavend was to dispense with an intermediate camp and start at night. At 10.45 p.m. on 27 August, the six of us stumbled up a rough track on the outskirts of Rehneh in thick mist and blundered into a hamlet where we had to beat off a pack of dogs with volleys of stones directed by torchlight. In the confusion, we lost the path. Two hours later, the cloud lifted to reveal, impossibly high above, the white cone of Demavend luminous in the moonlight. Below lay a wave-tossed cloud-sea – cold, immobile and impassive. I shivered uncontrollably when at dawn we stopped for breakfast to force down hard-boiled eggs, sardines and chocolate and then retched the whole lot up.

By 6 a.m. the sun was dazzling and the sky intensely blue. With a thousand metres still to go, seams of black lava gave way to gleaming snowfields interspersed with fantastic towers of sulphurous, yellow rock. For the next six hours the climb assumed a surreal quality. Stopping for breath every fifteen steps and vomiting at intervals, I had to fight off an almost irresistible yearning to lie down and go to sleep. The sunlight was blinding, yet it remained intensely cold with the wind blowing in fierce gusts. Drunkenly, I followed up a broken rib of yellow rock almost asphyxiated by nauseous puffs of Zohak's sulphurous breath and after collapsing on a heap of scree fell fast asleep.

On waking, I vomited again but felt better. Ahead and above, two figures were silhouetted on what I assumed must be the summit. One was definitely Julian and the other was surely Bill. Rousing myself for a final effort, I joined them fifteen minutes later only to find that Bill was in fact David. Bruce, plodding steadily behind, came in next with Bill shortly after. The roof of

Iran was a shallow, snow-filled crater fringed by ochre rocks covered in graffiti, miscellaneous placards and rubbish. Diaphanous clouds floated by like phantoms out of an inky-blue sky. Below, billowing up from a colossal gulf, cumulus clouds closed and parted. The descent felt like the dreamland and twenty hours after starting, five of us reassembled at the road head. Keith had somehow got detached on the way down, but turned up halfway through supper having had to walk several extra miles.

The sensible thing would have been to crash out then and there. But the prospect of Tehran's garages closing over the weekend led to the near-catastrophic decision of driving straight through to Gulhak that same night. When I fell asleep at the wheel and drove into the mountainside, the impact burst another good tyre. If I'd veered just a little the other way, we'd have gone over a precipice. That crazy night drive turned out to be a wasted effort for it took another week to get the jeeps repaired. This time round, our reception in Tehran was less than enthusiastic. Mr J.B. Ventham, BP's chief in Iran, and his charming wife were exceptionally hospitable. But the diplomatic ramifications of our 'North Persian' tag rumbled on. Reggie Burrows's farewell party was cancelled 'unavoidably', and Miss Palmer Smith's promised invitation to meet some 'Persian ladies' never materialised. A popular tale doing the rounds was that the CNPE had stumbled on to the embassy's Lar Valley camp after being lost for several days. However, there was still the prospect of a grand reunion with Aki to look forward to, though perplexingly, there was no message from him at the embassy. Bill traipsed off to the Mountain Federation's offices to find out what had happened to him and eventually tracked down Colonel Kachpiss.

'I must offer you and your friends my warm congratulations,' said the colonel. 'Captain Ghaffari has already given me a glowing account of your exploits which have been well covered in our local newspapers. However, I must inform you that our Iranian team traversed the Haft Khan ridge a few days before you did. I do hope you are not too disappointed.'

After Bill had given the colonel a frank assessment of the mountains of Palur he was less effusive, but offered lukewarm congratulations on our 'fast' ascent of Demavend.

'To commemorate your achievement, you will be sent a special photograph of Demavend signed by the Shah himself!'

He was surprised that we had heard nothing more from Aki, but promised to arrange a meeting as soon as possible. Two days before our departure, a scribbled note arrived from Aki inviting us to lunch at his house.

After waiting for half an hour at the appointed street-corner rendezvous, a scruffy little man appeared with a written message. 'Very regrettably, Captain Ghaffari has had to take his wife to hospital, and will not therefore be able to receive you.'

Back in Cambridge, Bill wrote to both to Aki and Colonel Kachpiss expressing the expedition's warmest thanks together with a detailed account of our climbs. Neither replied, nor did Bill ever receive the Shah's signed photograph of Demavend. Some years later, when serving with the Colonial Service in Aden, I bumped into Colonel Kachpiss who happened to be passing through leading a visiting Iranian climbing team. I asked him if he remembered the Cambridge North Persian Expedition. Charming as ever, he confessed that he had no recollection of it whatsoever.

The CNPE's twenty-eight day, 4,800 mile return journey back to Cambridge was another incident-packed race against time in order to make the start of the Michaelmas term. With Julian Huxley's *From An Antique Land* as our guide, Bill's 'Cultural Swan' included the mosaic faience mosques of Isfahan, a carpet factory in Hamadan, the coppersmith's bazaar in Baghdad, the Sassanian arch of Ctesiphon, the Street That Is Straight in Damascus, the Phoenician port of Byblos, the millennium water-wheels at Hama, Homs, a desert drive to Palmyra and the great souk of Aleppo before crossing the Taurus and on to the Anatolian Plateau where it was already bitterly cold at night. Apart from being arrested in Syria we were generally met with kindness and I count it a particular privilege to have seen the wonders of this ancient land before their wanton destruction at the hands of ISIL.

On 5 September 1956, only one day late for the start of term, SXB 206 and 205 drove slowly down Kings Parade exactly 104 days after we had left Cambridge on that balmy midsummer's morning that now seemed light years away. Within weeks of our return, the Soviets had invaded Hungary and the botched Anglo-French invasion of Suez signalled the end of Britain's status as a world power. It was a miracle that both jeeps should have finished the course despite a final count of sixteen new tyres. Years later, SXB 206 was spotted still driving around Cambridge. Six night drives on the homeward journey left me with involuntary eye-blink, which persisted throughout the Michaelmas term, but otherwise we had survived unscathed.

The CNPE had cost £1,600, perhaps £24,000 in today's money. A month before we graduated in June 1957, a £300 deficit had been reduced to an overdraft of £138 14s 11d, thanks largely to vehicle and equipment sales and receipts from newspaper and magazine articles, but no thanks to the War Office which made us pay dear for tentage 'wear and tear'. Keith and Bruce's natural history collections, which included sixty-eight new Persian plant species, five small fishes, miscellaneous lizards and an unusual snake, were well received by the British Museum of Natural History. Bill's description of Elburz birdlife was published in *Ibis* and Julian's account of tribal life in the *Geographical Magazine*. Both Bill and Keith later exhibited their Elburz watercolours and I wrote up the expedition in the 1957 *Himalayan Journal* illustrated by David's painstaking sketch map. A year later, this was superseded when the 1958 *Alpine Journal* reproduced Dr Hans Bobek's masterly *Karte der Takht-e-Sulaimangruppe* accompanied by a gushing encomium from Douglas Busk.

Without the Mount Everest Foundation's grant, the CNPE would never have left England. Whether the expedition had made a contribution to '*the exploration of the mountain regions of the earth*' is debatable. I later discovered that 113 years before us, the Austrian botanist, Theodor Kotschy, had spent several weeks in the Hazarchal and that in the late nineteenth century, Beresford Lovatt had crossed Orim Nizwa on horseback. The *Moscow Atlas* puts its height at 3,720 metres or 12,231 feet. The 1963 edition of Bartholomew's *Middle East* 1:4,000,000 map still referred to '*Kuh-i-Niswa, 18,000*', but it no longer features in Bartholomew's *Times Atlas of the World*. Sir Claremont Skrine remained our loyal champion to the end. Chairing a Royal Central Asian Society's meeting on 5 December 1956 at which Bill gave a lecture illustrated by Keith's film, he described this as 'quite exceptional among the various travel talks and films we have seen since the war ... an admirable specimen of the modern expedition of the youth of England, and, in fact of Europe!' The Honorary Secretary to the Mount Everest Foundation's assessment was more circumspect. When responding to Bill's expedition report, he asked for further and better particulars about expenditure and concluded, 'I am glad that you thought the expedition worthwhile'.

For us, the Cambridge North Persian Expedition had been a defining experience. First love, first mountain, first expedition are ones you never forget. Many years later, I went some way to repay the MEF's generous grant when acting as the Foundation's Honorary Legal Adviser from 1980 to 1995, including six years as a member of the board of management. During this time, I helped to dissuade one of its chairmen, George Lowe, from dispersing the whole of the MEF's capital fund rather than restricting expedition grants to income and was also responsible for the appointment of professional managers to look after its investments. The MEF flourishes and since its inception has dispensed over a million pounds to British and New Zealand mountaineering expeditions.

ENVOI

Iran is an exception to the rule that you should never go back. Fourteen years after that Cambridge expedition, I did so by stopping over in Tehran when returning home from Australia in December 1970. My hosts Anthony and Sarah Wood were happy that we should spend a weekend in the Elburz so we drove to Rudbarek, which had become a popular tourist resort. The Iranian Mountaineering Federation had built its new headquarters here and it was no great surprise that the chief guide should be our old muleteer Safar Ali Negani now married with several children, one of whom subsequently climbed Everest. Safar's reception room was stuffed with photographs and citations from foreign mountaineering expeditions, yet for all his newfound fame, he remained modest and unaffected and agreed to accompany us for a two-day trek into the mountains.

The sky was cloudless when the four of us set off up the Sarchal Valley with a single mule. The Mazanderan forest had thinned out, but Takht-i-Sulaiman, resplendent in winter snow, could even have passed for a Persian Weisshorn. On reaching Vanderbon, I had an overwhelming urge to follow up the Barir Rud to get a nostalgic glimpse of Alam Kuh's great north face. High up its snow-choked gorge, the face's eastern edge came tantalisingly into view. But with dusk approaching, I had no time to go any further so raced down the gorge to rejoin the others before night fell. Next morning, after a frosty night at the Chaikhana Chasamir Ali, the sky was overcast and the leafless-trees forlorn. Safar said that we had been lucky to get this far as for much of the previous winter, Rudbarek had been knee-deep in snow.

Thirty-five years after the CNPE, I returned to Iran once again, this time with my wife Georgina, John and Patricia Ducker and Alan Pardoe. My aims were to climb Kuh-i-Sabalan, the great volcano in Azerbaijan that Sir Roger Stevens has described as *'the most haunting of all the mountains of Iran'*, and to follow Freya Stark's original 1931 route across the Elburz. Since 1970, the Pahlavi dynasty had been replaced by Ayatollah Khomeini's Islamic Republic and Iran was still recovering from a devastating decade of war with Iraq which had been armed by America. Even so, most people we met were frank and friendly and the young thirsted for closer ties with the West. Never once did I hear the muezzin's call to prayer or see a beggar crying for alms. Our principal guide, Mehran Etemadi, was a charming young undergraduate reading archaeology at Tehran University who spoke exemplary English and dug pop, rock and heavy metal. Our mountain guide, Parviz Pashazadeh, fifty-four and married with three children, was a Karate and Judo expert with the uncompromising mien of a revolutionary guard. Both men looked after us like good shepherds.

Our journey began with a cable-car-assisted day-trip to the summit of Tochal where jolly groups of men in shorts and unveiled female trekkers strode out purposefully in every direction. We then flew on to Ardabil to visit the tomb of Sheikh Safi-ad-Din the founder of Iran's glorious sixteenth century Safavid dynasty where a full-scale replica of the Victoria and Albert Museum's famous 'Ardabil' carpet was being rewoven on a giant loom. At the local Zur Khaneh, or 'House of Strength', a seventy-year-old performed jaw-dropping feats of weight lifting and twirled twenty-kilo clubs around his head like skittles. Originating as Sassanian martial arts training to take on the Roman legions, this extraordinary performance was accompanied by drums, cymbals, rhythmic chanting, dervish-style dancing and exhortations to Allah. Georgina detected the smell of hashish mixed with more honest sweat.

At 4,711 metres Kuh-i-Sabalan, Iran's third highest mountain, is complex in structure, holds snow throughout the year and is where Zoroaster composed the *Avesta*. Parviz had climbed it twenty-five times and much preferred it to Demavend of which he had made fifty-three ascents. Our first camp at Shabil overlooked the stupendous Shiven Barch Gorge, a haven for wolf and bear. From here, we trekked up to the Hoseini Moghadas Refuge past black, goat-haired tents through the sparse summer pastures of the Shahsavan, an Azeri-speaking branch of their Elburz cousins. The refuge, an unusual combination of mosque and mountain hut, was half-filled with snow and housed twenty-five boisterous young men up from Isfahan. One of them, in the best Iranian poetic tradition, recited to me his ode to the mountain:

> *Sabalan be proud, most beautiful creature*
> *We suffered to climb upon you*
> *And now gaze in wonder on your lovely form*

The ascent of the mountain in summer is little more than a tough, 2,000-metre scramble up scree, boulder fields and snow-couloirs. However, a sleepless night on an ice-covered, concrete floor compounded by diarrhoea and altitude sickness reduced our summit party to Parviz, Mehran, Georgina, John and me. Georgina was first to reach the frozen lake that marks its summit crater. With dark clouds gathering, our descent was hastened by snow flurries and thunder.

Back at Ardabil, the male section of the Municipality's hot-spring baths was filled with trimly muscled men wearing underpants to conceal their manhood.

In the ladies section, the matrons went naked and the young women wore bikinis. We moved on to camp by the Caspian shore where, under the discreet surveillance of lurking protectors of public morals, Georgina and Patricia swam in all-enveloping black cowls, while John passed the time spotting commoner feathered species. After a night at Qaswin, famous in pre-Ayatollah times for its 'Qaswin Number Six' wine, we returned to the heart of the Elburz over a 2,560 metre pass dotted with blue bee hives. The road then spiralled down to the valley of Alamut, an oasis of wheat and rice fields, orchards, poplar thickets and walnut groves surrounded by bleached hills. Dominating a corner of this hidden valley is the Great Rock of Alamut on which Hasan-i-Sabah, the 'Old Man of the Mountains', built the impregnable castle from where he despatched his hashish-fuelled *Hashishin* on the death missions that disposed of six Caliphs of Baghdad. Hulagu Khan, a grandson of Ghengiz, eventually broke the power of the Assassins and destroyed Alamut's priceless library in the process. Their ghosts still haunt these mountains and their deadly legacy reaches to all corners of the earth. In a Persian garden below the rock shaded by walnut trees, a dignified old man summoned his grandchildren to bring us baskets of cherries and bowls of yoghurt for our picnic.

Like Freya Stark, a night was spent at Garmerud, an ageless village of tiered, verandahed, mud-brick houses overlooking a mountain torrent. Early next morning, Parviz led our caravan of four muleteers and mules up the ancient trade route that crosses the Elburz to the coast. Beyond a clutch of alpine chalets, their roofs piled high with newly harvested wheat, we pitched our tents at Pichuban on a bright meadow knee-deep in orchids and were soon invaded by a horde of inquisitive village children. Shortly after dawn, the caravan climbed on to the ruined *caravanserai* marking the Salambar Pass from where Freya had taken the photograph of Solomon's Throne that had so stirred my youthful imagination. Overcome by nostalgia, I stared across a shadowed gulf to where the deeply furrowed ridges of the Elburz converged on Solomon's squat pyramid and Alam Kuh's unmistakeable prow. Only the sight of the once familiar Caspian mists creeping up the valley broke my reverie.

When descending to the coast by the vestiges of a path that hugs the lip of the Gelza Rud Gorge, we met an extended caravan of heavily laden mules, old women riding donkeys and fathers shouldering children coming up to establish themselves in their solid, stone houses for the summer. Further down, I rounded a bend in the path and stopped dead in my tracks. Framed by converging, forested ridges and picked out in clear relief, the north-west faces of Takht-i-Sulaiman and Alam Kuh burst into view to bring a host of half-forgotten memories flooding back. Yet distance lends enchantment to the view. Parviz had frequently climbed Steinauer's North-East Buttress and assured me that the Ice Curtain had long since melted and the glaciers all but disappeared.

At our last camp by the Caspian, Mehran regaled us with jokes about slothful Turks and hapless Caspians, 'A Reshdi comes home after work to find a queue of men taking turns to pleasure his wife.

"Why don't you get a divorce?" says one of them to the cuckold.

"No thanks", replies the Reshdi, *"I'd only have to go back to the end of the queue!"*

But Mehran also had harrowing tales of suppression, persecution, torture and of the 300 journalists still locked up in Tehran's dreaded Evin Prison. Iran, with its proud, sophisticated people and a heritage of three great civilisations going back 2,500 years, will always be a land of paradox.

2

AT THE CROSSROADS

The immediate after-effects of the Persian expedition – involuntary eye-blink and amoebic dysentery – didn't do much for my final year's studies, though didn't stop me from playing rugby, then my first choice sport, as captain of my college's Rugby XV. At the end of that Michaelmas term, I hitch-hiked up to North Wales for the CUMC's winter climbing meet at Helyg where my newfound climbing companions were John Scott, a rugby-playing Trinity contemporary, and Mark Bicknell, a cerebral Wykehamist. Both were self-assured scions of old-established mountaineering families and one of Scott's uncles was the legendary Tom Longstaff, a veteran of pre-First World War expeditions to the Caucasus, Rockies, Himalaya and Tibet and the medical officer on General Bruce's 1922 Everest expedition. We climbed nothing of note, but afterwards Scott suggested that I join him, Bicknell and an Oxford friend, Jim Graham, for a week's climbing in the Tarentaise the following June. Their dates happened to fit in with Bill Norton's invitation that I team up with him and Tony Delafield for a fortnight's climbing at Zermatt a month later, by which time I hoped to have graduated from Cambridge, preferably with a degree.

Few would dispute R.L.G. Irving's judgement that the Alps are 'the best of all ranges in the world'. I had only once caught a brief glimpse of them from a Milan-bound sleeper on Trinity's 1955 groundbreaking rugby tour of Italy, so the prospect of actually climbing them was tantamount to seeking my holy grail. Money was again my problem, but instead of taking gainful employment during the Easter vacation to pay for what was going to be my last holiday before embarking on the real world of work, I took up the offer of a six-week exchange studentship at Uppsala University, Sweden, awarded by a Trinity don, Professor Broad, for my long-standing, if somewhat spurious, membership of his Cambridge Scandinavian Society. When my long-suffering father lent me £50, I promised to repay the loan by flogging British-made nylon climbing ropes, which were then rumoured to be in short supply in Italy.

Whereas the great peaks of Zermatt are generally serious undertakings, those of the Tarentaise serve as an ideal introduction to alpinism for a novitiate. On 27 June 1957, I caught the train from Victoria with a through-ticket to Bessans in the Arc Valley intending to rendezvous there with Scott and Co. Weighted down with one large rucksack forward, containing my own climbing equipment and another stuffed with three nylon climbing ropes aft., I further encumbered myself with a suitcase filled with clothes to grace various social engagements in Milan and the Riviera that I hoped to fulfil between climbs. That year, severe floods had severed all road and rail communications into the Arc valley and no public transport operated beyond Pralognon. After a torrid day, alternatively hitch-hiking and walking along France's near-deserted roads, I forwarded the suitcase FOB to Milan and then spent another two days walking to Bessans where a *poste restante* message informed me that my prospective companions were already ensconced at the Averole Hut. Reaching it late that evening, I learned that Scott and Graham had time for only one more climb before heading home.

Our traverse of the Levanna Occidentale and the Aiguille Percée ('a first rate expedition' according to the guidebook) was never as demanding as my slog up the Arc Valley. The owner of the sports shop at Bessans had no interest in buying my ropes, but suggested that I try Courmayeur. This Mecca of alpinism was only forty miles away, but to reach it by either road or rail with France's transport network in chaos would have involved a complicated and expensive circular journey. Bicknell suggested instead that we walk through the Paradiso National Park after crossing the Col du Carro and Nivoletta to Ceresole Reale from where a regular bus service went up the Aosta Valley to Courmayeur. We did just that in perfect weather and I then vowed that I would return to that magical area some other day.

Courmayeur is the base for the longest and hardest climbs on Mont Blanc. In 1957, it would still have been recognisable to J.M.W. Turner as the alpine village he had painted in 1802. When viewed from Chamonix, the glittering snowfields and flowing glaciers of Mont Blanc's North Face present a vision of the sublime. When viewed from Courmayeur, the cyclopean architecture, grim ramparts, soaring rock arêtes and chaotic icefalls of its South Face inspire wonder and awe. For all the mountain grandeur that surrounded it, the little town had a chic yet friendly atmosphere so I lost no time in presenting myself with my ropes to Courmayeur's head guide. He courteously heard me out before delivering a gentle put-down: 'My dear young man, I have to tell you that our Italian sports shops are bulging with these nylon ropes and at much more competitive prices than those you are offering me. Should you require confirmation, I suggest you walk up the main street and visit Toni Gobbi's climbing shop. He has an excellent selection of nylon ropes as well as the most up-to-date climbing equipment.'

Gobbi was no mere shopkeeper. The following year he and Walter Bonatti became Italian national heroes after their epic ascent of Gasherbrum IV in the Karakoram. But having lugged those wretched ropes round the Alps for over a week, I felt utterly deflated. My face must have shown it and, on seeing my discomfiture, the great man softened.

'I tell you what my friend. As a gesture of goodwill, I will buy two of your ropes for the price you paid for them in England.'

The violent thunderstorm that flooded our bivouac that night signalled the end of the good weather and any immediate prospects of climbing on Mont Blanc. Mark went back to England while I caught a bus to Milan. My suitcase had turned up intact, but my wild appearance failed to pass muster with my protocol-minded Aunt Phoebe, the wife of the British Consul General. So I moved on to the Riviera to take up an invitation from Joelle, a demure French *demoiselle* I had befriended at Cambridge, to stay at her parents' luxurious villa at Antibes. Her eagle-eyed mother acted as Joelle's chaperone for a breathless round of gourmet luncheons and candlelit dinners at expensive restaurants, which Joelle assured me was *normale*. Back at Milan, Aunt Phoebe's reception was warmer second time round. We saw *Simon Boccanegra* at La Scala, dined at the famous sixteenth century Villa d'Este above Lake Como, and heard the legendary pianist Benedetti Michelangeli give a private recital in her apartment in the Via St Andrea. On 21 July, I came down to earth to share a leaky tent with Bill Norton in a sodden alpine meadow at Winkelmatten above Zermatt.

In the words of the distinguished Swiss mountaineer Charles Gos: '*Switzerland finds its summing up in Zermatt*'. Dominated by the iconic Matterhorn and ringed by Switzerland's greatest peaks, Zermatt's long historical association with British mountaineers is attested by the many plangent memorials to the fallen that fill the English Church's graveyard. After alighting from the train,

I was propositioned for custom by a posse of young guides sitting on the wall opposite the Monte Rosa hotel and intoning the mantra 'So you climb zee high mountains?' The *Tariff des Guides* made it clear that their services were strictly for rich Americans.

By my novice standards, Bill and Tony were relatively experienced alpinists. They had already planned a packed climbing programme, but over the past few days, bad weather had put the high peaks out of condition and only on the following morning did the clouds begin to lift. There followed a week of settled weather when the three of us climbed the Adlerhorn, Strahlhorn, Zinalrothorn, Wellenkuppe/Ober Gabelhorn, and Weisshorn in quick succession. Nothing remarkable but no big alpine climb is a pushover. And for me, the long hut marches through cool pine forests; the convivial atmosphere of the huts; the nervous anticipation of pre-dawn starts; the wonder of alpine dawns and the satisfaction of completing a demanding climb were revelatory experiences.

Everything had gone swimmingly until our ascent of the Weisshorn's east ridge when I had felt a sudden, sharp pain in my right hip as if something had snapped. The hip had taken a hammering over the past few weeks, but the intensity of this pain was something new and I reluctantly recalled Professor Trueta's strictures of the previous year. We completed the climb without mishap, but back in camp that evening my hip developed a dull ache that made even walking a trial. I reckoned that my first alpine season was over, but rather than sharing my concerns, I gave Bill and Tony the excuse that I was now so broke that I would have to make tracks for home.

The following day, 1st August, was Switzerland's national holiday and the day after happened to be my 23rd birthday – cause for a double celebration. As we gazed down from our hillside eyrie to Zermatt, now lit up by the flashes of exploding fireworks, Bill turned to me.

'Very sorry John that you're having to go home tomorrow. According to Bernard Biner, this spell of good weather's only going to last for a couple more days, so Tony and I have decided to have a crack at the Taschhorn/ Dom traverse. Biners say it's a great climb and hasn't yet been done this season. Great pity that you can't join us.'

Biner was a famous Zermatt guide and a true friend to British climbers. However, the traverse that Bill and Tony were proposing was at least a grade higher than anything we had done to date. Charles Evans, leader of the successful 1955 Kangchenjunga expedition, had devoted a whole chapter to it in his book *On Climbing*. The guidebook's description: 'magnificent though in bad conditions the time required can be doubled', convinced me that I couldn't possibly miss out on this one. Next morning, there was not a cloud in the sky and over breakfast I told Bill that I had changed my mind; borrowed some Swiss francs to tide me over and entrained one of my two rucksacks for Visp, Zermatt's railhead in the Rhone Valley. Shortly after noon, the three of us set off for the Tasch hut, five hours away and all steeply uphill. Inside, it was filled with noisy British trekkers just in from the first day's stage of the high-level walking route from Saas Fee to Chamonix. Outside, the Austrian guide Kuno Rainer, Hermann Buhl's climbing partner, was grilling himself in the sun. After supper, the grizzled hut warden confirmed that no one had attempted the complete Taschhorn/Dom traverse that year, but warned us about dangerous double cornices on the Taschhorn's north ridge.

At 2 a.m. we crept out of the hut and plodded up the Weingarten glacier with the eerie silence broken only by the sound of the frozen snow squeaking under our crampons. Dawn saw the sun-kissed rim of the Taschjoch beckoning from on high and on reaching this belvedere the Matterhorn emerged from the bowels of its misty valley glowing like a golden phoenix. To the south-east, beyond the dark trough of Saas Fee, a billowing cloud-sea of light and shadow swelled up from the lakes of Lombardy. The Taschjoch marks the start of the traverse proper. After a snatched second breakfast, we moved off up the Taschhorn's southern flank, a tapering neck of snow and ice whose flanks plunged giddily to the glaciers far below and then merged into an open slope whose loose shale was overlaid by frozen snow. It offered no belays, so there was no point in roping-up. Always to our left, the mountain's sinister south face dropped 2,000 metres sheer to the glacier. First climbed at the turn of the century by Ryan and Winthrop Young with the Lochmatter Brothers and Josef Knubel, this daring and dangerous route was not repeated until 1943 by a powerful Swiss party who were astonished by Franz Lochmatter's leads made without modern aids and equipment.

I was beginning to feel desperately insecure on this treacherous, unprotected slope where any slip could have been disastrous. During one rare moment of inattention, I glanced between my legs to see two other climbers waiting patiently below, reluctant to follow because of the rubbish we were dislodging and showering down the mountain. Freezing on precarious stances to allow them to scuttle across to the security of the south-east ridge, their route proved better than ours for they reached the Taschhorn's summit only minutes behind us. Here, both parties huddled together for warmth in the lee of some rocks. The Swiss tucked into a large tin of black cherry jam and drank hot coffee from a Thermos flask. The Brits gnawed at a greasy sausage and were reduced to sucking icicles off the rocks because our water bottles had frozen solid.

Although the weather was still holding, the Swiss had decided to go no further. Glancing down the Taschhorn's north ridge, I understood why. In a good year, most of it is solid granite. Now, only an occasional rock spike poked through a quivering fin of virgin snow that plunged down like an arrow with either side falling away into nothingness. Saas Fee lay 1,800 metres below, snug and secure in its misty valley. Up here, we might have been on another planet. Taking the lead off the summit was like walking the plank with no means of climbing down the ridge's fluffy, unconsolidated snow except by straddling it with one leg on either side. Ice axe belays were purely psychological and one slip would have sent all three of us to kingdom come.

On reaching the Domjoch at 3.30 p.m., I glanced back up the Taschhorn's north ridge where our steps appeared as a clean-cut line hugging its razor-sharp snow crest and then faced up to the challenge of the massive, crumbling gendarmes sheathed in snow and ice that guarded the citadel of the Dom. Tiring now, I moved across to its shadowed east flank to avoid them only to find myself on a black precipice of ice-smeared rock. The sudden transition from sunlight to shade completely changed the complexion of the climb and not for the first time that day I was seized by cold fear. The rock was insecure and at the end of one delicate traverse I found myself perched on what might have been a window ledge on the Empire State Building with a 2,000-foot drop below. Wedging my ice axe between a tongue of ice and a niche before hammering home with a stone to fashion a makeshift belay, I shouted across the void to Bill: 'Come on! I'm well belayed.'

Even as I spoke, the axe fell out with a dull clang. I just managed to stop it with my foot before it fell plumb to the glacier. It was years before I told Bill what had happened.

Despite some mutterings behind about route finding, some awkward, scrambling pitches up flaky walls brought me back on to the ridge's firmer rock, just as the Dom's summit snows were turning yellow in the late afternoon sunlight. At 6 p.m. we stood atop Switzerland's highest mountain sucking at the last of Tony's 'snowade', our hands benumbed by a bitter wind. The Dom Hut was still another 1,500 metres below, but as we raced unheeding in the gathering dusk across the teetering snow-bridges and the shattered ice blocks fallen from the monstrous ice cliffs of the Festi Glacier, I was too elated to bother about crevasses or much else.

The Dom Hut had long been deserted by the time we got up next morning. Stretched out in the sun on a low parapet, I gazed across the Mattertal to the Weisshorn, the Queen of the Alps, to trace the route we had done only three days before. Had we really climbed that shining mountain? We had indeed, but it was definitely the Taschhorn/Dom traverse that would remain the defining experience of my alpine apprenticeship. Two years on, two of Cambridge University's most promising undergraduate mountaineers, Peter Mayo and John Spottiswode, fell to their deaths while descending the Taschhorn's south flank having all but completed the first Dom/Taschhorn traverse of that season.

After a snatched breakfast, we descended to earth down one of Switzerland's steepest hut paths passing en route groups of toiling weekend climbers as we nurtured that smug feeling of having ourselves safely got off a great climb. At Randa there is a simple inn where we shared our last meal together, for here our paths divided. Bill and Tony were heading back to Zermatt while I would be hitchhiking to England. A short way down the track, I swung round to wave them a last goodbye. Their dim figures were still standing by the doorway and they waved back. At that moment, I remembered with warm gratitude the many adventures that I had shared with Bill over the past two years. It never crossed my mind that he and I would never climb together in the Alps again.

SKYE RENAISSANCE

At Cambridge I had read economics and law with no great enthusiasm for either subject and had left with the firm intention of becoming neither an economist nor a lawyer. Advertising was then in vogue so I followed the trend and joined the old-established firm of Charles W. Hobson of Chandos Street, London W1 on 9 September 1957 as a trainee account executive at £650 a year plus luncheon vouchers. The firm's managing partner, Nicholas Kaye, was an aesthete who also published high-quality travel books as a sideline. Somewhat out of character, he had just brought out a mountaineering manual by J.E.B. Wright, one of Britain's few professional guides, which he asked me to review. I did so with unflinching arrogance. Kaye thanked me politely for my trouble, but never used the review. Some years later, he published an English edition of Frison-Roche's *Mont Blanc and the Seven Valleys* translated by Wilfred Noyce and illustrated with Pierre Tairrez's superb photographs.

I had realised that advertising was not my style long before Kaye commissioned me to find a tame leopard to be used as a macho logo to launch a poncey line in Italian shoes. Leopards don't tame, but the firm's creative department wouldn't accept this and when the drug-benumbed animal refused to cross a mock-up zebra crossing led on a chain by a terrified male model wearing a pair of purple shoes, the photographers and press melted away, the campaign folded, and the agency lost a valuable client. I moved on to apply for a job with the British Antarctic Survey, then a responsibility of the Colonial Office. That particular venture was never a starter for Professor Trueta's original prognosis had proved correct, so in February 1958 I was admitted to hospital for major surgery on my tubercular hip. After two months stretched out on my back in traction, I emerged with a withered right leg half an inch shorter than the other. After my discharge, I asked the surgeon how soon I could start climbing again.

'I'm afraid you've lost most of the muscle in your right leg. We can probably get you walking normally with a built-up shoe, but I can't see the possibility of your ever climbing again.'

We left it at that. I was determined to prove him wrong.

During a nine-month convalescence at home with my long suffering parents, a visiting nurse pumped daily injections of streptomycin into my left buttock. To pass the time, I embarked on an over-ambitious literary project about Iran which was never completed, but to get back into physical shape I set myself an ambitious regime of physio-therapeutic exercises starting with simple walks and short runs before graduating on to longer tramps around my native Gower Peninsula. As I grew stronger, I made solo excursions into the hills of my boyhood, the Brecon Beacons, the Black Mountain of Carmarthenshire and the Great Forest of Breconshire whose Welsh myths of witches and wizards, fairies and goblins, magic springs and haunted lakes with buried treasure had been embedded in my consciousness since child-hood. After walking the twenty-five mile stretch of the Roman road Sarn Helen from Neath to Brecon where I swore I heard the tramp, tramp, tramp of the legionnaires feet above the soughing wind, I felt confident enough to ask John Scott if we might go climbing together in Skye. It was just short of a year since my release from hospital.

The choice of Skye had been fired by my ambition to traverse the Cuillin Ridge, Britain's closest mountaineering experience to an alpine climb. The Hebridean quality of Skye's light, an ever-shifting pattern of colour produced by its juxtaposition to the Atlantic and the island's synthesis of wildness and beauty, had made it a place of pilgrimage for British painters from J.M.W. Turner to William Daniel. Its mountaineering interest was first appreciated by Professor J.D. Forbes, the 'father of British mountaineering', after he had climbed Sgurr an Gillean, the Cuillin Ridge's culminating peak, in 1835. Thereafter, ascents of the Cuillin's two highest mountains, Sgurr Alasdair and Sgurr Dearg in 1873 by a Scot, Sheriff Nicolson, stirred Norman Collie, (another 'father of climbing' though in his case in Norway), to visit the Cuillin and pave the way for a strong Alpine Club contingent to descend en masse on Skye in 1890.

The Scott/Harding plan was to hitch-hike to Skye and base ourselves on Glen Brittle from where we intended put in ten days' rock climbing before tackling the Cuillin Ridge itself. For me, this was going to be as much a make or break test of my hip as a mountaineering challenge. Before setting off, I stayed for a few days with John at his parents' house at Speen to get to know him better. His collection of mountaineering books would have graced a college library, but what really impressed me was his musical accomplishments. He had played chamber music with Jacqueline du Pré and known both Vaughan Williams and Gerald Finzi, whose widow kindly invited us for tea.

On 18 March 1959, we took to the high road to Mallaig and over the next two days hitched thirteen separate lifts to Fort William. Hitch-hiking has long gone out of fashion, but in the 1950s it was a cheap and sometimes adventurous form of transport that got me round Britain, Sweden and the continent. Our lifts included those from an ex-SAS Liverpool-Irish lorry driver who had fought in North Africa, Italy, France and Korea ('Koreans eat dogs!'); a former Wehrmacht Eastern Front veteran; and a monosyllabic 'trunker' who manoeuvred his thirty-gear behemoth like a Formula One racer. The romance of the road took the shapely form of Angela, a gorgeous, auburn-haired Lancashire lass with a liberated smile who picked us up after dark on a rain-swept corner of Warrington that first evening in her red Renault Dauphine sports car. When she ran over a stray dog, a passing policeman dismissed its demise with 'Just too bad, Miss. Carry on!' Our luck eventually ran out four miles from Fort William when, after standing on the roadside for three hours, we had to trudge back to the railway station before catching the train to Mallaig and camping that night on the hill that overlooks the town.

When I peeked out through the flaps of John's boy-scout tent next morning, the world seemed born anew. Mallaig's bustling harbour was bright with the white sails of fishing boats fluttering in the breeze. Across the Sound of Sleat, the mountains of Skye rose from out the sea like some ghostly apparition. Mr MacBrayne's steamer dropped us off at the Kyle of Lochalsh from where the Kyleakin ferry sped our way over the sea to Skye. That long day ended with an eight-mile walk from Carbost to Glen Brittle where our kind hosts,

Mr and Mrs McCrae, revived us with pints of tea and platefuls of scones before giving us the use of a hayloft whose straw became our bed for the next ten days.

Old Mr Macrae had shepherded his flocks on the Cuillins long before the Forestry Commission had bought up most of the land during the 1930s depression. He regaled us with tales of Gavin Maxwell's ill-fated basking shark fishing venture at Soay and Menlove Edward's solo row by night in a tiny boat to climb on Rùm: an exploit for which he was fined £3 for breaking wartime security regulations. On waking next morning, we looked out across the white sand beach at the mouth of the glen to see Rùm emerging from the sea like a misty fortress with its cone-shaped summit peak, Askival, over-topping a bank of cloud. Skye's weather is notoriously fickle so before it changed its mind, we climbed Sgurr Alasdair and celebrated our first Skye scalp with a skinny dip in the ice-fringed Loch Coire a Ghrunnda. After drying off in the sun, we felt like young gods.

It had been a brilliant start, but that was the last decent weather for the next eight days. From now on, our routes on the Cioch, Sgurr Dearg, Sron na Ciche and the Grundda Face from Loch Coruisk were mostly done in rain, sleet and storm. The daily round of fording burns in spate and tramping through sopping wet heather, bracken and brambles to reach the slippery slabs of some distant rock face became a war of attrition. John's heel became badly bruised and the coarsely crystalline gabbro left our fingertips raw. The itching that we had first assumed to be a legacy of the hayloft's fleas was eventually traced to the ticks that abounded in the heather. With no let-up in the weather, the prospect of our Cuillin traverse was becoming increasingly remote and though he didn't say so directly, Mr McCrae clearly thought so too.

The eight-mile-long Cuillin Ridge gets its reputation as 'the best day's mountaineering in Britain' because it involves 10,000 feet of ascent and descent; four recognised rock climbs and long stretches of exposed scrambling. Modern record-breaking freaks have completed in preposterously fast times what, until 1911, was thought impossible to achieve within a single day. The first all-woman traverse in 1928 took thirty hours and the first to be done in genuine winter conditions was in 1965 by the four-man team of MacInnes and Crabb; Patey and Robertson after several previous attempts had failed. Success can depend on Skye's unpredictable weather. By making our bid in late March, we were riding our luck.

But as the holiday had progressed, I had felt myself getting stronger and more confident and when, on the evening of 29 March, the temperature dropped and the Cuillin Ridge became clear of cloud for the first time in over a week, everything seemed possible. The alarm clock went off at 3 a.m. and after breakfasting on porridge, sausages and eggs, we stepped outside to a night sky bright with stars and the loch shimmering silver under the light of a half-moon. At first, it was easy to pick up the path to the foot of Gars Bheinn, the peak which marks the start of the traverse, but 3,000 feet of scrambling up slippery frost-coated rocks in the dark left us bad tempered with bruised shins. The sun was rising as we breasted the summit to reveal in silhouette the spiky, black peaks of the Cuillin Ridge snaking away to the north before it swung round to the east like a gigantic bow. From here, its culminating peak Sgurr nan Gillean looked impossibly far away.

At this point, I was already wondering whether we weren't crazy to be taking on this traverse. The distance from our start point at Glen Brittle to the finish at Sligachan was fifteen miles, yet it had already taken us three hours just to get this far.

'What d'you think John?' I asked him.

We hadn't said much to each other on the way up for he hadn't been going that well.

'It's this bloody heel that's troubling me,' he grunted. 'I'm going to have to strap it up if I'm going any further.'

He wound a crepe bandage round the heel, but then had to struggle to get his boot back on again.

There was not much snow on the crest of the ridge, but the rocks were coated in ice and on reaching a deep gap festooned with abseil slings, we assumed it must be the Thearlaich Dubh, the last unclimbed section of the traverse until Norman Collie did it on his second attempt in 1890. John abseiled down in quick time, but my traditional 'over the shoulder and round the crutch' technique was rusty and after some faffing around the rope got jammed. To free it, I had to climb both up and down, thereby wasting a good forty minutes and bruising my shoulder in the process. On reaching the true Thearlaich Dubh Gap, John promptly abseiled down its icy basalt, but my shoulder was so sore that I had to climb down unroped. John was singularly unimpressed by this performance.

'If you don't mind me saying, that was a bloody silly thing to do!'

'Agreed,' I muttered, somewhat shaken. 'But we've got to make up time.'

At 10.15 a.m. we stopped for a quick bite and a drink before attacking the south end of Sgurr Mhic Connich. John was now looking wan and unsteady on his feet.

'How are you feeling?' I asked him.

'Not too good I'm afraid, and this damned heel is making it difficult to walk properly. I'm also worried about the time. It's taken us six hours to get to here with only one third of the ridge completed and some tough parts still to come.'

'I'm also pretty knackered.' I replied. 'And I don't like the look of this King's Chimney dead ahead. It's completely iced up.'

We ducked the chimney and reached Mhic Connich's summit by a variant route, though by now were so far behind schedule that I couldn't see how we could possibly complete the traverse before dark.

However, the chimney up An Stack seemed to galvanise John and after swarming up Sgurr Dearg's Inaccessible Pinnacle and then abseiling down the far side, we had reached the ridge's halfway mark. By now, it was so hot on the open ridge that our water bottles had long been emptied and we were forced to eat snow to avoid dehydration – a sure way to getting diarrhoea. Knees, hips and feet were taking a pounding, but we were now moving together in sweet harmony. The intimidating face of the Bhastair Tooth yielded without fuss and our scramble up Sgurr nan Gillean's west ridge was cheered on by a couple of jolly Lancastrians perched on the summit. At 5.40 p.m., ten and a half hours after leaving Gars Bheinn, we joined them and shared our last orange together.

Throughout that long day I had thought of little else but the beers we'd sink and the gourmet dinner we'd demolish at the Sligachan Hotel. But on taking our seats in the dining room, we were both too tired to manage anything more than soup before slumping off to bed. So ended the Cuillin adventure. It had marked a new chapter in my mountain life and I shall always be indebted to John for his friendship, good humour and stalwart companionship that went so far in restoring my own self-confidence.

A month later, I applied to join the administrative branch of the Colonial Service. Idealism and public service had influenced this choice of career, but so had the prospect of long leaves and adventure. After a series of interviews and a daunting final board, I was accepted subject to passing the medical examination and soon after was offered one of the Service's most coveted appointments as a District Officer in Kenya. Kenya Colony had always been my first choice for a posting, but the winds of change sweeping Britain's African territories towards independence, persuaded me that Aden, Britain's last imperial foothold in the Middle East, might have marginally longer-term career prospects. The Persian expedition had also given me a taste for antique lands and although work in Aden Colony sounded a bit humdrum, its wild protectorate, where tribal blood feuds and frontier dust-ups were part of everyday life, promised adventure in spades.

For reasons more closely connected to heart than head, I deferred my South Arabian posting. While marking time before starting the prescribed Arabic course at the School of Oriental and African Studies that autumn, I tried to complete my Persian *magnum opus* in the British Museum's reading room eking out a precarious London existence writing hack newspaper articles while working for Geoffrey Handley-Taylor, an affable Yorkshire man and friend of Vera Brittain. Geoffrey was a literary impresario who promoted an ingenious line in worldwide literary and musical who's-whos to target American academic egos. When my savings ran out, Geoffrey urged me not to waste more time 'in vile gloom in the shady streets of literature' but to join the Colonial Service forthwith as I was, as he put it, 'the right stuff'. Still riding my emotional roller coaster, I again postponed my appointment and bluffed my way into Peter Lumley's, then London's top modelling agency. After a sticky start, the money started rolling in, but the offer of the very lucrative Gibbs toothpaste-ad slot was a mugshot too far. I put in my resignation fearful that the Colonial Service's recruitment officer would take exception to my toothy grin enlivening the pages of *Woman's Own*.

In those last golden days of September 1959, I said goodbye to my homeland hills in the company of fleet-footed Anne, a Diana in the chase whose loving companionship had lightened the past locust year. Over four glorious days, we hiked from Myddfai to Brecon across the Great Forest of Breconshire, for 400 years the exclusive hunting preserve of lords of Brecon, climbing every mountain, swimming every lake and never once meeting another soul along the way.

3

SNOW ON THE EQUATOR I: MOUNT KENYA

On 1 January 1960 I boarded the *SS Leicestershire* bound for Aden to take up my first Colonial Service appointment as a cadet assistant adviser based in Mukalla. This Arabian Nights-style port, 300 miles up the coast from Aden and capital of the Eastern Aden Protectorate's Quaiti Sultanate, was one that Sinbad himself might have sailed from. Dominated by a bare, bleak mountain called Jebel Qarat, the multi-storied lime-washed merchants' mansions that lined the edge of Mukalla's ancient harbour crammed with ocean-going dhows, sambuks, and skiffs attested to its former prosperity. In that now-vanished world of despotic sultans and larger-than-life British colonial characters, my task as a junior assistant adviser was to help lay the building blocks of a civilian administration; establish a modern fishing industry; promote agricultural development and road building, and run a military and administrative school for aspiring Arab soldiers and civil servants.

Paucity of Her Majesty's government funding, an incoherent political strategy and local obscurantism could make routine work intensely frustrating. But beyond Mukalla's tired sophistication and the sky scraping, mud-brick cities of Shibam, Saiun and Tarim in Wadi Hadhramaut, there was adventure in plenty for a young Political Officer whose job it was to control the fringes of the Empty Quarter. Here, along a frontier drawn in the sand, a string of *Beau Geste* forts manned by the Hadhrami Bedouin Legion commanded the key wells that kept feuding Bedouin in check and deterred Saudi and Yemeni territorial incursions.

South Arabian summers were stupefyingly hot and female company non-existent. For all Far Arabia's exotic marvels, I sometimes wondered what had induced me to have chosen to serve the golden years of youth in this barren land which offers little to its own and even less to the stranger. Nonetheless, hours spent battling with obdurate Arab bureaucracy and fruitless parleyings with intractable tribesmen in flea-infested forts at least offered the inestimable perk of generous leaves of which I was determined to take full advantage. Despite my boss's mantra that 'leave is a privilege not an entitlement', I applied for three weeks' local leave on completion of my first year's service to fulfil a long cherished ambition of climbing Mount Kenya.

This project had taken wings on my first day in Aden when, on reporting for duty to Aden Colony's Chief Secretary, Ken Simmonds, I was so taken aback on seeing the full-length black and white mountain photograph that filled the entire wall space behind his desk that I blurted out: 'What a superb photograph! That has to be the North Face of Mount Kenya!'

'Correct,' beamed Simmonds, as he swivelled round to trace with his forefinger a tenuous line up the mountain's awesome face.

'I did most of that route with Arthur Firmin just before the war. We only just failed to make the summit.'

I was duly impressed. Simmonds had been a president of the Cambridge University Mountaineering Club in the 1930s. Firmin had been Kenya's outstanding post-war mountaineer before his death in the Himalaya in 1955.

From that moment on, I reckoned that Mount Kenya was within my grasp. However, I did wonder how on earth I was going to get fit enough to tackle a serious snow and ice mountain well over 5,000 metres high when I was stuck on the tropical shores of South Arabia. Fortunately, in the scarred, pink limestone bulk of Jebel Qarat, its ochre-tinctured screes riven by skeletal black basalt ridges, I had a 430-metre training peak literally at my doorstep. Yet to reach its bleached summit up those clinkered slopes that radiated heat even in winter, represented a challenge particularly from the prominent ridge that was barred halfway up by a friable, vertical step. After several unsuccessful attempts, I finally overcame this obstacle, less concerned about falling off than being torn to pieces by the vicious pack of pye-dogs that roamed the Jebel's upper reaches. I had already had one brush with these brutes when unwittingly disturbing them. After a nervous standoff, I began a stealthy tactical retreat just as the gnarled leader dog launched itself downhill towards me snarling and foaming at the mouth. Attack seemed my only hope of not becoming mincemeat and so, armed with a sun-hat full of stones, I charged uphill yelling hysterically as I hurled my missiles at it. Just as all seemed lost, the brute sheered off, whereupon the rest of the pack slunk away.

Life in Mukalla took a steep upward trajectory with the arrival of Stewart Hawkins, a member of the Climbers Club and a protégée of Wilfred Noyce who was on secondment for a year's stint as a cadet political officer in between taking his Arabic degree at Oxford. Along with Eamonn Conboy of the Eastern Bank, we systematically explored the virgin limestone cliffs that lined Mukalla's twenty-mile-long beach and rounded off the day with dehydrating treks into the wild wadis of its desiccated hinterland.

But none of these activities solved the problem of with whom I might climb on Mount Kenya. Enquiries with John Blacker, the hut secretary of the Mountain Club of Kenya in Nairobi, had drawn the discouraging reply 'It would be very difficult to find anyone here who knows the mountain and is capable of leading the standard route.'

With less than three weeks to go, I still had only one taker: Ruth Drake, a forty-two year old divorcee working as a government architect in Nairobi who was 'mad keen to climb Nelion, though Batian might be too much for me'. A last-minute flurry of correspondence added Tony Garman of RAF Aden and Mick Fearn of RAF Salalah to the party and then, out of the blue, Professor Per Hoel, a Norwegian working at Massawa, wrote to ask if he could come along because *'as a humorous example of my physical fitness, I walk easily on my hands.'*

Garman had done some hard Scottish climbs. Fearn was a novice. Drake and Hoel were unknown quantities. The prospect of attempting Mount Kenya with four people whom I had never met, made me wonder what I was letting myself in for. My only Alpine season had been four years before and since my hip operation, serious rock climbing limited to Skye. But it was now too late to pull out and when the Aden Airways plane touched down at Nairobi airport on 16 January 1961, I was met, somewhat embarrassingly, by both Ruth Drake and a very recent Aden-based girlfriend Sabrina. After partially resolving this little local difficulty, Ruth invited me to stay at her house on the outskirts of Nairobi. I rode pillion on her rackety Lambretta through the Nairobi Game Park nervously eyeing zebra, giraffe, gnu and the occasional lion.

After Arabia's heat and dust, Kenya was paradise enow. From the palm-fringed beaches of the coast to the high-savannah tableland, its skies were as wide as heaven and the whole place pulsated with the drumbeat of Africa. After staying a couple of days with Ruth, we met up with the rest of the team at Nairobi's New Stanley Hotel, though only after Hoel and I had wasted two and a half hours in adjoining reception rooms waiting to identify one another.

After summary introductions, Ruth took me aside, 'I'm sorry to have to tell you John, but this Hoel is the same gloomy, humourless man with whom I had a blazing row on Kilimanjaro last August.' She never explained quite why.

Hoel had brought nothing with him but his boots and an anorak, so we spent the remains of that day scouring the *dukas* of Nairobi for equipment. It was an unpromising start for a group of strange bedfellows.

Descriptions beggar that first sight of Mount Kenya as it floats above the burnished high plains of Equatorial Africa and on a clear day you can see it from Nairobi. From the air; its 1,000-metre-high summit peaks, the crystalline remnants of an ancient volcanic core, resemble a clutch of sharp pimples perched atop a colossal dome 3,500 metres from its savannah base and encompassing the distance between London and Birmingham. Although its snows had been familiar to Arab slave traders long before its first European discoverer, the German missionary Krapf, reported seeing what the Kikuyu called Kirinyaga, 'The Mountain of Whiteness', from a distance of 100 miles in 1849 Krapf was laughed to scorn by European geographers. But in 1899, Halford Mackinder, 'the Father of British Geography', made the first ascent of the mountain's highest peak, the 5,199 metre Batian, with the Courmayeur guides Ollier and Brocherell. His month-long trek from Nairobi to the mountain's base with 160 porters through what was then totally un-administered country, surviving en route strikes, desertions, lootings, food shortages and repeated attacks from hostile Kikuyu tribesmen, was an epic in itself. Another thirty years passed before Batian was climbed again (and its 5,188 metre twin-summit Nelion for the first time) by Eric Shipton, a footloose twenty-one-year-old, newly arrived coffee planter, and Percy Wyn-Harris, a Colonial Service District Commissioner. A year later in 1930, Shipton teamed up with H.W. ('Bill') Tilman, a highly decorated First World War hero who was then farming in Kenya, to begin one of mountaineering's most famous partnerships. Despite their very dissimilar temperaments and nine years age difference, they made first ascents of most of Mount Kenya's principal peaks within a fortnight including the traverse of Batian and Nelion by Batian's west ridge, a climb Shipton later described as the hardest he had ever done. Subsequently, all three of these Mount Kenya pioneers became notable 'Everesters' and died within three years of one another.

In 1961, Kenya was a Crown Colony with dark memories of the recent Mau Mau Emergency still lingering. Yet, there were no travel restrictions, permissions or park fees required to climb Mount Kenya and of several possible approaches, I chose the Burguret route as had Shipton and Tilman thirty-one years before. Ruth had already done all the necessary spadework by hiring zebroids from Raymond Hook, a grizzled ex-big-game hunter who had first settled in Kenya in 1912. Although she ungraciously describing him as 'a madman', he gave us a gamey lunch for free before presenting us with an exorbitant bill for zebroid hire as the payback. After camping near his farm that night, we set off in column next morning, 22 January, with six pack animals carrying 120 pounds apiece and three Kikuyu muleteers dressed in surplus British Army battledress and armed with pangas.

The two-day approach march to the 4,795-metre-high Arthur Firmin Hut involves 3,000 metres of vertical ascent through successive bands of outsize stinging nettles; hardwoods three arm-spans in girth; sunless thickets of ten-metre-high bamboo; heather as big as trees; chest-high tussock grass; giant lobelia and groundsel resembling monstrous cabbages. When I peered out from the tent I was sharing with Ruth on the second morning, the ground was frozen solid and the twin pillars of Batian and Nelion, buckled by colossal rock slabs and festooned with hanging glaciers, loomed up above us. At this critical point, the shutter of my camera jammed. The new Firmin Hut, built by the Mountain Club of Kenya as a memorial to the country's outstanding mountaineer, is only twelve-metres lower than the summit of Mont Blanc and the latter stages of the approach march through wet, tufted grass and up seemingly endless scree slopes left me with a splitting headache and severe altitude sickness.

Next day, I didn't feel up to anything more challenging than a trudge up Point Lenana, 200 metres above the hut. Now become a popular trekking peak, it will always have special associations with the Italian prisoners of war Benuzzi and Balletto who, after escaping from the British prison camp at Nanyuki in 1943, bravely attempted to traverse Batian's formidable north-west ridge equipped with camp-forged crampons and ice axes. The altitude seemed to have no effect on Hoel who raced up and down an easy first. But Mick Fearn had developed a temperature of 104 degrees, which Ruth diagnosed as incipient pulmonary oedema, a potentially fatal condition. We should have gone down immediately to a lower altitude. Instead, we took a chance and held our collective breaths.

The party's common objective had been to climb Nelion, and maybe Batian too. But fundamental differences now emerged as to how this might be done. I wanted to get fully fit and acclimatised before making any attempt. Fearn was incapacitated, but Garman and Drake were determined to make their bid as soon as possible: Hoel expressed no opinion. This lack of cohesion was already creating subtle rifts. After two days acclimatisation, I felt fit enough to do a test-run traverse of Sendeyo and Tereri, two subsidiary peaks at the northern end of Mount Kenya's crater rim distantly joined to Point Lenana by a three-mile-long ridge. No one else shared my enthusiasm, so at first light on 26 January I set off on my own in brilliant sunshine with the air crackly crisp. From the summit of Lenana, the snow-flecked reaches of the upper Mackinder Valley fell away 4,000 metres before merging into a pattern of muddy browns that marked the savannah. A kilometre on, beyond Simba Col, a heavily indented ridge curiously reminiscent of the Cuillin rolled on towards the cathedral-like spires of Sendeyo and Tereri. They looked discouragingly far away, but for the first time in five days I was feeling on top form. After racing down to Simba Col, I began a rollercoaster four and a half hour ride over a succession of gendarmes and towers before coming up short against Sendeyo's south-east face. Split by a well-defined chimney which I identified as the original route taken by Howard and Gabrioli in 1945, I powered my way up it and twenty-five minutes later stood on Sendeyo's summit.

So far, so fast. Yet the brilliance of early morning was fading. A cold wind had sprung up and dark clouds were settling over the brooding bulk of Batian. With half of the equatorial twelve-hours span of daylight already gone, the sensible thing would have been to make tracks for home there and then. Tereri's towers reared up on the other side of a deep notch rapidly filling up with mist, yet so temptingly close that I knew I couldn't let this one go. After a false start, I made a zigzagging, nerve-stretching descent down flaky, volcanic rock towards a glimmer of snow that marked the bottom of the gap. From here, I made another false start that ended up at the top of a teetering gendarme. Reversing this with difficulty, I eventually clambered to the top of Tereri's broken summit duly chastened.

It had taken eight hours to get this far. With only four hours of daylight left, it was now too late to reverse my outward route. The only feasible way back to the hut was to drop down into the upper Mackinder Valley and then re-ascend Lenana, three miles away and a thousand metres higher. The business of getting off Tereri by a diagonal girdle traverse across verglassed rocks and ice-choked gullies, remains a nightmare memory. At one stage, I found myself off-balance halfway up a vertical chimney whose exit was blocked by a frozen waterfall. With a frenzied burst of energy, I bridged both sides and propelled my upper body over the lip before collapsing at the top in a quivering heap. An hour and a half later I was sitting on the screes of the upper Mackinder Valley stuffing down my last bar of chocolate drained by the physical and mental strain of the past three hours.

In fast fading light, Lenana was dimly visible on the skyline. I set my course towards it, crossed the top of the Mackinder Valley and then began to climb up a seemingly endless moraine. At first, the scree was fine as sand, but became progressively chunkier and less stable higher up leaving me gasping for breath every twenty-five steps. I had already lost all sense of time when night fell like a blanket and an impenetrable mist enveloped everything around. I kept plodding on upwards by instinct with my reserves of energy gradually seeping away. Once, after falling flat on my face, I lay there prone for minutes unable to get up. Eventually, the mist cleared and when the moon came up to silhouette Lenana, I spotted my morning's footprints in the snow. Faintly now, but unmistakably, someone was shouting my name and a light flickering on the skyline ridge. Thirteen hours after leaving the hut, I was shaking hands with Tony and Mick on Lenana's summit.

My integral traverse might even have been a first, but I had stuck my neck out to do it and it was no surprise to learn next morning that the others had been hatching their own plans. When Tony announced that he and Mick were going to recce the Shipton/Wyn-Harris route on Nelion the following day, I assumed that Ruth and Peter Hoel would be climbing with them.

'Certainly not!' Ruth snapped. 'Nothing would induce me to climb with that man. He's got no proper rock-climbing experience and hasn't a clue how to abseil. I shall be going with Tony and Mick.'

After the trio set off, I took Hoel for a training climb on nearby Tilman Peak. Quiet and self-contained, he was immensely strong physically and climbed as effortlessly as a gymnast. Late that evening, a glum-looking Garman returned to the hut, followed by an exhausted Fearn.

'Sorry John, some bad news. Your abseil rope got jammed halfway up Nelion. Mick and I will retrieve it tomorrow when we'll be making our summit bid.'

'What about you, Ruth?' I asked, taken aback.

'Frankly, I'm far too tired after today's climb' she replied. 'I'll be taking a rest day tomorrow.'

Party unity was beginning to fracture. Ruth was refusing to speak to Hoel and my own relationship with her had soured ever since we had shared a tent on the way up. Dalliance seldom mixes with mountaineering and while her motives for climbing were complex, mine were clear. I was also worried whether the gutsy but inexperienced Mick Fearn, now lying comatose on his bunk, was really up to it. Neither he nor Garman owned a watch between them. Whatever their plans, I was determined that before attempting Nelion, Hoel and I should have a serious workout together on Point Pigott, the fourth highest peak on Mount Kenya. Shipton and Tilman had made the first ascent in 1930 by its North-West Face, but the more difficult South Ridge had only been done two years before. Having seen Hoel in action, I had no worries that we could manage it, but was more concerned about my feet. The brand-new Robert Lawrie boots sent out from London were half a size too small and had left both my heels raw and several toenails blackened.

To reach the base of Pigott involved a 1,000-metre descent down boulder-strewn moraines to Two Tarn Hut. Hoel set off at a cracking pace leaving me wincing with pain as I stumbled along in his wake. The first section of the South Ridge was straightforward and an hour and a half's climbing took us to the col below its final section where the rock steepened dramatically.

'Better stop here for a rest and a quick bite.' I said to Peter as I gazed across the void that separated us from the Forel Glacier's ice cliffs and Batian's majestic West Ridge.

'This is where the real climbing starts.'

After munching some chocolate in silence, I turned to him: 'Ready to go Peter?'

He glanced back and shook his head.

'Sorry John, but I'm not feeling too good. I'm afraid I can't go any further.'

I wondered what could be wrong with him. Up until now, he had been moving fast and confidently. However, if he was unwell I couldn't possibly push him. Could I go on alone? After my scrape on Sendeyo and Tereri, the last thing I wanted was another solo epic, yet having got this far, the urge to reach the summit was overwhelming.

'Okay Peter. You stay put just here. I'm going on, but please don't go home without me!'

The ridge now narrowed to a thin edge, sometimes surfaced with a veneer of ice, with tremendous exposure on either side. I felt extremely vulnerable, but only when confronted by the 'Second Tower' and its 'extremely serious' Grade VI pitch did my nerve fail. I couldn't risk attempting this without the support of a second, so dropped down on to the North-West Face and found a weathered abseil sling suspended from the top of an overhanging chimney. By jamming my body up and over it, I regained the ridge well above the tower and fifty minutes after leaving the col, stood on Pigott's summit. The descent was easier than expected and I found Hoel sitting in exactly the same place I'd left him. Without a word, he took off at great speed, led all the way down to Two Tarn Hut and then, without pausing, raced up the screes to the Firmin Hut leaving me limping behind.

Back at the hut, all was confusion. Two climbers from Tanganyika, Anton

('Axe') Nelson and Dave Goodall, having trekked up from the roadhead in a single day had taken possession with a noisy gang of porters. Garman and Fearn had climbed as far as Mackinder's Gendarme, the halfway mark on Nelion, but had been forced to retreat when Fearn had almost collapsed. He was now lying in his bunk breathing heavily. Ruth sat alone in a corner, fussing and distressed. After ten hours on the trot, I was too tired to be either sympathetic or sociable and left my formal introductions to the following day.

Nelson, a rangy, all-American employed by the Government of Tanganyika, was the current president of the Tanganyika Mountain Club. Goodall, a dour Yorkshireman, was a Colonial Service agricultural officer. Four years before, this pair had made the first ascent of Kilimanjaro's impressive Heim Glacier. Nelson's go-go personality lightened the hut's stale atmosphere and when he and Goodall returned that evening declaring that Point John's Grade IV climb was 'an imposter' and that they were going to climb Batian by Mackinder's Diamond Glacier route the following day, I was relieved to think that there would be at least two competent climbers on the mountain.

But who would be climbing Mount Kenya with whom now that Fearn was out of contention? Ruth, blowing hot and cold, was barely speaking to either Hoel or me, but had established a good rapport with the easy-going Garman. This left me to climb again with Hoel who seemed none the worse for Pigott. Nelson's enthusiasm was infectious, but I was apprehensive about tomorrow's climb and before falling into a fitful sleep reread the guidebook's route description by torchlight committing it to memory mindful of John Blacker's warning that unless Nelion's summit was reached by 10.30 a.m. to carry on to Batian would result in benightment.

At 4.20 a.m. on 30 January, I was cooking bacon and eggs for four. An hour later, Hoel and I followed Garman and Drake across the Lewis Glacier to the base of Nelion's south-east face. The mountain was intimidating, but as the sun came up the rock warmed to a reddish tint and its seemingly blank face assumed a reassuring pattern of gullies, ledges, pinnacles, and buttresses. On this third attempt, Garman was on familiar ground and we reached Mackinder's Gendarme by 8 a.m. He and I led through the crux pitches of Shipton's and Rickety Crack up until when both Drake and Hoel had been climbing confidently. But on Rickety, Hoel struggled and Drake came off, though was safely held by Garman. The rest was straightforward and we reached the summit together at exactly 10 a.m. well within guidebook time.

So far, everything had gone to plan. Ruth was tired but ecstatic.

'Now I've done Nelion, I'm going on to Batian,' she declared excitedly.

'Few other women have ever done that.'

From here, Batian's summit was only 150 horizontal-metres distant across a deep notch called the Gate of the Mists which links the twin peaks. I imagined that it could only be half-an-hour away and was puzzled that the guidebook allowed three to four hours for the round trip. When I peered down into the gate I could see why. The recommended route is to make a forty-five-metre diagonal traverse across the upper lip of Nelion's North Face. In dry conditions, this would have been straightforward, but with the rocks now encased in ice, hours of step-cutting would have been necessary and to save weight, none of us had brought crampons.

These conditions changed the whole nature of the climb. Garman was game to carry on and Ruth blithely unconcerned, but at this *moment critique,* Hoel delivered another bombshell.

'I'm sorry John, I'm not going any further. I've climbed Nelion and that's good enough for me. I have no wish to climb Batian. I shall stay here until you return.'

At first, I didn't believe him. Was this a repeat of Pigott? I tried reasoning, but nothing would change his mind.

'Okay Peter, you stay put here. We'll pick you up later.'

Time was slipping by. To keep up to schedule, I decided to abseil down into the gate to reconnoitre the way ahead. Unfortunately, the 200-foot abseil rope in Hoel's rucksack was so badly knotted after Garman's second attempt that I wasn't prepared to lose more time straightening it out, so abseiled down on my doubled 120-foot climbing rope. It was a bad mistake. I had misjudged the distance and found myself stranded on an ice-encrusted boss with the gate still some way below. I left the rope hanging free; nicked a line of steps through the ice to the gate, and then traversed its corniced ridge. Suspended in space over the Diamond Glacier on one side and Nelion's 800-metre North Face on the other, I wondered what lunacy had brought me to this pass. After safely reaching the Batian side of the gate, I shouted up to Tony to follow. Ruth insisted on a complicated abseil arrangement and on joining up berated me for not taking the normal route. To force the pace, I raced on up the ridge to Batian's summit to be followed by an unruffled Garman and flustered Ruth forty-five minutes later. Ruth's had been a gutsy performance, but the effort had exhausted her and by taking three hours to get this far meant certain benightment.

Without more ado, I scuttled back down to the gate to work out how best to regain Nelion's summit. Barely a hundred feet below, I was amazed to see Goodall stuck under an overhang and Nelson shouting instructions below him. Preoccupied with our own problems, I'd completely forgotten about them.

'We followed you as far as Mackinder's Gendarme and then traversed across to climb this God-almighty Diamond Glacier.' Nelson yelled up.

'We've had to give the bloody thing away. The ice is so effing hard we couldn't get our crampons into it. We're settling for Nelion if we can only get up these effing rocks.'

I left them to it and assessed our own options. The diagonal ice traverse was definitely out and then, losing all touch with reality, I tried to shin up the rope I had left hanging. In no way was this going to work, and as I swung like a pendulum back and forth over space, I remembered that Hoel must still be on the top of Nelion. Retracing my steps to Batian, I could see him sitting on his rucksack seemingly oblivious to the dramas unfolding below.

'Peter' I shouted up to him. 'Get yourself a belay and give me a top rope!'

He must have heard, but didn't budge a muscle. Even when Tony and Ruth joined me to take up the call, Hoel would not be moved. As the late-afternoon mists descended, the gate echoed with a cacophony of shouts and cries from five despairing climbers. Eventually, we gave up.

We had reached a *moment critique*. With the mist thickening, it now began to snow. Goodall and Nelson had taken a line further round Nelion and were now out of sight. From the gate, the only line of weakness I could see was a vertical, twenty-metre iced-up chimney, just to the right of my abseil rope. There was nowhere to take a secure belay, but Tony closed up to take up a precarious stance. I had already stuck my neck out on Tereri and Pigott, but if I came off this time there was precious little chance of Tony holding me and not just one but three lives would be lost. I braced myself, offered a silent prayer and then, with the adrenaline pumping furiously, attacked the chimney forcing my way up it, shoulders and hands jamming simultaneously and boots scrabbling on the ice, my body propelled by sheer will power. At the top I hauled Ruth up like a stranded fish. It then took four throws before Tony could catch the top rope.

Reunited on Nelion at 4 p.m. Hoel got to his feet and then walked across to meet us, his face expressionless.

'What on earth was the problem Peter?' I burst out. 'Couldn't you see that we were in dire straights and needed a top-rope?'

'I'm sorry, John. I completely lost my nerve. I simply couldn't move.'

At least I admired his honesty. He was, after all, a family man.

Ruth, white-faced and strained, badly needed food and a rest. Another precious fifteen minutes were spent untangling the knotted abseil rope. Nelson and Goodall joined us briefly, but were well on their way by the time we were ready to follow. On the thirty-metre abseil above Windy Gap, Hoel went down like a rocket, but Ruth's nerve and technique deserted her. On reaching Mackinder's Gendarme, night fell like a blanket and it began to snow really heavily. By now, Nelson and Goodall were out of sight, but Tony, who had twice climbed down from this same point, was determined to carry on, as was Ruth. I wanted to follow suit, but Hoel insisted on staying put. Sensible enough. Two climbers had been killed the previous year when descending this same passage after dark.

As the clouds lifted, the bobbing light of Garman's head torch marked their slow but steady descent. Far below, across the Lewis Glacier, the lights of the Firmin Hut twinkled like a solitary star. I thought of Mick Fearn waiting there alone, anxious and apprehensive. Later, the moon came up so bright that every detail of the descent route was clearly visible, so at least the others would soon be safely down. When it became intensely cold I took my boots off, stuffed my feet into my rucksack and gingerly eased myself into a flimsy plastic bag. Although overwhelmingly tired, I could only doze off intermittently and spent the next ten hours shivering and shouting with my teeth chattering uncontrollably. Hoel sat it out on the coiled abseil rope: silent, impassive and seemingly impervious to the cold.

At 6 a.m. my boots were frozen solid as the sun's first rays began to melt the verglas off the red-tinged rocks and bring back some vestige of life. As I shook out a cascade of ice crystals from the plastic bag, Hoel pointed towards the horizon.

'Look over there John, it's Kilimanjaro. Amazing! It must be 200 miles away!'

It took another two hours to thaw out before beginning our descent. At the foot of Nelion, Goodall and Nelson had come across from the hut to meet us. We walked back together to find Mick Fearn waiting in the doorway with steaming mugs of hot chocolate.

The rest is short in telling. The following day, Tony Garman, the real hero of the Nelion/Batian twenty-nine-hour epic, led a restored Mick Fearn up Shipton's route on Midget Peak and then survived a desperate scrape in descent. Nelson, Goodall and I did a circuit of the main peaks and on the morning of our last day, Ruth and I made up our differences by climbing Point John together. Peter Hoel left a day early to catch his plane. He wrote to me later to report that although he had got lost for a time in the bamboo forest, he was overjoyed to have become only the second Norwegian to have climbed Nelion 'When I am climbing, I suffer and curse, but when I am away from it, I long to be back.' Many of us have felt the same.

4

OLYMPIAN HEIGHTS: GREECE AND ANATOLIA

Kenya had opened new perspectives. The prospect of returning to Mukalla to renew battle with the Quaiti Sultanate's obscurantist bureaucracy left me with a certain sinking feeling. However, on passing through Aden I was unexpectedly summoned to the Secretariat, the Aden Government's headquarters, by a senior officer, Robin Thorne, who came quickly to the point.

'The Head of the Lands Department, Cecil Kenyon, is long overdue home leave and his deputy has had to fly home on emergency sick leave. As a result, we have no administrative officers currently available to fill the gap. You read law at Cambridge so we're offering you Kenyon's post in an acting capacity. It would mean having to extend your tour by another eight months. However, acceptance would mean promotion to a much higher pay scale. Think about it and give me your decision as soon as possible.'

This was effectively a royal command so I didn't think about it.

Sad in many ways to be leaving Mukalla's empty beaches, Hadhramaut's sky-scraping cities and the limitless sands of the Empty Quarter, I took up my new appointment on 1 April 1961, All Fools Day.

The year of 1961 was an exciting time to be working in the British Crown Colony of Aden, the finest natural harbour on the Arabian peninsula. As the headquarters of Britain's Middle Eastern Command, it supported a 10,000-strong British garrison; had become the second biggest bunkering port in the world and a major port-of-call for transoceanic liners from Australasia, the Far East and

South Africa. This 'Hong Kong of the Middle East' and 'Eye of the Yemen' had reached the apogee of its prosperity with land, its most valuable resource, selling at much the same price as in the City of London. The Lands Department was responsible for the allocation and administration of this Crown Colony's land and when Kenyon went on leave it became my job to run it. Faced with a welter of unfamiliar problems in the energy-sapping heat of my second Arabian summer, I had little time to think about mountaineering, or much else for that matter.

For what would have been my first long leave, I had originally planned a bumper season in the Alps, which would now have to be put on hold. Instead, I reverted to a plan originally hatched during my Arabic course at the School of Oriental Studies before coming out to Arabia. When browsing around Probsthain's Oriental bookshop opposite the British Museum, I had picked up a first edition of Lord Percy's *The Highlands of Asiatic Turkey* which described a journey he had made through the mountains of Hakkiari in Turkish Kurdistan in 1899. Percy's photographs of what, to me, was a completely unknown range of alpine peaks and glaciers had come as a revelation. Through Bill Norton, I got the address of Sidney Nowill, an Alpine Club member living in Istanbul, and wrote to him about the prospects of climbing there. His reply was deeply pessimistic: 'Kurdistan has so far defied almost every attempt by travellers to get into it. There is no climbing club in Turkey and nowhere where one can recruit a climbing companion. The 'Mountain Club' in Istanbul devotes itself entirely to fencing, tennis and, as an afterthought, skiing. On account of the area's political sensitivity, I can see no immediate prospect of anyone getting permission to go there.'

Further enquiries got me nowhere and when confiding my frustrations to Bill he replied,

'Sir Claremont Skrine tells me that *the* man to get in touch with on Turkish Kurdistan is C.J. Edmunds CMG, CBE.'

Edmunds was unquestionably *the* expert on Kurdistan. However, after Ottoman Turkey's dismemberment after the First World War, it was on his advice to the 1925 Boundary Commission that the former Ottoman territories of Mosul and its oil fields were given to Iraq. The dire consequences of this advice are still with us today and made Edmunds as unpopular with the Turks as Skrine had been with the Persians. I decided not to pursue this line of investigation any further.

Nonetheless, I didn't give up on the possibility of climbing elsewhere in Turkey, and as a fall back, planned to make an exploratory visit to the mountains of Greece on my way back to England. At first sight, Greece was an unlikely choice, for although classical literature abounds with references to Olympus, Parnassus, Ossa and Pelion and though mountains make up eighty per cent of its land mass, I could find no accounts of anyone who had ever climbed there. So I wrote to Athanassios Tsartzanos, the honorary secretary of the Hellenic Alpine Club in Athens, for advice on climbing Mount Olympus in late November.

'This is not the ideal period for climbing', he had replied. 'The weather being liable to be bad or just cold. Bring along a light raincoat.'

By now, Sidney Nowill had also written to say that he 'might be able to take a few days off for climbing in December as we are having to stay with us a girl called Nigella Blandy (aged twenty). She is an excellent climber and happens to be Whymper's granddaughter.'

Whymper's granddaughter! I didn't know that he had one, though like any self-respecting mountaineer, I well knew the story of Edward Whymper's first ascent of the Matterhorn and its tragic aftermath.

Following a lengthy exchange of correspondence, Sidney suggested that after I had climbed Mount Olympus, his wife Hilary would be delighted that I stay with them for a week in Istanbul. Thereafter he, Nigella and I could sally forth to explore the mountains of Anatolia. 'Hilary is expecting a baby so will not be joining us, but it would be useful if you brought a tent. Turkey's very cold in winter. We may all have to squeeze in together.'

Late on 15 November 1961, I boarded the Europe Australian Line's *Bretagne* with four suitcases, two rucksacks and a load of emotional baggage. As the liner slipped anchor and slid off into the night, I stood transfixed at the ship's rail until the lights of Aden disappeared over the horizon. With a lump in my throat, I kept thinking of Susan, the golden-haired girl I was leaving behind me in Steamer Point. The *Bretagne*, a former British liner was now Greek-owned and jam-packed with testosterone-fuelled young Australians bound for the UK. During the ship's one and only lifeboat drill, the lifeboats remained resolutely stuck fast because an overdose of paint had gummed them to the davits. My shipboard social life centred on a stunning trio of Hardy Amies models, Gaynor, Rania and Helen, loosely escorted by the firm's ex-guardee director/minder Bill Akroyd MC. I tagged along with these beautiful people until our last, tearful dinner together in Athens. Bill later wrote me to say that the final leg of their voyage had been a disaster as the *Bretagne* had mysteriously caught fire off Piraeus leaving its passengers to make the rest of their journey back to England by train.

Olympus! The very name evokes imagery, divinity and aspiration. The *altius* of the Olympic motto; birthplace of the Titans; home of the Gods from where Zeus despatched his thunderbolts and from where Prometheus stole the sacred fire and paid the price chained forever on the frosty Caucasus. Yet Homer's portrayal of Olympus as a paradise *'not shaken by the winds, not wet with rains, nor touched with snow'* could not be further from the reality. The name 'Olympus' is generic for any number of mountains scattered around Greece and Turkey, though the most famous is the Thessalian Olympus, a limestone massif whose triple summit lies some eighteen kilometres west of the Aegean and which covers an area larger than the Bernese Oberland.

Apart from its mythological reputation I knew little about Mount Olympus and had never seen a photograph of it until I visited Athanassios Tzartzanos at the Hellenic Alpine Club the day after the *Bretagne* left Piraeus. The sight of the mountain's daunting 500-metre north face plastered in snow prompted my involuntary low whistle for it bore not the remotest resemblance to Homer's paradise. Certainly, I was going to need more than a light raincoat for this one.

'Is that really Mount Olympus?' I asked him.

'Yes, of course it is' he replied with pride. 'It is the finest mountain in Greece.'

'Is there anyone in the area with whom I might climb it?'

'I'm afraid not. The only local guide is Costas Zolotas, but he's currently away in Munich. Anyway, no one would dream of climbing Olympus at this time of year.'

I didn't waste his time any further, but before leaving the club bought a copy of its illustrated publication *Olympus* as my guide. From this, I was surprised to learn that the first ascent of its highest peak Mytikas (2,917 metres), 'the Needle', had only been made in 1913 by the Swiss Boissonas and Baud-Bovey, 244 years after the Ottoman Sultan Mehmed IV had made an unsuccessful sally on horseback and fifty-six years after Whymper's first ascent of the Matterhorn. This I found puzzling given the nineteenth century rediscovery of Greece by a host of European travellers, poets and painters. Part of the explanation lies in the fact that at this time Greece's mountains were infested by brigands, so that of Britain's Victorian mountaineers, only the indefatigable clergyman Henry Tozer made the first serious, but unsuccessful, attempt to scale Mytikas in 1865. It was another sixty-one years before W.T. Ainslie made the first British ascent of Mytikas, and Olympus only emerged from climbing obscurity during mountaineering's 'iron age' when, in 1934, the brilliant Italian Comici delineated the first modern rock-climbing lines that inspired Greek climbers such as Costas Zolotas to pioneer their own hard routes.

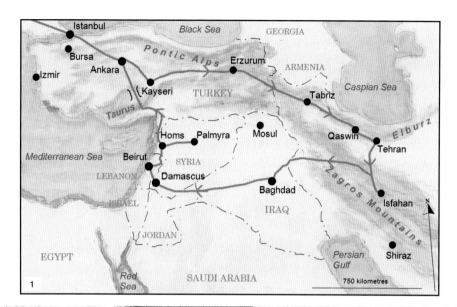

1 The Middle East. CNPE 1956 *Overland Route*.
2 CUMC Ben Nevis Meet 1955 at the Steall Hut. Standing L–R: ANO, Neil Macpherson, Pinney, Urquart.
Sitting L–R: Wright, Bill Norton.

3 CNPE outward bound. Camp on Anatolian Steppes. **Photo**: Bill Norton.
4 CNPE reception at Royal Palace, Tehran with HRH Prince Golum Reza Pahlavi (right). L-R: Author, Bruce Anderson, David Cook, Keith MacDougall, Captain Ghaffari. **Photo**: Unknown/untraceable.
5 Mule caravan in Mazanderan Forest. Sardab Valley. **Photo**: Keith MacDougall.

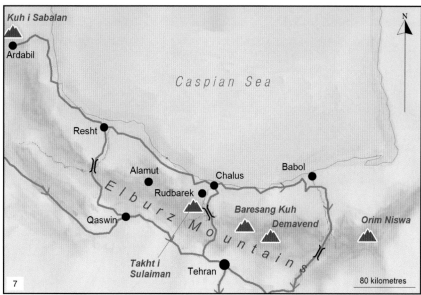

6 Group at Vanderbon. Back L–R: Author, Captain Ghaffari, Front L–R: Keith, Bruce and others.
   Photo: Julian Mustoe.
7 Elburz Range, Iran.

8 Hazarchal Base Camp. L–R: Bruce, author, David, Bill Norton, Julian Mustoe. **Photo:** Keith MacDougall.
9 Keith and Saphar bag a moufflon at Hazarchal. **Photo:** Bill Norton.
10 Captain Akbar Ghaffari, 'The Tiger of Tehran'. **Photo:** Bill Norton.
11 Bill on the summit of Alam Kuh.

11

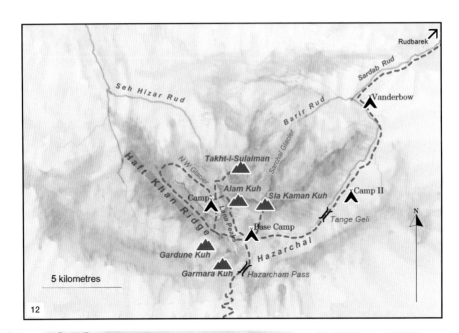

12 Takht-i-Sulaiman Massif, Elburz.
13 Alam Kuh north face from Takht-i-Sulaiman.

14 Saphid Arb. Shahavan encampment. **Photo:** Julian Mustoe.
15 Shahsavan migration from Saphid Arb.
16 Parviz Pashazapeh. Kuh-i-Sabalan in background.

17 Alps 1957, Tarantaise. Traverse of Levanna Occidentale.
18 Alps 1957. At the Dom Hut after the Taschhorn/Dom traverse. Weisshorn in background.
 L–R: Tony Delafield, author, Bill Norton. **Photo:** Unknown/untraceable.

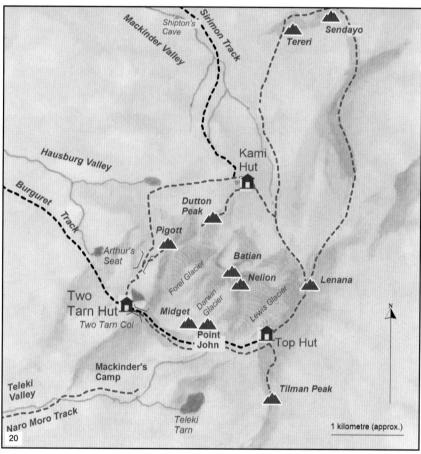

19 Cuillin Traverse, Skye 1959. Scurr nan Gillean ridge. John Scott and author.
    Photo: Unknown/untraceable.
20 Mount Kenya.

21

21 Mount Kenya 1961. North face of Nelion and Batian from near Sendeyo.
22 Mount Kenya 1961. Loading up at Raymond Hook's Farm.
23 Mount Kenya 1961. Camp at Hook's Farm. L–R: Tony Garman, Ruth Drake, Mick Fearn.
24 Mount Kenya 1961. Sendeyo and Tereri.

25 Mount Kenya 1961. Author on summit of Tereri.
26 Greece 1961. Mount Olympus, north face of Mytikas.

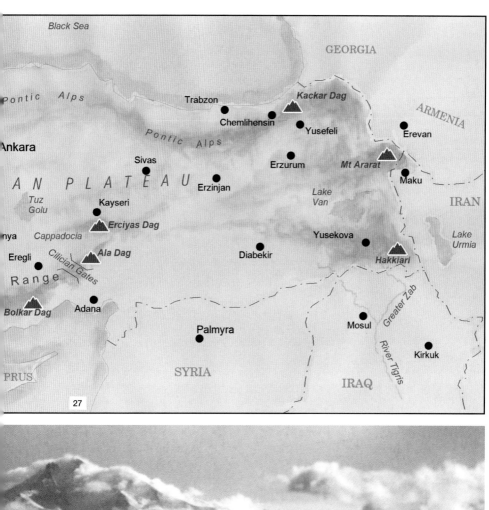

27 Turkey.
28 Turkey 1961. Ergiyas Dag north face.

29 Turkey 1961. Ergiyas Dag east face from Cuc Dag.
30 Turkey 1961. L–R: Nigella Blandy, Sidney Nowill, Mahmud, Ibrahim and Ali Safak at Camardi.
31 Scotland 1962. An Teallach traverse. Neil Macpherson.

32 Scotland 1962. Beneath Beinn Eighe. L–R: Bill Norton, Stewart Hawkins, author.
33 Aden. Jebel Shemsan.

34 Little Aden Aiguilles. John Ducker and Tony Boyle.
35 South Arabia. On patrol in the Radfan mountains.
36 Socotra. The Haggier Mountains.

Mindful of Sidney's request to bring a tent, I spent the next three days in Athens trying to extract my brand-new, UK-express-despatched Robert Lawrie's Everest Meade tent from the clutches of the Greek customs who were demanding £175 duty (£2,000 today) before releasing it. Athanassios knew exactly how to deal with this sort of nonsense and got it out for free. I never used it in either Greece or Turkey. On 24 November 1961, I boarded the Athens/Salonika express saddled with eight pieces of heavy baggage and a one-way ticket to Litochoro Limani, the nearest railway station to Olympus. With winter drawing in, the journey north past dun, lifeless fields backed by harsh, uncompromising ranges captured a different flavour of Greece and for fully an hour we steamed past the great mass of Parnassus, another mountain touched with the wand of divinity and already streaked with snow.

Nine hours up the line, there were neither whistles, lights nor porters to announce the train's arrival at Litochoro Limani, so when the train slowed to a barely perceptible stop, I hurriedly off loaded my baggage before it slipped away into the night. Alone on an unlit platform, the only audible sound was that of waves lapping the nearby strand. Eventually, I located and roused a resentful station master who, after emitting a string of oaths, raised an equally bolshie taxi-driver to take me nineteen kilometres to Litochoro's tourist hotel, a miserable place devoid of either food or heating. After repairing to the town's only taverna, I forced down a foul-smelling sausage and was violently sick.

Litochoro, at the foot of Mount Olympus's most easterly approaches, straddles the turbulent Enipeus River before it debouches from its spectacular gorge on to the coastal plain. To early European travellers, it was a place of ill repute with banditry rife. In 1961, it had barely emerged from the shadows after a decade of war that had devastated Greece and killed 600,000 of its inhabitants. The village's sullen, hostile atmosphere recalled a notorious civil war atrocity in 1946 when the communist leader Zachariadis attacked and destroyed Litochoro's police barracks in reprisal for the disembowelling of three left-wing ELAS functionaries.

I slept badly that night and the following day, the lowering pall of black cloud that shrouded the mountain's upper reaches seemed to reflect Litochoro's bitter past as I wandered around its gloomy streets showing Tzartzanos's letter of introduction to anyone likely to speak a common language and to find someone who might confirm that the Spilios Agapitos mountain hut was open and whether any local guide was available. The village tailor assured me that 'Jimmy' was my man and would meet me at the tourist hotel tomorrow at 7 a.m. Predictably, Jimmy did not turn up at the appointed hour, so I went in search of him myself bent double under the weight of a rucksack stuffed with tinned food, cooking equipment, climbing and abseil ropes, crampons and enough pitons for a north-wall siege. After Kafkaesque wanderings, I bumped into a man whom I assumed must be Jimmy. He had a tweed jacket slung over an ex-Wehrmacht day-sack and spoke no English, but I took it on trust that the hut would be open. As we made our way out of Litochoro with Jimmy in blue jeans and sandals and me feeling quite ridiculous in heavy cavalry-twill climbing breeches and duvet jacket, a bystander called out in English, 'You've got the right man!'

Without that wretched rucksack, the hut march might even have been a pleasure for by now the sky had cleared to reveal a cluster of snow peaks lining the western horizon and the path picked its way through successive bands of maquis, mixed forest and magnificent stands of 1,000-year-old Black pine which, unlike so much of upland Greece, had generally been spared from the depredations of charcoal burners. But by the time we reached the Stavros spring, fouled by a milling throng of sheep and goats, I was already flagging. The extent of my most recent training had been to race our Egyptian guide up the Great Pyramid of Cheops during the *Bretagne's* break in Cairo, a vertical interval of 135 metres as compared with 1,800 metres to the hut. Jimmy insisted on taking turns with the rucksack, but brand new, narrow-fit Italian climbing boots were giving me the red-hot blisters that made that nine-hour hut march an ordeal. I came in a very bad second to be greeted by Jimmy at the hut with hot tea and a blazing log fire.

Next morning, Mytikas was just visible as the culmination of a jagged ridge over-topping the curious, horizontally striated flanks of Olympus's south-east face. The snow above the hut was deep and the weather uncertain. Jimmy was fit as a chamois, but even he could go no higher in open sandals. I was dressed for the Himalaya, but still felt nauseous from the altitude and that disgusting sausage. Besides, my feet were killing me and the German occupation map that Athanassios had given me in Athens would be useless for navigation in bad weather. Nonetheless, having come this far I couldn't back out now and so, after leaving Jimmy to 'guard' the hut, I trudged upwards through the snow with leaden thighs to the summit of Skala, the stepping stone to Mytikas. And now, as if on cue, the clouds lifted to reveal my path to the summit of Olympus. From here, it was only fifty metres higher and 300 metres further, but to get there would have involved a tricky descent over slippery, sloping slabs to a narrow col from where the summit ridge soared upwards in a succession of steep, snow-covered steps overlooking the Megala Kasania's 500-metre precipice.

I now understood why it had taken so long for mere mortals to reach the 'Throne of the Gods' and settled for the nearby peak of Skolio. It was only six metres lower than Mytikas, but it might have been a mile.

Two days later, I arrived by bus in Istanbul and presented myself at the Nowills' spacious flat at the top of their apartment block in Moda on the Asiatic side of the Bosphorus. Overlooking the pretty harbour of Kadikoy, the ancient Chalcedon, Seraglio Point lay only half a kilometre across the historic stretch of water that separates two continents. Even now, whenever I hear the Janissaries Chorus from Mozart's *Die Entführung aus dem Serail,* I see in my mind's eye that transcendent skyline of swelling domes and pencilled minarets veneered with snow that glinted gold in the December sunshine.

I was intensely curious to meet the man with whom I had corresponded so often over the past fifteen months. Apart from sharing a common passion for mountains, all I knew about him was that he was thirteen years my senior and the director of a Turkish public company. His welcome was friendly but guarded and it took time to discover that Sidney Edward Payn Nowill was a polymath who not only spoke fluent Turkish, French and German, but was also an economist, political analyst, painter, photographer, writer, art connoisseur, gourmet, wine-buff, and worldwide traveller. And as I learned many years later, Sidney had also worked for the British Secret Intelligence and from 1947–1949 under the despicable traitor Kim Philby who was then head of mission in Istanbul. Philby's feline charm had duped almost everyone from his boss 'M', Sir Stewart Menzies, downwards. Ignorant then of the depth of Philby's treachery, Sidney nonetheless 'cordially detested' the man. A clue to Sidney's own covert activities was hinted at by his choosing as his literary *nom de plume* 'Ashenden', Somerset Maugham's fictional secret service hero.

As the last working resident member of the British mercantile community whose dynasties had, for over two centuries, dominated the commercial life of the Levant, Sidney had already written the first volume of his autobiography *The Mountains of My Life* when aged only thirty-three. The book has a haunting, lyrical quality that reveals more about his motivations and character than anything he wrote or said about himself in later years. It lovingly describes his early upbringing in the family's decaying mansion at Bournabat, a once-exclusive international enclave above Smyrna that had been the richest and most cosmopolitan city in the Ottoman Empire before its catastrophic destruction by the Turkish Army in 1922. Sidney had been educated in England, but his heart remained in Bournabat from where, as a sickly child, he could see from his sickbed the distant, snow-clad Nimph Dag, the peak that had first stirred his passion for mountain adventure.

After a youth impaired by ill health, Sidney had climbed with the zeal of the reborn. He had had few opportunities to meet fellow British mountaineers so his Alpine climbs had mainly been done with professional guides. Nigella, whom he had met in Zermatt and climbed with in the Dolomites, was an exception. I was a touch apprehensive about meeting the granddaughter of Edward Whymper whose marriage at the age of sixty-six to a woman of twenty had lasted only four years. There had only been one child, Ethel, a fine climber in her own right. Nigella was Ethel's daughter. I didn't doubt that she would be a competent mountaineer, but the Mount Kenya imbroglio had made me wary of climbing 'blind', particularly if emotional baggage became involved. However, any misgivings vanished the moment I met Nigella, an auburn-haired, no-nonsense stunner with a winning smile. It was Sidney and Nigella who were taking a punt, not me.

In 1961, the mountains of Turkey were little known to British climbers. Sidney's plan was that he and I should spend three days on the Ulu Dagh above Bursa to get to know each other. Thereafter, the three of us would drive on to Kayseri from where Nigella and I would attempt the 3,916-metre Erciyes Dag before we all headed east to the Dolomitic peaks of the Ala Dag. After a week's sight-seeing in Istanbul, I bought a two-shilling ferry ticket to make the two-hour trip across the Sea of Marmara to the port of Yalova from where I shared a *Dolmus* taxi to drive to Bursa to meet up with Sidney.

Spread about a bosky plain dotted with vineyards, poplars and cypress and dominated by the snow-clad Ulu Dag, the garden city of Bursa had been the Ottoman capital during its most formative period and is where six sultans are buried and boasts 200 honey-coloured mosques. The 'Great Mountain' that overlooks it is a twenty-mile-long, six-mile-wide massif whose rolling, twelve-mile-long summit ridge culminates in the 2,543-metre Karateppe. Originally known as the Bithynian Olympus, it had been a place of pilgrimage from the earliest times with the memory of the Byzantine monks who had frequented its slopes still preserved in its older Turkish name 'Keshish Dag', the Mountain of the Monks. Until quite recently, snow from the névé of its northern cirques was laboriously transported down the mountainside to Yalova and thence ferried across the Sea of Marmara to cool the Sultan's sherbet.

Sidney's Delphic instructions had been to meet him at 'the club': wherever that might be. I could only assume that the Land Rover with the Ponds Face Cream insignia parked in Bursa's main square was Sidney's. And so it proved.

'Glad you've made it at last' said Sidney frostily. 'I'd have liked to have shown you something of Bursa, the most beautiful city in the Middle East after Isfahan, had you only been on time. However, there's not enough of that left now as we must reach the Becheren Refuge before dark. It's 2,000 metres higher up the mountain and the road's likely to be snowed-up.'

The road soon deteriorated into a rough track that twisted upwards through a dense pine forest with snowdrifts piled high on either side. When our driver Mahmud changed down into low-ratio Sidney broke a long silence: 'Remnants of a great blizzard that swept through three-weeks ago when I was up here with Nigella and my cousin Phillippa Treadwell. Incidentally, this refuge we're going to is privately owned by Mehmet Bey. He's had to smarten it up a bit because skiing has become quite popular on the Ulu Dag and he's having to compete for custom with the big hotels in Bursa.'

Snow lay thick around the refuge. Though unguarded, it was clean and well-maintained with sheets and blankets provided. After Mahmud had lit the stove to get up a good fug, Sidney relaxed.

'You know John, I've got a very special feeling for the Bithynian Olympus and this is probably my fortieth visit. As a first outing tomorrow, I suggest we climb Kuskakli by the west ridge and descend its south-west face. It's an old favourite of mine. Nothing much to it'.

Next morning, it was still snowing with the clouds masking the top of Sidney's 'Marble Mountain'. When we eventually made a start, I spotted some huge paw marks in the snow just outside the hut.

'Too big for a wolf, but too small for bear,' observed Sidney.

'Must be a Karabash, the Anatolian sheepdog. A very ancient breed, tawny-yellow in colour with a black head, hence the name. Stands as high as a Great Dane and males can weigh up to fifty kilos. The shepherds use them to guard their flocks from wolves and put iron spikes round their collars. Sometimes they even cross them with wolves. They can be quite ferocious, so let's just hope we don't meet any.'

Though twice as high, the Ulu Dag's climbs are Scottish in scale and character. The ascent of Kushakli was little more than a rocky scramble, but the descent on snow-encrusted rocks by what Sidney called 'the organ pipes' was tricky and I couldn't understand why he hadn't brought a rope. Was he giving me some sort of test? The tops had been shrouded by cloud and mist all day, but as we raced back to the refuge in late afternoon the cloud suddenly lifted and the sun burst through for the first time. Away to the west, beyond successive bands of light and shadow and the stark silhouettes of lone pines, a turbulent cloud-sea opened and closed to reveal a receding line of whaleback ridges beyond which a slither of light reflected the sinking sun.

'The Aegean', observed Sidney drily.

For our last climb on the Ulu Dag, Sidney chose Zirvay, the third summit of the range. Its northern cirque, sheathed in snow and ice, brought to mind the cliffs of Ben Nevis. Sidney's route traced a tenuous line up its western edge by a series of rock ribs leading to the upper snowfields. Once again, his insistence of climbing without a rope seemed perverse as an unprotected fall with no one else near the mountain could have been disastrous. On gaining the ridge, we met the sun for the first time that day only to have our faces frozen by a bitter east wind. A gracefully curving cornice-line followed the ridge eastwards before culminating in a distant summit.

'Karateppe', said Sidney, motioning towards it with his ice axe. 'Looks a lot closer than it really is. A summit too far for today. Better get down before it's dark.'

With that, he set off at breakneck speed down the mountain leaving me floundering behind. Forcing our way through the gloomy pine forest in the darkening evening mist, I was left in no doubt that on this Turkish Olympus, gods of a harsher temper dwelt.

Nigella's midnight arrival off the express ferry from Istanbul denied her a *filet mignon* dinner at the Celik Palace Hotel and a massage in the *hamam* of Bursa's finest fourteenth-century domed thermal baths. After breakfasting off buffalo milk and honey, the Pond's Land Rover headed eastwards through Ionia's fertile vales and gentle woodlands for the Bolu Pass which marks the true geographical divide between Europe and Asia. Here, in the thinner air of Anatolia, autumn had become winter with the stolid earth frozen and snow already spreading its monochrome mantle over the Anatolian Plateau. Eastwards, the steppe unfolded – illimitable, immobile and impassive.

What had taken our Persian expedition two days and nights to drive from Ankara to Kayseri now took five hours. The Plateau's billowing cloudscapes reminded me of East Africa, yet not even that first sight of Mount Kenya was as dramatic as that of Erciyes Dag. Resplendent in winter snow and rising 3,000 metres clear from the Cappadocian plain with its ridges and recesses sharply etched by the sun, even Sidney was moved to leap out to record this tremendous spectacle with his Linhoff plate-camera. The Greeks had called it 'Argos Oros', the 'Silver Mountain', and Strabo had reckoned it to be the highest in the world. Hamilton, the first European to climb it in 1837, had searched in vain for the remnants of Noah's ark.

'Are we really going to climb that thing?' I muttered to Nigella.

'It looks one helluva big mountain and we haven't even got a map.'

'Proper maps are unobtainable in Turkey due to military security,' broke in Sidney. 'But don't worry. From here, we're looking directly at its north face. From the other side it's not particularly difficult and you'll be starting from the Tekir Refuge which leaves you with only 1,740 metres of vertical height to climb to the summit.'

To me, it still seemed one helluva long climb.

At Kayseri, Sidney insisted on visiting the director of physical education to confirm that the Tekir Refuge was open. When a tough-looking Turk with a mountaineer's mien told him that the director wasn't in, Sidney retorted sharply: 'Never mind that. The refuge is supposed to be open and permanently guarded in winter. Anyway, we can't hang around here. I've got to get my friends to Hisarlik as soon as I've finished my business in town.'

Sidney's business took longer than expected and when we eventually reached Hisarlik in late afternoon, he insisted that Mahmud continue driving up the mountain track until it became completely blocked by snow.

'I'm afraid we're going to have to leave you here,' said Sidney. 'Just keep following those footsteps through the snow. They're bound to lead to the Tekir Refuge eventually. See you both in four days time!'

The refuge was ten miles away and another 500 metres higher. The sky was still clear, but our rucksacks felt very heavy. Barely started, two enormous Anatolian Karabash sheep dogs spotted us from a high ridge and, after detaching themselves from their flock, came charging down the hillside barking and snarling.

'That's all we need,' I groaned to Nigella. 'Dump our rucksacks and have ice axes at the ready. Go for their balls if necessary!'

Luckily, it never came to that. The huge beasts sheared off at the last moment and reluctantly returned to their charges.

More worrying were the black clouds fast enveloping the Erciyes's summit. As it disappeared from view, a penetrating wind sprang up. Fresh snow, getting deeper with every step, was obliterating the track and when night fell no moon was visible. Two hours later, it was snowing in earnest. When we came across a deserted barn, I said to Nigella: 'Don't know about you, but I'm not a bit happy about this. According to Sidney's altimeter, we haven't gained much height and the weather's fast deteriorating. We could do a lot worse than hunker down here for the night.'

'But this can't possibly be the hut,' she replied firmly. 'I think we should bash on.'

We did just that, but it might have been our last bash, for soon we were battling through a full-scale blizzard. The track had long since vanished, but a line of telegraph poles was still faintly visible through the maelstrom. Pray God, I thought, let them lead to the refuge. Four hours later in the black of night, visibility was virtually nil and I was worried stiff that we had overshot the refuge. A forced bivouac didn't bear thinking about.

And then, ghostly yet unmistakable, the sound of a bell rang Lutine-like through the storm. Changing direction slightly, we followed its ringing to the outline of a building and then, finding a door, burst through it encased in snow. Our arrival was greeted with loud applause, followed by hearty handshakes and backslapping all round from what turned out to be the entire Turkish national ski team. Clustered round a central stove, they were wearing nothing but their underpants. Only when Nigella removed her tasselled cap and shook out her auburn hair, did their smiles turn to panic. A woman! The room emptied as a dozen devout Moslems covered up their manhood and rushed off to don their salopettes.

'I never thought that anyone would be crazy enough to come up here at night in this weather,' said Turan, after the excitement had died down.

'When your friend spoke to me so roughly in the director's office it was already far too late to start, so I assumed you'd be coming up tomorrow with the mules. We rang the bell just in case. You have been very lucky to have got here alive!'

Turan turned out to be Mount Erciyes's chief guide and was up here to train the Turkish ski team. The refuge's two resident guardians, both cross-eyed, assumed that Nigella and I must be married, so allocated us a cosy little room to ourselves with its own stove.

The mules never made it next day because the storm never let up. I was minded to do a recce, but when a couple of venturesome skiers came back encased in ice, thought better of it. That evening, with one precious day already gone, I asked Turan about our chances of climbing Erciyes the following day by Sidney's recommended route, 'The Devil's Gulley'.

'It would be madness to attempt that climb in these conditions,' he snorted.

'This weather's not going to clear for another twenty-four hours and higher up, the snow will be waist deep and liable to avalanche. Even in summer, you should allow fourteen hours for that climb.'

'Thanks, Turan. But I think we'll probably give it a go anyway. We can always turn back if things look too bad.'

He stared at me aghast. Nigella didn't blink an eyelid.

I set the alarm for 1 a.m. The hut was so well insulated that I couldn't hear the wind outside and when I peeped through the door, the blizzard was blowing harder than ever.

'No point in starting now,' I told Nigella. 'Better go back to bed.'

Although she never told me at the time, Nigella was not feeling at all well. There was no change in the weather at either 4 a.m. or 5 a.m. At 6 a.m. after a quick brew of Nescafe, we left the hut and set a compass bearing on Erciyes. Visibility was down to twenty metres; driving snow lacerating our faces, and the noise of the wind made normal conversation impossible. For the next four hours, we bashed on without exchanging a word. I was beginning to accept that this was mission impossible when I cupped my hand over Nigella's ear and shouted:

'Let's at least get to the Devil's Gulley.'

'Fine by me, if we can only find it', she yelled back. 'But I've no idea where we're going.'

As we climbed higher, the wind and cold intensified. Knee-deep snow made trail blazing a trial of will and the whiteout made it impossible to get the feel of the slope or the lie of the land.

After another hour, I stopped to consult the altimeter.

'I just don't believe it,' I gasped. 'It's already taken us five hours to climb only a thousand metres. We don't know where the hell we are, but unless we call it a day now, we'll never get back to the hut in daylight.'

As much by instinct as compass bearing, sometimes swimming chest-deep through the snow, we hit off the refuge three hours later. Turan was inside, positively glowing. His remonstrations began in English, but soon switched to Turkish. We quickly got his gist.

On waking late next day, 15 December, I peered out of the window to see the Turkish ski team practising their turns on the slopes above the hut. The sky was cloudless and the buttressed rim of Erciyes's semi-circular crater bowl looked so tempting that for a wild moment I seriously contemplated another attempt. We settled instead for Cuc Dag, a nearby satellite peak that gave panoramic views of Anatolia's snow-clad ranges fringing every horizon. When we said goodbye to our Turkish friends that afternoon, the guardians refused any payment for our three-night stay, but insisted that we telephone them from Hisarjik village to confirm safe arrival. That twenty-mile descent to Kayseri's tourist hotel wading through knee-deep snow is best forgotten. By 5 p.m. it was already dark with an icy wind blowing face-on. At Hisarjik I couldn't find a telephone anywhere. Racing on, I slipped on the ice, cannonaded into a wooden door and almost knocked myself out. Thereafter, I wasn't at my best. Nigella remained cool, calm and collected throughout.

Sidney had always intended that the red limestone peaks of the Ala Dag should be the expedition's climax, particularly as he had unfinished business to settle with Demirkazik, the 'Iron Stake'. At 3,756 metres, this is not only the highest peak in the range, but also the highest and grandest of all Mount Olympuses. Sidney's obsession with what he called the 'DK' stemmed from his first attempt to climb it in 1951 with Pauline Eshir when they had been forced to make a high bivouac on a narrow snow ledge with Sidney racked by cramp and Pauline suffering from altitude sickness. After surviving a very uncomfortable night, they managed to climb down much chastened. The Ala Dag had the additional attraction to Sidney as being virtually unknown to British mountaineers for although numberless armies and caravans treading the historic highway from the plateau to the Mediterranean coast would have passed this way, not until the twentieth century did any Europeans – inevitably German and Austrian expeditions – attempt to climb them. Their first British pioneer had been Edward Peck, then serving at the Ankara Embassy. After a brief visit in 1942, he returned the following year with Robin Hodgkin and L.A. Hurst to make the third ascent of the Demirkazik by the eponymous Hodgkin/Peck Couloir. On the summit, Peck substituted the faded swastika emblem left by Spreitzer's 1938 German team with his own 'staid calling card'.

Nigella and I had to make a pre-dawn start from Kayseri and a 112-kilometre taxi ride in order to rendezvous on time at Nigde where Sidney was waiting with the Land Rover. The hills around sparkled with fresh snow, but deep drifts soon blocked the road so we had to walk the rest of the way to the village of Camardi where Sidney's faithful muleteer Ibrahim had been waiting patiently for hours with his mules packed up and ready to go. But to do what, exactly? During that long snow trudge, with the frozen black wedge of the Demirkazik looming ever closer, I had been churning over in my mind quite what we were hoping to achieve in this wild range in the middle of winter. When the late afternoon sun sank behind a bank of cloud, the DK's sheer north face looked utterly intimidating. At Camardi the snow lay thick on the ground, but higher up everything would be choked in the stuff. My feet were in ribbons; I had a racking cough and felt very tired.

Was Nigella feeling the same? She had a streaming cold and didn't look at all well. But I didn't want to be the first to back off, so I turned to Sidney who was intently studying the ground with his Zeiss binoculars.

'What d'you think about climbing in these conditions, Sidney? Doesn't look too good to me.'

'I've never seen the Ala Dag like this before,' he replied. 'Just to get within range of the DK and establish a high camp up the Narpiz Gorge would take the best part of a day. Moreover that gorge is an avalanche trap and frankly I wouldn't contemplate the DK in these conditions. Again, I don't like the look of the weather and the last thing we want is to get stuck here in Camardi with all road exits blocked. I suppose we could hang around for a day to see if things improve, but I doubt that they will.'

Sidney was responsible both for his family and his charges. I knew that he would be feeling as disappointed as Nigella and I were at finding the prize slipping away.

'However,' he continued, 'having driven halfway across Turkey to get here, might I suggest an alternative plan? We could visit the Cappadocian Troglodyte valleys, drive through the Cilician Gates to the coast to inspect a couple of crusader castles and then cross the Taurus via Konya to see its dancing dervishes. The Ala Dag will not go away and we can always come back another day.'

Sidney could indeed come back another day, but I wondered if I ever would. He was still leaving a door slightly ajar, but did I really want to give it a push?

'I think you're probably right Sidney' I said at last. 'Let's fall in with your plan B.'

The following year, Sidney did return for another attempt on the DK. That too was abortive, but a year later in June 1963, he, Nigella, Elizabeth Parry and his cousin Phillipa Treadwell climbed it by the Hodgkin-Peck couloir in the course of a thirty-hour epic. Nigella and Elizabeth then drove back to England and stopped off in the Alps to finish their season with ascents of Col Dolent, the Grepon and Mont Blanc by the Innominata Ridge.

On the way back to Istanbul, we saw all the wondrous sights that Sidney had promised. When I asked him why the country was not full of tourists, he replied:

'The Turks have a saying which might roughly be translated thus: "*We are Turks. Two fingers to the rest of you*". Basically, they are a very hospitable people, but deeply conservative with an unshakeable self-confidence instilled in them from the time when the Ottoman Empire ruled the world. I can never see tourism taking root.'

For once, Sidney got it wrong.

On the eve of my departure for England, Sidney, Hilary, Nigella and I dined at the newly built Hilton Hotel overlooking the Bosphorus. There, for a delicious half-hour, Nigella and I danced cheek to cheek at the hotel's nightclub before making a last-minute dash so that I could catch the midnight Orient Express. The train was already moving away from the platform as we kissed goodbye. I can never forget those days on the Erciyes and those nights at the Tekir Refuge when Nigella stole all our hearts away.

5

SNOW ON THE EQUATOR II:
MOUNT KENYA AND RUWENZORI

My journey home on the Simplon-Orient Express never justified the cost of the first-class wagon-lit ticket. The train's lack of facilities would have deterred James Bond (let alone Hercule Poirot) from repeating the experience. The through service to Istanbul finally collapsed in 1977 and today's tourists get no further than Venice in revamped carriages which only faintly recreate the glamour of pre-First World War travel *de luxe*. My eight pieces of luggage made movement within the confined space of the compartment that I shared with a grotesquely fat Turk almost impossible. Nonetheless, apart from the tiresome interruptions of customs officials as the train was shunted to and fro the Greek and Bulgarian frontiers, that first night passed without incident.

Next day, we chugged on unhurriedly through a Balkan countryside thickly covered in snow. There was no food on the train and when it ground to an unscheduled halt at 10 p.m. in the middle of the Bulgarian plain, I carried on reading *Anna Karenina* in my bunk leaving my companion to investigate the situation. When he failed to return after half an hour, I bestirred myself to find our carriage completely deserted. Dressing in panic, I leaped outside into a blizzard to see that the wagon-lit carriage had been uncoupled from the main train, which was now gathering steam another fifty-metres down the line. Dragging my impedimenta through the snow, I scrambled aboard just as it moved off into the night.

Inside, all was panic and confusion. Both the heating and lighting had failed and in the intense cold and pitch darkness, distraught passengers were struggling to find themselves seats. Abandoning my luggage, I forced my way through the melee and eventually located a compartment unoccupied save for an individual wrapped in a blanket moaning and shuddering convulsively. Plague or cholera? Past caring, I moved in. At dawn next morning, a young Syrian student broke blanket-cover and insisted on sharing with me salami, bread and halva, my first food for eighteen hours. After recovering my luggage, I spotted a spare seat and wedged myself between my former Turkish companion and a lubricious Italian girl called Lidia Lazzero. We spent most of that day in cosy proximity stuck in a siding at Belgrade's railway station and arrived in Trieste on Christmas Day, twenty-four hours late. The spirited Lidia led a passenger protest to the stationmaster's office and was promptly arrested before our noisy demonstration secured her release. That same evening we kissed goodbye on Milan's railway station, a brief encounter with no exchange of addresses. Late on Boxing Day, I joined my parents and sister Jane at the Swiss ski resort of Pontresina for our first family reunion in two years.

This was the first time that I had ever been skiing. To ski had always been a boyhood ambition, but to ski well you'd best start early so I never achieved that distinction. Nonetheless, after two days in the beginners' class, I could negotiate the basic turns. Thus enthused, I then spent the best part of February at Champery and Kitzbuhel working on a survival technique that I hoped would enable me to graduate from the piste to ski mountaineering. Precious days of home leave sped by, though not without a week in the north-west Highlands with old climbing chums Neil Macpherson, Bill Norton, John Scott and Stewart Hawkins selecting our routes from W.H. Murray's classic *Undiscovered Scotland*. The trip's social highlight was tea at Achiltibuie with John Scott's still sprightly uncle, Tom Longstaff and his artist wife Charmian. Our best expedition was the traverse of An Teallach, 'The Forge', Murray's 'ideal mountain', having the finest ridge in Scotland outside the Cuillin. High on the flanks of Sail Liath, a wind-slab avalanche broke away just below its corniced ridge and took all five of us several hundred feet down the mountain with it. As I tumbled down, over and over, half-buried in a black void, all I could think of was a maxim I had once read in a Swiss mountaineering manual,

'Keep hold of your ice axe whatever else. To lose it means disgrace.'

We came to rest just before the slope dropped sheer away. Miraculously, no one was injured and so, after dusting ourselves down, we regrouped to regain the Forge's airy ridge. Diaphanous clouds opened and closed; a pair of golden eagles wheeled above; a Brocken spectre lighted our way and a 1,000-foot glissade down An Teallach's north flank closed a memorable Highland day.

On 29 April 1962 I was recalled to Aden fully expecting that my next posting would be to the Western Aden Protectorate (WAP), an area described by Aden's more traditional colonial officers as a 'Cowboy and Indian Madhouse'. To my chagrin, I was posted instead to the Secretariat, the government's administrative headquarters in Aden and quickly discovered that my titular responsibilities for overseeing a preposterously large portfolio of governmental business was seamlessly managed by the Colony's highly competent technical officers. By way of compensation, I was given a new brief to develop South Arabia's speculative tourist industry. Many thought this risible particularly as it had long been official policy to prohibit tourists from entering the protectorate for fear of offending local sensibilities and custom. A more important consideration was security. Not only were dissidence and unrest rife along the Protectorate's virulently hostile frontier with the Yemen, but many parts of the WAP had never known the *Pax Britannica* or indeed any other.

Yet had there then been a measure of peace and security, what is now the Yemen Republic, once known as *Arabia Felix* and described by Tim Mackintosh-Smith as 'indecently well-endowed ... and inexhaustibly photogenic', could have been a magnet for tourists. But as it was then, and as it is now, the energetic but desperately impoverished peoples who inhabit this roof of Arabia remain riven by the sectarian and internecine feuding that has bedevilled their country's progress for centuries and spawned the habitual dissidence that so easily translates itself into anarchy, warfare and terrorism.

Nonetheless, I seized this as an opportunity to explore some of the least known corners of the WAP where the Arabian Gulf's deserted beaches ran for miles; where multi-storied, stone-built forts commanded every eminence, and where dizzying ravines, patterned by a thousand metres of stone terracing, hung as if suspended from the sky. The highest mountains in Arabia are also to be found in this south-west corner of the peninsula, but much of the rock is shattered and friable and was anyway inaccessible for security reasons. On my last Arabian tour, as adviser to the sultanate of Lahej, my parish included Subeihi – as wild a tract of sand, stone and mountain as existed in the WAP. In its sere uplands and around the 2,766-metre Jebel Kharaz, the highest and most spectacular of the extinct line of volcanoes that run from Perim Island to Aden, were still to be found ibex, baboon and even leopard. I passed by this impressive mountain on several occasions, but recreational climbing in Subeihi was never on the agenda and for tourist visits at least a platoon of heavily armed tribal guards would have been necessary to prevent looting, kidnapping or worse.

Prospects for tourism were more promising in Aden Colony where adventure sports included sailing, surfing in shark-infested waters, and rugby played on salt-encrusted pitches that lacerated knees and elbows. For climbers and scramblers, Jebel Shamsan, the 1,740-foot extinct volcano around whose skirts the original port of Aden had been built, offered a form of rock climbing that had originally been introduced by the French entrepreneur Anton Besse whose Aden-made fortune enabled him to found Saint Anthony's College, Oxford. Besse had initiated Evelyn Waugh into the sport during the author's pre-war visit to Aden, and by his own account, Waugh enjoyed the experience.

For John Ducker, Tony Boyle and me, the exploration of Shamsan's desiccated ridges made a change from swimming, surfing, sailing and snorkelling. Having exhausted their scrambling potential, we turned our attentions to Little Aden whose teetering aiguilles were clearly visible across the sparkling bay that separated the two peninsulas. These shattered peaks, at whose base the British Military Cemetery of Silent Valley was sited, were occasionally climbed by suicidally inclined members of the British Armed Forces. John, a fellow Colonial Service officer, had already done some climbing. Tony, a dashing RAF flier and currently the governor's ADC, was a novice but proved himself a natural even in tennis shoes. Unfortunately, the rock was so friable that when, after our third visit, the top of one tottering pinnacle collapsed in a cloud of dust leaving me hanging on to what little was left of it, we decided to leave Little Aden to the marines. Tony went on to play a crucial role in organising covert SAS resistance to the Egyptian occupation of Yemen between 1963 and 1967, personally flying sixteen arms-dropping sorties out of Tel Aviv to support Yemeni Royalist Forces.

As Arabian climbing stunts went, the most hare-brained was undoubtedly the challenge that John Malcolm, Godfrey Meynell, Peter de la Billiere and I issued to the Royal Marines to race to Shamsan's summit. At the height of the Aden summer, this was as masochistic as sport gets. In the event, the 'Shamsan Scramble' was effortlessly won by a Somali schoolboy who had come second in the Middle East cross country championships. I came in an exhausted runner-up, but the marines just beat us on team aggregate.

Apart from flogging up and along the ragged ridges of Radfan on military patrols during my last tour, I did no more recreational climbing during my service in South Arabia. But forty years on, I happened to spend a fortnight's holiday with my wife Georgina and friends on the island of Socotra, 250 miles south of Aden, and formerly part of the Eastern Aden Protectorate. Socotra, the jewel of the Pink Arabian Sea and latterly a UNESCO World Heritage Site, was where the Phoenix died in a nest perfumed with frankincense and where the Sumerian hero Gilgamesh came to learn the secret of eternal life. Its particular attraction to the climber lies in the 1,500-metre-high Haggier Mountains that form the island's spine and comprise some of the world's oldest rocks. Protruding from a forest of frankincense and dragon's blood trees (whose red resin Stradivarius used to lacquer his violins), the Haggier's spiralling granite pillars offer a plethora of new routes to those rash enough to brave the hazards of modern Yemen.

In January 1963, Aden's accession to the Federation of South Arabia ended 126 years of direct British rule and ushered in the final chapter of Britain's South Arabian connection. That April, I was unexpectedly promoted to act as the Deputy Ministerial Secretary (security) with direct administrative responsibility for Aden's internal security, Aden's police force and security liaison between MI5, the British armed forces and the federal government. At this time, HMG and the federal government's principal security concerns resulted from the previous year's revolution in neighbouring Yemen, which had ended a thousand years of Imamate rule and precipitated a bloody civil war. After the newly-declared Yemen Republic had allied itself with President Nasser's United Arab Republic, a 30,000-strong Egyptian army promptly invaded the country with the aim of transforming the political map of the Arabian Peninsula by wiping out what was left of Yemen's royalist opposition; ejecting the British from Aden, and eventually seizing the Gulf's oil. The presence of a well-equipped Egyptian army on the Yemen frontier ratcheted-up the dissident guerrilla activity throughout the Protectorate and precipitated the Radfan war which encouraged the terrorist campaign in Aden that was to force Britain's ignominious withdrawal four years later in 1967.

The demands of this new job inevitably meant extending my tour and kyboshed any plans for that long-promised alpine summer season. Instead, when my leave fell due in December 1963, I decided to embark on a second East African mountain safari taking in both Mount Kenya and the Ruwenzori. Once again, the problem was to find climbing partners. My main contact in Kenya, John Blacker, was keen to climb the Ruwenzori 'but not Mount Kenya again!' At this juncture, Jane Fenton a keen naturalist whom I had met skiing earlier that year and who was currently staying with friends in Nairobi, entered the picture. Jane was a walker rather than a mountaineer, but when I mentioned my plans in a letter she replied by return.

'I would love to come as a baggage bearer/cook/climber to either Kenya or Ruwenzori or both. PS: I have just met your friend John Blacker.'

Within days, I got a letter from Blacker to say he had bumped into Jane at Lukenia, the Mountain Club of Kenya's local rock-climbing playground near Nairobi.

'Jane's a very nice girl,' he wrote, 'but came wearing atrocious footwear and fell off an easy climb. John Hull and I have been giving her instruction, but I'm beginning to doubt whether she will make the grade and frankly don't think that she should attempt either Nelion or Batian.'

With only three weeks to go before my leave began, Jane and I were still the only starters for Mount Kenya mainly because most of the Mountain Club of Kenya's regulars were already booked to celebrate Kenya's Independence Day, 12 December 1963, on the summit of Batian. I had almost given up on the project when, out of the blue, I was telephoned by Hamish McNish, a thirty-year-old Scot working with a firm of quantity surveyors in Aden. Hamish had climbed in Scotland, Norway and the Alps, but had no climbing equipment with him. This could be put right in Nairobi, but to embark on another Mount Kenya venture with one non-climber and the other coming on spec seemed crazy. Later, I would owe Hamish my life.

My last weeks in Aden were fraught. On 22 November the world held its breath on the news of President Kennedy's assassination in Dallas. Kennedy's nerve might have saved the world from nuclear catastrophe, but his Middle East policy of supporting Nasser to counter Russia's growing influence had fatally undermined Britain's precarious position in South Arabia and encouraged dissidence in the federal states and terrorism in Aden. Eleven days before my departure, an attempt was made to assassinate the British High Commissioner, Sir Kennedy Trevaskis, and a delegation of federal ministers at Aden Airport, as they were about to leave for a constitutional conference in London. Fifty-one people were seriously wounded and two killed including a senior British political officer who threw himself into the path of a grenade. A state of emergency was declared, the Yemen border was closed and I was given a week to devise a scheme to register Aden's estimated 100,000 aliens. The Aden Airport outrage presaged a terrorist campaign that was to cause Aden 2,000 casualties including 800 British servicemen and civilians. When I boarded the British Airways comet for Nairobi on 21 December, I felt I was deserting a sinking ship.

The flags and bunting of the new Republic of Kenya that fluttered wearily in Nairobi's streets augured ill for Britain's longer-term tenure of South Arabia. Nonetheless, five frantic days of partying with the Happy-Valley set and the less inhibited members of the mountain club induced a more buoyant mood. Hamish flew in from Aden to celebrate Christmas Day and on Boxing Day, he,

Jane and I drove 135 miles to Raymond Hook's farm at Burguret in a borrowed Land Rover. Hook, looking even more grizzled than I remembered him from two years before, was absurdly pleased to see us.

'But why on earth have you come to climb the mountain at this time of year?' he growled. 'The rainy season isn't finished yet, so the Burguret track will be one big bog and I certainly don't fancy conditions higher up. Those idiots who tried to plant an Uhuru flag on the top of Batian at midnight had a dreadful time of it as the whole mountain was covered in snow. They only got as far as Nelion and I'm tempted to say "Serve the silly buggers right!" Anyway, I won't be around much longer to see that sort of nonsense again. I've lived in this country since 1912 and for the past thirty-five years have hired out my mules to everyone from Wyn-Harris and Shipton onwards. But all that's coming to an end. This new government will soon dispossess me of my land. Never mind. I'm giving you my best muleteer Daburu. You'll remember him from your last visit. Camp here tonight, and make sure you get moving early in the morning.'

Hook took the trouble to see us off next day standing besides his farm gate: a lonely old man and sad relic of Kenya's white tribe.

As Hook predicted, the Burguret track was unrecognisable from what I remembered three years before. Our two muleteers had their work cut out hacking through the freshly grown bamboo thickets with pangas. The giant-heather zone was thigh-deep in liquid mud and light rain persisted throughout the day and into the night. After rigging up three army 'poncho' capes for a shelter, all five of us huddled under it for the night with Daburu constantly feeding the log fire to keep predators at bay. The following morning, as we sloshed through the knee-high tussock grass of the alpine zone, the clouds suddenly parted to reveal Batian's tremendous south-west face sheathed in a mantle of fresh snow.

At Two Tarn Hut, I paid off Daburu and retired to bed with a splitting headache. Jane, ever cheerful, seemed unaffected by the 4,500 metres of height while Hamish broke the ice of the tarn and gave himself a strip-wash. Our plan to climb Tereri after inspecting the newly built Kami Hut en route on the other side of the mountain got no further than a scramble up to Arthur's Seat, but on the third day I suggested to Hamish that we have a shot at Midget Peak, the spectacular aiguille that rises like a cathedral's spire at the far end of the lake. Midget had a certain reputation and might have been Shipton and Tilman's last climb. On their way down, the weather broke and the inexperienced Tilman slipped off a snow-covered ledge and concussed himself. Shipton somehow managed to climb down to Tilman, bearing his companion's dead weight on his shoulder, before shepherding him off the mountain.

I hadn't climbed seriously for eighteen months and never before with Hamish, so it was foolhardy to have started late in the afternoon. We made the summit in good time, but this left barely an hour to get down in daylight. During Shipton's dramatic descent, he had made eight successive abseils hacking off lengths from his 120-foot climbing rope with a stone to make belay loops. I had a knife and plenty of abseil slings, but after a couple of botched starts reverted to sending Hamish on ahead on a tight rope. We were still only halfway down when night fell like a blanket and it began to snow heavily. The holds became impossible to see properly and for the next two hours I clawed my way down the face like a crab, pitch after pitch, relying on feel and instinct. Back at the hut, Hamish went straight to bed, but staggered up again at midnight to celebrate Hogmanay with Jane's hot chocolate and whiskey. Next morning, I stepped outside to find that yesterday's storm had left a foot of snow around the hut and Midget sheathed in ice.

Our Midget adventure had not fazed Hamish who was now impatient to do the Shipton/Wynn Harris route on Nelion. The weather relented as we began the 1,000-metre climb to the Arthur Firmin Hut through knee-deep, breakable crust encouraged by a ballooning cloudscape rising from the plains below suffused with warm tints. But a wall of frozen snow blocked the hut's door and inside it was like a refrigerator with the bedding sopping wet. To get water from the Curling Pond, I had to hack through six inches of ice. When another storm blew in that night and lasted until midday, I settled for my fifth ascent of Lenana. That same evening, Reynold Coyne, ex-OUMC, and Jeff Thompson, ex-CUMC, rolled in having driven 600 miles from Tanganyika before spending another three days trekking up the Naro Moru route in sleet and snow. When I tried to persuade them to join us to climb Nelion the following day, Jeff's reply should have warned me off: 'Sorry John, no go! We're completely knackered. And in these conditions, we wouldn't go near that climb anyway.'

At 4 a.m. next morning it was still blowing a gale. While I was cooking bacon and eggs for two, Hamish spent the time easing himself into his frozen boots. We hadn't said a word to each other until I noticed the size of his rucksack.

'What on earth have you got in there Hamish?'

'Both my Icelandic and Polar sleeping bags if you must know, just in case we have to bivouac.'

A sharp exchange lightened his load by ten pounds.

The wind never dropped and halfway across the Lewis Glacier – the largest on Mount Kenya but already shrunk to half the size it was sixty years before

– our clothes were already coated with rime. I hadn't noticed the transition from night to day when we began what I remembered as an easy scramble up the Donkey Walk but had now been transformed into a serious crampon climb up an ice-filled couloir. Another thirty minutes were spent trying to negotiate the Rabbit Hole, where the rock became recoated with *verglas* faster than I could scrape it off. After two hours, we had climbed a mere 250 feet. I broke off the engagement but during the descent, Hamish managed to get himself stuck under a waterfall for half an hour during his second abseil and almost froze to death. Back at the hut, the sun came out for the first time that day.

We retreated to Two Tarn Hut that same evening with Jane weak from diarrhoea and Hamish in a sorry state with his baldpate festering with sun-sores; his eyes puffed up like balloons, and his feet a bloody mess. Over supper he blurted out: 'Look, John, I'm very sorry but I've really had my fill of this bloody mountain. I haven't got that much leave left and I'd like to get away tomorrow so that I can climb Kilimanjaro before I go home.'

'Tell you what Hamish, we're all feeling a bit battered, but give it a day and we'll see things very differently. The barometric pressure's rising and from this hut there's a fine route up Nelion that's well within our compass.'

Jane smiled sweetly, but said nothing.

At 5 a.m. next morning, the moon was full and the night sky brilliant with stars as we stumbled across the moraines of the Darwin Glacier below Nelion's south face. Hamish was limping badly and I had picked up Jane's diarrhoea. Nonetheless, by 6.45 a.m. we had reached the topmost *névé* of the Darwin Glacier where I spotted an old abseil sling hanging from the rocks above.

'Must be the route up there,' I said to Hamish. 'Doesn't look that difficult. I'm sure we can manage a more interesting variant.'

Hamish looked less than enthusiastic, but I was now feeling on form and without further chat launched myself up an open corner formed by two converging rock walls. The next hundred metres of near-vertical rock split by ice-filled cracks and chimneys gave me the hardest and most sustained stretch of climbing I had done to date. After two and a half hours, I reckoned I had cracked it on reaching a point just below the lip of an easy-angled snow slope that led to the base of Nelion's summit rocks.

'Nearly there!' I shouted down to Hamish who had cunningly secreted himself into a niche in the rock overlooking the Darwin Glacier. I began a delicate traverse across the face towards a large granite block that abutted the snowfield. It had looked firm enough until I grasped it, but at a touch, the whole thing broke away taking me and several tons of rock with it.

Hamish fielded a shower of rock fragments on the rucksack he had stuck over his head while I was left hanging in space ten metres below him.

My head was singing; my forehead was streaming with blood and my right eye was closing up. My shoulder and hip felt as if I'd been hit by a ton of bricks.

'You okay John?' asked Hamish.

'Buggered if I am,' I grunted. 'But at least we're still on the same rope. Thank God your belay held. Are you alright?'

'I'm fine,' said Hamish.

Actually, I was both shocked and dazed, yet sufficiently fired-up to consider carrying on with the climb, now that the difficulties were behind me. Still hanging free on the rope, it was the intense pressure around my waist that brought back a glimmer of sense and the realisation that I must get back on to the rock face before the rope squeezed the life out of me. Yet, to get lodgement wasn't that easy for with only one eye operative, I couldn't focus properly. Eventually, I reconnected with the rock and Hamish climbed down to join me. The loss of a couple of slings and karabiners during the fall didn't make abseiling any easier and it took seven hours to reach the bottom of the glacier just in time to avoid stone and ice avalanches sweeping down from Nelion's sun-loosened upper slopes.

Back at the hut, Jane got busy with hot tea and bandages. Later that evening Daburu arrived with the mules. The following day's walk out to the Gathuru Forest station in thick mist was another trial by tussock grass, mud and bamboo thicket. Conversation was limited as Hamish's feet were in tatters; Jane was exhausted with diarrhoea; and I kept stumbling about like a drunken man having lost all perspective. We blessed the local forestry officer who gave us a lift from the road head to the Silverbeck Hotel, but were too tired to face supper. I saw a doctor next day and swore that I would never climb without a helmet again. One could write volumes about Mount Kenya for it has no peer in Africa and few elsewhere. In Tilman's words, 'On Kenya is to be found climbing at its best … few countries have such a symbol and an inspiration.'

On the 9 January 1964, Jane and I left Nairobi to begin the 800-mile drive to Mufindi in southern Tanganyika to deliver a beat-up, open Land Rover to a big-game hunter. Jane might not have been the greatest climber, but her support on the mountain had been rock-solid and she now proved herself a dauntless driver. On our way down the dirt road that masqueraded as the Cape to Cairo Highway, we spent four days touring the game parks and four nights at luxurious game lodges with scarcely another tourist in sight. The snows of Kilimanjaro became the backcloth to our meanderings through herds of elephant, prides of lion and the occasional rhino with the blue hills of Africa ever rolling away to the deep south.

At Mufindi, whose climate at 7,000 feet is as English as exists in Africa, our hosts were Jane's old friend Mary and husband Jonathan Niblett. He was just back from a week tracking down the rogue bull elephant that had been wrecking several hundred square miles of the Brooke Bond tea plantation that he managed. After a three-day idyll, Jane and I turned about to catch the East African Express at Dodoma for a 400-mile train journey to Mwanza on Lake Victoria at an average speed of fifteen miles per hour. A thirty-one hour crossing of the lake on the *SS Victoria* took us to Kampala where, after a night at Makere University, we met up with John Blacker and Charles Richards to drive to Fort Portal, the road head for the Ruwenzori.

John had settled the composition of the Ruwenzori party some months before. Although we had corresponded often, I didn't know much about him save that he had been working in Nairobi with the East African High Commission for several years as a demographer. It was from Charles that I learned that John had boxed at Eton; rowed in the winning 1950 Oxford boat; was currently the Mountain Club of Kenya's vice president and its acknowledged expert on mountain cuisine. Unlike John's suave grandfather Carlos, whom his great friend Oscar Wilde described as 'the best dressed man in London', John cared little about outward appearances and never minced his words. When I had suggested to him that two of East Africa's leading climbers, Axe Nelson and Mike Adams, might be included in the Ruwenzori party, he replied, 'Nothing would induce me to go with either. Nelson never stops talking and Adams climbs in order to bolster his *amour-propre.*'

I had liked Nelson for all his chat, but was less sure about Adams. During some earlier correspondence with him about rock climbing in Aden, I had been disconcerted by his casual aside: 'An acquaintance, Percival, got killed there some years back'.

John's preference was for Charles Richards, a former MCK president who had spent most of his life as a medical missionary in Africa. Charles was also a scholar who had edited the OUP's *East African Explorers* and was one of the few Europeans who spoke Bakonjo, the language of the Ruwenzori tribe that supplied porters for Ruwenzori expeditions. John's description of Charles as 'Slow, and no great shakes as a climber, but one couldn't ask for a nicer companion', was exactly right.

John Buchan once described the Ruwenzori as one of the world's 'last secrets'. For 2,500 years these fabled 'Mountains of the Moon', as depicted on

Ptolemy's famous map, were thought to be the source of the Nile yet had defied all efforts to discover them. When Nero's exploratory expedition failed to return, the river's elusive source became one the world's most intractable geographical mysteries and one for which Europe's most adventurous nineteenth-century explorers were prepared to risk their lives. When, in 1867, the Royal Geographical Society instructed Burton and Speke to find the Nile's 'coy fountains', their specific task was to discover the Mountains of the Moon,

Speke's claim to have identified Lake Victoria as the Nile's primary source, though vigorously disputed by both Burton and Livingstone, was eventually confirmed by Stanley during his thousand-mile crossing of Africa in 1874. Even then, the existence of the Ruwenzori remained a matter for conjecture until Stanley got proper sightings of the range from the shores of Lake Albert during his 1888 expedition. Lake Albert is the White Nile's secondary source and the Ruwenzori's snows are that lake's main feeders. Ptolemy had almost got it right all along.

Stanley's discovery encouraged a flood of European scientific expeditions to explore the Ruwenzori. However, its climbing history effectively begins and ends with the Duke of Abruzzi's monumental Italian expedition in 1906 which employed 300 porters and twelve Europeans, including the photographer Vittorio Sella and the Courmayeur guides Ollier and Brocherell – the first summiteers of Mount Kenya with Mackinder seven years before. In the space of thirty-six days, Abruzzi's mountaineers and surveyors climbed every peak in the range, which Abruzzi named after members of the Italian and British royal families. The photographs taken by his photographer Vittorio de Sella are still unsurpassed and five of Ruwenzori's six snow massifs he named after African explorers – Stanley, Speke, Baker, Gessi and Emin – while the sixth bears his own name Luigi di Savoia as the Royal Geographical Society's tribute to the greatest mountaineer-explorer of his day.

The riddle of the Ruwenzori's very existence was largely due to its proximity to the Congo's equatorial forests whose rain-sodden winds blanket the range with dense cloud for most of the year. Doctor Noel Humphreys, who made the second ascent of Margherita, the range's highest peak, in 1926 enjoyed only one day without rain during six separate expeditions. Fully aware of its reputation, we didn't fancy our chances so wasted no time at Ibanda, the headquarters of the Bakonjo tribe, where Charles recruited a headman and nine porters for our ten-day trek within the space of an hour. Douglas Busk, of Elburz fame, had considered it necessary to hire *sixty-two* porters for his five-man, ten-day visit in 1953. Carrying loads of fifty pounds apiece in near-freezing temperatures and wearing little more than Mr Ahmed Bhimji's flimsy cotton shirts and shorts, these Bakonjo porters were the real heroes of our own expedition.

Climbing in the Ruwenzori had become less of an expedition since the end of the Second World War when the government of Uganda subsidised the Mountain Club of Uganda's hut-building programme. Nonetheless, given its reputation for bad weather, we were prepared for the worst when our caravan set off in column up the Bujuku Valley on 19 January. Yet whereas the weather had persistently been against us on Mount Kenya, it stayed fine for most of our time in the Ruwenzori. The network of huts took the sting out of its notorious approach marches and, apart from a brush with a column of soldier ants, the familiar tales of impassable torrents, the 'bottomless' Bigo Bogs, and the impenetrable Jabberwocky Forest proved misplaced. On the morning of our third day we were comfortably ensconced at the 13,000-foot high Bujuku huts, already occupied by five Brits who had driven overland for £80 a head; three Germans without a single item of climbing equipment between them; and two others who were living off a diet of porridge and rock hyrax.

With the weather set fair, we set the bar high. On 23rd January all four of us climbed Speke's Vittorio Emanuele peak by its heavily crevassed glacier. On the following day, we moved up to the Irene Lakes Hut to squeeze into its tiny aluminium shelter prior to Blacker and I making a dawn start to attempt Margherita (5,109 metres) by its north-east ridge. All went well until I was halfway up a steep and exposed section of rock filmed with ice. I was suddenly seized by a paralysing attack of vertigo, something I had not experienced since my earliest climbs. Visions of my fall above the Darwin Glacier crowding back, my nerve failed and I could climb no further. At this, John calmly took over the lead and after reaching the top of the step, we threaded our way through a maze of fantastic ice mushrooms, to reach Margherita's summit only three and a half hours after leaving the hut. With progress so fast, we decided to carry on to Alexandra by a traverse whose practicability depends on the state of cornices, which can be impassable. Barely started, the mists descended and for twenty minutes we could only wait impatiently before a momentary clearing revealed a maze of yawning bergschrunds at our feet. Nothing ventured, we plunged on down and fifty minutes later were staring back from Alexandra to the fantastic confection of snow and ice that festooned Margherita's summit.

The original plan had been to rejoin Charles and Jane at the Irene Lakes Hut after dropping down to the hut from the Stanley Plateau. But at this point, a thick mist reduced visibility to a few metres. The plateau is a featureless snowfield, covering over two square miles and fringed by ice-cliffs. Shipton and Tilman had spent a couple of days wandering around it blind. To chance our arm descending the cliffs in these conditions was asking for trouble so we retraced our steps and eventually came across a line of tracks that could only have come up from the Elena Hut, two kilometres further down the Elena Glacier. Following them until the clouds lifted as unexpectedly as they had fallen, we diverted to bag our third peak of the day, Moebius. From the Elena Hut, a contouring traverse around Stanley's eastern flank led back to the Irene Lakes Hut where Charles and Jane were waiting anxiously. That ten-hour traverse of Mount Stanley, involving 1,525 metres of ascent and descent, was one of the most rewarding climbs I ever did and marked the high point of our Ruwenzori expedition.

The following day, with the weather still holding, we decamped; rejoined the porters and moved on to the superbly sited Kitandara Lakes Hut where a leopard raided the porters' camp. As was his wont, Blacker insisted on having a skinny dip in the lake and without thinking I dived in after him from a high rock into water so cold that my body went into temporary paralysis. From the Kitandara base, all four of us climbed Mount Baker's summit peak, Edward, leaving Blacker and me to continue along the ridge to bag Baker's subsidiary peak, Semper. An attempt to reach Lac Vert on the Belgian Congo side of the range next day was frustrated by helichrysum, an everlasting shrub, which at this altitude proved virtually impenetrable.

As a *grande finale* to mark our last full day, Blacker and I decided to make a bid for Savoia, at 4,979 metres the highest and remotest peak in the southern Stanley Group. Inevitably, the weather broke. After cramponing up the lower Savoia glacier, dense cloud and a howling wind made it impossible to fix our exact position. A line of snow-covered slabs led to an obvious ice gulley up which we cramponed on front points to a bleak summit where the mist momentarily cleared. Staring across a blank space to what was patently a higher peak, John uttered an uncharacteristic expletive and then groaned, 'Bloody hell! We've climbed the wrong mountain! That must be Savoia on the other side of the glacier. There's not a hope of reaching it today.'

Nor was there, and then, as if to rub it in, John skewered his right calf with a crampon while reversing the gulley and twice we both fell through crevasses on the glacier. Back at the hut Charles offered some comfort after concluding that we had unwittingly done a new route on Philip. To celebrate this low-key triumph John opened the last tin of *coq au vin* for supper.

We left the Ruwenzori by the Mubuku Valley, the route originally taken by the British pioneers whose names, thanks to Abruzzi, are preserved in the nomenclature of the range – Stairs, Scott-Elliot, Moore, Freshfield and Wollaston. From the Freshfield Pass, John pointed to a shapely peak marking the eastern end of Mount Baker, first climbed in 1906 by Sandy Wollaston, a member of the 1921 Everest Expedition. In 1930, this eminent scholar/explorer was shot dead by a deranged Cambridge undergraduate. His author son, Nicholas, was one of John's closest friends.

Lower down the upper valley, where the track rides high on the hillside, we passed the Bujongolo rock shelter, which Abruzzi had chosen for his base camp. Giant groundsel now gave way to heather trees ten metres high and, as the last semblance of a path vanished, we spiralled down into the jungle by a succession of twisting steps and a 300-metre near-vertical slope besides a thundering cataract. It was here that Charles suddenly lost his footing. We watched helplessly as he clawed desperately at the tree roots that arrested a fall that would otherwise have been fatal.

The path in the trough of the Mubuku Valley had not been cut for several years. Marching single file in extended column, the porters had to hack their way through a mass of interlacing roots and branches that formed a vegetal mattress several feet off the ground. Soon, we were having to ford streams and squelch through fetid swamps strewn with the carcasses of decaying trees draped in cushions of moss, brushing aside the creepers, lianas and giant nettles that barred the way. Forcing a way through the sunless bamboo thickets, we often had to squat and sometimes even crawl to get through. The march never seemed to end, but late that night the silhouette of Nyambitaba Hut, from where we had set out eleven days before, emerged through the gloom.

After an almost uninterrupted spell of good weather, it is easy to over-enthuse about the Ruwenzori. In a normal season, the Bujuku route could have taken twice as long and the Mubuku route been impassable. Only three weeks before us, a German party had never managed a single day's climbing in ten and has been chased up a tree by an elephant. Many have had good cause to curse Ruwenzori's weather yet without it, the range's glaciers and snowfields, much larger than those of Mount Kenya and Kilimanjaro combined, would cease to exist. And unlike those great volcanoes of Kenya, Kilimanjaro, Meru and Elgon, the Ruwenzori is a proper range of mountains, sixty-miles long and thirty wide with its forests and flora more bizarre and exotic than imagination can conceive. Here, by the shores of its icy lakes and in the depths of its hidden valleys, you may still hear the shriek of the hyrax and the cough of the leopard as you gaze up in wonder at the Mountains of the Moon.

6

KURDISH HAKKIARI

When I flew into Nairobi in December 1963 for my second African climbing safari, the three territories that had formerly made up Britain's East African empire – Uganda, Tanganyika and Kenya – had already become independent republics. The prospects of British South Arabia weathering the winds of change were fading fast, so when I returned to England after the Ruwenzori adventure in February 1964, I reckoned that it was time to investigate my prospects for longer-term employment.

Clearly, any future career change would severely limit the mountaineering opportunities that had been offered by generous Colonial Service leaves. Accordingly, I put in as much climbing and skiing as I could during the remainder of that leave. A week in the north-west Highlands brought together scions of alpinists of the Golden Age in Nigella Blandy, the granddaughter of Edward Whymper, and John Wills, a grandson of Alfred Wills who had been the Alpine Club's president when Whymper climbed the Matterhorn. We traipsed up Ben Loyal and Ben Hope; traversed An Teallach without being avalanched and climbed Liathach by the Northern Pinnacles Ridge route that had defeated me two years before. Nigella and I never climbed together again, but we remain in close touch. As a climbing partner and friend, none was better.

Before returning to the heat and dust of Arabia, I was determined to graduate from skiing to ski mountaineering. The best way of achieving this was to join the Eagle Ski Club (ESC) because membership was open to all-comers. Originally founded in 1925 at the Swiss resort of Maloja as a genteel ski-touring club, most of its early members were skiers turned aspirant mountaineers so professional guides were usually employed to lead tours. Yet the competitive downhill racing ethos was reflected in the gold, silver or bronze Eagle badges that were awarded for perceived ski-touring competence. Later, I was instrumental in having these somewhat artificial distinctions abolished, though the Eagles never lost their cutting edge and have become Britain's most successful ski mountaineering club.

Before the Second World War, Arnold Lunn's Alpine Ski Club (founded in 1908) had pioneered British ski mountaineering. After it, the ESC revived what had become its near-moribund body. The man primarily responsible for this renaissance was Neil Hogg who, like his elder brother Quintin Hailsham, had climbed and skied extensively in the Alps between the wars. After his retirement from the Diplomatic Service, Neil took over the management of the Hogg family's Hotel Seeburg in Lucerne and used the Chalet Herrschaft in Grindelwald as a base from which to introduce new ESC members to ski mountaineering under the aegis of Swiss guides such as the peerless Hermann Steuri who had led the first guided ascent of the Matterhorn's North Face.

When attending Neil's ESC training meet at Concordia in late April 1964, the frailties of my skiing technique were mercilessly exposed. Nonetheless, and despite some atrocious weather, we almost climbed the Finsteraarhorn and skied the length of the Aletsch Glacier, the longest in the Alps. After this exhilarating experience, I felt unjustifiably confident enough to hire a phlegmatic Grindelwald guide, Hans Ruedi Kaufmann, to ski the Haute Route from Zermatt to Chamonix with my old climbing chum Tony Delafield, a much more experienced skier than me. Originally pioneered by members of the Alpine Club in 1861 as a summer trekking route, the first complete ski crossing of the Haute Route was accomplished by Marcel Kurz and Professor Roget in 1911. For decades thereafter, it was regarded as somewhat exceptional to have done it and even as late as the mid-1950s, no guideless British party had completed it. My own inspiration to attempt it had been Robin Fedden's *Alpine Ski Tour*, which describes his own 1955 guided crossing. In 1964, ski mountaineering equipment had changed little since the 1930s. Permeable leather boots froze at night; cable bindings were unreliable, and skis measured from floor level to a height of an arm's stretch above the head challenged poor technique. Electronic avalanche-rescue devices, mobile phones and GPS were unheard of.

We left Zermatt in fine weather on 29th April and after climbing the Pigne d'Arolla, progressed to the Chanrion Hut, which marks the Haute Route's halfway mark without seeing another party. Holed-up in the hut for twenty-four hours by a blizzard, my growing angst about future prospects for a meaningful post-Colonial Service career reached a bizarre climax. In this disturbed state of mind, I penned a letter of resignation to the director of establishments in Aden. Due to massive accumulations of fresh snow, Kaufmann sensibly decided to abandon the final stage of the tour to Chamonix to avoid avalanche risk. After descending to Orsières, I got the letter stamped at the local post office. But some innate instinct held me back from posting it. Forty-five years later, I came across it unopened.

Nonetheless, the wheels of change had been set in motion. On first leaving Cambridge, I had vowed never to open a law book again. Now it was a case of needs must. Three days before sailing for Aden on 2 June 1964, I had an investigatory interview about career prospects as a solicitor with Francis Tufton, a senior partner in the old established City firm Markby, Stewart and Wadesons. On reporting for duty in Aden, I learned that I had been appointed to serve in the Western Aden Protectorate (WAP), a posting for which I had been badgering the Establishments Department for years. Also awaiting me was a letter from Tufton offering me articles of clerkship on the completion of my current tour. Had I only known about my WAP posting before leaving England, I might never have bothered with that fateful interview. As it was, the prospect of throwing up a promising new career opportunity posed a dilemma that became the more difficult to resolve as that fateful tour progressed.

My initial appointment as adviser to the Sultanate of Lahej involved responsibility for devising and implementing four major development schemes and overseeing the construction of the new military road to Dhala, a key military base on the Yemen frontier. I was then appointed as political officer responsible for the establishment of a tribal administration and the rehabilitation of Radfan whose vertiginous mountain fastnesses had been devastated by the only significant modern military campaign that the British fought in South West Arabia. This tour proved to be the most exciting and fulfilling of my five and a half years service in South Arabia, but growing disillusionment with HMG's disingenuous policies; the trauma of a broken marriage engagement; and the realisation that if I didn't make a fresh start now, it would soon be too late, prompted my formal resignation. For years after, I regretted that decision though eventually came to accept that the romance of Arabia was a dissolving dream and has since become a veritable nightmare.

Three years of training as a solicitor's articled clerk was going to condemn me to very meagre holidays, so I was determined to make the most of my last home leave when my tour ended in June 1965. I had never forgotten those photographs of the heights of Hakkiari as portrayed in Percy's *The Highlands of Asiatic Turkey*, so I wrote to Sidney Nowill suggesting that we make a joint venture to the range. Since my first approach to Sidney in 1961, the political situation in Kurdistan had changed dramatically. Despite the vicious guerrilla war still being waged on the Turkish/Iraq border by Kurdish fighters under the inspired leadership of Mullah Mustapha Barzani, the recent opening of a CENTO road through Eastern Turkey to Iran had induced the Turkish government to relax travel restrictions to Hakkiari.

However, Sidney's reply was as discouraging this time as before, though now for different reasons: 'I would love to climb with you – if free. But at the moment I'm committed to join Robin and Renee Fedden, Peter Lloyd and Peter MacColl in Hakkiari subject to agreement on start dates.'

Sidney had hitched his star to a formidable team. Robin Fedden was not only a distinguished mountaineer and ski-mountaineer, but also a famous writer and near-east authority. His wife Renee was herself a competent climber while Peter Lloyd, whom Sidney described as 'a pretty tough mountaineer', much more than that having been a member of several pre-war Himalayan expeditions including Tilman's 1938 Everest expedition. McColl, was an eminent botanical scientist. Patently, I was out of my class.

Although disappointed, this setback made me the more determined to get to Hakkiari and not just on account of its mountains. I had gleaned from Percy's book that the area had a most unusual and tragic history and that the subsequent career of Percy himself, then the heir to the Duke of Northumberland and already the MP for Kensington and Chelsea at twenty-four, was enigmatic. The primary aim of his fact-finding mission to Turkey and Hakkiari in 1899 was to assess the political mischief that both the Germans and Russians were up to. A secondary objective was to investigate the plight of the Nestorians, a Christian sect whose stubborn insistence in maintaining that Mary was not the mother of the son of God, had condemned them as heretics ever since the Council of Ephesus in AD 431. Scattered to the winds from their original Syrian homeland by Tamerlane in 1400, they had fled to the fastnesses of Hakkiari to pursue their primitive faith, only to find themselves living in fractious proximity to much longer-established Muslim Kurdish tribes.

Percy correctly predicted both that the proposed German scheme to build a strategic railway from Constantinople to Baghdad would be a threat to British India and that the visits by well-intentioned British missionaries to Hakkiari would arouse the worst suspicions of both the Porte and local Kurdish tribes.

His prophecy that Russia's interference in Eastern Turkey would eventually precipitate the Kurdish genocidal massacres that effectively wiped both Armenians and their co-religionist Nestorians off the map proved correct. But the precipitate end to what had been a meteoric political career raises some unanswered questions. After becoming Balfour's Secretary of State for Foreign Affairs at the age of thirty-two in 1903, Percy died six years later in a second rate Paris hotel having booked in under the name 'Mr Percy'. Although the official cause of death was pneumonia, it was rumoured that he had been killed in a duel by Winston Churchill's brother Jack. It was alleged that Percy had had an affair with Winston's future wife, Clementine Hosier.

In 1965, as it is today, Hakkiari was a *terra incognita* to British climbers generally. But it was not ever thus. At the turn of the twentieth century, the exploration of its mountains had been an exclusively British affair because of the permanent consular posts Britain then maintained throughout Eastern Turkey. In 1897, Lieutenant Colonel Francis Maunsell, the British consul in Van, not only climbed Galianu Peak (3,685 metres) in the Cilo group of the range, but narrowly failed to reach the summit of its culminating peak Resko (4,170 metres). Twelve years later, another British Consul, Mr B. Dickson, explored the neighbouring Sat Dag group. Predictably, German and Austrian expeditions took all the prizes between the wars, and not until 1957 did two Scots, Tom Weir and Douglas Scott (not to be confused with his famous Everest namesake who led a barnstorming Nottingham Climbers Club expedition to the Cilo Dag in 1966), become the first Britons since Dickson to explore the range. Weir described it as 'a paradise with superb mountaineering ... the most rewarding of any in which I have travelled'.

Despite my aspirations, I might well have consigned Hakkiari to another pipe dream had I not received another airmail letter from Sidney in late March 1965 with the breathless opening sentence: 'It's on!'

Apparently, the Fedden/Nowill equipe, theoretically made in heaven given that both men were aesthetic polymaths, had imploded. The ostensible reason was a disagreement about start dates, but according to Sidney, a more serious bone of contention was women, 'Peter Lloyd hates women on a party, and Hilary felt that she was being let in on sufferance.'

Sidney, on the other hand, much preferred to climb with women and had already tried to recruit regular members of his loyal harem for Hakkiari, but unfortunately none were currently available.

Yet Sidney's version of events didn't quite ring true. Renee Fedden was always going to come and Peter Lloyd, a happily married man, is unlikely to have held such a prejudice. A more fundamental disagreement concerned the commissariat. Lloyd insisted that there should be porridge for breakfast, while Sidney was in his 'Grape Nuts only' phase. A compromise should have been possible, for Sidney was a gourmet and Renee Fedden acknowledged to be the best amateur cook in London. Unfortunately, Sidney had got it into his head that his role would mainly be that of interpreter. More likely, this was simply a clash of personalities.

I had no objection to being enlisted as an eleventh-hour substitute though had no idea, at the time, that Sidney was set on a clandestine race to be first into Hakkiari before either Fedden or another British party led by Monica Jackson, leader of the first British all-women's 1955 Himalayan expedition. The prospect of climbing 'the marvellous, virgin face of Geliasin' (Resko's summit peak), had so excited Sidney that he now wrote, 'Lloyd and Fedden think they will be the conquerors. What a lark if they weren't!'

To up the ante, Sidney instructed me to bring along 'etriers and slings, rock pitons, extra thin and flat splayed … a small tear-gas pistol, thunder-flashes or noise guns as a precaution against bears (extremely troublesome in Hakkiari) plus a few potted shrimps, a one pound tin of butter and (for your own use) a one-man tent and an extra cooker.'

None of these items (except butter imported from Kenya) were available in Aden, nor did I have any alpine gear with me. I had to prevail on my parents to dispatch a small trunk-load by express sea freight to Aden. The trunk's non-arrival delayed my final departure from Arabia by five days. A year later it turned up at Harwich having circled the world. To make up a climbing kit, my ex-Radfan chums in 45 Royal Marine Commando issued me with army boots, a sleeping bag and rucksack. Smart Tailor of Steamer Point, Aden knocked me up a pair of climbing breeches from Harris Tweed (the only 'cold climate suiting' available) within twenty-four hours. The saga of the missing trunk meant that I had to scrap the first leg of my luxury cruise from Alexandria to Izmir on the Italian Adriatica Line's *Bernina* and fly instead to pick the ship up at Beirut. Unlike the *Bretagne,* there were no beautiful people on board the *Bernina* and my permanent table companion, an uncommunicative Egyptian gentleman wearing impenetrable dark glasses was, I felt sure, an Egyptian Intelligence Service plant.

To steal a march on his rivals, Sidney had decided to drive the entire 2,400-mile round-trip to Hakkiari and back in a battered Chevrolet chauffeured by Qadr who doubled as guard and general factotum. We left Moda on 11 June and at Ortahisar, Sidney insisted on doing a 'warm-up' climb up the 'west face' of a crumbling monolith overlooking the town. His travelling regime was to make a pre-dawn start with breakfast in individual pre-prepared snack boxes; have a quick lunch stop and then settle down for a leisurely dinner at a restaurant, preferably accompanied by a ferocious red wine called 'Buzbag'. Before bedding down for the night at wayside hostelries, Sidney would undertake a microscopic inspection of the mattress linings for bed bugs. If no beds were provided, we all slept in the same room on air mattresses.

Parts of Eastern Turkey were unfamiliar even to Sidney with stretches of the road beyond Malatya littered with tortoises and blocked by herds of water buffalo. On the shores of Lake Van, Qadr served a special luncheon while we relaxed on easy chairs and gazed across its azure waters to the snow-streaked slopes of the extinct volcano of Suphan Dag. Sidney and I braved an icy swim in the lake, so naturally chlorinated that no fish can survive in it. Van itself was a miserable dump with dark memories that still lingered on from the early twentieth century Armenian and Nestorian massacres. Its population, then little more a few thousand, has since grown to half a million. Sidney cajoled the venal reception clerk of its only hotel to give us its one available room, which had just been vacated by a Kurdish woman whose jealous husband had locked her inside it for several days. The stench was overpowering. After moving all the stinking bedding and furniture into the corridor, we slept side by side on the floor like sardines.

Beyond the sentinel castle of Hosap, perched imperiously on a crag overlooking the road, Hakkiari's distant snow peaks became visible for the first time from the 2,750 metre high Gunzeldere Pass. The Chevrolet's dizzying descent into the bowels of the awesome Greater Zap gorge by a road blasted out of a perpendicular wall of rock eventually led to Colmerik, a nondescript town embowered with poplars and surrounded by snow-capped mountains. This, Hakkiari's administrative capital, was where Sidney had made prior arrangements to meet the Vali (provincial governor) Jalal Caya Khan a twenty-seven-year-old Istanbul Turk who wore an open-necked bush shirt and an 'Ataturk' cap pulled down flat over a pair of dark glasses. He smoked incessantly, spoke rapid English and positively radiated energy.

'Sadly, there is no hotel in Colemerik', the Vali explained. 'But you may stay in my roads department's rest house.'

Sidney would much have preferred to drive on to Yuksekova to make a flying start close to the mountains. However, to refuse the Vali's hospitality would have been imprudent. The rest house had no beds, so we were installed in two of the hospital's dormitories, bereft of furniture save for iron bedsteads and slippers. Neither the lavatories nor the taps worked, but its two nurses were very friendly.

Back at the Vali's office, Sidney outlined our climbing plans while the Vali conducted his official business by simultaneously signing letters and dealing summarily with local petitioners. He then telephoned the commandant of police at Yuksekova with orders to provide us with a reliable muleteer and an armed guard.

'And now gentlemen, you must meet my wife at my house.'

Mrs Vali, an attractive brunette and graduate of Indiana University, shared Government House with both her mother-in-law, a worn-out, old peasant woman, and her own charming, sophisticated American mother. After some inconsequential small talk, a flutter of local ladies descended to pay their respects. It was light years away from Indiana.

'And now you must see something of my country!' exclaimed the Vali, patently bored with women's talk.

Seizing the wheel of his jeep, he ground up a murderously steep track for a brief stop at a restored Seljuk madrasah before plunging down to the bottom of the Greater Zap Gorge by a road freshly dynamited from out of the defile.

'We've only just opened this road,' explained the Vali. 'You are the first Englishmen ever to see it.'

Twenty-five kilometres further on, we crossed over a bridge spanning the foaming Zap and stopped at a village where the road ended abruptly against the mountainside.

'We're building a new road to those villages up there' he went on, pointing up to the mists. 'They can be cut off by snow for seven months in the year.'

On the return journey to Colemerik, the Vali expatiated on the problems of Hakkiari's internal security, employment, education and health and dealing with its deeply conservative and often hostile Kurdish peoples. I thought back to my own time amongst the tribes of South Arabia and was humbled by this man's drive, energy and commitment.

That night, the Vali invited us to dine at the garrison officers' mess to honour a visiting World Health Organisation delegation. The dining room was devoid of decoration save for representations of Ataturk in full uniform and Gallipoli-inspired posters of Turkish infantrymen leaping acrobatically into enemy trenches shouting 'Allah, Allah!' The mess waiters were conscript national servicemen, shaven-headed as a precaution against lice. Tumblers of raki helped me through a succession of impenetrable speeches and a diatribe on the evils of colonialism from a do-gooder English WHO nurse.

The newly built CENTO road made for a smooth, seventy-two-mile drive to our road-head Yuksekova, a scruffy village of low-slung buildings with Cilo Dag's snow peaks delineating the southern horizon. At its one coffee shop, Sidney tracked down the police commandant who escorted us to an officers' mess decorated with photographs of blowsy belly dancers. A dozen military men and government officials sat around smoking and drinking coffee.

'You've come here at a bad time,' said the morose government inspector from Tarsus who was plainly not enjoying his Yuksekova posting.

'Much too early in the season. There's far too much snow for climbing now, even though it's warm enough. But you should see this miserable place in winter when it's under a metre of snow and swept by blizzards! Anyway, why are you starting from here rather than Hirvata where you can at least cross the river by a bridge? Here, the river is impassable.'

Our start was delayed by the furiously moustachioed colonel who had eyed us malevolently from the start and had insisted on having Qadr questioned by the police on suspicion of spying. An hour late, our Kurdish guide Mehmet, an obsequious know-all who claimed to have climbed Resko several times, fetched up with a muleteer Ferech whose face resembled a limestone buttress. Ferech promptly demanded an exorbitant fee for the use of his donkey and three horses. Despite the army's remonstrances that two would suffice, Sidney settled for three at the equivalent of fifty-five pounds a day.

A ton of food and equipment was now tied into woven, goat-hair sacks as a prelude to the familiar charade of loading, load adjusting, unloading and re-loading. At 12.45 p.m. on 16 June, the caravan finally set off across the Yuksekova Plain, Ferech astride a donkey leading his three heavily loaded mares with the rest of us straggling along behind. Heading due south under a clear, blue sky towards a wall of snow mountains, our hearts were singing until we reached the river. For exactly as the government inspector from Tarsus had predicted, it was in spate. Sidney now remembered that he'd left his altimeter behind, so sent Mehmet and Qadr scurrying back to retrieve it, leaving Ferech in charge of route finding.

Ferech advised that the only way to cross the river was to make a long detour upstream. As the day merged into late afternoon, we seemed to be moving further and further away from the mountains, yet deeper and deeper into a marsh of ten-foot high reeds. Ferech, having earlier removed his rubber galoshes, was now wading barefoot through knee-deep water when I first saw a snake with distinctive V markings along its back squirming away from under my boots. I shouted across to Sidney, 'For God's sake! Watch out for snakes!'

And then realised that the whole marsh was seething with them.

On reaching dry land we caught up with Ferech calmly replacing his galoshes.

'Why in God's name did you take us through that dreadful marsh?' demanded Sidney. 'The whole place was alive with poisonous snakes!'

'Snakes?' said Ferech. 'Yes indeed there were snakes. But how many of them remained under my feet?'

Four hours after our parting, Qadr and Mehmet caught up with us none too pleased at having had to swim the river. The afternoon's trudge over undulating ridges strewn with giant poppies, larkspur and hollyhocks and interspersed with icy streams eventually led to a grassy hollow in sight of a village. Here, we camped, too tired to eat anything save a mug of tepid soup. At dawn, a swarm of ragamuffin children descended on us like flies. It was at this village that the police commandant had instructed Mehmet to draw a rifle as a protection against bears, but the only weapon available had already been appropriated by a local shepherd. On learning this Mehmet demanded that Sidney give him a written guarantee absolving him from any further responsibility for our safety. Sidney refused point blank.

With Sidney quietly fuming and Mehmet in a sulk, Ferech now took over the lead into the heart of the range. By early afternoon, we had reached a 3,000-metre snowy col overlooking the next valley fringed by jagged peaks and vertical cliffs from where there was no obvious way for the horses to get down to the bottom. Mehmet now redeemed himself by finding a route through an unlikely funnel of rock that led to a narrow gangway across a cliff face with overhanging sides that threatened to unbalance the heavily loaded horses. Just as the last horse negotiated this *mauvais pas,* a shaggy bear covered in yellow hair slid down a snow couloir dead ahead. The horses began to rear and panic, but when everyone yelled in unison the bear lumbered off.

Reassuming his role as guide, Mehmet now chose an incomprehensibly unsuitable route up the trough of the snow-filled valley. The horses kept falling through the snow crust up to their girths and despite Ferech belabouring their rumps with a stick while attempting to haul them out by their tails, the wretched animals would not be budged. So we had to go through the charade of unloading, manhandling them on to firmer ground and then re-loading them. Tired and bad-tempered, the caravan breasted the Demirkapu, or 'Iron Gate', as the shadows lengthened. The spectacle dead ahead caused even Sidney to stop and draw breath. Across the yawning gulf of the Tegui Savi valley, the biggest glacier in the Middle East came tumbling down from the base of Resko's half-domed summit to its very bottom. As magnificent as it was unexpected, we stared in wonder as black clouds came rolling in from the west to hasten the descent that might have ended the expedition.

The direct route down into the Tegui Savi would have involved a 500-metre climb down very rough scree. This was patently impossible for the horses and the only alternative was to traverse a steep snow slope below the col that led to safer ground. Ferech looked uneasy, but managed to coax two of the horses across the slope. The third stopped halfway, shaking and terrified. Meanwhile, Ferech's donkey, having taken an independent line a little higher up the slope, slipped and fell heavily against the stationary horse, knocking it off balance. Ferech, moving with astonishing speed, grabbed its bridle and hauled it to safety. Mehmet seized the donkey by the tail and held it tight. Either fall would have been fatal.

Both animals and men were exhausted by the time camp was established at Erbish Yaila, a level patch of ground tucked inside a shepherd's stone-enclo-sure in the lee of an enormous erratic boulder. Towering above, rose a ring of superb peaks and the snout of Resko's glacier. After rigging up my tent, I crawled into it feeling too sick and cold to face another alfresco supper. Despite our ton of equipment, Sidney had brought neither a mess tent nor cover under which we could eat together and share the day's adventures. Once the sun went down, it was too cold to sit around in the open. It was a curious omission for such an experienced traveller, but Sidney admitted later that this was the first time that he had brought a tent on any of his expeditions. He and Hilary were snug and insulated in theirs: I less so. Mehmet and Ferech slept soundly under their shepherds' cloaks, but Qadr made do in the clothes he stood up in.

By reaching the secret heart of Hakkiari so early in the season, we had avoided the noxious insects and flies that plague the place in high summer and now found ourselves in a botanical paradise with the ground emblazoned with giant mauve crocus, primulas, gentians and orchids wherever the snow had melted. The slopes around were pitted with the tracks of chamois and ibex and we became almost blasé about seeing bears every day. Ferech assured us that they were a menace to flocks; raided fields, gardens and orchards, and even killed the odd shepherd.

The scenery was grand and Erbish made a superb campsite. Yet having come so far at considerable cost, I was disappointed that Sidney's schedule had left only one week for climbing. After one fallow day's idling, all three of us embarked on a 1,000-metre climb up the heavily crevassed glacier to examine Resko's uncompromising north-east face. This was enough to convince Sidney that this particular climb was best left to Fedden and Lloyd, though by way of compensation an airy scramble up a detached rock tower at the glacier's edge gave Hilary her first virgin summit. The following day, an attempt to reach the Mia Hvara Valley, where Weir and Scott had camped in 1957, was frustrated by our selecting the wrong col. Sidney then decided that a better view into this elusive valley would be from the summit of the 3,869 metre Maunsell Peak, a day-long outing up interminable scree-strewn slopes and snow gullies that was eventually rewarded by a summit view of the Mia Hvara and Resko's north-west face that Sidney declared to be 'unsurpassed in Hakkiari' and the first British ascent of Colonel Maunsell's mountain.

With time slipping by, Sidney was determined to make the second British ascent of Resko. However, unlike the route taken by Weir and Scott from the north, he wanted to do his from Serpil Zoma on the south side of the mountain. This meant dropping down 300 metres into the Rudbare Sin gorge and then climbing up another 800 metres to the zoma. Unsurprisingly, both Mehmet and Ferech were dead against it. Mehmet because this was not the traditional way to climb Resko, Ferech because, at 2,930 metres, Serpil Zoma was too high for his horses. Sidney would have none of it and on the way round picked up a Kurdish shepherd at Serpil Yaila as a substitute guide.

Past the junction of three torrents crossed by a bridge of plaited branches overlaid by flat stones, the track to Serpil Zoma climbed steeply up a broken hillside infested by thistles with spines that left a painful sting. Mehmet took exception to my reverting to a hard tongue of snow to avoid them and complained to Ferech, 'See how that wretched infidel moves … like some cursed snake.'

Snakes there were in plenty: slithering off the path into the undergrowth with Ferech pursuing them with his heavy stick. Serpil Zoma was perched on a level, grassy platform that seemed to float in space. Two thousand metres below, the River Zap raged through the mighty gorge of the Rudbare Sin. To the east, the peaks and glaciers of neighbouring Sat Dag were spun with gold in the setting sun. Sidney considered it 'the most splendidly sited camp I have ever made.'

Mehmet had assured Sidney that Resko could easily be climbed 'without hands' by its East Ridge. But the ridge was invisible from our camp and so, to get a proper sighting of it I made an early morning recce along Resko's long, outlying south ridge as far as a high col from where every detail of the mountain's immense south face and east ridge themselves were plainly visible. It looked as if Mehmet might be right about the East Ridge, though to get there would mean losing much of the height so hardly gained by camping at Serpil Zoma.

At 2.30 a.m. on 24 June, the Nowills and I slipped away from camp under a blazing constellation of stars. On reaching yesterday's col, Sidney looked at me askance.

'This isn't at all what I had imagined and can't possibly be the right way. Hilary and I are certainly not going to attempt to climb those huge rock buttresses protecting Resko's south face.'

'Absolutely,' I replied. 'But if we climb down into the snow amphitheatre below, there's a straightforward route along the crest of the east ridge to the summit.'

After a laboured descent into the amphitheatre, Sidney was still looking unhappy. So was I, though for somewhat different reasons.

'What the hell!' I thought to myself. 'I've moved heaven and the earth to get to Hakkiari, so we can surely do better than Mehmet's hands-in-pocket scramble.'

'Tell you what, Sidney,' I suggested, 'Why don't I make a short recce up the south ridge to see how it goes. I can always come down if it looks too difficult.'

After half an hour's grappling with friable rock and hard ice, I realised that the south ridge was a serious climb, so rejoined the others to reappraise the situation. We then agreed that Sidney and Hilary would cross the amphitheatre to attain the east ridge and that I would carry on up the south ridge. Thereafter, we would meet up where the two ridges joined and press on to the summit.

Even then, I realised that this was damned silly plan. The rock on the south ridge's shattered yellow towers quickly deteriorated and I only managed to extricate myself with difficulty from what had become a suicidal climb. Changing course by a tortuous diagonal traverse to reach the crest of the east ridge, I heaved myself over its lip three hours later lathered in sweat and then stared anxiously down its broad back for signs of the others. To my intense relief, two tiny figures were making steady progress upwards. Sidney might reasonably have blown his top when we met up. Instead, he gave a deprecatory smile and merely commented that he would have preferred not to lose 800 feet of height in getting here. There were no further difficulties save for an unprotected traverse across an unlikely band of *sastrugi* inconveniently coating the slabs below Resko's summit. Concealed in its rough, stone cairn was a zinc box containing a summit book recording the ascents of Hans Bobek's 1937 Viennese expedition and those of three subsequent Austrian/German expeditions including the first ascent of Resko's north-east wall three years before in 1962. Hilary's was the first by an Englishwoman.

Early next morning, Serpil Zoma was invaded by shepherds, sheep, goats and ferocious dogs. We retreated down the valley and camped short of Serpil Yaila, only to be plagued by a gaggle of giggling children coming up for a peep. A survival of the Carduchi who harassed Xenophon's 10,000 Greek mercenaries some two and a half millennia ago, the Kurds have successfully defied all efforts to tame them and continue to assert their independent spirit and fighting prowess to this day by taking on both Turkish and ISIL forces alike. Some of the men wore Ataturk flat caps and ragged suits; others affected the traditional baggy trousers with long woollen stockings. Their unveiled women were dressed in brightly patterned, embroidered dresses. Their children ranged from fair-skinned, blue-eyed Circassians to dark Turanian types. While the men tended the sheep, the women milked and spun. I might have been back at Saphid Arb.

The hills were alive with the cries of their bleating flocks and the soil was bursting with spring flowers. It seemed idyllic, yet life for these proud people who insisted on giving us yoghurt, eggs and pungent cheese, was anything but. Disease was rampant; most of the children had streaming noses and dreadful eye complaints. The fine-featured young women who rocked the goat-skins of milk to make curds and cheese would all too soon become the same work-worn shrews who lurked in the darkest corners of their foul-smelling goat-skin tents, cooking meagre meals over smoky, dried-dung fires. Brief summers would soon give way to long winters when everyone retreated to the valleys to escape ordeal by snow and ice. Some would doubtless have swapped their traditional way of life for the sops of modernity that the Vali promised.

But not all. And down in the Rudbare Sin there were terraced fields watered by irrigation channels, fringed by hedgerows and shaded by giant almond and peach trees in which urchins shook down the ripened fruit into wicker baskets below. The air was filled with the buzzing of insects, and as we followed the uneven road back to Yuksekova, clouds of swallowtails rose and then settled back along the way. As the day wore on, a fiery heat radiated off the rocks; out-size horseflies tormented the horses, and our caravan became over-extended. For a spell, I fell in with a group of fleet-footed Kurds led by a man carrying a three-metre-long stave with which he propelled himself over obstacles on the path like an Olympic pole-vaulter.

The foaming Zab had long been left behind when our straggling band eventually caught up with itself on the 2,720-metre pass that divides Cilo Dag from Sat Dag. Looking longingly across to Sat's soaring peaks and glinting snow-fields, I could only regret that Sidney had cut our stay so fine. He could always come back – and did – but for me the towers of Sat Dag remain a dream. Below the pass, we pitched our tents for the last time in a lush meadow covered with giant buttercups, scillas, gentians and primulas. That night, Ferech nearly lost his mares after they broke their hobbles to join a mob of frisky wild stallions. It took him four hours to retrieve them. While crossing Yuksekova's drear plain next day, we had first to ford a tributary and then cross the main river on horse-back before getting back to the Chevrolet. Stopping over at Van that same night, we bumped into Renee Fedden and Peter McColl in the flea-ridden tourist hotel. They could not have been friendlier or more charming.

On the drive back to Istanbul, just short of Kayseri, Sidney ordered Qadr to stop the car when an effulgent Erciyes Dag burst through the clouds. After a protracted photographic session, he turned to me and said, 'Why don't you have a crack at it, John? We can drive direct to Hajilar for you to pick up some food. If you move fast, you could bivouac near the base of the north-east face this evening and be up and down by tomorrow afternoon.' I could never forget the adventures I had shared with Nigella on Erciyes and Sidney must have known what the mountain meant to me. His offer was typically generous, for he and Hilary were already overdue in Istanbul.

At 5.30 p.m. I set off from Hajilar with a mule, a muleteer and a couple of small boys in tow. The muleteer proved to be a thoroughly unpleasant man who persistently lagged behind prodding the wretched animal with a pointed stick. I summarily dismissed him on reaching the Zoma of a Yuruk family. The tribesmen pressed on me tea and yogurt and insisted that I stay the night. I excused myself politely and then bashed on for another half-hour after dark before making a rough bivouac in the shelter of some rocks.

It was bitterly cold that night and I could only doze in snatches. At 3.30 a.m. in faint moonlight, I brushed the frost off my clothes and stumbled across the intervening stony ground and tufted grass toward the dark bulk of Erciyes. By 5.30 a.m. I had reached a point on the face where the snow slope steepened sharply into rock-hard *névé* and then ice. Sidney's borrowed crampons, two sizes too small, were giving me excruciating blisters and I had some anxious moments on the upper section of the glacier, but at 6.45 a.m. I breasted Erciyes's east summit. The sky was inky blue and far below faint wisps of smoke rose from scores of Yuruk encampments scattered over the Anatolian Plateau. Five hours later, I rejoined the others at Hajilar.

That ascent of Erciyes should have been the perfect ending to our Hakkiari adventure. But back in Istanbul a letter from home awaited me with the shattering news that my younger brother Owen had gone missing. I caught the overland bus to Munich that evening and then the train to London. Not long after my return home, they found his dead body in a wild and lonely place. After commissioned National Service with the Welsh Guards, he had graduated from Cambridge with a degree in anthropology and archaeology. He had taken his life aged twenty-seven. His death broke my parents' hearts and changed the course of the lives of both my sister and me. I could still have returned to South Arabia as Sir Richard Turnbull, the high commissioner, had urged, but I now had other priorities to confront and had set my course on a new career. There could be no going back.

7

ANTIPODEAN VENTURES I

DOWN TO EARTH, DOWN UNDER

Resignation from the Colonial Service and Owen's tragic death brought me painfully down to earth. Lifestyle adjustments would now have to be made with five and a half years of adventure about to be replaced by the grind of articles of clerkship and the business of coming to grips with the unfamiliar world of Britain's swinging sixties. The transition was bumpy and I might even have given up my prospective legal career had I not got married. The catalyst for this had been an Easter skiing holiday in the Cairngorms in 1966 with a party that included some old climbing chums, a young flame and, at the eleventh hour, my future wife Georgina. After the fun and games were over, I proposed to Georgina on the banks of Loch Ness, assuming that the very place where she had recently spent several weeks working as a 'Nessie Spotter' with Peter Scott's Loch Ness Enquiry Research Bureau might be ideal for popping the question. My proposal fell flat, but persistence eventually won my fair lady and we were married on 24 September 1966. Bill Norton was my best man.

For many men, marriage marks the end of serious mountaineering. Selfishly, I carried on. Throughout our married life Georgina allowed me this indulgence after realising that our honeymoon ascent of an erupting Mount Etna during a blizzard dressed only in beachwear was a foretaste of things to come. Thereafter, we were to share many other mountain adventures together and had it not been for Georgina's earnings as an MP's secretary, we would have been hard pressed to survive those early years of married life living in South Kensington on an article clerk's salary of £650 a year.

Visits to the mountains were now severely curtailed. Even so, in March 1967 we managed a low-budget skiing holiday in Courmayeur staying at the apartment of a friend, Elizabeth Gordon. While an *enceinte* Georgina knitted a child's matinee jacket, Kit Power and I skied from the Pointe Helbronner on the south side of Mont Blanc to Chamonix without seeing another soul en route. A few days later, we climbed the Breithorn on ski from Cervinia with an old Arabian chum Chris Beadle and celebrated our modest achievements at La Brenva, Montenvers, where its twelve-course Savoyard dinner cost £3 a head. That September I squeezed in a week of classic rock climbs in Glencoe and on Ben Nevis with Tony Delafield, John Blacker and Geoff Newham. It was my last Highland fling for seven years.

During those drear years in articles, I sometimes wondered if I wouldn't have swapped a week in South Arabia for a year in the City. An eighteen-month stint drafting little but corporate legal documentation led me to the despairing measure of applying to join the World Bank. After only a couple of interviews, I was offered the plum job of secretary to the bank's board of executive directors in Washington at a salary fifteen times that I was currently earning. Confronted by this life-changing decision, I concluded reluctantly that to have resigned from one career and then ducked out of another without qualifying might be imprudent so I refused the bank's offer by telegram. At 6 a.m. the following morning, while Georgina and I were still abed, the telephone rang and a girl with a breezy transatlantic twang informed me that I was being connected to Mr J. Edgar Haag, the World Bank's head of personnel.

'Hey John', said Mr Haag, 'We're very sorry that you've refused our offer. Is money your problem?'

Money was indeed our problem. Heart thumping, I explained to him as calmly as I could that I still had unfinished business to complete, so would not be accepting the bank's generous offer.

In July 1968, I completed my articles assuming that I had assuredly put the Law Society's final exams behind me. Georgina agreed that we celebrate the occasion with an alpine holiday on condition that she brought along a girlfriend, Rosemary, the feisty niece of an Irish earl who had never spent a night under canvas, let alone set foot on a mountain. None of my erstwhile climbing chums were free that year, so when Nick Allen, the nephew of an elderly neighbour, introduced himself one evening after visiting his aunt, we persuaded him to come on board. Nick was something quite exceptional. After coming up to Oxford on a classical scholarship from Rugby, he had read medicine before switching to oriental studies, anthropology and philosophy. He spoke six modern languages, was a consummate musician and an expert on art both ancient and modern. He was also the only British mountaineer at that time to have done the Philipp-Flamm route, reputedly the hardest rock climb in the Dolomites. Disconcertingly modest, he was scarcely known to the Oxford University Mountaineering Club's elite because he had done most of his student mountaineering with the hard school of Munich climbers in Germany. Nick sported a prodigious beard, eschewed creature comforts and was totally disinterested in what he ate.

On 16 August 1968, the four of us left England for the Bernese Oberland in our brand new Morris Traveller. Nick had selected this area because he was 'not too keen on an exclusive diet of Chamonix rock and wanted to concentrate on snow and ice'. During the outward journey it never stopped raining. Georgina and I were snug enough inside my Meade Everest tent – at last put to good use – but Nick's 'fairly light two-man tent' was a relic of his days as a boy scout. Despite leaks and intense discomfort, Rosemary shared it with him for most of the next four weeks and survived the experience.

Our immediate neighbours at the Grindelwald campsite were a group of grinning kamikaze Japanese climbers bent on the Eiger Wall. Quiet and well behaved, they managed to squeeze all six of them into a two-man tent. For a change of scene, we repaired to Neil Hogg's Chalet Herrenshaft to enjoy his wit, generous hospitality and wise counsel. Neil, an honorary member of the Alpine Club, had been my inspirational mentor four years before on my first Eagle Ski Club Alpine meet. When he died in 1995, I showed a draft of the obituary I was writing for the *Alpine Journal* to his elder brother Quintin Hailsham. After correcting a grammatical infelicity, the former Lord Chancellor paid his younger brother the compliment of his being 'the most talented man I ever knew'.

The Oberland was experiencing such bad weather that, after a training climb up the Mittelhorn, we moved across to the Engelhorner for better conditions and what Nick described as some 'hardish rock'. Our first sally up the Rosenlauistock's West Kante, was quickly followed with the Vorderspitze's West Kante, 'one of the finest routes in the Engelhoerner', according to the guidebook. On the crux pitch, as Nick powered past a German pair struggling with their *etriers* I realised that he was in a different rock-climbing league to mine. Back at Grindelwald, he and I set our sights on a traverse of the 4,078-metre Schreckhorn, the 'Peak of Terror' and the last of the great Oberland peaks to capitulate. On 25 August the four of us set off for the old Strahlegg Hut,

1,718 metres higher and one of the longest hut marches in the Alps. Years later, when Nick had become a distinguished Oxford don married with children, he was appalled to learn that Georgina was already four-months pregnant when she completed that seven and a half hour trek.

The Shreckhorn was still plastered in snow from recent storms. Throughout the ascent of its heavily iced-up south-west ridge, we were followed closely by a guided German party who, by the time we left the summit to descend by the south-east ridge, had dropped far behind. Well below the headwall of the Schreck Glacier, Nick and I took our first break of the day, relieved to be safely off what had been a demanding climb. Wondering how the Germans were getting on, I glanced back to the high col from which we had just descended which separates the Schreckhorn from the Lauteraarhorn. At that very moment, three black dots came hurtling down the length of the face. We struggled back up the glacier through deep, slushy snow to find a tangled mess of bodies. Only one of them, the guide, could get on his feet. His two clients lay groaning in the snow tinged red with blood. All three were shocked and injured, and one had broken his arm. The bemused guide insisted that they could get back to the hut unaided, but without arguing the toss we loaded their rucksacks on to ours, raced down the glacier to the hut to raise the alarm and then plodded back up again to help bring them down. A Swiss rescue helicopter picked the wounded up from the hut that night. The German guide didn't thank us in so many words, but stood us a beer before taking off.

Back at Grindelwald, Neil presented me with a copy of Christoffel's *La Montagne and la Peinture* as a memento of our Schrekhorn saga. We wanted to stay on in the Oberland, but bad weather aborted an attempt on the Lauterbrunnen Breithorn, so we moved on to Pontresina where Nick and I climbed the Piz Morteratsch by the Cresta de la Speranza under heavy snow. More bad weather enforced a week's culture-break in Venice when Nick insisted on attending the *avant garde* Bienalle art exhibition on three successive days while the rest of us settled for less elevated pleasures. Artistic appetites thus satiated, the party then headed north to the Dolomites where Nick suggested the north face of the Crozzon de Brenta and traverse of the Cima Tosa as our final climb. It was as well that I never got a proper view of the Crozzon's immense face 'so rich in its architecture that it has attracted every "extreme" climber since Paul Preuss's day' (*Extreme Alpine Rock* by Pause and Winkler), until we were fully committed to the climb. Our route was not the *Direttissima*, but still involved 1,000 metres of steep climbing up snow-covered rock using techniques previously unknown to me. The weather got progressively worse as the day wore on and on the Crozzon's summit an electric storm set our ice axes zinging and sent Nick's matted hair and beard standing on end. It was still that way when we stumbled back into camp sixteen hours after leaving it. Nick and I did one north Wales weekend together later that year before our paths divided. Cool, courageous and combative, he was the most brilliant rock master I ever climbed with.

By the following year, my stuttering legal career had almost ground to a halt. Nonetheless, I was still hanging in there when, in early April 1969 Richard Brooke and I set out from Chamonix to do the Haute Route on ski. The start had to be delayed by three days due to my tearing a calf muscle while descending the Vallée Blanche with Richard and our friends Kit and Penny Power. Penny's robust physiotherapy treatment got me as far as the Trient Hut by which stage I had run out of time, so would have to go home once we got down to Orsières. That evening at the hut, I tried to persuade a group of young Frenchmen to invite Richard to join them so that he might finish the course. They shrugged off the offer with Gallic disdain.

Richard was one of the finest men I ever had the privilege of mountaineering with. Strong, calm and totally dependable, his climbing record was immensely impressive. But he was also pathologically modest, a quality which the Frenchmen totally misread. When trying to conduct negotiations what I should have said was: *'This man is a former Royal Naval officer who's done more big climbs in the Alps and elsewhere than you've had baguettes for breakfast. He was on the British Rakaposhi expedition, has climbed in New Zealand and with Hillary in Antarctica. He's worth the lot of you put together and you'd be bloody lucky to have him in your party!'*

Unfortunately, it didn't come out quite like that and my failure to inject enough braggadocio in my inarticulate French made no impression on them.

In the event, we all left the Trient together in the very early hours next morning to descend to Orsières. The sky was clear and starry on starting, but halfway down the Combe d'Orny we were hit by a tremendous storm and the French party disintegrated. It was too late to retreat to the hut and for the rest of that *sturm und drang* descent they were only too glad to be ferried down behind us. At Orsières, the French implored Richard to join them, which he did with good grace. Unfortunately, the rest of their tour had to be abandoned two days later when an avalanche broke Richard's skis and French morale.

Richard's tales of his climbs in the New Zealand Alps had set me thinking. Disenchanted with the solicitor's profession and minded to seek new horizons, Georgina and I decided that we should follow the example of her father who, in 1950, had thrown up his own English legal practice and three days' hunting a week, in exchange for pioneer farming in western Australia. Australia itself had no mountains of significance, but New Zealand just across the Tasman Sea had them in spades.

On 30 August 1969, we emigrated to Western Australia as £10 Poms with our two young daughters, Emma and Victoria. Georgina had spent some of her early years in the Wide Brown Land, but for me it was *terra incognita*. The notion that I might find some agreeable niche farming was comprehensively dispelled within weeks. Mustering mobs of stubborn Merino wethers with fly-blown bottoms as a prelude to injecting, drenching and shearing them in dusty paddocks in a hundred degrees of searing Australian sun, brought it home that I would need loads of lolly, bags of expertise and that particular brand of Aussie toughness to survive the hardships, setbacks and climatic vagaries of farming in Australia. At least the experience added some new expletives to my vocabulary.

Farming might be an uncertain occupation, but in most other respects these were heady times to be working in the 'lucky country' which was just emerging from the days when its economy rode on the sheep's back. A rip-roaring mineral boom was making Perth an epicentre for new money and its stock exchange resembled a betting shop where outback farmers, having abandoned their land, hung around just to catch their brokers' eye. In this frenzied atmosphere, I almost got myself a job with Lang Hancock, the billionaire mineral magnate who, with his partner Wright, had first discovered the Hamersley Range's iron-ore deposits and would have enlarged Port Headland's harbour with a nuclear bomb had the Western Australian government let them do so. Their respective daughters, Gina Reinhart and Mrs Michael Bennett, subsequently became two of the richest women in the world. At that time, Hancock's HQ office was a modest bungalow in Subiaco, a suburb of Perth. My interview there was short because my face didn't fit. I settled instead for a humdrum job with the Perpetual Executor and Trustee Corporation of Western Australia.

While marking time for something better to turn up, I ran into an old East African hand Mike Adams, John Blacker's *bête noire*. He and Claude Girardin, another former Mountain Club of Kenya president, had recently founded The Climbers Association of Western Australia (CAWA) with a membership of itinerant Poms leavened by enthusiastic indigenes. With Adams filling the roles of president, chief instructor, guide, and premature 'grand old man', the CAWA had already adopted the full trappings of elected officers, training meets, lectures, and annual dinners.

Rock climbing was already well established in Australia's eastern states, but the more serious pursuit of 'bush whacking' had a stronger following in Western Australia. Under the aegis of the CAWA, Adams was determined to change all that, even though climate and geography were against him.

Australia is not only the driest and hottest of the world's continents, but also the flattest with landscapes that generally lack either variety or dramatic elements. And yet, in this last refuge of primitive man, marsupial beast and primeval vegetable works, there remains much for those with a bent for expeditioning and an appreciation of unusual country to discover. And once you venture beyond the city's suburbs into the brilliant light and illimitable horizons of the Outback, you must hazard that unique wilderness that the Australians call 'the Bush', where European consciousness has still to find a place.

Under Adams's generalship, the CAWA's top guns practised the gamut of *avant garde* climbing techniques at weekends in stone quarries around Perth. The more serious winter season meets were held in the Stirling Range, some 240 miles to the south. Driving down from Perth through the pancake-flat peneplain of Western Australia, this fifty-mile-long range is the only prominent feature visible for thousands of square miles. From afar, its half-dozen summits of just over a thousand metres resemble a clutch of vegetated, rounded humps. Closer to, the greensward reveals itself as a matting of plant, scrub and tree so closely plaited together that you need a machete to get through it. The peculiar qualities that have enabled the Stirling's flora to survive in a climate which can vary from sub-zero to 100° Fahrenheit in a matter of hours, manifests itself in unique flower species sometimes confined to individual peaks, and an obdurate bush whose spiny leaves are guaranteed to shred any known fabric within a weekend and the skin of your hands, shins and knees in an afternoon. Designated a national park in 1957 to preserve its floral integrity, only the Stirling's park authority was allowed to cut tracks through the bush to give authorised access to four specified peaks.

The highest and wildest of these are faced with 700-foot bluffs of sandstone and quartzite that combine the roughness of gabbro with a plethora of holds that make for superb rock climbing. During our time in Western Australia, I managed three separate visits to this unusual range the first of which coincided with the CAWA's 'spring manoeuvres weekend' in early October when Adams had given advance notice that he was going to forge a new route up the north face of Bluff Knoll, at 3,597 feet, the highest peak in the range. His successful ascent of *Hell Fire Gulley* with Brian Lever, followed by a triumphal return to the CAWA's campfire made talk of lesser routes superfluous. Next day, after climbing another Adams original on *Toolbrunup*, Georgina, our two-year-old daughter, Emma and I had had enough of baths in sand holes lined with polythene and the bush flies that made life near intolerable in our stiflingly hot tent so decamped to the deserted white-sand beaches of the Great South to recover.

At about this time, I ran into Peter Riddey an itinerant ex-Oxford University Mountaineering Club renegade who was then working as a geo-physicist and essayer for Poseidon, the nickel-mining company whose shares had gone ballistic and subsequently ruined many a punting Pom. I was nonplussed when Riddey confided that no nickel had actually been mined by Poseidon to date. Although Adam's had ordained that the Australian summer, November to March, should be treated as close season in the Stirlings, Peter and I decided to breach protocol one December weekend, and discovered that it was actually considerably cooler then than it had been in the spring.

We set our sights on the north face of Porongurup, the third highest peak in the range, sited deep in territory hitherto unpenetrated by the CAWA. Thick mist masking the tops made for cool conditions and my first serious essay in bushwhacking. According to native-born Australians, 'bush craft', that essential perquisite to safety in the Outback, can never be fully developed by Pommie bastards. When, after three exhausting hours, we had covered only two miles and were still far short of our target, we abandoned Pyrongorup and settled instead for the virgin face of Isongurup. Its only evident line of weakness was an enormous crack, which gave 300 feet of Mild Very Severe climbing on steep, sound rock. Returning to Perth with shredded trousers and bloodied hands, I wondered whether one and a half hours of climbing compensated for seven spent in the bush. Nonetheless, our climb *Redemption Grove* was grudgingly recorded as a CAWA first.

Three months later, Riddey and I came back for another crack at Pyrongorup accompanied this time by Robin Smith, a 'dare all and be kin to the gods', globe-trotting Kiwi then in the process of writing his uncompleted masterwork *Mountains and Man* as a prelude to assaulting the six most famous north faces of the European Alps. Led this time by a genuine bushwhacker, we reached the base of Pyrongorup's 700-foot face in under two hours and promptly attacked what looked like its least unpromising line up a chasmic chimney whose water-smoothed, slimy back wall led to an insurmountable overhang. After wasting two hours trying to climb it, we abseiled off for a less demanding route up the airy edge of Pyrongorup's north buttress.

Riddey suggested that as this was likely to be my last climb in the Stirlings, I had better lead it. Two hours and 400 feet of sustained climbing later, I came up against a thicket protecting the last few feet between me and the summit, which was so dense that even Smith was defeated by it.

'Bugger this effing bush,' said Smith, 'We'd best get off the bastard before dark. It's half-past four already.'

I hadn't noticed the time, but Riddey was so anxious to get back to the girl-friend he had abandoned in his car by the roadside that he had to be restrained from abseiling down the entire face using two ropes of unequal thickness. The correct knot to be used in such circumstances is the Fisherman's Bend rather than the Fisherman's Knot. One holds firm, the other doesn't. Abseiling, especially by the traditional 'rope slung over the shoulder' method, is inherently dangerous and after completing mine, I was horrified to discover that the thinner rope was within two inches of slipping out of its knot.

Smith's bush craft eventually got us off Pyongorup without further incident, but we still had to get back to Riddey's car. Night found us floundering through thicket, thorn, root and snare – sometimes headlong, sometimes horizontal – as our clothing, hands and shins became progressively more lacerated. Back at the car, Riddey's incandescent girlfriend was about to drive off and report us missing so it needed a keg of Swan lager to restore amity and celebrate the first ascent of Pyrongorup's north face.

Twenty-five miles south of the Stirlings lie the Porongurups, a range wholly different in climate, vegetation and character. Ten miles long and 2,000-feet-high, these basalt domes rise like giant bollards from a forest of Karri trees whose 200-feet-high boles grow as straight as the Pillars of Jupiter. In spring, when the Porongorups resemble a wildflower garden, Riddey and I made a couple of tentative investigatory visits. However, without bolts and bongs we could make no impression on the vestigial cracks of these miniature El Capitans.

Furthest south, all that remains of Australia's three-million-square-mile, sun-baked continent is a narrow littoral of green farmland fringed by granite cliffs and white-sand beaches washed by the rollers of the Great Southern Ocean. Early one morning, Georgina and I walked four miles along a deserted beach and then forced our way inland through the bush to reach the summit of Mount Manypeaks, an isolated basalt dome, 1,800 feet high, covered with rare flowers and overlooking the sea. We saw no other living thing that day save the red kangaroo and on that lonely peak I sensed the reality of the Australian dream.

SNOWY MOUNTAIN SAGAS

My job with Perth's Perpetual Executor and Trustee Corporation was never intended as more than a stopgap. I had originally toyed with an offer of appointment with the Australian Department of External Affairs, but having twice been flown 4,500 miles from one side of Australia to the other for interviews with prestigious eastern states universities, plumped for an administrative/legal post in the brand new Canberra College of Advanced Education (CCAE) which not only offered the highest salary, but was also closest to Australia's highest range, the Snowy Mountains.

To make the transcontinental move to Canberra, Georgina agreed that I would drive the 2,800 miles from Perth with all our worldly goods and she would fly across with the children after I had found suitable family accommodation. To cross the Nullarbor, I recruited through the local newspaper one Laurie Seiber to be my co-driver. It had taken the Victorian explorer Eyre six months of dreadful privation to make this desert crossing which, even today, must rank as one of the most boring of its kind. In a thousand miles, only the shadowed rim of the 100-mile long Eucla Basin broke the monotony of a landscape whose shrivelled features had all but been obliterated long before the advent of man. One 300-mile section of 'dirt' was booby-trapped with giant potholes and took eight hours to negotiate by night. After dropping Seiber off at Melbourne, I completed the rest of the journey to Canberra on my own by driving up the deserted Bonang Highway through Gippsland's silent eucalypt forests, marvelling at the giant stands of *Eucapyptus regnans* which is the tallest hardwood in the world.

Unlike Australia's other major cities, which cling umbilically to the continent's seaboard, Canberra lays a hundred miles inland at an altitude of over 500 metres. Cupped within a bowl of rolling blue hills, Australia's capital city has up to six months of frost and the occasional snowfall. The Snowy Mountains, only three hours drive away and the only range on mainland Australia with recognisably alpine features, culminates in the Main Range which has six peaks of over 2,000 metres. It covers much the same area as the Cairngorms and shares with its Scottish counterpart a common architecture of isolated granite plateaux and some vile weather. In the best mountaineering traditions, the first ascent of its highest peak Kosciuszko (2,230 metres) is hotly disputed. Kosciuszko was chosen by the celebrated Polish botanist and explorer Count Strzelecki because he unflatteringly compared its shape to the burial mound in Krakow of the eponymous Polish patriot. Strzelecki indisputably reached the summit in 1840, but a compatriot Doctor Lhotsky doggedly maintained that he had got there four years earlier. Lhotsky's clunky 'Mount King William the Fourth' was never going to cut the mustard and the better Australian view is that indigenous white stockmen were grazing its summit pastures years before either pesky Pole appeared on the scene.

But in this ancient land of heat, drought and sand, the wonder of the Snowys is that they maintain their snow cover for most of the year. Besides, Australians insist that their mainland's winter snow cover, stretching along a 300-mile arc from Mount Buller to Mount Bimberi, is greater than that of Switzerland. Be that as it may, Kosciuszko regularly registers 100 inches of precipitation and it is certainly true that Australian/Norwegian gold miners founded the Snow-Shoe Ski-Racing Club at the gold-rush village of Kiandra in 1878, thus predating the first European ski club by over a decade. Initially, the sport's popularity proved ephemeral, but when the Snowy Mountains hydro-electric scheme opened up tracts of previously inaccessible mountain in 1949, this led to the creation of the 2,100-square-mile Kosciuszko National Park and the construction of Thredbo, one of the world's most expensive ski resorts which boasts its own FIS international downhill run. Although popular in the way that Australians take any sport, the scope for piste skiing in the Snowys is somewhat limited, but the undulating ridges and rounded summits of Kosciuszko, Townsend, Twynam and Carruthers offer entertaining ski touring and are accessible from both Thredbo and Guthega as either one or two-day expeditions.

Between May and November 1970, I made six separate visits to the Snowys, though only once did the sun shine bright out of a brilliant blue sky as you expect to be your due in Australia. My companion on these outings was usually a CCAE colleague, Hugh Mahon, a self-deprecating academic whose skiing never matched his bushwhacking skills. The aim of our first expedition, to climb Australia's two highest peaks, Kosciuszko and Townsend, was also the least successful as neither of us could handle the langlauf skiing technique to which Hugh had been converted without having previously put principle into practice. Equipped with the Kiandra-era, second-hand wooden boards without metal edges that I had picked up through a small ad in the *Canberra Times*, we set off for the heights from the top of the Thredbo chairlift following the tracks of two genuine langlaufers whose vigorous poling action soon saw them glided out of sight.

Kosciuszko eventually came into view as an unmistakable hump on the horizon four miles away. In summer, this mountain goes one worse than Snowdon in having a just-about motorable summer track to its summit. But winter is different and confronted with the first gradient of the day, Hugh confessed that he had forgotten to bring along the one ski wax that conditions demanded. Two hours later, the view from Kosciuszko's summit was prodigious and the only clear one I ever got in the Snowys. From here, the Main Range took on the form of an island lapped by the waves of an immeasurable forest sea, broken only by a succession of undulating snow crests that receded to a southern horizon marked by the delicate white line of the Victorian Alps. A challenging descent through powder snow, ice and 'sastrugi' confirmed my preference for Alpine skis and persuaded both of us that Townsend (2,209 metres) was better reserved for the following day.

That night at the Lake Albina Hut, nestling in a tiny glaciated cirque over-looking a frozen lake, was the coldest I ever spent on the Australian mainland. The last party to report in that evening was incredulous to learn that we were using langlauf skis in this corner of the range, but their wine flowed copiously and we were soon the firmest of mates. Next day, we woke to a blizzard of Antarctic origins that put paid to the Townsend project. Our companions urged us to stay put, but time was running out and after taking compass bearings on Thredbo, Hugh and I marched off in Indian-file through a blinding blizzard across the featureless cold pole of Australia. Benumbed by cold and deafened by the wind, we took brief refuge in the miniscule Seaman Hut noting the plaque that commemorates Laurie Seaman's death by blizzard in 1928. Five hours on, we were more than thankful to drop off the high plateau and slide gently down towards the lights of Thredbo through ghostly groves of snow gum, that most beautiful of all Alpine trees, whose bark turns through a succession of reds, browns, greens, greys and white as the season progresses. Safely returned, we learned that the Victoria Alps ski-resort of Perisher was buried under fifty feet of snow.

Our second attempt on Townsend on 25 September took the much longer and wilder approach from Guthega, but was again frustrated by bad weather. Instead, we bagged Mount Twynam, the third-highest peak in Australia, and a month later I made a solo ski ascent of Mount Carruthers after spending a night in the back of our car to ensure a dawn start. As the skiing season drew to a close, Hugh and I mothballed our skis and decided that the best way of climbing Townsend would be to do so on foot up its western spur, the longest and finest ridge in the Snowys. Involving a 1,615-metre ascent, it was only accessible from the remote Geehi Valley on the far side of the range and as we could find no record of anyone having done it before, assumed that we might bag a first.

More important matters now intervened. When Georgina gave birth to our third daughter Joanna in Canberra on 7 October 1970, we had already taken the difficult decision to return to England for good at the end of that year. Australia had opened up brilliant new horizons, but our British roots were too deeply embedded to change allegiance forever. It was therefore agreed that Georgina and our three daughters would take the slow-boat back to England via South Africa in November while I would fly back in advance to find gainful employment. My *quid pro quo* was a week's stopover in New Zealand to climb Mount Cook.

I had already heard a lot about Mount Cook from Richard Brooke who had climbed its equally impressive neighbour Mount Tasman twenty years before. Fritz Stammberger, a former Austrian guide who ran Canberra's only skiing and mountain equipment shop and had himself climbed extensively in the Mount Cook National Park, was pessimistic about my chances.

'The whole area gets the most bloody awful weather with storms that can last for weeks, particularly in November which is when you're going to be there. That's far too early in the season and to allow only a week is ridiculous! You'd be darned lucky just to get up Footstool.'

My climbing ambitions were beginning to look like a poor excuse for making the 3,000-mile detour to New Zealand, though of more immediate concern was my level of fitness. Neither the odd rock climb on the nearby Boroomba Rocks, where a profusion of 100-metre granite routes made it a popular venue for rock-jocks of the Australian National University's Mountaineering Club, nor cycling to work (then regarded as a Pommie novelty and ridiculed by red-blooded Aussies) was enough to get me into shape. And so, for my last Australian venture, I suggested to Hugh that we bring forward the Townsend spur project. The logistics of this trip were complicated because the only weekend Hugh could manage happened to be my last in Australia and coincided with the date when my family were sailing from Sydney – Friday 13 November 1970.

If that date augured ill, worse was to come when Hugh pulled out at the eleventh hour. His place was taken by Terry Birtles, the head of the CCAE's geography department, but otherwise an unknown quantity. Having driven 170 miles to Sydney on Friday morning to see Georgina and the girls safely on board *SS Akaroa*, I returned to Canberra that same night and early the next morning picked up Birtles to drive another 150 miles to the far side of the Snowys. This 500-mile trip left me completely drained physically and emotionally.

The weather, which had been very unsettled all day, was fast deteriorating when we reached what we took to be a road head. Terry now suggested that the sensible thing would be to return to Canberra 'without any further messing around'. However, at that very moment, the clouds lifted to reveal the

Townsend Spur for the first time. Facing us squarely on the opposite side of the Geehi Valley, it emerged from dark-hued forest skirts and then, like some irresistible force of nature, surged upwards in a series of giant steps before vanishing into the mists above the snowline.

'Good grief Terry, just take a look at that!' I burst out. 'What a challenge! We can't let this one go. The Geehi River can't be more than 300 metres below us. If we move fast, we can reach it in half an hour and then cross the river by the footbridge shown on your map before following the track up to the abandoned Snowy Mountains Scheme camp. If we make a dawn start tomorrow, we could be up and down the mountain by nightfall and be back in Canberra by Monday morning!'

Terry nodded resignedly and folded away his map.

Terry was a distinguished geographer, but neither of us had made any allowance for the regenerative qualities of the Australian Bush, which had completely obliterated the old Snowy Mountain Scheme tracks. He was certainly plucky, but his shortcomings as a bushwhacker and his outrageously large rucksack, which snagged every giant tree fern that crossed our path, meant that the descent to the river took an hour and a half. Where the map marked a footbridge, all that remained was a faded wooden sign 'Danger! One person to cross at a time only!' We waded thigh-deep across the ice-cold Geehi, but could find no vestige of a path on the other side where dense thickets of peppermint, red stringy bark and alpine ash overshadowed matted undergrowth as impenetrable as anything in the Stirlings. As dusk closed in and the rain belted down I sounded the retreat.

The fun had only just begun. Swelled by the rain, recrossing the Geehi without a rope proved extremely hazardous and Terry was almost swept away by the current. No moon was visible and when night fell black as pitch, neither of our torches were working. With water deluging down from all angles, the slope descended earlier that day became almost un-climbable. Soaked through and miserable, Terry had been flagging even before he sat down for a breather on a nest of soldier ants. When they started to bite, he leapt up with a yell and then trod on a venomous snake. The pace quickened, but near the top of the bank he slipped, sprained an ankle and managed to lose his ultra-expensive US Everest Expedition sleeping bag in the process. After removing the leeches that festooned my arms and legs, I spent my second successive night in the back of the car. When a bleary dawn came up next morning, heavy clouds obscured the Townsend Spur and the rain had turned to hail. We spent the best part of the morning searching for Terry's sleeping bag and eventually found it just short of the car. With no more talk about the Townsend spur, we then headed back to Canberra.

MOUNT COOK

New Zealand, the 'Land of the Long White Cloud', is as different geographically from Australia as any country could be. When Polynesian seafarers first discovered this green oasis in the wilderness of the Southern Ocean a thousand years ago, it was as close to an earthly paradise as existed. Its age of innocence ended abruptly with the coming of the Europeans who felled the primeval forest for sheep runs and imported a ragbag of alien fauna including rats, foxes and deer which consigned to oblivion its unique range of indigenous flightless birds and irrevocably altered the balance of nature. Despite this fatal impact, the Southern Alps of New Zealand remain one of the world's least spoilt natural wonders with mountains that rival those of the European Alps and the biggest glaciers in the world outside Central Asia and the polar regions.

I had always intended to see this mountaineering Eden for myself before leaving the Antipodes, but from everything I had been told about Mount Cook, the prospect of climbing it seemed infinitely remote. Nonetheless, on 21 November 1970, exactly six days after the Townsend spur debacle, my plane was approaching New Zealand's west coast when Mount Cook's mile-long triple-summit ridge thrust itself through the clouds as if to confirm its Maori name Aorangi – 'The Cloud Piercer'. This tremendous sight moved even the Queenslander sitting beside me to stare in wonder. He soon recovered his composure and assured me that there were higher mountains in his native Australia.

Richard Brooke had prepared my way in New Zealand with an introduction to Mike and Dot White who invited me to stay with them in Christchurch. That night, Mike, a member of Hillary's Antarctic Expedition to Mount Herschel, opened the doors to New Zealand's climbing fraternity by having Jim Wilson, another Antarctic and Himalayan veteran and author of a Mount Cook monograph, *Aorangi,* to supper. After dining off Canterbury lamb, slides were produced, climbs relived and a congenial evening spent by all. Neither Mike nor Jim were starters for Mount Cook and Jim's frank assessment of my chances of climbing it merely confirmed that of Fritz Stammberger.

To get the feel of New Zealand's mountains, the following day Mike generously offered to introduce me to the Arthur's Pass National Park which is only ninety miles from Christchurch and offers genuine alpine routes within a day.

But then, New Zealand is full of surprises. Its South Island alone has six major national parks and the 240,000-acre Arthur's Pass established in 1901 predates the first British national park by over fifty years. The initial drive across the bone-dry Canterbury Plains bore no resemblance to the lush pastures of Kent and gave way to skeletal eastern foothills in the rain-shadow of the Southern Alps that had more in common with the steppes of Anatolia. But on rounding a bend in the road above the Waimakiriri River, a tableau of heavily forested ridges of southern beech backed by a classic alpine mountainscape of shapely peaks and glittering snowfields burst into view. Our ascent of the south-east face of Mount Phipps took the style of a minor alpine climb in Scottish spring conditions and through gaps in the baggy clouds, there were tantalising glimpses of the park's wilderness area and Mount Rolleston, the monarch of the park and source of three glaciers. Amazingly, we were back in Christchurch in time for supper that same evening.

Early next morning, I caught the first bus from Christchurch to the Mount Cook National Park. After crossing the desiccated Mackenzie Country (named after a cattle rustler, the Kiwi equivalent of Ned Kelly) the bus juddered to a halt on the shores of Lake Pukaki. At this mandatory tourist stop, everyone piled out to photograph the colossus that is Mount Cook. Although only 3,764 metres high, it rises almost 3,000 metres clear of the lake's shimmering waters, making its vertical scale comparable with that of Mont Blanc. It was a breath-catching sight and an irresistible challenge to adventure.

Seven hours after leaving Christchurch, I was installed in the New Zealand Alpine Club's Unwin Hut in the heart of the 173,000-acre Mount Cook National Park, a UNESCO World Heritage Site which has within it seventy-two named glaciers and a clutch of superb mountains. Not a cloud flawed the sky, yet the hut was deserted save for its guardian. When I asked if he knew of anyone I might climb with, he eyed me suspiciously and said: 'No, mate, you've come much too early!' and then went about his business. To confirm the truth of this, I walked three-miles down to the Hermitage whose early history is interwoven with the birth of New Zealand mountaineering as the headquarters of that tough breed of Kiwi guides – Adamson, Fyfe, Clarke, the Grahams, Williams and Bowie. The original Hermitage Hotel was destroyed by a flood in 1913 and its replacement by a disastrous fire in 1957. Since rebuilt as a luxury hotel catering for intercontinental tourists, within its bowels was housed the offices of Alpine Instruction Ltd, a guiding, instruction and mountain-rescue outfit run jointly by a charming Kiwi, Lynn Crawford, and an ex-Yorkshire, Himalayan and Andean veteran Peter Farrell. Both were household names in New Zealand climbing circles having made the first ascent of Mount Cook's notorious east face in 1961.

'You've come at just the right time – at least in one respect,' said Crawford. 'There's been an unprecedented spell of settled weather for the past fortnight which has enabled four of our mates to make first ascents of Cook's *Caroline Face*. Unfortunately, I doubt that you'll find anyone else around to climb with as it's too early in the season. So far as I'm aware, the only people left on the mountain are the boys just about to finish our aspirant guides course. They've already climbed almost everything on their programme and will be coming down tomorrow. Just on the off chance, I'll give Pete a buzz on the walkie-talkie this evening to see if anyone's interested in joining up, though I doubt it. Your best bet would be to get up to the Ball Hut tomorrow to meet them for yourself. But I must warn you that this good weather's bound to break soon and when it does you'd best be safely grounded down here.'

What was it about Mount Cook's weather? The problem lies in the prevailing winds that blow from out the hot heart of Australia and which, while crossing the Tasman Sea, become saturated with moisture. On hitting their first obstacle in 1,400 miles – usually Mount Cook – the impact produces an annual precipitation of 300 inches and a pattern of spring and summer storms that defeated the attempts of the early pioneers and countless others since. It seemed that my luck had already run out, but having come this far I was determined to chance it so bought four days' food in the Hermitage village and then wandered back to the empty Unwin Hut wondering why I was here and what it was all costing.

The weather was still holding next morning. To save myself the ten-mile trek to the Ball Hut, I joined a busload of American tourists come to ogle at the eighteen-mile-long Tasman glacier. The hut itself was deserted and as the sun rose ever higher into a cloudless sky, I stared down on to this enormous glacier and wondered gloomily whether this really was the last of the good weather. Just after noon, my married man's ennui was interrupted by the breathless arrival at the hut of a posse of vibrant young aspirant guides, exultant at having climbed Cook, Tasman and much else besides.

'I got Lynn's message all right, John,' said their instructor, Farrell, 'but I doubt if I can help. This lot have just finished a great course and will want to get straight home. We've had a fantastic spell of good weather, but it's not going to last.'

I felt ridiculous and spare; a pallid Pom sitting awkwardly on his own like a lemon while these bronzed, laughing young Kiwis were noisily reliving the adventures of the past ten days.

Over a snatched bite of lunch, Farrell interrupted the chat and glanced over in my direction.

'John here is looking for someone to climb Cook with. Gather he's climbed a bit and has brought up plenty of food. I reckon that there's still one more day of good weather left. Anyone interested in joining him?'

The room went silent. Where was the drum roll that would call one of these heroes to arms? I shrank into the back of my chair as the seconds passed like minutes. Was my great adventure in danger of deteriorating into farce? And then, at last, someone at the back of the hut cleared his throat and said, 'Okay Pete, I'll give it a go. But I don't know anything about this bloke and he doesn't seem to have brought that much climbing gear with him.'

It was a Wagnerian moment. The speaker, Mike Browne, was sitting apart from the rest. Apparently, he had missed out on the mass ascent of Cook because his climbing companion had twisted an ankle. Save for Mike subsequently disclosing that he was reading zoology at Christchurch's Canterbury University, his character was to remain an enigma to me but his motivation was transparent. Farrell agreed to make good my lack of equipment with the apparently 'indispensible' north-wall hammer. His last words were:

'Good luck John. Mike's a good goer. But to reach the Plateau Hut tonight, you'll have to move bloody fast up the Haast Ridge. Above all, don't take any chances with the weather.'

Browne and I left the Ball Hut at precisely 2 p.m. After dropping down on to the Tasman Glacier, the problem was how to get off it again in order to reach the foot of the Haast Ridge. A century before, the glacier's lip ran higher than the Ball Hut, but had since shrunk sixty metres below the lateral moraine which now took the form a near-vertical wall of stones embedded in detritus. I was already beginning to regret my comradely gesture of agreeing to carry all the food when Browne tackled this by cutting steps up it without bothering to rope-up. At the top of the moraine, he turned to me with the glimmer of a smile, 'Bad place this. It's where a lot of them come off!'

Save for Browne's occasional silhouette high on the ridge above, I saw nothing more of him for the next three hours. The Haast Ridge was unlike anything I had encountered in the European Alps. The semblance of a path up mostly rotten rock cunningly concealed two vicious indigenous growths: the prickly bush lawyer and fighting Spaniard, both of whose spines can lance your fingers at the touch. Staggering into the King Memorial Hut four and a half hours after leaving the Ball Hut, I found Browne waiting for me in the doorway with ill-concealed Kiwi satisfaction at the sight of abject Pom discomfiture. I would have given good money to stay put there for the night, but as we were already one and a half hours ahead of guidebook time, Browne insisted that we bash on after filling me up with mugs of hot tea. We reached the Plateau Hut three and a half hours later long after dark and had to cut ice steps up the last fifty metres to the doorway.

To Browne's surprise, the hut was already occupied by the Horsley Brothers jubilant at having just completed the grand traverse of Mount Cook's triple summit. Any ascent of Mount Cook has something of a cachet, not so much because of the standard route's technical difficulties, but on account of its weather and the frequency of avalanches. In 1882, the Reverend W.S. Green had travelled round the world to climb it with his guide Ulrich Kaufmann and the Swiss hotelier Emil Boss only to have the prize snatched from them by a terrific storm when only sixty metres from the summit. Twelve years later, on Christmas Day 1894, the New Zealanders Fyfe, Graham and Clarke made the mountain's first ascent, just forestalling Edward FitzGerald and his Swiss guide Matthias Zurbriggen.

There are harder modern climbs on Mount Cook than the grand traverse, but it remains the mountain's blue riband and was first achieved by the English-born, Australian-nurtured Freda du Faur with her New Zealand guides Graham and Thomson. Freda, who championed female mountaineering and emancipation throughout her life, was the first person to climb all five of New Zealand's highest peaks during four remarkable seasons in the Southern Alps. The First World War put an end to her brilliant climbing career and the premature death of devoted partner Muriel Cadogan unhinged her. In 1935 she committed suicide aged fifty-three. Seventy-one years later in 2006, a group of New Zealand climbers placed a memorial stone over her unmarked grave at Manly Cemetery, Sydney to commemorate one of the most outstanding woman mountaineers of any age.

Freda had done her traverse without crampons. The Horsleys had taken a lot longer; had been forced to bivouac en route and lost both a rope and a rucksack. Regaled over supper with their epic, I was just about to turn in when the normally monosyllabic Browne said: 'Yer know John, if we've a cat's chance in hell of climbing Cook before the weather breaks, we'd better get going early!'

'What do you mean by *early*, Mike?'

'Like one o'clock tomorrow morning, mate. That's the only time when the Linda Glacier will be in condition.'

Was he being serious? I was still feeling shattered after that ghastly hut march and to carry straight on seemed like complete lunacy. However, when the Horsleys confirmed Brown's weather forecast, it seemed that the Reverand Green's original Linda Route might be an even bet notwithstanding the Linda's bad reputation for ice avalanches. Anyway, according to Mike, it was now back in fashion.

As I lay sleepless on my bunk awaiting the dread 1 a.m. reveille, my thoughts were concentrated on the prospect of climbing over 1,200 metres with a man I didn't know, without a guidebook or map and up a mountain which, up to 1950, had only been climbed by seventy other parties. Munching our way silently through a Kiwi-style breakfast of fruit, cereal, omelette, bread, butter, jam and coffee, whatever Mike might have been thinking about this Pommie bastard, he kept to himself. Just as we were leaving, he broke silence to quiz me on my knowledge of ice belays and prusik loops, a standard aid for crevasse rescue. Fifteen minutes out, his worst suspicions were confirmed when I admitted to having forgotten my camera.

We eventually got started at 2.50 a.m. and promptly blundered into a maze of crevasses after straying on to the wrong side of the Linda Glacier. By dawn, I was breathing hard but going strong. High up on the Linda, the sun brought down a shower of ice blocks, which we avoided with some Phil Bennett-quality side-stepping. An exposed traverse along a fragile snow-shelf led across to the north-east ridge and then on to the 120-metre rock-band that guards the summit. Once above this key passage, I sensed that nothing could stop us and as we cramponed up Mount Cook's ice dome, shoulder to shoulder, my heart was singing. At 8.25 a.m. on 25 November, my fifth day in New Zealand, we were shaking hands on the summit of Mount Cook. The climb had taken only five and a half hours and we almost seemed to have floated up the mountain. Now, on the apex of some gigantic bow, the curvature of the earth was clearly visible to both north and south, as the snowfields, peaks and glaciers of the Southern Alps stretched away to infinity.

Return to earth down the rock band required constant care. When Mike's progress unexpectedly dropped to a crawl, I tried to force the pace; slipped momentarily on the ice and, on checking myself, was seized by the darker side of the mountain's awesome personality. Throughout the remainder of that plunging descent, the sight of Mount Tasman's hanging glaciers, falling tier upon tier like the layers of some monstrous wedding cake to the bottom of a dizzy gulf, held me mesmerised. Once off the ridge the pressure eased, though the effort of keeping up with Mike as he bulldozed his way beneath the Linda's tottering séracs, seemingly oblivious to ice fall or avalanche, was

37

37 Mount Kenya 1963. Midget Peak after the storm.
38 Mount Kenya 1963. Two Tarn Lake with Midget Peak and Point John.
39 Mount Kenya 1963. The Darwin Glacier beneath Nelion. **Photo**: Hamish McNish.

40 Mount Kenya 1963. Retreat from Nelion. **Photo:** Hamish McNish.
41 Kenya 1963. At Two Tarn Hut. L–R: Jane Fenton, Hamish McNish and author.
42 Ruwenzori 1964. Approach march through Jabberwocky Forest. John Blacker.

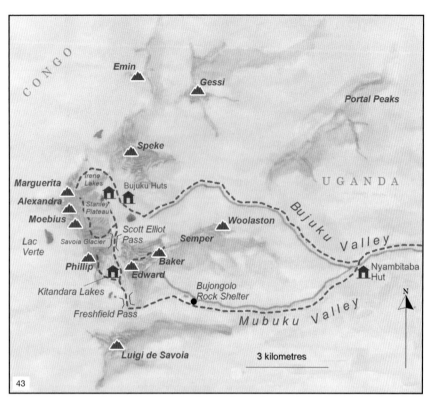

43 Ruwenzori.
44 Ruwenzori 1964. Mount Baker from Bajuku huts.

45 Ruwenzori 1964. Descent from Margherita.
46 Ruwenzori 1964. Margherita from Alexandra. John Blacker.
47 Ruwenzori 1964. Coronation Group. Savoia Glacier and Philip.

48 Hakkiari, 1965. Approach march. Ferech leads the way to the Cilo Dag.
49 Hakkiari, 1965. Resko from Demirkapu Pass.
50 Hakkiari, 1965. Kurdish summer camp at Serpil Yaila.

51 Hakkiari, 1965. Kurdish family at Serpil Yaila.
52 Hakkiari, 1965. Camp at Serpil Zoma. Sat Dag in background.
53 Hakkiari, 1965. March out with Ferech. Sat Dag in background.

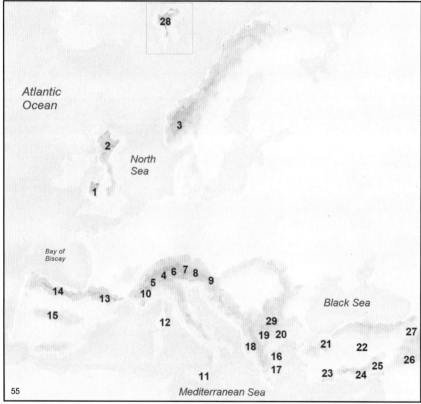

54 The Alps 1968. L–R: Rosemary Ross, Nick Allen, author and Georgina on Strahlegg Glacier.

55 Europe and Turkey – •1 Wales. Ch. 1 & 2   •2 Scottish Highlands. Ch. 1, 2, 5 & 11   •3 Jotenheim Mountains, Norway. Ch. 1   •4 Pennine Alps. Ch. 2 & 8   •5 Mont Blanc. Ch. 7, 9, 10 & 17   •6 Bernese Oberland. Ch. 7   •7 Bernina. Ch. 7   •8 Dolomites. Ch. 7   •9 Julian Alps. Ch. 17   •10 Monte Viso. Ch.17   •11 Sicily. Ch. 7   •12 Corsica. Ch. 15   •13 Pyrenees. Ch. 8 & 11   •14 Cordillera Cantabrica: Picos de Europa, Fuentes Carrionas, Mampodre. Ch. 11   •15 Sierra de Gredos. Ch. 11   •16 Mount Olympos. Ch. 4 & 15   •17 Parnassus and Vardousia. Ch. 16   •18 Pindus and Tymphi. Ch. 16   •19 Smolikas. Ch. 16   •20 Falakro. Ch. 16   •21 Ulu Dag. Ch. 4   •22 Erciyes Dag. Ch 4 & 6   •23 Takhtali Dag. Ch. 15   •24 Ala Dag. Ch. 4 & 13   •25 Bolkar Dag. Ch. 13   •26 Hakkiari. Ch. 4 & 6   •27 Kackar Dag. Ch. 14   •28 Spitsbergen. Ch. 15   •29 Pirin Range. Ch. 15.

56 The Alps 1968. The Schreckhorn, south-west ridge.
57 The Haute Route 1964. Tony Delafield and Rudi Kaufmann beneath the Dent d'Hérens.

58 New Zealand 1970. Mount Cook from Plateau Hut.
59 New Zealand 1970. Summit of Mount Cook. Mike Brown and author.
60 New Zealand 1970. Mount Tasman from Mount Cook.
61 New Zealand.
62 The Pyrenees 1974. Arête de Gaube on the Vignemale. John Blacker.

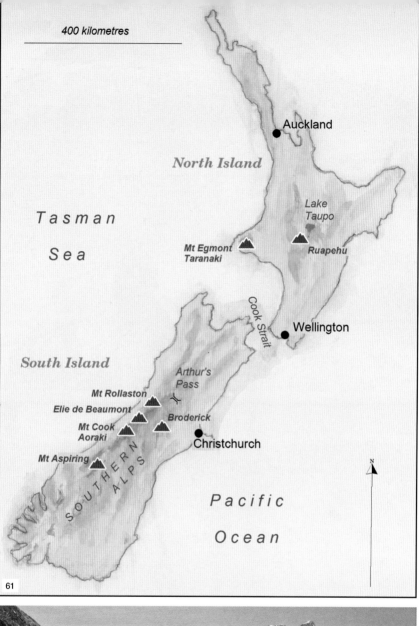

61

400 kilometres

Auckland

North Island

Tasman

Sea

Lake Taupo

Mt Egmont Taranaki

Ruapehu

Cook Strait

Wellington

South Island

Arthur's Pass

Mt Rollaston

Elie de Beaumont

Broderick

Mt Cook Aoraki

Christchurch

Mt Aspiring

SOUTHERN ALPS

Pacific

Ocean

N

62

63

64

63 Mont Blanc 1975. L–R: Paul Stibbard, Bill Hicks, Georgina.
64 The Alps 1976. Gran Paradiso Traverse. Charlie Clarke.

65 The Alps 1976. L–R: John Longland, Charlie Clarke, Peter Mould.
66 The Alps 1979. Aiguille de Rochefort. Steve Town.
67 Scotland 1983. Highland crossing, Corrour station. Alan and Nick Wedgwood.

68 Spain 1993. Fuentes Carrionas, Cordillera Cantabrica.

69 Spain 1986. Picos de Europa. Peña Santa de Castilla. L–R: Rupert Hoare, David Seddon, Roger Childs.
70 Spain 1996. Mampodre. Peña de la Cruz. Roger Childs.

lung-blowing. But I was determined to stay with him and in the home straight leading up to the hut, matched him stride for stride as we broke the tape together at 12.45 p.m.

The round trip had taken us just over ten hours. As adrenaline levels plummeted, reaction set in. There were compelling reasons to get off Mount Cook there and then before the weather broke. Instead, Mike went to bed for the next four hours while I mooched around desultorily writing up my diary and observing a kea, the razor-beaked New Zealand mountain parrot, doing its best to destroy Mike's crampons. Sensibly enough, we spent that night at the hut before making a very early start next morning. We tore across the Grand Plateau Glacier to Cinerama Col as the sun's first rays highlighted the soaring ice ridges of Tasman and Lederfield and the 1,800-metre-high *Caroline Face* which had first been climbed earlier that month. And now, as the sky became blurred with ominous clouds, a race to beat the weather encouraged an unhealthy spirit of competition to speed that final descent. Finishing strongly across the Ball Glacier, I just pipped Mike back to the Ball Hut. That same evening, we took a farewell drink off Lynn Crawford at the Hermitage's Tavern Bar now reserved for the hotel's staff, roadmen, climbers and the like, and then celebrated our various successes with the Horsley Brothers for a slap-up supper in the more convivial Glencoe Lodge.

Mike Browne and I were never going to be best buddies, but I respected him and we had shared a great adventure together. Four years later, he moved across to the west side of the Mount Cook National Park and became a founder member of the New Zealand Mountain Guides Association. With his wife Carrol, he subsequently established Fox Glacier Guiding, which today employs over sixty staff with an open invitation to 'experience our friendliness and hospitality for yourself'.

Back at Christchurch the following evening, Jim Wilson suggested that as my Kiwi finale, we have a crack at Mount Rollaston's Otira Face, 'the best route on the mountain'. Next morning saw us slogging up its sopping-wet glacier in rain and sleet under a blanket of mist with Jim wearing tennis shoes to save his leather climbing boots for the climb proper. At the start of the day, I had no idea what the route involved and was little the wiser at the end of it, though for the record, the vertical interval from Arthur's Pass to Rollaston's 2,272-metre summit is 1,340 metres of which half was on relatively sound, if greasy, rock and the ascent took six hours. Soaked through and shivering, we tucked into sausages, eggs, and salad drenched in mayonnaise under an overhanging rock before making a speedy descent down the glacier as the nor'westerlies began to blow up for something special. Back in time that evening for one of Dot White's sumptuous high teas, I marvelled at my luck with the weather and the hospitality of my New Zealand friends. The following day, I boarded the plane back to England to face a dank December and an uncertain future.

8

MIXED FORTUNES

In his book *Seasons in the Sun: The Battle for Britain, 1974–1979,* Dominic Sandbrook describes the 1970s as Britain's economic, political and cultural nadir. The shrinking value of sterling; the stagnation of a once vibrant economy; the decline of manufacturing industry in thrall to union militancy; miners strikes; carnage in Northern Ireland, and a catalogue of other national disasters faintly reflected my own family's fortunes during the early years of that troubled decade. When I flew back from Australia in December 1970 to our cramped flat in South Kensington to prepare the ground for their return, my first task was to find gainful employment. The sunlit days of Canberra were now replaced by the grey skies of a London whose streets were filled with mounds of rotting rubbish caused by the dustmen's strike. Readaptation to a demoralised Britain after sixteen months of easy living in the 'lucky country' determined that I must at last settle down to forge a respectable career as a solicitor. Experimental spells with law firms in the West End, Cheltenham, the West End again, and then Brecon, reflected my own uncertainties and the alarming gulf in quality that separated British law practices.

It took me two and a half years to find the right niche. Yet I shall always be grateful for my time with Tackley, Fall & Read of Wimpole Street under the aegis of the firm's senior partner, John Mather, a fine lawyer, an inspiring mentor and a sympathetic guide whose indulgence (and Georgina's) allowed me a week's mountaineering holiday in September 1971. My companion was Michael Baker whom I had first met earlier that year climbing in Derbyshire. Michael, a thrusting young barrister, a former president of the Oxford University

Mountaineering Club and shortly to become an outstanding honorary secretary of the Alpine Club, had already chalked up some fine Alpine routes. As a member of the Ullswater Foot Hounds, he kept himself disgustingly fit chasing foxes up and down the Lakeland fells. When he suggested that we do a short alpine season together based in Zermatt, I stifled any feelings of married man's guilt without realising what I was letting myself in for.

As was then customary, we travelled out to Zermatt by rail, sitting up overnight. Michael wanted to climb as many peaks as possible in the shortest possible time so after booking in at Paula Biner's Bahnhof Gasthaus, we caught the train to Riffelalp that same afternoon and five and a half hours later were ensconced in the Betemps Hut at the foot of Monte Rosa. Without drawing breath, the following day we attempted the classic traverse of the twin 4,000-metre peaks of Pollux and Castor. On the summit of Pollux, I had a dreadful headache and couldn't stop vomiting. To my relief, Michael agreed to abandon Castor and we made tracks back to the hut.

'Tell you what', said Michael over supper that evening. 'We're now well placed to have a crack at either the *Cresta Rey* on Monte Rosa or the *Lyskamm traverse* – maybe both if the weather holds.'

I was less enthusiastic.

At 2 a.m. next morning, the din of rain beating down on the hut's roof never sounded better. I rolled over and slept soundly until dawn. Daylight confirmed the wisdom of that decision. Yesterday, the peaks had been bare of snow: now they were plastered in the stuff. Immediately after breakfast, the hut's other occupants sensibly retreated to Zermatt leaving Michael and I to mooch around arguing the toss. At midday, Michael reluctantly agreed that we should do the same and then led the way down the moraines to Zermatt at a furious pace, kicking up clouds of dust in his wake.

The last time I had stayed at Zermatt was in 1964 just before Tony Delafield and I launched out on the Haute Route. In the intervening six years, new buildings had sprung up everywhere; few climbers were in evidence and the shops were already stuffed with skiing equipment for the winter season. Bulky clouds obscured the high mountains and when Michael suggested that we should abandon Zermatt and go rock climbing in the Karwendal instead, I wondered whether my journey had been worth it. Both disgruntled to greater or lesser degrees, we wandered off on our own separate ways to reappraise the situation.

Back at the Bahnhof that evening, the mood lightened when Paula suggested that we should have a shot at the *Rimpfischhorn* traverse.

'The weather's about to clear. It's a lovely climb in good conditions. But you must be careful when descending the North Ridge. It will be tricky now with the rocks covered in snow.'

Next day, we bashed up to Flualp where a hippy-type guardian named Taugwalder was having his work cut out to feed a boisterous group of chamois hunters. When he flatly refused to give us a 3 a.m. wake-up call with it being 'too cold at this time of year' we doubted that he could possibly have been related to 'Old' Peter Taugwalder, the Zermatt guide falsely accused of cutting the rope during Whymper's disastrous descent from the Matterhorn in 1865.

At 4 a.m. next morning, we stole out of the hut into a thick mist that totally obscured the route we had carefully reconnoitred the previous evening. Gradually, it melted away to reveal the great ring of Zermatt's peaks lifting their heads from out of a cloud-sea that blanketed the valley below. It took four hours to reach the Rimpfischorn's summit, but as Paula had forecast, the North Ridge was smothered in snow. A premature descent off the ridge necessitating a tiring re-mount was followed by an over-cautious abseil complicated by a cats-cradle of tangled ropes and karabiners. The first serious pitch presented itself as the heavily iced-up Grande Gendarme. I wanted to take it direct; Michael preferred to turn it. The compromise involved a time-consuming top-roped descent which landed us on the mountain's north-east face and a paralysingly cold traverse across its snow-covered rocks which taught me the lesson of never wearing permeable leather gloves in fresh snow: mine had frozen solid. We made it back to the Bahnhof in double-quick time to find Paula distraught at the death of one of her guests, a young Irish climber, who had been killed earlier that day while abseiling off the Obergabelhorn.

With only three climbing days left, Michael was determined to bag a couple more classic routes before calling time.

'How d'you fancy our chances on Monte Rosa's *Cresta Rey*, Paula?'

'I don't see why not,' she replied. 'It's a splendid route on excellent rock which takes you direct to the Dufourspitze. The forecast is for more fine weather and most of the recent snow should have melted by now.'

For the second time that week, we flogged up to the Betemps Hut and at 4.30 a.m. the following morning were grinding up the Grenz glacier. After overtaking one guided party to Michael's obvious satisfaction, we managed to fall through two small crevasses before reaching the base of the ridge. In spite of a minor route-finding disagreement as to where the climb actually began, the Cresta Rey's clean, dry rock yielded gracefully all the way to Switzerland's highest summit, the Dufourspitze. Here, a beaming Michael seized my hand.

'Good going that. The guidebook allowed three to four hours for that climb. We've done it in little more than two!'

Back at the Betemps Hut, I would happily have left things at that. A surfeit of moraine bashes, glacier flogs and galloping descents to Zermatt had left my feet a mess of blisters. Michael, on the other hand, was only just getting into his stride.

'We're now perfectly positioned for the *Lyskamm traverse*,' he announced that evening.

'According to Marcel Kurz, it's an even better climb than the *Norman Neruda* route on the face – and safer too. In fact, the guidebook rates it as 'one of the finest ridge traverses in the Alps!'

A succession of noisy parties arriving throughout the night made sleep impossible and as the dark hours dragged by, the challenge of the *Lyskamm traverse* assumed ever more fantastic proportions in my fevered imagination.

Although the hut's guardian again failed to wake us at the appointed hour, we got away an easy first and stumped off into the night with our head torches cutting a swath through the darkness. After dropping down on to the heavily crevassed Grenz glacier, Michael realised that he had forgotten his prussic loops, so I gave him a couple of mine. The day's crevasse fall-through tally eventually ended up as Baker four: Harding one. Yesterday's climb had been cold but bearable. Today, it was so cold that I lost all feeling in my left hand. I was also feeling weak from diarrhoea even before we breasted the Lysjoch where the climb proper begins. Dead ahead, the Lyskamm's south-east ridge reared up like a ship's prow, steep and sharp. It was also heavily corniced and overlooked the mountain's stupendous north-east face, festooned with ice cliffs and plunging 800 metres to the Grenz Glacier. Michael glanced at it and observed drily, 'That's the *Norman Neruda* route okay!'

I could never catch Michael in descent, but we were reasonably well matched in ascent. However, this time he attacked the ridge as if he had more to prove than just leaving me in his slipstream. We reached the Lyskamm's 4,527-metre summit in half the guidebook time, but the effort of climbing 1,760 metres almost nonstop since leaving the hut left me gasping. Even so, apart from one route-finding hiccup, the long descending traverse of the Lyskamm's north-west ridge went smoothly enough. Our real troubles began on reaching the Grenz Glacier where the route's character changed abruptly. What had been a day of brilliant sunshine now turned to darkest shadow even though, having narrowly avoided frostbite on the ridge, I now felt uncomfortably warm.

From here, the hut wasn't that far away, but to reach it meant having to cross the glacier at its most chaotic. Once again, our somewhat different approaches to mountain craft led to a disagreement about tactics. Michael's insistence that the guidebook directions must be right reflected his rigorous textbook training. My more *laissez-faire* approach favoured the ski-map's route down the middle of the glacier. In fact, there was no obvious way to the hut and the issue was left unresolved until my chosen 'path' became blocked by avalanche debris that had peeled off the ice cliffs above only minutes before. At this, Michael exploded.

'This can't possibly be right. This bloody route is typical of your fatalistic attitude. It's quite obvious that you don't play bridge.'

'Actually, I do, though only under pressure,' I replied, trying to jolly things along. 'But I can assure you that I'm quite as keen as you to get shot of this ghastly glacier.'

Silently now, keeping our thoughts to ourselves, we wandered from side to side of the glacier edging through its labyrinth of yawning lateral crevasses and teetering séracs that seemed to have assumed grotesque, animalistic forms. I had almost begun to despair that we would ever find our way out of this horrendous maze when we chanced on an escape runnel down the middle of the glacier. Michael graciously conceded that I might have won a trick, but neither of us were minded to spend another night at the Betemps Hut. I was well into my third beer when Michael took off like a rocket for Zermatt. I saw little of him until the Riffelberg where an importunate American's misreading of the railway timetable lost us the last train down from Gornergrat. Stumbling and cursing all the way down the path as dusk turned to night, Paula Biner's mugs of sweet tea at the end of that seventeen-hour day restored my faith in humankind. Michael had decided to stay on awhile in Zermatt and our slap-up, farewell supper at the Hotel Derby that evening restored good humour, amity and camaraderie. 'After all,' said Michael. 'We did knock off four respectable routes in seven days.'

It was another four years before I returned to the Alps, mainly as a consequence of some unfortunate career decisions. Of these, that of swapping the certainties of John Mather's estimable law practice for the speculative prospects offered by Major Howard Llewellyn MC, sole partner and practitioner of his eponymous solicitors firm in Brecon, was undoubtedly the worst. Brecon was a country town that had changed little since its medieval heyday and its xenophobic tribal politics matched anything I had experienced in South Arabia.

I had imprudently burned our London boats by buying 'County House', a handsome Grade II listed Queen Anne townhouse which had, until our purchase, been the lodgings for the judges of the recently defunct Breconshire Assizes. Soon to discover that in Brecon you were either 'in or out', we remained irredeemably 'out' and as Howard's assistant I was earning less than the local postman.

Howard, a brave soldier, was a doughty advocate in the Rumpole-mould, but his other qualities might better have suited service with Captain Henry Morgan on the Spanish Main. By challenging the morals of local dignatories in public and the mores of Howard's practice in private, I played a bad hand. After only a couple of months, I realised that I had made a ghastly career mistake so began looking for employment elsewhere. Now aged thirty-nine, with little to offer save a bewilderingly variegated CV, I was lucky to get an interview with the City of London law firm Norton Rose Botterell & Roche. When the firm's senior partner closed my interview by asking whether the firm might have the privilege of getting six-weeks' work out of me before I moved on, I assumed I had blown it. Just before leaving the firm's offices, its administrator Dick Clifford, a former Tanganyika District Commissioner, took me aside: 'Let me give you a spot of advice, John. If they make you an offer, at whatever the salary – take it!'

I took it.

Joining Norton Rose in 1973 marked the start of a legal career that took me to retirement. Even so, the Brecon imbroglio came at a high price. I had put several local noses out of joint including that of the High Sheriff, the town's leading estate agent and when I instructed another firm to sell County House, he made sure that its sale took another three years to materialise. During that time I commuted weekly between Brecon and London leaving Georgina to cope with our three small children. Nonetheless, by 1974 we were sufficiently secure financially to embark on the first of several Cairngorm Easter family skiing holidays as guests of the skiing-mad Macphersons and that same summer Georgina and I also decided to break new ground with a holiday in the Pyrenees. This was inspired by Robin Fedden's *The Enchanted Mountains*, which describes, in gem-like prose, the three Pyrenean climbing seasons that he, his wife Renee and Basil Goodfellow made during the 1950s. Our choice was sealed by Bill Wade's recommendation.

Bill had been my tutor at Trinity. His Olympian intellect and lucidity of expression reduced the most abstruse legal complexities to comprehensibility.

However, I never expected that our relationship would survive after I had the gall to ask him if he could give me some insight into the mind of the examiner of the real property paper in my final Tripos examination. He made it clear that not only was he setting and marking the paper, but would pay particular attention to mine. Thirteen years later, I bumped into Bill at the Alpine Club's annual dinner at the Cafe Royal having just flown in from New Zealand flushed with my triumph on Mount Cook. I expected the cold shoulder, but he greeted me like an old friend and so we remained for the rest of his life. Professor Sir William Wade, Master of Gonville and Caius College (as he became) was a connoisseur of mountain ranges worldwide, yet the Pyrenees remained dearest to his heart and he rated its yellow liqueurs as highly as those of Chartreuse.

Our Pyrenean venture kicked off on 1 June 1974 when John Blacker, Sarah Wood, Georgina and I disembarked at Bilbao and squeezed into John's battered Land Rover. It was seven years since John and I had last climbed together and four since Sarah and I had trekked in the Elburz. At this time, Spain was still in General Franco's iron grip. The streets smelt, the atmosphere was oppressive and at one of our camps we were arrested at gunpoint by the Gardia Civile. Beyond Pamplona, the baking heat, shrivelled vegetation, and eroded mesas of the southern foothills of the Pyrenees reminded me of the Yemen. From our first campsite at Torla, we trekked through the pine and beech forest of the magnificent Ordesa Canyon to the sunlit alpine meadows at its head where we had planned to spend a night at the Goriz Refuge prior to climbing Mont Perdu, the 'Lost Mountain'. That trek had a dreamlike quality, but we came to earth on finding that the newly built Goriz Refuge had not yet opened for the season.

The only alternative was a broken-down *cabana* lacking either table or chairs with rough boards for bunks and its mud-floor littered with empty cans, broken bottles, and rotting food. From an adjoining lean-to, the stench of excreta was overpowering. Sarah opted to share John's one-man tent while Georgina and I moved into the *cabana*. Later that evening, we were joined by two young Spaniards who sang and danced the whole night through to the accompaniment of a recorder and mouth organ. The following day, using a postcard as our guide, Georgina and I climbed Mont Perdu by a snow couloir with one ice axe and a three-metre waist-loop making this her first graded climb.

A 120-kilometre, bone-shaking drive along pot-holed mountain roads led to the village of Benasque set high in the upper Esera Valley. Once a fashionable summer resort for the Aragonese nobility escaping the heat of the plains, the faded escutcheons that embellished the stone portals of their crumbling eighteenth-century mansions recalled a long-vanished age. Here too Hilaire Belloc, once a prodigious walker, had been inspired to write *Tarantella* with its 'fleas that tease in the High Pyrenees', a nostalgic paean to Belloc's lost youth when he had explored the Pyrenees from end to end and later written the range's first monograph in English.

Like Belloc, we had come to Benasque as a base from which to climb Aneto, the culminating peak of the range. In the stultifying heat of mid-afternoon, time stood still in Benasque's deserted, dusty square so we decided to move on to the *Cabana de Llosas* in the upper Vallebierna, disregarding a hirsute student from the Moray College of Further Education's remonstrances that camping was prohibited. John forced the Land Rover up the valley's boulder-strewn track until it could go no further, but the *cabana* was nothing but a heap of granite rocks piled up in the lea of a boulder roofed over with pine boughs. Its earthen floor was overlaid with dirty straw, old newspapers and plastic sheeting so Sarah again opted for John's tent. Georgina and I made do with the *cabana*.

Despite the *cabana's* fleas, the Pleta de Llosas was the most romantic campsite I can remember. A dancing meadow ran to the edge of a thinning treeline where the blanched branches of solitary dwarf pines had been clean-polished by the wind. Clusters of violet and white crocuses thrust up their heads through the retreating snows and by the banks of the infant River Llosas we bathed and washed our clothes. From high above, a skein of screes spilled down from an immense granite amphitheatre crowned by saw-tooth ridges. The place was touched by the wand of enchantment and it was here that I fell in love with the Pyrenees.

At 3,404 metres, Aneto forms the apex of the sprawling Maladeta massif. The mountain was first climbed fifty-six years after Mont Blanc, a curious fact given that it is 1,403 metres lower, but partly explained by Aneto's relative inaccessibility at a time when banditry was rife in Spain, and partly on account of Pierre Barrau. This superstitious local chamois hunter set himself up as the mountain's guardian and guide, yet believing implicitly the Maladeta's myth of inaccessibility, never pressed on to the summit. Barrau's last climb on Aneto was in 1824 when, after resolutely refusing to rope up with his French clients, he disappeared down a crevasse. His fate was seen as divine retribution by the locals and greatly enhanced the Maladeta's reputation as the 'Accursed Mountain'. Its spell was only broken in 1842 when Count de Franqueville and a Russian Imperial Army officer de Tchihatcheff climbed Aneto from the Vallebierna by the route that John and I intended to follow.

When John woke me to a cloudless dawn, I had toothache and he had diarrhoea. Nonetheless, we soon reached a high brèche on the crenelated Cresta de Llosas that overlooks the gloomy depths of the Valle de Coronas. On breaking out into the sunlight, our crampons took wings up the broad Coronas Glacier and thence to the airy Bridge of Mohammad that leads to the cross of Madonna marking Aneto's summit. To east and west, wave after wave of snow peaks stretched along the spine of the Pyrenees to the shores of the Mediterranean and Atlantic. On this lonely peak, I dreamt that one day I would traverse the entire range on ski.

To get the feel of the French Pyrenees, we crossed the range to the once fashionable resort of Cauterets where Spanish heat and sunshine were replaced by Atlantic cloud and rain. Our plan was to walk up the Val de Gaube to the Oulettes refuge from which to climb the Vignemale's *Arête de Gaube*, which Bill Wade had recommended as a classic. At 3,298 metres the Vignemale, the highest and grandest Pyrenean peak wholly in France, will forever be associated with Count Henri Russell, the French-born Irishman who climbed the mountain thirty-three times; courted it like a suitor, and consummated his bizarre union by hacking out a series of grottos from the living rock in which he spent weekends and entertained friends to dinner in evening dress.

Russell and his bosom friend Charles Packe, a landowning Lincolnshire squire, are generally credited as the first British Pyrenean pioneers. In fact, that honour falls to Anne Lister, the chatelaine of Sibden Hall, Halifax who, having narrowly missed becoming the first woman to climb Mont Blanc in 1827, forestalled the Prince of Moscow, son of Napoleon's Marshall Ney, to make the second ascent of the Vignemale by a new *Assez Difficile* route the following year. In later life, Anne took over the management of her family's famous engineering company Listers. A recent BBC documentary made much of her lesbianism, but failed to mention her exceptional achievements as a mountaineer.

Having taken on trust the *Syndicate d'Initiative's* assurances that the Oulettes Refuge would be guarded and open, we blithely set off up the Val de Gaube. On emerging from the woods below its famous lake, the huge, triangular wall of rock that closed the valley's head could only be the Vignemale's north face with our chosen arête flanking it. The Oulettes hut's guardian was *not* in residence and only the winter room open. The scenery outside was grand: the room itself mean and filthy. After scouring its one fat-congealed frying pan with twigs and snow, Georgina and Sarah knocked up a delicious supper of veal chops, mushrooms and courgettes over a smoky fire. Late that evening, two dishevelled young Frenchmen burst in. They had just climbed the *Arête de Gaube*, but had taken eleven hours for the round trip.

'Zee climb is in good condition, with three pitons in place. But we had many problems finding zee vay down the Ossoue Glacier in the mist.'

'Three pitons!' exclaimed John. 'I thought this was supposed to be a straight-forward classic climb. What's the grading of this route anyway?'

'According to the French guidebook, it's *Assez Difficile Superior*,' I replied.

'Huh!' grunted John. 'Is it now. Let's just hope there's not too much *Superior* about it.'

I hoped so too. I hadn't done a serious climb for over three years.

Early the following morning, John and I were well established on the *arête* to confront the first challenging pitch as it merged into the Vignemale's north face. I clipped a running belay into a piton and then ran out another thirty-five metres of rope which meant that John had to close up behind to find a decent belay. There wasn't one, but I climbed on anyway, first up an awkward chimney leading to slabs before veering diagonally upwards to an overhanging cleft. On reaching a tiny stance, I stopped to scan a convex bulge of rock that barred the way ahead. At my feet, the face plunged a thousand metres sheer to the Oulettes Glacier. Searching ever more frantically for the French pitons, my calves began to quiver. I was already off balance, and given John's non-existent belay, retreat from this desperate place seemed supremely unattractive, so I shouted down to him: 'I can't hang about here any longer or I'll peel off. Hold tight, I'm just having to go for it!'

I did so bald-headed knowing that if I didn't maintain momentum I'd certainly come off and we'd both end up as mash at the bottom. The intensity of that pitch remained with me for years. Back at the hut, we checked the guidebook's description and worked out that we must have been off route for the last third of the climb.

In later years, John and I shared many mountain adventures together in Greece, Turkey, Kenya, the Alps, Bhutan and Sikkim. But it was in the Pyrenees that our lifelong friendship was sealed. Late that afternoon, the four of us wandered down the Val de Gaube through meadows carpeted with wild flowers. The slopes around were garnered with azalea, gentians and orchids and with the dying sun playing on the waters of the Lac de Gaube, fishermen cast their four-metre-long rods for trout. It might have been Arcadia and indeed, in the words of Count Henri Russell it is in the Pyrenees that 'the smiles of the artist and the heart of the poet will always turn'. I could never have imagined then that five years later I would be struggling down this same valley in winter with broken skis and sticks, shocked and despairing of how I would break the news to my cousins back in England that their son Alain had been killed by an avalanche coming off the Vignemale.

9

MOUNTAINS OF PARADISE

That first Pyrenean summer holiday had changed my mountain focus and in March the following year, with my professional career with Norton Rose now assured, I returned to the range as a member of an Eagle Ski Club team led by Michael de Pret Roose and the Swiss guide Martin Epp. It was over five years since I had done any ski mountaineering and my technique showed it. The heavily indented Pyrenean terrain proved to be harder graft than the Alps and the huts were more primitive and sometimes filled with shoulder-deep snow. The weather was so unrelentingly bad that the tour had to be cut short due to avalanche risk. For all that, the wildness and remoteness of the Pyrenees in winter caught my imagination as much as in summer and I came back hooked on 'La Frontiere Sauvage'.

But I had not turned my back on the Alps and that same summer Georgina and I slipped off for a week's holiday at the entrepreneur/yachtsman Ron Amey's luxurious chalet in Les Praz de Chamonix. This indulgence was Ron's way of thanking Georgina for taking in his daughter-in-law's three young children after they had been unceremoniously dumped on our doorstep at County House, Brecon, by their distraught and depressed mother. To make up the alpine party, we invited Georgina's cousin Bill Hicks and friends Paul Stibbard and Chris Verney to join us. Only Verney had any previous alpine climbing experience.

Our first venture, a standard ascent of the Aiguille du Tour, encouraged me to lift our game to attempt the Aiguille du Plan. Halfway up, avalanche-prone snow precipitated a tactical withdrawal. As a parting shot, I then suggested we climb Mont Blanc via the Aiguille du Goûter. On the way to catching the Tramway du Mont Blanc to the Nid d'Aigle terminus, the sky had been flawless save for a tiny cloud hovering over Mont Blanc's summit. By the time we set off for the Tête Rousse Hut at the foot of the Aiguille du Goûter that innocuous cloud had got a lot bigger. In Alan Blackshaw's magisterial handbook *Mountaineering*, there is a photograph of lenticular clouds gathering over Mont Blanc with the caption 'A storm usually follows the appearance of these clouds in a matter of hours.' At the Tête Rousse, Mont Blanc was already shrouded in cloud and as peals of thunder began rolling around an agitated guardian rushed about telling everyone to get off the mountain – quick. We did just that. It was a disappointing end to the holiday, but as many have found to their cost, the lesson of Mont Blanc is never to chance your luck with its weather.

The following year, 1976, I returned to the Gran Paradiso National Park to recreate memories of the enchanted walk I had done with Mark Bicknell nineteen years before. Although Victorian members of the Alpine Club had been the first to explore the Paradiso's peaks, it had since suffered neglect from British climbers. Our party shook down to John Longland, Charlie Clarke and Peter Mould. I had known Longland ever since he burst on to the Cambridge climbing scene as a *wunderkind* who already knew everyone worth knowing in British mountaineering circles. During my first CUMC novice-climbing meet in north Wales, he literally broke the ice with a pre-breakfast dip in the Helyg stream. Self-assured and opinionated maybe, but John was also a sympathetic mentor with a profound respect for moun- taineering's traditions. On becoming the CUMC's president in 1956, he had already notched up 300 British climbs over the previous two years and during his *annus mirabilis* in 1957, he and Simon Clark, both twenty-one year- olds, led the undergraduate expedition that made the first ascent of the Andean peak Pumasillo, the highest virgin peak in the world outside Asia. John was now head of Unilever's public relations department, but the promise of youth was fading. Drinking and smoking too much, he hadn't climbed in the Alps for years. Charlie Clarke, also ex-CUMC but a generation younger, was a consultant neurologist and already a veteran of eight Himalayan expeditions including Bonington's successful 1975 Everest South-West Face expedition. Peter Mould, the party's oldest member, was a committed Christian and, like me, had served in the Colonial Service. He had half a dozen alpine seasons behind him and had put up some new routes in Greenland. Climbing together in the Lakes earlier that year, he had come across as an ambitious, if painstak- ingly methodical rock climber.

We drove out to Italy and, on 11 July 1976, pitched Longland's two Barry Bishop US Everest box tents at Pont in the Val Savaranche, a lovely alpine valley once regarded by an earlier generation of Alpine Club members as being at 'the extreme limits of Alpine civilisation'. Formerly a hunting reserve of the dukes of Savoy, it was later designated as Italy's first national park with the royal lodges converted into mountain huts. Late that afternoon, despite much puffing and wheezing from Longland, we reached the Victor Emmanuel II Refuge, which has recently been refurbished, to accommodate over a hundred guests and were promptly allocated a cosy four-bunk *salle privée*.

The particular climb on which I had set my cap was the *Paradiso/Herbetet traverse*, first accomplished by Captain J.P. Farrar DSO, the Alpine Club's president during the First World War whose list of climbs occupied seven pages in Mumm's Alpine register. The guidebook described the traverse that he and his lifelong friend and guide Daniel Maquignaz had pioneered in 1876 as 'magnificent', though even they had been forced to make one bivouac. To get ourselves into shape, the nearby peak of La Tresenta looked good for starters. Unfortunately, Longland's attempts at ingratiating himself with the guardian through the unlikely medium of Spanish left the bemused Italian with the impression that we were intending to traverse the entire Denti di Broglio/Monciair/Ciaforon chain, a feat as yet unaccomplished. To have bagged a mouse after boasting of elephants would have lost all credibility, so John assured the guardian that our real objective was the north face of the Ciaforon.

Clearly visible from the hut, this dome-shaped peak has a heavily glaciated face split by two overhanging sérac barriers. The direct route was unanimously vetoed in favour of a less heroic line which offered a convenient cop-out if things got tough. With Charlie and me shakily in the lead, the large chunk of ice we dislodged to hit John's forearm sent him and Peter scuttling over to the north-west ridge for cover. Forty-five metres of step cutting up black ice with my new and unfamiliar Horeschowsky 'North Wall' ice-hammer reduced my calves to jelly so we also chickened-out to join the others on Ciaforon's rubble-strewn summit.

On the way down, Peter shed a crampon, which would have ended up 300 metres below had it not lodged itself on a rock ledge. Our clumsy retrieval operation was witnessed by a group of marvelling Bersaglieri who lost no time reporting the episode to the guardian's wife thereby confirming her already low opinion of the braggadocio British. A face-saving ascent of the understandably 'somewhat neglected' Becca di Monciair's north-east ridge the following day did little to restore our reputation and when John incautiously disclosed our Paradiso plan and then asked the lady for a twenty-four-hour weather forecast, she gave him a dismissive shrug and jerked her head in the direction of two Italian guides propping up the bar.

Apart from us, the only other climbers who left the hut at 1.50 the next morning were a trio of Italians laden with ice screws to do battle with the Ciaforon's north face. I hadn't slept a wink thanks to weekend local carousing both inside and outside the hut throughout the night. The moon was so bright that head torches were unnecessary, yet despite yesterday's recce, the complexities of the boulder field above the hut temporarily split the party leaving Longland muttering darkly about 'someone's bloody awful route finding'. At differing speeds and by diverse routes, we cramponed up the Gran Paradiso Glacier keeping uncharitable thoughts to ourselves. The sun hit the mountain's topmost rocks just as we reached Madonna's statue silhouetting Mont Blanc like a cardboard cutout on the northern horizon. It was intensely cold and during the short traverse along the ice-encrusted ridge leading to the Gran Paradiso's true summit, Charlie dropped a glove. I held my breath as it vanished down a narrow chimney. Fortuitously, it stopped a little way down and I managed to retrieve it.

The serious part of the climb was now about to begin. I gave a low whistle as I stared down the Gran Paradiso's north north-east ridge, which curved down to the Piccolo Paradiso Col in a graceful 200-metre shark's fin of glinting ice. To our left, the Gran Paradiso's north-east face plummeted 600 metres sheer to the Paradiso Glacier. To our right a bulging, convex hump of ice overhung the Tribolazione Glacier.

'What the hell are we taking on?' I thought to myself, marvelling at the courage and daring of Farrar and Maquignaz who, exactly 100 years ago, had launched themselves down this terrifying ridge in their nailed boots with no crampons and one flimsy hemp rope. My thoughts were suddenly concentrated on my family and whether I had updated my will.

'Bloody hell Charlie, what d'you make of this one? There's damn all security. I can't see how we begin to take belays.'

When he muttered something about 'ice-axe belays' I replied, 'Okay then, we'll do it in short pitches. But if I fall, just jump over the other side and let's hope the rope jams tight on the crest.'

Of two possible ways to tackle the ridge, that of straddling it *à cheval* and cutting out bucket steps would have taken hours. The alternative was to drop down on to the Tribolazione side, face inwards and traverse crab-like under its crest relying on my crampon points to hold me on the ice. In fact, I had to choose this method anyway for I had foolishly decided to swap my long-shafted Simond ice axe for the Horeschowsky North Wall Hammer which didn't have a cutting adze and was proving difficult to grip.

'Okay. Charlie. Here I go!'

The top layer of snow was frozen solid and belays purely psychological. But I soon got into a rhythm and kept going doggedly with Charlie following close behind. On reaching the col, we stared back in silence watching John and Peter making an ultra-cautious descent, which seemed to take hours. When they eventually joined us, all four let out whoops and John shouted 'We've cracked the key passage!'

And then, without thinking, I sheathed my Horeschowsky axe into a karabiner attached to my waist-loop. The hammer end was too short to fit in securely and slipped out. As it slid across the frozen snow towards the lip of a precipice. I stared in disbelief rooted to the spot. Miraculously, it stopped within inches of the edge.

Switching leads, John and Peter now went ahead to tackle the five exposed pinnacles at mid-height that led to the Col di Montandeyne which marks the halfway point of the traverse. Without a break for eight hours, we were now well within guidebook time, but I was getting worried about a catalogue of silly mistakes – Charlie dropping his glove and Peter his snow goggles and me almost losing my ice hammer. And then, just before settling down for a quick bite, both John and I had near-fatal slips on the ice. Patently, we were losing concentration and badly needed a rest, but the short break became a long one. Swapping leads once more, I led up the sound rock of the Becca di Montandeyne's south ridge only to find that its north ridge was studded with disintegrating pinnacles that triggered stone avalanches at a touch. The slow, laboured descent to the Finestra Dzasset took hours and on reaching it I took stock.

'We'd better have a rethink of where we're going from now on.

It's already taken us sixteen hours to get this far so there's not a hope of completing the traverse before dark. It'll take three hours just to climb the Herbetet from here and at least another three to get down from there to the Leonessa Bivouac.'

'I've no intention of either bivouacking or crossing the Leonessa glacier in the dark,' said John. 'I vote that all bets for Herbert are off and that we make tracks for the Sberna Bivouac.'

The Sberna Bivouac lay on the far side of the Montandeyne Glacier still some way below, but a better bet than the Leonessa. After one false start down a potentially lethal couloir, we found a safer route from the Col Bonney down to the glacier though tiredness and timid cramping technique again slowed the pace. As we trudged through soggy, knee-deep snow in the gathering twilight, I prayed that the faint, black dot on the ridge ahead could only be the Sberna Bivouac and that it was open. It was, though had we arrived a day earlier, its five bunks would have been occupied by members of the South Wales Caving Club whose hut book entry described their ascent of the Herbetet as 'like climbing a Welsh slag heap'. A lively melt-stream coursed across the hut's wooden floor, but there was no shortage of damp blankets and Charlie generously lent me his duvet boots to help thaw my frozen feet. After a mug of soup, I went straight off to sleep. We had been nineteen hours on the trot.

From the Sberna, the quick way back to the Victor Emmanuel hut next morning cut across the Montandeyne and Laveciau Glaciers. Trying to force the pace, I fell through one crevasse and John spiked his leg doing the same while Peter needed all three of us to haul him out of a third. Back at the VE Hut, the guardian's wife didn't give us a glance, but the fat cook couldn't stop laughing when we told him that we had spent a night at the waterlogged Sberna Bivouac.

Later that afternoon, we drove round to Cogne in the Val Nontey with the aim of climbing the Grivola from the Pousset Chalets. The path from Cretaz climbed steeply past newly scythed hayfields humming with crickets before diving into a dark forest carpeted with pine needles where clouds of butterflies rose at our approach and then settled like snowflakes. The chalets, tucked away at the end of a narrow valley was a place of ghosts and on a smooth cliff-face high above, some long-forgotten Wehrmacht detachment had painted 'A Gruppe 1944'. It was raining hard when Peter's alarm went off next morning and had turned to sleet at the Col Pousset. From here, the sight of the 'Grey Lady' stripped of snow and revealing nothing but scree-strewn thighs was enough to terminate the engagement. Pounding down the Val Lauson past herds of disinterested ibex and chamois, the shrilling cries of urchins shouting 'Bravi Escalatori' spurred us on to the ice-cream parlours of Cogne.

Early on, there had been some brave talk about doing one of Mont Blanc's great South Face routes. However, when the guardian of the Val Ferrat campsite above Courmayeur warned us off climbing on the Italian side and that conditions were much better on the French, we settled for a twenty-course gastronomic Everest and 3.79 litre of chianti at La Palud's Maison de Filippo before driving through the tunnel to France. By the evening of the following day, most of the wine had been sweated out on the moraines up to the Albert Premier hut from where we planned to traverse the Aiguille du Chardonnet by the famous *Forbes Arête*. The weather had looked settled, but when the guardian failed to give a 3 a.m. reveille next morning and none of the guided parties had bothered to get up, there had to be a reason. Nothing ventured, we followed three young Frenchmen out into the night and wended cautiously past the notorious crevasses of the upper Tour Glacier.

The French had difficulties surmounting two large bergschrunds barring the icy *bosse* that marks the start of the *Forbes Arête* and while they took a break, we slipped past them and stormed the ridge. But by now, ominous clouds were welling up from the valley and just short of the Chardonnet's summit the weather closed in and the rocks began to hum with electrical charges. Peals of thunder, followed by snakes of lightning, caused pandemonium behind with the Frenchmen yelling '*Laissez l'arête! Laissez l'arête!*' We did just that, but when Charlie leapt down one side of it leaving me stranded on the other and Peter followed Charlie's suit, both ropes got jammed between the rocks. Charlie was still feeling the afterglow of the Maison de Fillipo and it needed a time-consuming exercise to unravel the ropes before the four of us could regroup below the ridge crest.

Snow was falling heavily as the French went steaming past and had vanished by the time we reached the summit. Assuming that they had continued the traverse down the West Ridge, we were stunned when another two Frenchmen emerged from the murk. Without a word they began cramponing down a narrow couloir at breakneck speed with Gallic gesticulations.

'Must be the right way,' I said to John.

'Suppose so,' he replied, looking unconvinced.

We followed on, but soon lost them. Rope-length after rope-length the couloir spiralled downwards: always steep, icy and dangerous before petering out at the lip of near-vertical wall of ice.

'Bloody hell!' I yelped, peering down into a gulf of swirling cloud. 'This can't possibly be right. We must have landed up on the North Face! Charlie – for God's sake give me a tight top-rope and I'll take a quick peek. It may not be as desperate as it looks.'

It was. But I went over anyway, front-pointing furiously inwards and bashing the pick of my north-wall hammer into the diamond-hard ice like a piston. It felt like climbing down the side of an ocean liner.

'No go, Charlie!' I shouted up at him. 'It's quite hopeless. Hold me tight. I'm coming back up.'

Squirming back over the lip huffing and panting, I was astonished to see that we had now been joined by all five Frenchmen, one of whom suggested that we form a single rope to get back to the Chardonnet's summit.

'And after that?' I asked him.

'We reverse zee arête of course! Zee only solution for zee party's *securite*!'

He might have been right, but the prospect of a multilingual rope of nine was more than EU *amité* was worth.

'Thanks for the suggestion,' I said. 'We'll follow you back to the summit, but after that we're going to complete the traverse down the West Ridge.'

He shook his head, mouthed an expletive and then shot off with his companion without another word. As the other three trailed after them, I heard one of them muttering *'Fou, fou, les Anglais. Fou, fou!'*

Back on the Chardonnet's summit at 7 p.m. we hit off the West Ridge correctly this time. Now on a single rope, I went first followed by Charlie and Peter with John bringing up the rear. Without a break for fifteen hours, blood sugar levels were falling fast and flaws in technique surfaced.

'We simply aren't going fast enough,' I kept repeating to myself and anyone else minded to listen. 'We must reach the Col Adams Reilly before it's dark.'

When Peter, seemingly in a dream, began hammering in an ice piton, my patience snapped.

'You can't possibly need that damned thing here, Peter. John's got you absolutely secure. Charlie and I must bash on to find this col before we can't see a bloody thing.'

'Agreed', said John, as if on a Sunday walk. 'Scout out the site for a snow hole. We're going to have to bivouac tonight.'

Charlie and I reached the Col Adams Reilly Superior as night fell. He was desperately tired, but cheerful as ever. I began digging frantically to excavate a snow hole but could make little impression as the snow overlaid hard ice with bedrock beneath. By 11 p.m. we had excavated a shallow trench, just as John shepherded in an exhausted Peter. I slit open my polyurethane survival bag to make a rough cover over the trench. It was too narrow to fit in all four, so bits of Charlie were left sticking outside. The night passed as such nights do: shivering, shuddering and squashed up against each other trying to find the least uncomfortable positions to stave off hypothermia and cramp. I couldn't sleep yet dared not look at my watch for fear that the passage of time had stopped.

Came a grey dawn with the clouds still low. John's hands were frost-nipped and one of my boots frozen solid. Faint shouts came wafting up from the glacier far below, so we assumed that the Frenchmen must have got down safely. After thawing out, the descent to the Tour Glacier was almost frustrated by a huge bergschrund barring the way, but once on the glacier the cloud lifted momentarily and the hut became visible on its far side.

'No problems now,' said Peter, but Charlie was sceptical.

'I don't like this damned glacier one jot. I fell into one of its bloody great crevasses only a couple of years back. We *must* keep up high, just as we did yesterday.'

'But Charlie,' protested John, 'we're very much lower down than yesterday. The hut can't be more than forty-five minutes away and there's a perfectly good line of tracks leading across it.'

I agreed with John, but Charlie remained unconvinced.

'I'm going ahead to lead this one as I'm the only silly bugger on this trip who hasn't yet fallen down a crevasse.'

Barely started, the mist came down like a blanket and the tracks disappeared. And then, without a sound, Charlie disappeared. Now you see him, now you don't. I'd given him sufficient slack and had no trouble holding him. However, when John and Peter crawled to the lip of the crevasse, they couldn't see or hear him.

'Where the hell are you, Charlie? Are you okay?' John shouted down repeatedly.

'Thanks for nothing. I'm still alive – but only just!' at last came up his sepulchral voice. 'I must have knocked myself out on the way down. Just get me out of here will you *asap* – and I've lost my Everest ice axe, dammit.'

It wasn't that easy. Charlie's no lightweight and was hanging free in his harness five metres down. The lip of the crevasse was overhanging and the rope had cut so deeply into the snow that man hauling didn't work. Charlie eventually had to extricate himself using his own prusik loops.

'I told you silly buggers that it was the wrong bloody route!'

'We'll do it your way from now on Charlie,' I assured him.

The cloud never lifted and route finding across fragile snow-bridges through the maze of crevasses became another nightmare. Taking the lead, I went straight through a big one and only just managed to fling myself forward to reach the other side. Eventually, we picked up yesterday's tracks and staggered into the hut thirty-four hours after we had left it. The hut book recorded that five Frenchmen had got back at 5 a.m. that morning after reversing the entire *Forbes Arête* and that nine climbers had been *totalement deroute* on the Aiguille de Chardonnet. The voices that we had heard from the Col Adams Reilly had been those of twenty *Chasseurs Alpines* looking for our bodies at the bottom of the north face.

10

END OF AN ERA

The Paradiso circus had not been copybook alpinism and reinforced the lesson of never chancing your arm with alpine weather. But it had been a lot of fun and it was a sadness that I never climbed in the Alps with any of that *equipe* again. Big-hearted Charlie, who introduced us to High-Low Poker Everest Base Camp style, was bound for higher things as Chris Bonington's first-choice medical officer and Peter disappeared from our lives until Georgina and I joined his 1991 Alpine Club 'Green Expedition' to Bhutan. And then, only months after our Paradiso adventure, John died from a brain tumour aged fifty-five on Christmas Eve 1976. His death was a grievous loss. Nothing he did later in life quite matched his brilliant triumph on Pumasillo, an ascent immortalised on the cover of George Band's book *Summit* that commemorates the Alpine Club's 150th anniversary. John's latter years were marred by ill health and the breakdown of his marriage, but I shall always remember him for the innate mountaineering ability, judgment and an imperturbability that made him the ideal climbing companion. Also, for his courage, humour and easy gift of friendship.

The following year, 1977, marked my last career crossroad when, at the mature age of forty-three, I became a partner in Norton Rose. Two months later, we bought 'Lingmell', eight Heathview Gardens, a Soames Forsythian villa set in the middle of Putney Heath which was to become our family home for the next twenty-five years. Serendipitously, Heathview Gardens had a raft of mountain and adventure associations. The name of our house had been chosen by its original Cumbrian owners to remind them of Scafell's main outlier.

Number seven, the house next door, had briefly belonged to Ernest Shackleton. In number thirteen, 'The Corner House', lived Lord Hailsham, an honorary member of the Alpine Club and brother of my ski mountaineering mentor Neil, while the house opposite his had been that of Walter Haskett Smith, the 'Father of British Rock Climbing', whom was still fondly remembered by an elderly neighbour being driven daily by his liveried chauffeur in a Rolls Royce to his barrister's chambers in the temple. And yes! Sean Connery had once lived just round the corner.

Shortly before we bought Lingmell, it looked as if I might not be around to enjoy it. This was a consequence of my having a ridiculous bicycle race with two cheeky young city slickers who regularly overtook me on the Embankment in the course of my daily ride to my firm's Moorgate offices. To turn the tables, I bought myself a brand new bike, but the outcome was the same. Not only was I worsted but also finished up in the Intensive Care Unit of Saint Bartholomew's Hospital with a suspected heart attack. Georgina arrived at my bedside waving a mortgage agreement that she insisted that I sign before my demise. Happily, the purported heart attack turned out to be nothing more than a nasty viral infection and I was discharged after a week.

A fortnight later, I joined Alan Wedgwood's party for a fortnight's ski touring in central Switzerland. I had only met Alan earlier that year during a Climbers Club meet in north Wales when, on a particularly foul January day, we had found ourselves scrambling together up the *Parson's Nose* on Snowdon's Crib y Ddisgyl. The wind was howling, the rocks were plastered in snow and Alan was in his element. A scion of Josiah Wedgwood, Alan was a former president of the Oxford University Mountaineering Club and a current member of the elite Alpine Climbing Group with a physical presence that made him look several sizes larger than his six-foot-two. His party also included three highly competitive and talented lady ski-mountaineers, Sally Westmacott, Alan's wife Janet, and Michael Baker's wife Sarah, leavened by Pip Hopkinson for light relief. Under Alan's unflurried leadership we climbed three decent peaks; crossed a couple of high passes and got storm-bound for twenty-four hours in the Corno Hut. Our final bid to climb Monte Rosa from Zermatt was frustrated by bad weather. The tour had been fun and games throughout and in Alan I discovered someone who shared my own ski mountaineering philosophy and who became the anchorman of the early stages of my Pyrenean ski traverse.

The following year, 1978, I was invited to serve on the committee of the Alpine Club, the world's oldest mountaineering club. Founded in 1857, its members were originally culled from what *Kelly's Handbook* termed

'The Official Classes' with election to its exalted ranks requiring both a proposer and seconder. The Alpine Club's presidents were not only renowned mountaineers, but also men of public distinction such as Peter Lloyd, its current incumbent. Apart from his notable Himalayan achievements, Peter was an eminent scientist who had worked on the development of the jet engine during the Second World War and been head of British defence research in Australia.

When first elected to the club in 1966, I imagined I had entered Valhalla. However, until we returned to London in the mid-1970s to live there permanently, I had had few opportunities to meet fellow Alpine Club members. Both Lloyd and I had climbed in Hakkiari so I had hoped that on joining the committee we might swap yarns about our respective climbs there. However, at my first committee meeting he neither greeted nor introduced me to any other committee member. Business was conducted without a scintilla of levity and the general atmosphere seemed to confirm the club's reputation for being stuffy and unfriendly. When I got to know him better, I discovered that Peter was a generous, warm-hearted man with whom I shared a common bond through our mutual Australian connections.

But at this time, the Alpine Club was undoubtedly going through a staid patch. Despite the post-war revival of British mountaineering, particularly in the Himalaya, it had lost its momentum in large part as result of its inter-war years legacy when the achievements of British mountaineers in the Alps had generally fallen far behind those of continental climbers. In 1952, to improve the standards of British alpine climbing, a breakaway group of young activists had formed the Alpine Climbing Group (ACG) to recruit a new breed of ambitious British climbers. In 1967, to bridge what had become an ever-widening gap between the AC and mainstream British mountaineering, a putative merger between the AC and ACG was proposed.

Initially, this was strongly opposed by AC die-hards who questioned whether the ACG were 'decent, clubbable chaps'. I happened to attend the acrimonious general meeting when the issue was first debated and it took a magisterial speech from Lord Tangley to put the AC's history of feud, dispute and rivalry into perspective. Even so, the AC/ACG union was only consummated in 1972. A more contentious merger was that between the AC and the Ladies Alpine Club, founded in 1907 with its own distinguished history and traditions. When this merger motion was proposed, I was sitting immediately behind that redoubtable misogynist H.W. Tilman who, after leaping to his feet incandescent with rage, swung round on the assembled members and announced that he would rather resign than see it carried. In the event, Tilman did not resign, but thirty-five LAC members did, including some of the most outstanding women mountaineers of the day.

Both these mergers took time to gel. The transition might have been smoother if members had been given the opportunity to get to know each other better through what had once been the customary AC annual summer alpine meets. In recent years, this tradition had lapsed and to revive it, George Band proposed that there should be an informal AC meet that summer. To show willing, I volunteered to co-ordinate it after persuading Ron Amey to lend us his chalet at Les Praz de Chamonix as a base 'for any AC members interested in doing classic routes on Mont Blanc'. The dates of the meet were chosen to dovetail with the Harding family's holiday plans for a prior visit to the Pyrenees.

This Pyrenean trip began and ended badly. The three-day outward drive was a chapter of accident and it was so hot at the Arrens-Massou campsite that after only one night, camp was shifted to the snowline where the tents became infested with biting flies. Eight-year-old Joanna's verdict, 'I'm absolutely fed up with this and will not be going another step on Dad's stupid expedition', was unanimously supported by her sisters. Although my stock went up when our eldest daughter Emma, Neil Macpherson's daughter Kirsty and I climbed Pic Batboucou, the next outing was a near-disaster.

Back at Arrens-Massou we had rendezvoused with Jean-Pierre Leire, the Pau hotelier with whom, during the closing stages of my second Pyrenean ski tour earlier that year, we had made a *sturm und drang* escape down the *Arête de Gaube* as avalanches boomed all around. Jean-Pierre had originally suggested that he and I climb the Balaitous together, but due to 'bronchial troubles', now decided to pull out. With Georgina fighting-fit, it seemed a pity to give away the Balaitous's *'Facile voie normale'* and so, after trekking up to the Larribet Hut for the night, we gave the hut's *Petite Guardienne* strict instructions that the children were not to move an inch from the hut until we returned the following morning.

Came the dawn, with the initial approaches to the Balaitous straightforward enough. However, once beyond the Col Noir which marks the Franco/Spanish frontier, the contours on the French map disappeared. Descending hard névé on the Spanish side of the col, Georgina spiked her calf with a crampon but gamely carried on without either of us realising the extent of her injury.

'Why don't you have a good rest here while I investigate the way ahead?' I suggested brightly.

Georgina didn't bother to reply. But rather than discuss the situation further, I pressed on up the Frondella Glacier only to realise halfway up that I was forty-five degrees off course. Instead of retreating, I took a new line to reach the crest of the ridge. This soon deteriorated into a nerve-wracking scramble up loose rock, which sent chunks of it crashing down the mountain.

'You bloody, bloody fool. You've really landed yourself on this stupid, pointless climb,' I kept muttering to myself, though by now it was safer to climb on than descend. Clambering on to the summit much shaken, I found that I had mistakenly climbed the *Frondella Centrale*.

When I rejoined Georgina, she was sitting on a large boulder angrier than I had ever seen her before or since. Back at Arrens-Massou the ministrations of a young French doctor put things right but Dad was in disgrace. We left the Pyrenees the following day. For the children, the week's camping in the mountains had been a magical experience and Mum was voted 'simply wonderful'. I never climbed solo again.

Three days of lazing on the beach of Saint Pierre sur Mer almost restored marital relations and on 27 July we exchanged our leaky tents for Ron Amey's chalet. Of the ten Alpine Club members who had originally expressed some interest in the meet, only Steve Town and his chum Graham Luker turned up that evening. Denis and Gwen Greenald had left a terse message that they were 'somewhere in the area'.

I had not previously met Steve, a senior civil servant who, despite having done eight alpine seasons and become a member of the Alpine Climbing Group, had only been elected to the Alpine Club the previous year because he knew so few other AC members. Blunt, unmarried and ten years younger than me, he came across as a skilled and ambitious mountaineer. Graham Luker, a more sensitive soul, had read geology at Swansea University, so we shared a tenuous connection.

'D'you have any particular climbs in mind, Steve?' I asked him over supper. 'No one else has fetched-up so far. Maybe I could join up with you and Graham?'

'Graham and I have done quite a bit of climbing over the past fortnight, here and at Zermatt,' he replied, eyeing me cautiously. 'We've got in mind the north-west face of the Bionnassay and then the old *Brenva* route. How does that grab you?'

Both routes were within my compass had I been fit and acclimatised, but I was neither. And after the *Frondella Centrale* affair, I was certainly not going to stick my neck out.

'I'd have to get a lot fitter to do either climb without slowing you up,' I replied, glancing in Georgina's direction.

'Think it over,' said Steve. 'We'll come round early tomorrow morning to see how you feel and what the weather's doing. Someone else may have turned up by then to give you a wider choice of climbing partners.'

To date, I had only nibbled at the fringes of Mont Blanc and would happily have settled for the normal *Aiguille de Goûter* route which had repulsed us three years before. I realised that this would not have satisfied Steve, but when thinking things over that night, I recalled Richard Brooke's enthusiasm for a Mont Blanc traverse that he had done some years before and which the guide book described as 'Magnificent … one of the finest in the Alps.'

When Steve and Graham turned up the following morning, I told them that I'd found a climb that might suit all three of us.

'What's that?' asked Steve, looking dubious.

'The traverse of Mont Blanc from the Tré la Tête to Chamonix across the Domes de Miages and Aiguille de Bionnassay.'

'We can't possibly do that in one day!' exclaimed Steve.

'Agreed,' I replied. 'It's at least a two or even a three day expedition so we can spend the second night at the Durier Refuge.'

'That's still one helluva long second day,' grunted Steve after perusing the map. 'A lot will depend on the weather. The snow's very low this year. Anyway, this isn't at all the sort of climb that Graham and I had in mind. We'll have to think about it and give you our decision at lunchtime.'

We were lunching on the verandah *en famille* when they returned.

'We're on for your climb, John. But we'd better get cracking if we're going to make the Tré la Tête this evening. We'll take my car as far as Les Contamines.'

When I turned to Georgina, Steve said, 'Don't worry about the old man. Graham and I will take good care of him!'

The hut march to the Tré la Tête hotel took a breathless one and a half hours. The hotel was empty save for two guided parties and noisy French youth. At 3 a.m. next morning, I caught a Frenchman attempting to make-off with my treasured Simond ice axe. After a brief, heated exchange, we stormed up the Tré la Tête Glacier to come in an easy first at the Conscrits Hut. Continuing up the ridge to the 3,425 metre Aiguille de la Bérangère, I witnessed one of the greatest views in the Alps with every detail of the Cyclopean architecture of Mont Blanc's tremendous South Face etched out in stark monochrome.

Its shining summit, marking the culmination of a nine-kilometre frontier ridge that only once fell below 3,350 metres, was magnificent but looked immeasurably far away.

The weather was holding, the situations were spectacular and although the ridge was heavily corniced, the climbing was never difficult. Shortly after noon, we reached the Refuge Durier, a flimsy wooden shack, perched like a rook's nest on a rocky platform overlooking the Miage and Bionnassay glaciers. Already occupied by four Germans, there was just enough room for three more. After nine and a half hours going non-stop, my exhaustion was compounded by altitude sickness and a raging headache so I took to my bunk. The Germans were in their sleeping bags by 5.30 p.m. Steve and Graham followed a couple of hours later as shafts of evening sunlight streamed through the hut's tiny window.

Altitude sickness saps energy and morale. During the night, my courage reached a low ebb. Between snatches of sleep, nightmare visions woke me to the reality of tomorrow's climb to which imagination lent insuperable difficulties. The Germans had already recce'd the route the previous day and when their alarm went off at 1.30 a.m. and they raced to action stations, it was like a scene from *The Guns of Navarone*. Yet by the time they eventually got going one and a half hours later, the Brits were at their heels. And now, miraculously, my altitude sickness left me and I felt raring to go. There was no moon, but it was easy enough to follow the dancing beams of the Germans' head torches reflecting off the snow ahead. When the slope narrowed to a rock ridge, the gap between the two parties closed and Steve brusquely forced his way past the Germans to take the lead. It was light at 5 a.m. when Graham attacked the terminal rocks of the Bionnassay's south ridge and then graciously gave me the lead to its snow-capped summit. Traversing the Bionnassay's famous east ridge, an exposed fin of snow stretched tightly across a void before merging into the Dome de Goûter, the route led on past the Vallot Hut; mounted the *Bosses Ridge* and thence took us to Mont Blanc's summit. After a round of back-slapping and pumping each other's hands, our hubris was short lived when Pete Scott, an ACG member who recognised Steve, came across to greet us.

'Done anything good, Pete?' asked Steve.

'Yep,' said Pete. 'We've just completed the *Peuterey Ridge*. A few days back we also did the *Sentinelle Rouge* after doing *Route Major*.'

On the way down, we bumped into our German friends settling in for a night at the Vallot Hut.

'Better do a weather check,' said Steve, glancing at his altimeter. 'I don't like the look of those black clouds coming in from the west. If the weather breaks, I don't fancy descending the Goûter. Better go straight down to Chamonix by the Bossons Glacier.'

Nineteen hours after leaving the Durier, we reached the Chamonix Valley with the rain bucketing down. I shuddered to think what it would be like for the Germans up above. We couldn't find a taxi, so I walked the rest of the way to the chalet to fetch our car and pick up the others. Happily reunited, Georgina then broke the bad news over beer and a bite.

'The Greenalds turned up after you'd left for the Tré la Tête. They said they'd try to meet up with you on the summit of Mont Blanc after doing a training climb on the Petites Charmoz. Unfortunately, Denis fell when only a few feet off the ground and fractured his leg in three places.'

Next day at the hospital in Chamonix, the children were fascinated to see Denis's leg totally encased in plaster and another British climber, Peter King, prone in the next bed with a large metal pin sticking through his ankle. King had somehow survived falling down the length of the east north-east buttress of Les Courtes in his sleeping bag. That night, at Argentiere's Le Dahu restaurant, we celebrated our Mont Blanc traverse and my forty-fourth birthday after Steve and Graham had presented me with a superb Pierre Tairraz photograph of Mont Blanc inscribed 'To our gallant leader'. It hangs in our cloakroom under another favourite photograph, that of Mount Kenya taken from Sendeyo.

In April the following year, on the third stage of my Pyrenean high route, an avalanche coming off the Petit Vignemale killed my cousin Alain and would have done for the rest of the party had not one member, Richard Reynolds, avoided burial and dug us out. This tragedy made me reassess whether the inherent risks of mountaineering were worth it. It is a question that most mountaineers will have faced up to at some time or other. Rightly or wrongly, I decided that unless I was to quit altogether, I had better return to the fray as soon as possible. Sally Westmacott's Climbers Club family meet at Bosigran that July accompanied by our three daughters was a starter, but a more realistic test was likely to be the joint Alpine Club/Association of British Members of the Swiss Alpine Club meet in Courmayeur that August.

I had hoped I might climb again with Steven Town, but he had already agreed to team up with Brian Chase whose wild-man reputation as the iconoclastic president of the CUMC in the mid-1960s went before him. Brian had done some hard Alpine routes; led an expedition to the Peruvian Andes and had climbed in the Hindu Kush. He also wrote poetry. Tall with reddish hair, laconic and self-assured he agreed to give me a lift to Courmayeur in his beat-up Ford Escort, insisting on driving all the way and sticking to *Route Nationale* roads to avoid paying *Autoroute* tolls. We camped the first night in steady rain in a ploughed field in northern France. Just short of the Jura, Brian decided to change the car's brake linings and finished the job inside twenty minutes. On reaching Chamonix late that evening, he made straight for the Bar National. Bursting through its wild-west-style swing-doors, he glared around the heaving saloon to see if any hirsute, beer-swilling Brits were 'up for it'. Apparently, no one was, so he turned on his heel and reluctantly agreed to have a bite in a less high-octane establishment. In the early hours the following morning, we fetched up at Courmayeur's 'Camping Peuteret' and happened by chance to pitch my tent bang next to Steve Town's.

Of those AC members present, the only one I knew was Douglas Hogg, assured, effervescent and with a refreshing sense of humour. Unfortunately, he was already committed to climb in the Paradiso over the next couple of days so when Steve suggested that I join the Chase/Town *équipe*, I was delighted to accept having already established that Brian was married and had not climbed in the Alps for several years. If I imagined that some of this might have taken the shine off him, I had second thoughts when he outlined his sport plan.

'I'd like to get up to the Estellette Bivouac this afternoon so that we can climb the Tré la Tête's south peak and traverse the Petit Mont Blanc tomorrow and then spend that night at the Giovanna Montagna Bivouac before coming down.'

I calculated that this little outing was going to involve six kilometres of challenging climbing at an altitude of over 3,500 metres. Steve had just completed a week in the Paradiso and Bernina. Brian was clearly determined to live up to his hard-man reputation.

The hut march to the Estellette Bivouac from the Val Veni involved a stiff 700-metre scramble up a steep rock ridge. As if to prove themselves, Steve and Brian raced into the lead but in their haste went inexplicably off-route. With an element of unhealthy competition creeping in, I was damned if I was going to come in last and, after a lung-bursting effort, reached the Estellette ten-minutes ahead of them. It was a bad mistake. This tiny Nissen hut, perched astride a narrow ridge overlooking the de la Lex Blanche and Estellette glaciers, had barely room enough for the three of us. And then, without missing a beat, Steve suggested that we carry on with an unroped recce up the Tré la Tête's south-east ridge to prepare for tomorrow's climb. Twenty minutes on, I was overcome by altitude sickness and vertigo. I managed to totter back to the Estellette behind the others before collapsing and being violently sick. Steve heaped some blankets over me, but I couldn't stop shivering.

As I lay there semi-comatose, I overheard the other two discussing the situation.

'We've got three options,' said Brian. 'First, we can carry on as planned, leaving him to make his own way down. Secondly, we can do a short training climb and come back to pick him up. Thirdly, we all go down together first thing in the morning.'

I felt pathetically weak and demoralised. Just to descend the ridge on my own now assumed ridiculous proportions.

'I'm sure I'll be feeling much better by tomorrow,' I piped up feebly.

'Perhaps I could start out with you and see how things go.'

'That's not really on,' cut in Brian. 'If you were to have another collapse, retreat would be that much more difficult for all of us.'

I couldn't dispute his logic. It was left that they would settle for the Tré la Tête's south peak and be back at the hut by 9 a.m. tomorrow.

They eventually left the Estellette at 4.30 a.m. Now feeling better, my offer to join them was declined. Three hours later, a solitary Italian climber Paolo Moretti dropped by to limber up for a solo ascent of the *Bonatti Route* on the Grand Capucin. Stepping out on to the hut's narrow gangway to meet the sun, the terrors of the night dissolved like the morning mist. We followed Steve and Brian's snail-like progress across the Glacier de la Lex Blanche.

'They're not going too well,' said Paolo. 'If they're hoping to climb the south peak, they're already one and a half hours behind guidebook time. However, if you'll excuse me, I'm just going to finish my own climb. I'll be back soon.'

I cleaned up the hut and hung around feeling my age. At 10 a.m. there was no sign of Brian and Steve, so I reckoned that they must have reverted to Brian's option one. When Paolo returned, he suggested that we should go down to the valley together and then wait for the others at the Elizabetta Hut. I left an explanatory note and followed on. When Brian and Steve fetched up several hours later, I detected a distinct *froideur.*

'Of course, we had to cut our climb short,' said Steve bitterly.

'Brian and I have decided to go up to the Torino Hut this evening to do a proper climb.'

Back at Camping Peuterey, Steve admitted that he wasn't feeling too good himself and would now be staying put in camp. Brian promptly fixed himself up with the newly arrived Henry Day to do the north face of the Tour Ronde next day. Obligingly, Steve agreed to drive all four of us down to Courmayeur so that Brian and Henry might catch the last telepherique to the Torino and for me to take up a long-standing invitation to stay that night with an old friend, Elizabeth Gordon. Just before parting, Brian asked me to look after his car keys.

A decent meal, a hot bath and a good night's rest did wonders for morale and next morning, I bought myself a new climbing helmet at Toni Gobbi's boutique. Back at camp, I found Steve looking glum.

'What's the problem?' I asked him. 'Still feeling unwell?'

'No, I'm fine now' he replied gruffly. 'Henry's back, though for some reason, he and Brian didn't do their climb. Brian's still up at the Torino waiting to hear from me, but I can't get through to the hut by telephone. Apparently, he wants me to bring up some extra climbing gear from his car. He left you with the key. Please let me have it'.

I fumbled around in my pockets. No key. My search for it occupied the rest of that morning. The ramifications of losing Brian's key were only beginning to dawn on me when Douglas Hogg, having just returned from the Paradiso, produced his own car keys which happened to fit Brian's driver seat door. Unfortunately, they didn't fit the boot, which contained all his ironmongery.

'Nothing for it I'm afraid, Steve. I can only suggest we both go up to the Torino with whatever gear as we can muster. I'll then explain the situation to Brian.'

With a grim-faced Steve laden with pitons, karabiners, slings and enough tinned food for a week, we took the next lift to the Torino. There was no sign of Brian nor had he left any message. The guardian was certain that he had already gone down to Courmayeur.

'Tell you what,' said Steve after some cogitation. 'The weather's holding up for at least another day. I don't know what's happened to Brian, but if you were on for it, we could fit in the Aiguille de Rochefort by the west ridge tomorrow.'

The Courmayeur guides were holding their annual festival in town that day leaving the Torino Hut/Hotel almost empty save for a collection of hirsute Brits squatting over Gaz stoves. A professor of science from Aberdeen University was brewing up his AFD spaghetti bolognese on the floor, while in the Torino's modestly priced *ristorante,* a jolly crowd of Italian construction workers were tucking into the real thing and sloshing down litres of chianti.

Steve insisted that we join the Gaz-set. His tinned curried beef and rice gave me the squitters throughout the night. The late arrival of two Royal Marine mountaineers, Guy Sheridan and Duggie Keelan, lifted the tone and added some welcome levity. Twenty-four years before, Guy and I had both served in South Arabia's Radfan. Three years on, he was to lead the operation to recapture Grytviken in South Georgia during the Falklands Campaign.

Long before dawn next morning, Steve and I threaded our way across a floor littered with comatose climbers. Still feeling queasy from diarrhoea, too much chianti and a filthy headache, I took little notice of the guided parties hurrying past us towards the ghostly spire of Dent de Géant. But Steve had something to prove and on the rocks below the Dent, he forcibly pushed past a guide who let out a string of expletives. This exchange lifted my own game and by the start of the Rochefort Ridge, we had overtaken all other parties and never lost the lead thereafter. The ridge was delicate with terrific exposure on either side. While climbing the final summit rocks, Steve dislodged a stone which would have split my head open had I not been wearing my new Gobbi helmet.

On the way back to the Torino, Steve suggested that we round the day off by climbing the Dent de Géant. When I told him that I had already promised to do this climb with Douglas Hogg, he went all quiet. Rather than chatting side by side, we now found ourselves racing back to the hut in breathless competition. At the Torino, I suggested we have a decent meal at the *ristorante* to celebrate our successful climb, but Steve insisted on breaking into another tin. Ungraciously, I opted for the *ristorante*. On joining me later, he let fly.

'I'm dead worried about Brian. I can only imagine that he's fed up with you for letting us down at the Estellette and for losing his car key. In any event, you've made a real mess of our climbing plans'.

To have lost Brian's keys was indeed deplorable. But I could hardly have ruined their climbing plans. Steve had been non-combatant after coming down from the Estellette and it later transpired that Brian too had been unable to climb the Tour Ronde with Henry Day due to exhaustion. After this unhappy spat, the hut began to fill up: first with Douglas, later with Brian. The keys had never turned up and so, to get into the car boot, he had dismantled the entire rear wing. I apologised profusely, expecting an ugly showdown. Instead, he was cool and matter-of-fact.

The following day the weather broke. Douglas and I led the route down to Courmayeur in thick cloud and pouring rain. At the campsite we ran into a barrister friend of Douglas's, Alan Pardoe, and promptly repaired to Courmayeur for a slap-up lunch. In the square, an Englishman dressed in

1950s Robert Lawrie climbing gear and wearing boots nailed with tricounis kindly invited us to dine that evening with the Association of British Members of the Swiss Alpine Club at the *Ristorante Venezia*.

It was not the most sparkling occasion, but I had the privilege of sitting next to another grizzled veteran who spoke nostalgically of the Himalayan approach marches he had done in the 1920s. He never gave me his name.

Continuous bad weather put the kibosh on any further climbing from Courmayeur so Hogg, Pardoe and I drove round to the French side for better conditions, only to have a timid attempt on Mont Tondu aborted by wind, rain and snow. After another wet night at Camping Peuterey, the weather forecast was unchanged, so I decided to cut my losses and head for home. Speeding down the Arve Valley on the Paris-bound express, I glanced back for a final glimpse of Mont Blanc only to see it enveloped in black storm clouds. Brian ingeniously overcame the problem of the missing key and he and Steve finished their alpine season in fine style with some classic routes culminating in the *Taschhorn-Dom traverse*. I much admired Steve's mountaineering skills and judgment and saw a lot more of him after he became the Alpine Club's very efficient honorary secretary. We walked together in Bhutan and on the AC's 150th anniversary at Zermatt, but never climbed together again. Brian's life was cut tragically short by the cancer which killed him eight years later when he was only forty-four years old. I often wish I had got to know him better.

11

'SKI MOUNTAINEERING *IS* MOUNTAINEERING'

For me, the Alpine Club's Courmayeur meet had not been an unqualified success nor had it fully extirpated the feelings of remorse that still haunted me in the aftermath of the Vignemale avalanche disaster earlier that year. How to solve the avalanche enigma was something I hoped might be answered at the avalanche symposium arranged jointly by the Alpine and Eagle Ski Clubs and the Ski Club of Great Britain that same autumn which I helped to organise. Amongst the speakers at this event were my Pyrenean mentor, Martin Epp, Walter Good, the deputy director of the Swiss Avalanche Research Institute at Davos and André Roch, one of Switzerland's most eminent mountaineers. Roch put the avalanche dilemma in a nutshell: 'If you want to avoid them, there is only one way – don't go into the mountains!'

Walter Good in another way.

'Believe me John, your accident could have happened to anyone. However, much you think you know about avalanches, you can never be certain.'

These reassuring words, if not entirely comforting, at least helped dispel my own avalanche phobia. The symposium also confirmed a growing realisation that my mountain focus had definitely shifted from mountaineering unalloyed to ski mountaineering. Why the change? I was a relatively competent mountaineer, but never more than a survival skier. If the seeds of my conversion had originally been sown on Neil Hogg's ESC Oberland Meet, it was the de Pret Roose/Epp 1975 Pyrenean ski tour that brought it home to me that many mountain ranges are best explored on ski in winter.

Skiing, as we know it today, was originally a Norwegian invention and only imported to the Alps in the late nineteenth century. Initially, the British (notably Sir Arthur Conan Doyle who made a pioneer ski crossing from Davos to Arosa in 1894) were amongst its earliest practitioners at a time when the emphasis was on touring using animal skis for uphill traction because mechanical ski lifts had not yet been invented. To put the chronology of ski touring and down-hill skiing in perspective, the Haute Route on ski between Chamonix and Zermatt was first accomplished in 1911 by Professor Roget and Marcel Kurz nineteen years before the first World Downhill Championships. If Conan Doyle witnessed the dawn of British ski mountaineering it was an Oxford University undergraduate, Arnold Lunn, who laid its foundations when, in 1908, he founded the Alpine Ski Club (ASC) to which he recruited some of the most eminent British and continental mountaineers of that time as honorary members. Lunn, later to become the 'father' of downhill racing and inventor of the slalom, envisaged ski mountaineering as 'the marriage of two great sports' and had hoped that his ASC should become a bridge between the Alpine Club and the newly formed Ski Club of Great Britain (SCGB).

Lunn's dream never materialised though from its inception, the ASC promoted guideless ski mountaineering in the Alps and encouraged exploratory ski touring expeditions to the Himalaya, the Rockies and New Zealand. One of its founder members, the great German Central Asian explorer Rickmer Rickmers, put it to the Alpine Club thus, 'ski mountaineering *is* mountaineer-ing … the best method of mountaineering in snow'. Few fellow AC members took his message on board and although on the continent, in America and New Zealand ski mountaineering has for long been regarded as an essential component in a mountaineer's portfolio of skills, as exemplified by the first complete ski traverse of the Alps achieved in 1956 by the great Italian moun-taineer Walter Bonatti, in Britain it remains a Cinderella. In R.L.G. Irving's *A History of British Mountaineering* ski mountaineering gets only one mention, and that in a Scottish context, and in the *Alpine Journal's* Alpine Centenary number, none save in Arnold Lunn's magnanimous article *Alpine Controversies*.

For what is the most environmentally friendly of all sports (unlike downhill skiing it requires no infrastructure and leaves no traces) the reasons for this neglect are puzzling and complex. Between the wars, continental climbers made most of the running in the Alps and the Alpine Club not only lost its pre-eminence, but also got bogged down in some unseemly controversies particularly the bizarre dispute between Lunn and the Alpine Club's old guard about the role of skis in mountaineering. The anti-ski faction had a formidable champion in Colonel E.L. Strutt who edited the *Alpine Journal* between 1927 and 1937 and was notorious for his resistance to mountaineering innovation including the use of crampons. Strutt, a 1922 Everester, regarded Lunn as an *arriviste* who promoted new-fangled sports. Lunn, a former Balliol scholar, was an equally doughty controversialist who had once converted the atheist philosopher C.E.M. Joad to Catholicism. The Strutt/Lunn feud, conducted through the unlikely vehicle of *Country Life,* may have contributed to Lunn being blackballed from both the Alpine Club and the SCGB, even though he was subsequently reinstated as an honorary member of the former and a president of the latter. Later knighted for his services to skiing and commissioned by the Swiss Foundation for Alpine Research to write his mag-isterial *A Century of Mountaineering* (the only monograph to commemorate the Alpine Club's 1957 centenary), when Lunn died in 1974 he would have had the satisfaction of knowing that British ski mountaineers had again become a force to be reckoned with. Yet old prejudices die hard as I was to discover when, as a vice president of the Alpine Club in 1996, I unsuccessfully promoted ski mountaineering expertise as a qualification for AC membership.

Ski mountaineering is never a soft option. After stomping uphill on skins with a heavy pack in zero-visibility to attain some blizzard-swept col or peak, you must somehow get yourself down the other side through powder, crust or crumb. Ski mountaineers must not only be competent mountaineers, but have also mastered a range of skiing techniques as well as snow-craft, avalanche evaluation, weather and navigation skills. The Pret Roose/Epp 1975 ski tour through the *Parc Nationale des Pyrénées* had been an object lesson in coping with difficult snow and weather conditions. Yet even for them, one key passage undertaken in a blizzard and whiteout had been touch-and-go throughout.

Paradoxically, it was this tour that persuaded me that the Pyrenees might be tackled without the crutch of professional guides. Yet not until 1978 did I feel confident enough to take up the challenge when Alan and Nick Wedgwood and I completed, in equally bad weather, the route that had defeated the Eagles, albeit at the expense of Richard Morgan having to retire halfway through after injuring his back. Thereafter, and for the next ten years, my principal mountaineering preoccupation was to complete a west to east ski traverse of the Pyrenees. This personal odyssey, involving nine separate tours, sixty-eight stages, over twenty peaks and close on 100 passes, is recounted in my book *Pyrenean High Route.*

There were times when I was tempted to call the whole Pyrenean project off, due not only to numerous accidents and incidents incurred along the way, but also as a result of a shattering discovery I made as an indirect consequence of having had a bad fall above the Lac d'Oredon during the fourth leg of the traverse in 1981. This had left me with the severe concussion, which precipitated a ten-hour rescue operation by the French Mountain Gendarmerie. After releasing myself from hospital at Lannemezan, I was rummaging around St Lary's tiny *librairie* while waiting to rejoin the remnants of my original Anglo-French *equipe*, when I came upon a slim *Club Alpin Français* paperback entitled *Haute Route d'Hiver Des Pyrénées* by Robert Ollivier. Until then, I had been using his exhaustive four-volume *Pyrenees Itineraires Skieurs* to piece together a consecutive route along the Pyrenees. Ollivier had never mentioned in his exhaustive guide the existence of a Pyrenean Haute Route, yet in this more recent publication he gave a description of Charles La Porte's complete ski traverse of the range in 1968, a feat hailed by the distinguished French mountaineer Patrice Bellephon as '*un des plus remarkable exploits de sa genre*'. For the past three years, I had blithely assumed that we might even be the first to complete a Pyrenean Haute Route. In the event, we hadn't even been at the starting gate. This stunning news made me wonder whether my own traverse was still worth pursuing and to see things in perspective, I decided to take up a Kenyan client's invitation to fly out to Nairobi that autumn to help sort out her family affairs. Unblushingly, I took this as another opportunity to chance my luck on Mount Kenya.

The Republic of Kenya was much changed since my last visit seventeen years before. Many houses in Nairobi had armed guards permanently stationed on their gates. At the seaside estate of my client Tilly Dalton, the daughter of a Nandi chief, two ridgebacks, a pack of Jack Russells and a posse of Nandi tribesmen armed with bows and arrows routinely patrolled the grounds. To help manage her complex life, Tilly had the loyal support of three 'protectors' all members of Kenya's white tribe who were resolutely staying on in the land where they had forged their lives and staked their futures. I first stayed with Alastair Burn a former Second World War soldier who, since Kenya's independence, had switched from farming to property management and was currently acting for Jomo Kenyatta's widow and Lady Delamere. My next port of call was with Jane Prettejohn and her husband Mike whose lifestyle combined *Out of Africa* with *Happy Valley*. From their tourist/safari hotel Indian Ocean lodge, built in the style of an Arabian Nights coral palace, we flew to Galana River Ranch, a 1.5 million-acre tract of semi-desert and bush bordering Tsavo East National Park. Mike had originally run this for big-game safaris at a time when it had supported 6,000 elephants and 350 Black rhino. Since the imposition of hunting restrictions, he had extended his remit to farming 30,000 head of cattle whose excrement produced enough methane gas to power Galana's entire electricity supply.

Over dinner at Galana, table-talk turned from ivory poaching raids by Shifta bandits armed with AK-47s to Mike's big-game hunting yarns. He still bore in his left buttock the bullet that his bearer had fired to dispatch a buffalo that was about to gore him to death and his left leg was deeply scarred from a recent brush with a lioness who would have chewed it off had not his photographer stepson taken a candid-camera flash-shot that scared the beast away. That night, I opted to sleep in a tent and when a faint rustling outside roused me, I peered through the flaps to see the heads of a dozen giraffes silhouetted against a satin moon.

Having completed my official business, I rendezvoused with John Blacker at Nairobi's Muthaiga Club for our projected tryst with Mount Kenya. John, then working on UN demographic projects throughout Africa, had roped in John Hull (currently the *chairman* of the Mountain Club of Kenya, for in the Republic of Kenya there could only be one *president*) and Sarah Howard who was then working for the Church Missionary Society. Sarah's father John, a former Colonial Service District Commissioner, had pioneered several routes on Mount Kenya in the immediate post-war period.

The logistics of this lightning trip were complicated. September usually gives a brief weather window for climbing on the north side of the mountain before the 'short' rains make it virtually impossible until late December. Due to work commitments, we had only a week between 19 and 25 September to get up to the recently refurbished Kami Hut and down again by the Sirimon Track. The porters' closed-shop only operated from the opposite side of the mountain, so we would have to rely on them bringing up our food supplies unescorted by the Burguret Track which was often impassable at this time of the year. Additionally, John and I could only begin our trek up the Sirimon Track a day after John Hull and Sarah.

The two of us set off late afternoon on 20 September, aiming to reach the intermediate Liki Hut that night. The rain soon turned to sleet, which became progressively heavier the higher we climbed. After nightfall, we completely lost the path and two hours later came to a sodden halt. Exhausted, irritable and with no moon visible, neither of us had the wit to work out how to erect John's new-fangled tent, so ended up by sleeping on the heather under it unopened. I was frequently sick during the night and next morning realised that we had fetched-up in the wrong valley. Under a dark, brooding sky, we doubled back much of the way we had come the previous night to find the Liki Hut badly vandalised with an exhortation scrawled on one fire-blackened wall, 'Munt Averest is big but it did not defeat the courage of man'.

My own mojo was fast waning and my head splitting as we stomped up the Mackinder Valley with John always ahead. At a fork in the track, the mists suddenly descended and I had no idea which way he had gone. Retching and disorientated, I began to hallucinate imagining that I could hear voices and that the grotesque shapes of giant groundsel were wild animals. All I wanted to do was lie down and go to sleep and when John eventually found me I was reeling around in an anoxic stupor. After a short rest, we blundered on through the mist and eventually found the Kami Hut.

John Hull and Sarah were waiting anxiously at its threshold for they too had had their problems. Leaving the roadhead an hour before John, Sarah had failed to find the Liki Hut and been forced to bivouac that night on her own in the open. She and John had met up next morning, but bad weather forced them to make a second bivouac at the Shipton Caves. As a result, they had only reached the Kami Hut that same morning to find the interior trashed and the bedding and kitchen equipment looted. Outside, rotting heaps of rubbish fed a family of rock hyrax and a legion of rats.

Back in Nairobi there had been some talk about climbing Batian's north face by the original 1944 Firmin/Hicks route. Supposedly the least difficult route up Batian from this side, the mountain's brooding, snow-flecked buttresses soaring a thousand metres above the hut, didn't give that impression. To get ourselves psyched up, Sarah and I sloughed off altitude sickness and nipped up the seldom-climbed Point Dutton. Lithe and attractive, Sarah proved to be a determined and an elegant rock climber, which boded well for Batian. The following day, the four of us headed off across the upper Mackinder Valley to acclimatise and repeat the *South-East Chimney* route on Sendeyo that Sarah's father had pioneered with the Italian mountaineer Gabrioli in 1945. Twenty years before, I had swarmed up this very route solo in twenty-five minutes. This time, it took Sarah and me one and a half hours to do an only slightly harder variation.

When the two Johns joined us on Sendeyo's summit, I had a sense of *déjà vu* when we decided to carry on to Tereri. For this passage, which traverses the deep gut separating the twin peaks, was the one I had taken in January 1961. This time, conditions were completely different and on peering into the gap that was rapidly filling up with mist, I couldn't believe that I had once soloed this near-vertical wall sheathed in snow and ice.

'With the rocks like this, we can't possibly climb down this face without at least a couple of abseils,' I told to the others. 'If Sarah gives me a top rope, I'll climb down to see if there's a decent stance lower down for a second belay.'

I climbed down for twenty-five metres without seeing a suitable stance so I shouted up to Sarah: 'No go I'm afraid. We'd be putting our heads into a noose. I'm coming straight back!'

Halfway up, a hold broke off in my hands and I slipped clean off the face. Sarah held me tight, but I was still quivering when we regrouped. The mist now made it so difficult to see the way off Sendeyo that I had visions of another Mount Kenya imbroglio. However, after some faffing around, Sarah and I part abseiled and part climbed down while the two Johns opted to abseil after joining both our ropes together for their final pitch.

Back at the Kami Hut, the Sendeyo scrape made me realise that we were not remotely fit enough to attempt Batian's north face. Instead, we settled for *Shipton's route* on Point Pigott with me climbing with John Blacker for old times sake. After four clean pitches, the insidious afternoon mist again descended and when it began to snow heavily and thunder, we scuttled back to the hut. For our last meal on Mount Kenya John cooked the pilaff pre-scribed in his chapter *Catering on Mountains* in the MKC's 1963 guidebook. His culinary muses were Elizabeth David and Claudia Roden, but his own slim *Recipes Celebrating a Lifetime of Friendship* is the one we still lovingly use at home.

Throughout the long march back to the roadhead through hail, sleet and snow the following day, I kept congratulating myself that we were not battling for survival on Batian's north face. However, when flying back to London, two matters occupied my mind. First, my less than inspired showing on Sendeyo with its intimations of mortality. Secondly, the future of my Pyrenean traverse. The La Porte discovery had blunted any sense of urgency to return to the fray and so, to put what had become an obsessive personal challenge into further perspective, I joined up with Alan and Elsbeth Blackshaw the following year to do the Verbier to Zermatt Haute Route variant. Despite the initial loss of the Blackshaws' skis as a result of Alan's over-confident reliance on British Rail consigning them to Martigny, we achieved everything he had intended by bagging the Rosa Blanche, Pigne d'Arolla and Tête de Valpelline en route. However, there weren't all that many laughs along the way and with the huts so overcrowded with packaged ski tours that mealtimes had to be staggered, I realised long before reaching Zermatt that this sublime route was being vulgarised and that my heart now lay in the Pyrenees.

Yet the dispiriting experience of trying to keep up with Alan and Elsbeth, a pair of Highland-based hares, brought it home that I needed to get a lot fitter if I was to complete the remaining two-thirds of the Haute Route des Pyrénées. Bicycling sixteen-miles a day to the office and back had landed me with three nasty accidents and was not sufficient training for serious ski mountaineering. Typically, it was Alan Wedgwood who came up with the solution of a weekend ski touring in the Scottish Highlands with the ambitious plan of crossing from Corrour to Dalwhinnie on ski, climbing Ben Alder en route. Ben Alder was itself a rare prize described by the Caledonian guru W.H. Murray as one of the most 'remote, un-get-at-able mountains in Scotland' because it is set in the heart of a 250 square-mile roadless tract in the central Highlands making it almost as difficult to get at it over a weekend from Glasgow as it is from London.

And so it was that at 8 a.m. Saturday 12 February 1983, British Rail's *Highlander* dropped off the Wedgwood brothers and me at Corrour, the highest railway station in the British Isles from where we skied off the platform to begin our ski crossing to Dalwhinnie. With a herd of stags foraging in the snow, the mountain tops shrouded by cloud and an indeterminate horizon merging into a lowering sky, we pushed on to bag a brace of 'Munros', Carn Dearg and Sgor Gaibhre. Rather than lose precious height by descending to Ben Alder Cottage on the shores of Loch Ericht just below the cave where Bonnie Prince Charlie had spent a night after Culloden, we bivouacked in the snow in the western lee of Ben Alder. Snow fell during the night but the weather lifted somewhat next morning when 700 metres of climbing on skins took us to Ben Alder's summit. A challenging descent through *névé, sastrugi* and breakable-crust led down to the shores of Loch Ericht and thence to the Grampian Hotel, Dalwhinnie late that evening. From here we picked up the Sunday-night sleeper for London and the following morning I was back in my Bishopsgate office just in time for breakfast.

My first ever Scottish ski tour had been in 1967 when I had introduced Georgina to a modest Cairngorm venture. But it was that 1983 Highland crossing that caught my imagination and served as a precedent for a succession of Scottish ski touring weekends during the 1980s and 1990s when snow conditions were consistently good. With a wilderness area in their backyard remoter than anything in Europe outside Scandinavia, canny Scots had long recognised that the scale and physical configuration of many of their mountains make them ideal for ski mountaineering. Sandy Leven, a local laird, had organised three Eagle Ski Club Cairngorm meets in the late 1970s and in 1984 Alan Blackshaw's Glenshee meet signalled lift-off. Thereafter, the Eagles were to run regular weekend ski-touring meets based mainly on stops along the West Coast Railway line including Kingussie, Spean Bridge, Fort William, Blair Atholl, Bridge of Orchy, Corrour and Feshiebridge. Between 1984 and 1997, I attended fifteen such meets and climbed over sixty Munros on ski including some memorable traverses over the Grey Corries, Aonach Mhor, Ben a Ghlo, Ben Lawers and Ben Lui.

Although Scottish hills are relatively low, they should never be taken lightly and uncertainty is the name of the game. Because the Highlands are a climatic nodal point where Atlantic, continental and Polar systems collide, prolonged spells of good weather can never be guaranteed. Thus, if the wet southwesterlies have melted the snow, revert to heather skiing. But in the case of Arctic blizzards, which can reach well over 100 miles an hour, get off the mountain quick for there are few huts or safe places in which to shelter. During an attempted traverse of the central Cairngorms in 1984 from Lecht to Kingussie with David and Anna Williams and Roger Childs, we had battled for three days through storm and bullying winds before that venture came to a premature end when I failed to emulate David's forty-five degree jet-turn to avoid a heap of granite boulders when descending from Beinn a' Chaorainn Beagh. The ensuing fall dislocated my right shoulder and walking off the mountain to the Falls of Avon Refuge with the shoulder hanging off was the most painful experience of my life. Without David and Anna's heroic ten-kilometre ski to Luibeg that night to raise the RAF Sea King helicopter that flew me to Raigmore Hospital ten hours after the fall, I would have suffered permanent damage and disability. Next day, it did nothing for my *amour propre* to read the Inverness *Evening Express's* headline, 'Middle-aged hill walker on the mend'.

For a less austere form of long-weekend training, the mountains of Spain offered an attractive alternative and during the late 1980s and the early 1990s I made six separate Spanish ski tours. The first of these was to the Picos de Europa, arguably the most dramatic minor range in Europe, which earned its matronym by heralding landfall to treasure-laden Spanish galleons returning from the new world. Running parallel to the *Costa Verde,* Spain's northern coast, for forty kilometres the rugged limestone summits of the Picos rise to over 2,600 metres and form the apex of the 450-kilometre-long Cordillera Cantabrica. With an annual precipitation exceeding 152 centimetres, the Picos generally carry good winter snow, but with the Atlantic lapping its foothills, the outcome of any ski tour will depend on the weather and particularly the notorious *Nodest Pardo* wind which can persist for days and brings with it foul weather and serious avalanche risk.

The range's topography also poses unusual navigational challenges because its three distinct limestone massifs are dissected by a chaos of transverse and converse valleys, gorges, defiles and sink-holes – the *canals, gargantas, desfiladeros* and *hoyos* of local nomenclature. Above the containing walls of this maze rise another complex of crenelated ridges, towers, pinnacles, obelisks and monoliths. There are few easy ridges or cols and a paucity of good paths make for a geographical confusion that the Spanish maps then available to us were unable to untangle. Overall, the topography of the Picos presents an unusual challenge for the ski mountaineer compounded by avalanche risk.

Although my old Cairngorm mentor Fred Jenkins had, inevitably, climbed in the Picos, the only account of any ski tour I could find was that of the French *grand raide* specialists Berruex and Parmentier. And so, in early February 1986, Pyrenean veterans Rupert Hoare, Roger Childs, David Seddon and I foregathered at Heathrow to attempt a modified version of the French traverse. Neither literature nor imagination are substitutes for seeing the ground for oneself and on arrival at Bilbao, plans had to be recast on learning that Sotres, our intended start point, had been cut-off by snow for the past week. Reverting to an altogether less ambitious programme, we kicked off from the mountain hamlet of Espinama, where local women sported six-inch high-heeled wooden clogs to keep their feet dry of snow, and skinned up the Rio Nevandi valley through a metre of fresh snow. The weather never let up for the next two days, so we never caught even a glimpse of our intended objective, the Pena Viega. After one bitterly cold night at the Refuge Aliva, we made a feeble retreat to Espinama through veils of driving snow.

By the following morning the barometer was rising and from Fuente De we set off for the village of Valdeon along the southern ramparts of the Central Massif. The sight of fresh ski tracks ahead so aroused Rupert's competitive instincts that to assess the strength of the opposition, he forged a diagonal uphill route through dense beech thickets to secure the high ground. Having sized-up the challenge of a totally inoffensive Parisian *équipe*, there could only be one team in it. Seven hours later at Valdeon, Childs ingratiated himself with Leandra Perez, the martinet mistress of the Fonda Begonia with a soft heart who gave us her best rooms. Leandra turned out to be the granddaughter of the legendary chamois hunter Gregorio Perez who in 1904, with the Marquis of Villaviciosa, had first climbed the 2,510-metre Naranjo de Bulnes, the talismanic monolith of the Picos. Her *bouillabaisse* and *chorizo* with eggs piquant closed a highly satisfactory day.

But thereafter, it was downhill all the way. The eighteen-kilometre trek down and up the stupendous Cares Gorge enclosed by 1,000-metre-high limestone cliffs confirmed my worst suspicions about ski-mountaineering in the Picos. The skiable snow ran out at Cain, a tiny hamlet squeezed into a clearing just before the Gorge reaches its narrowest point, which is barely an arm's span in breadth. This Spanish Shangri-La, the remotest habitation in the Picos, had been cut off from the outside world for the past fifteen days. We were its first visitors that year yet without blinking, the *Señora* of the Hostal Pena Santa opened up for business with platters of home-cured *jamon* and *chorizo* while the man of the house, perched atop the stove, studied us incuriously as he whittled away at a gnarled bit of wood. Above the bar, a bronze plaque commemorating Gregorio Perez's epic ascent of the Naranjo served as a reminder that 'El Cainejo' himself was born here. Back at the Begonia that evening, well out of Leandra's earshot, an ancient local put us right about that famous ascent.

'*Señores,* the true story is that the Naranjo was climbed by local hunters at least fifty times before Perez got anywhere near it. Many brave men fell in the attempt and when they hit the ground their bodies exploded into small pieces which had to be carried away in sacks.'

According to Leandra, our next staging post, the Vega Redonda Refuge, had been destroyed by an avalanche. Instead, we made tracks southwards into a remote nature reserve frequented by deer, wild boar, wolf and bear to get a better idea of the terrain ahead. From the Cebollada, a panoramic view to the north persuaded even Rupert that the gorges of the central Picos were best bypassed. When returning to Valdeon, Childs swore that he had skied over a hibernating bear. Next day, to speed our slowing passage, Leandra's son Miguel agreed to drive us to Covadonga at the western end of the range for something less challenging. I was concerned to see that bullet holes riddled the bonnet of his Land Rover, until he explained that these were not the work of Asturian irredentists, but the result of his getting on the wrong side of the Mayor of Oseja's boar hunt the previous day.

Covadonga commands the entrance to the Onis Gorge that leads into the heart of the western Picos. It owes its place in Asturian history to the memory of the legendary battle in AD 718 that was waged for days through the Picos gorges and which resulted in the Visigoth hero Pelayo's defeat of the moors and signalled the start of Christian Spain's *Reconquista*. Pelayo's name graces

Covadonga's grandest hotel, a Parador in all but name. Its funereal reception hall was adorned with stag horns, animal pelts and stuffed bears while a monumental stone staircase, lined with the doleful portraits of Asturian kings, achieved an improbable synthesis between Scottish baronial and Spanish ecclesiastical.

The only guarded hut in the Picos lay three hours up the Onis Gorge besides the Enol Lakes. When we got there, its guardian Juan Louis Somonao warned of avalanches higher up, so we settled for El Diadelliou, an otherwise unmemorable peak, which gave a grandstand view of the superb 2,596-metre Pena Santa de Castilla whose ice-encrusted summit resembled a surrealistic wedding cake. This was to be our last throw in the Picos for although few ranges in Europe can compare, its spectacular gorges form near-insuperable obstacles to continuous ski traverses.

On our last evening in Spain, as I watched the fading evening sun play on the purple snows of the Cordillera Sueva before it plunged into the Atlantic, I reread Juan Louis Somonao's inscription in the copy of his *50 Excursiones Selectas de la Montana Asturia* that he had given me at the Enol Lakes hut, 'Always remember that Spain is not just a land of bullfighters and flamenco, but has many fine mountains too!'

This was speedily put to the test in February the following year, 1987, when Childs, Hoare, Arctic luminary Derek Fordham and I flew to Madrid for an extended weekend in the Sierra de Gredos, the highest massif in Spain's 150 kilometre-long Cordillera Centrale. Little known to the British, this choice was influenced by Childs's ownership of the *Finca Prado Lobero,* the Wolf's Meadow, an attractive estate set high in the Gredos foothills near the little town of Candeleda which was then John Major's summer retreat. The Gredos had formerly been a royal hunting ground for stalking *Capra montes Hispanica,* the talismanic Spanish ibex. After the First World War, King Alfonso VIII, a keen conservator, donated it to the Spanish Government which, in turn, designated it a national park in 1932.

The Gredos is a range of contrasts. When wintering in Candeleda, where the lace-makers and potato crisp merchants who sell their wares in its narrow streets are recognised as artists in their own right, you can pick oranges off the trees that line its avenues and drink coffee in the main square under the shade of palms, while 2,000 metres above, glittering snow peaks hang suspended from an indigo sky. Breakfasting al fresco the morning after our arrival on the sunlit terrace of the Prado Lobero, frost lay heavy on the meadows and the tinkling of goat-bells floated up from the shadowed plain of the Tietar.

Away to the north-west, framed between the broad shoulders of twin converging ridges, rose a distinctive triangular snow peak.

'What is that mountain?' I asked Roger.

'That is Al Manzour,' he replied portentously. 'The monarch of the Gredos.'

At 2,592 metres, Al Manzour is the highest peak in the range and was only climbed in 1899, long after all the major Alpine and Pyrenean mountains had fallen. Its Arabic name, 'The Victorious', was the sobriquet given to Muhammad ibn Ali Amir, the brilliant Yemeni general who temporarily restored Moorish dominion over tenth-century Iberia when Islamic arts, sciences and agriculture flourished and northern Europe still languished in the dark ages. Child's modest claim to have made one of Al Manzour's first British summer ascents so excited Rupert's competitive spirit that he swore to make the first British winter ascent.

To get within striking distance of Al Manzour, it was necessary to drive north across the spine of the range by a twisting mountain road that at times shadowed its near-perfectly preserved Roman predecessor as it wound through a forest of oak, ash and pine which, in turn, gave way to a dense *maquis* of rosemary, thyme, lavender, citrus, gorse, heather and broom. From the bar at Navarradonda in the Tormes Valley, the Gredos's northern aspect of rolling whaleback ridges capped by the occasional granite tor, bore a comforting resemblance to the Cairngorms. After dumping the car at Plataforma, we skinned off to the Llano Hut, a mere forty minutes away, to find it deserted and unheated, with no obvious facilities for either cooking or washing up and its darker corners filled with mouldering rubbish. A cheerless, cold supper was followed by an evening stroll to the peaklet of Antinuedo to watch the sun set over La Mira and give us the promise of a fine day tomorrow. Back at the hut, we stretched out our sleeping bags on its bare boards and settled down for the night.

The high jinks which began around midnight reached a ski-clattering, oath-spewing climax at 3 a.m. From the ebb and flow of testy, weekend skiers blundering around as they bashed their heads on seasoned chestnut beams and flashed their torches about to find an inch of empty floor space, it seemed that all central Spain had decided to stay at the Llano that Friday night. It was like some mad disco and when the expletives of the *compañeros* eventually died away, only their snores were left for insomniacs to construct fiendish scenarios of revenge. At dawn, we disentangled ourselves from the mass of comatose bodies that littered the floor and stepped outside to greet the sun. Gliding across pristine snow past pink-tinged, granite monoliths, the view from the nearest skyline ridge disclosed the gamut of the Gredos's inner secrets with a tableau of glaciated cirques, saw-tooth ridges and spiralling aiguilles radiating out from a clutch of 2,500-metre peaks. The summits of La Mira and Morezon gave further fine views of wild gorges debouching southwards before dissolving into veils of haze that marked the Tietar Plain. Back at the Llano, well pleased with our nineteen-kilometre round-trip, we found that a jovial guardian was now in residence dishing out lashings of *lomo* and fried eggs.

That night, the hut's decibel level reached new heights with the late arrival of two Alsatian dogs, yet by 8 a.m. next morning the place was completely empty with the guardian complaining that last night's customers had deserted the Llano for the superior comforts of the Elola Hut superbly sited at the head of the Gredos Cirque. We followed a veritable Pennine Way of tracks through the snow to the Cuerda de Cuento pass from where the dazzling spectacle of Al Manzour's snow-encased pyramid prompted Rupert's, 'We must strike now while the weather still holds!'

With Childs complaining bitterly that we were missing out on a very good lunch, things went well enough as far as the Col de Crampons. Here, a lone climber's imprints nudged round an awkward rock bulge before disappearing up a steep snow gulley whose containing walls were over-laid with black ice and over-hung with Damocles-like icicles. At this point, Rupert disappeared leaving Derek and me to climb this final pitch. Just short of its exit, a barrage of ice blocks came winging down past our unhelmeted heads. As Al Manzour had been the bane of medieval Spain's Christians, Rupert, that scourge of medieval mountaineers, had stolen a march on us by a different route and was now crowing his conquest on the summit. Rupert Hoare had become Al Manzour 'The Victorious' and when another ice fusillade nearly decapitated Derek, we scurried down for cover and denied ourselves a share of Rupert's glory.

With the first British winter ascent of Al Manzour thus secured, Rupert claimed the lead in a helter-skelter race back to the Elola. At first, it looked as if nothing would halt his triumphal progress until a rare lapse of concentration lost him the lead. In a desperate effort to regain it, he went wildly off route and had to be dissuaded from making an Eddie-the-Eagle-style jump off a thirty-metre-high cliff to catch up. That night, we had the Elola to ourselves, but the terrific storm that broke in the early hours ended three days of near-perfect weather. Retreat to Plataforma through wind, snow flurries and breakable crust served as a reminder of how quickly conditions can change even in sunny Spain.

The following year, a reconstituted Gredos team had another crack at Al Manzour. After a night of blizzards at the Elola, this second attempt folded just below the Col de Crampons, due – we persuaded ourselves – to avalanche risk. For me, the ascent of Al Manzour remains yet another unfulfilled dream, but the memory of that great Islamic champion from a forgotten age lingers on.

It was another four years before I returned to the Spanish mountains in winter. This time, in February 1992, it was to the Alto Carrion, a massif of shapely 2,500-metre peaks some thirty kilometres south of the Picos. This party comprised Spanish veterans Childs, Hoare and Fordham leavened by John Hayward, Simon Kirk, Richard Morgan and Jay Turner. After flying into Bilbao, two expensive taxis conveyed the eight of us across the steppes of High Navarre to the Parador National Fuentes Carrionas. Throughout that long day, not a vestige of snow had been visible and it transpired that I had chosen the worst Spanish snow-year in living memory for this venture.

The original sport plan had been to traverse the massif east to west on ski; climbing peaks and camping en route. From the 1,800-metre Col Hoyo Banquila, a bird's-eye view of the upper Carrionas Valley running into the heart of the massif, confirmed that only the north-facing slopes had even a smattering of snow. Yet there were surprisingly few recriminations when everyone, except John Hayward, decided to dump their skis at Lebanza and proceed on foot. John, on home leave from covert activities in Afghanistan, was by far the fittest and strongest member of the party and later justified his Sherpa-style carry with a ski-extreme descent down the north face of Consejo.

Although it was intended that the expedition should camp throughout, the sight of an isolated stone building set near a stream on the grassy meadow of the Vega Caballos gave every appearance of a mountain hut. Six empty wine bottles, some mouldy *chorizo* and a dead mouse on the kitchen table, was sufficient confirmation for four sybarites to settle in rather than share my brand-new North Face VR25 tent. Returning to camp late the following evening after the whole party had climbed Curavacas (2,525 metres) by routes of varying difficulty, we were confronted by the hut's irate owners who, having driven up in their Land Rover, now accused us of trespassing and the theft of the hut's wine and comestibles. A Guardia Civil summons might have terminated the tour prematurely had not Childs, in flowery vernacular, reduced the temperature with protestations of our innocence and then producing his trump cards as a Gredos *finca* freeholder and the *Señor* of a Santander-born *Señora*. Hostilities were suspended and an Anglo-Spanish accord cemented with rounds of *Rioja*.

The conquest of Curavacas preceded a string of first-British winter ascents of Consejo, Tio Celestino (a Hoare solo), Pico Murcia and Espiguete. These climbs were in no way remarkable, but that of the Peña Prieta, the Carrionas' highest peak, was enlivened by a desperate summit race when Rupert was uncharacteristically slow in twigging my stratagem to deny him priority. Awakening belatedly to the technical limitations of his own curious choice of a route up Peña Prieta's scree-strewn south face, he then galvanised himself into self-destruct mode in a frantic effort to overtake me as I strolled purposefully above him along the summit ridge. Alas, too late for he only reached the summit full two minutes after me – a fair exchange for the rebuff on Al Manzour. With good snow cover, a traverse of these attractive peaks would make a fine ski touring expedition and the Pension Meson in Cardano Valley offers a most hospitable base for climbs on Pico Mursia and Espiguette. But beware! Do not mistake private hunting lodges for non-existent mountain huts.

In 1996, the 'Siberian Express' and Northern Spain's coldest winter for a decade cut off 1,500 Asturian villages. To take advantage of these exceptional conditions, Childs, Patrick Fagan and I flew out to Asturias Airport in February with the object of making a ski ascent of the 2,417 metre Peña Ubiña La Grande, an isolated massif fifty kilometres south of Oviedo. In the city's smart shopping malls, fur coats were *de rigeur* to withstand the blizzards that had brought chaos to the streets and hardship to the countryside. When the tourist bureau confirmed that the Refuge del Meicin, from where I had hoped to launch our Ubina bid, was inaccessible due to metres of unconsolidated snow, we lowered our sights to the more accessible Peña Rueda after establishing ourselves in the comfortable Hotel Melchior, Cortes at the head of the Quiros Valley.

The Peña Rueda's shapely summit was clearly visible from the hotel's dining room, but with a metre of snow covering the village, the 1,255 metre climb to its summit was never going to be a dawdle. From a high col overlooking the immense Foz Gorge, the face-on view of the Peña Ubeda's Cyclopian precipices, festooned with snowy excrescences from which the wind was tearing tatters, left me much relieved that we were not going anywhere near it. Soon enough, even the ascent of the Rueda was giving us trouble as from the Vallina Grande, a sinister place moated by sheer rock walls, the way to its summit was masked by shifting clouds. After struggling up a seemingly endless succession of transverse ridges with the light fading and the wind gathering strength, we took stock. It had already taken six hours to get this far and to carry on would mean certain benightment. The soundest insurance policy is the instinct of self-preservation, so we turned tail and got back to Cortes that night after ten hours on the trot. The following day's excursion along the Cordal-La Vega ridge following the tracks of boar, deer (and, according to Childs, bear), eventually ended up in dense forest in a far-off valley where we would probably have spent the night had it not been for a chance lorry lift to Cortes with a gang of ex-miners turned hunters.

Six weeks later, there was still enough snow in the Cordillera Cantabrica for Roger Childs and me to take a punt on climbing the 2,190-metre Peña de la Cruz in the Mampodre National Reserve, a likely-looking peak I had first spotted from the Alto Carrion. At the tiny village of Maraña, graced by one pub and a Romanesque church, the early-April sun had burned away the mist to expose the spiralled peaks and snow-covered flanks of yet another mystery Spanish mountain. In reply to Childs's macho 'What-are-conditions-up-there-like?' chat-up line, a weathered cowgirl eyed us up and down, gave the withering put-down, 'You're both far too old. You are carrying too much weight, and you won't find any treasure up there!'

High above the Regato de Valverde's greensward, already carpeted with miniature daffodils, the sun had passed its zenith. We pressed on upwards towards an infinitely distant skyline ridge with the sweat stinging our eyes and the skis feeling like lead. Under the incurious gaze of a herd of chamois, we dumped sacs and skis at a col and after kicking steps to the summit, collapsed to enjoy a superb panoramic view of the Cordillera Cantabrica. Westwards, wave after wave of white-crested summits stretched away to an indistinct horizon. Eastwards there remained only one snow-covered range, the Alto Carrion.

Down at the bar at Maraña, Childs let slip that we had seen at least half a dozen chamois that morning. At this, a hoary local gave us a pitying grimace.

'*Señores,* when I was a huntsman in my youth, herds of forty or fifty chamois were commonplace. You've come here far too late!'

Those ventures into the half-forgotten valleys of the Cordillera Cantabrica where squat, stone houses roofed with red Roman tiles hug the earth for winter warmth; where sheep and cattle take priority; where grain barns are set on stilts to deter the rats as in the Elburz; where fishermen throng untracked riversides and where deer, boar, wolf and bear still roam the forests, gave glimpses of another Spain that still preserved ancient values. Here too, I experienced a sense of rediscovery rare in most European ranges that flatters the traveller and vindicates his quest.

12

ANTIPODEAN VENTURES II

On the 13 March 1988, I completed the final stage of the Pyrenean High Route and with that ten-year odyssey of tragedy and triumph at last behind me, Georgina and I took advantage of the three-month long sabbatical that Norton Rose generously gave its partners after completing a decently long period of service. Our round-the-world tour that autumn to Africa, Australia, New Zealand, Fiji and America would have been a good excuse for taking a proper holiday after it, for the programme involved twenty separate air flights, forty-eight nights with friends or relatives, twenty-two in hotels, and another twenty-two spent either in mountain huts or under canvas.

When I had first visited Kenya in 1961, it was a British colony with a population of seven million. Today, it stands at over forty-five million. Even since my last visit in 1981, things had changed and not necessarily for the better. The customs officers at Nairobi's international airport were aggressive, inefficient and corrupt. Later, when driving through Eldoret, we fell victim to a scam involving both the car hire company and conniving pedestrians who shouted out from the curb side that our rear-axle was leaking oil. After a local garage had carried out some bogus repairs, I was escorted out of town for a 'test-drive' by three heavies who then presented me with an extortionate bill. I negotiated a 'discount' with an IOU after secreting most of my cash in my shoe. Finally, on flying out of Kenya, we had to bribe our way through the airport's emigration control leaving only minutes to run across the tarmac to catch the onward flight to Harare.

Despite such unpleasantness, Kenyan hospitality was as warm as ever. Mike and Jane Prettejohn invited us to stay at their Sangare Ranch with its 6,000 acres enclosed by a two-metre-high, electrified fence to protect Jane's race horses; the late Raymond Hook's zebroids and Mike's fifty South African pedigree boar-goats from marauding lions. Yet it was depressing to learn that the Prettejohns' salad days were numbered. Their pioneering farming operation at Galana had already been closed down by the Kenyan Government with its big game slaughtered wholesale by Somali Shifta bandits. Sangare had just been used as a setting for the film *Happy Valley*, but the Prettejohn marriage was on the rocks. Some years after their divorce, Mike barely survived a burglary at his beloved ranch when a panga-wielding gang thrust a family sword through his abdomen. He subsequently donated Sangare to a wildlife conservation charity in order to preserve Kenya's rare mountain ibex, the bongo.

As we breakfasted on the veranda, the morning mists cleared. Twenty-five miles away, Mount Kenya emerged from a skirt of clouds with its summit peaks and glaciers glinting in the sun. Georgina turned to me, 'You know John, I really would like to get up to the Lewis Glacier. When my Uncle Charles was soldiering here with the Kings African Rifles during the 1930s, he lugged his skis the whole way up to that glacier to be the first person to ski on Mount Kenya.'

It sounded like a great idea, but my previous scrapes upon that mountain left me a touch dubious.

'What d'you think?' I asked Mike.

'It's quite the wrong season to get up there from this side,' he replied.

'You'd be better off using the Chogoria Track on the eastern side. But I must warn you that this year's weather has been the worst on record, so the roads will be as slippery as hell and the forest track to the Bandas may be impassable. Also, the Chogoria's a good bit longer than any other approach to the main peaks.'

We decided to give it a go anyway for the Chogoria Forest is larger and more variegated than any other on Mount Kenya with magnificent specimens of *Mutati*, meru oak, cedar, East African rosewood and giant camphor rising forty-five metres high. Mike's predictions about the track proved entirely correct and when the Isuzu 4x4 sank up to its axle hubs in liquid mud, our salvaging strategy of chocking the wheels up with logs and brushwood got nowhere. After three hours, I was beginning to wonder how to survive a night in the forest with a bad-tempered rogue elephant notorious for his dislike of Japanese 4x4s. Rescue eventually came in the form of five likely lads from Macclesfield who happened to be passing by and managed to lever out the car with tree trunks.

A night at the Chogoria Bandas left a sour taste when the manager tried to short-change us. Nothing daunted, trek prospects were looking good next morning with clear, blue skies silhouetting Mount Kenya's indented summit peaks on the horizon. An early start saw us nervously skirting a herd of buffalo and by noon, we had reached 3,750 metres on the Nithi Ridge with the dense bamboo thickets of the Chogoria Gorge spread out far below. Just to get down there was going to be challenge enough, but with Georgina nursing a splitting migraine and a strained leg muscle, I took stock. Certainly, we had enough food for five days but I now realised, too late, that to get from here to the Lewis Glacier and back could take at least a week. Trudging back to the Bandas past steaming mounds of fresh elephant droppings with close sightings of eland, forest hog and Mackinder's eagle owl, I pondered how I had again underestimated Mount Kenya. Just before nightfall, we chanced by the Macclesfield lads' camp to find three of them laid low with diarrhoea and altitude sickness. Feeling a touch smug, we decided that our twelve-hour trek had not been such a bad effort after all.

The object of driving to Kitale over 350 miles of lethally slippery dirt roads was to stay with another of Tilly Dalton's protectors, Sep and Helen Mayer at their Dutch colonial-style house built high on the slopes of Mount Elgon. As a former wartime soldier, Sep had been allocated a standard 1,300-acre plot by the British Government of Kenya which he had since converted from a forested wilderness into a self-sustaining farming operation that employed sixty Pokot tribesmen living in the fourteen staff houses and a school for 600 local school children which he had built himself. As one of only four survivors from the original 800 who took up the government's offer, Sep was definitely staying on. To give us a feel of the 4,321-metre Mount Elgon, the oldest and largest extinct volcano in East Africa, he volunteered to drive his Land Rover as high as axle-deep mud permitted. We lunched by the entrance of an enormous cave with its dark lake fed by a waterfall – a magnet for every type of big game to drink here at dawn and dusk. At midday, the place was taken over by screeching colobus monkeys and chattering baboons. Sep reminisced of how, in 1948, he had spent four days climbing to Elgon's summit with fifty porters and the local district officer who always changed into black tie for dinner.

Our last days in Kenya were spent with Tilly Dalton at her beach-hut retreat at Malindi where she insisted that Georgina should pad out her bathing costume to enhance her physical attributes to best advantage, African-style. This was to be my final farewell to the country, which, over twenty-seven years, had given me so much pleasure and set the stage for some of the most defining experiences of my mountaineering life.

From Nairobi we flew on to Harare and thence to Western Australia where, in-between stays with family and friends, we revisited the Porongorups and Stirlings. Our final Australian destination was Tasmania whose tag 'England Down Under' is as misleading as its geographical classification 'temperate maritime', for although it shares the same latitude as Spain's Atlantic coast, it lies in the path of the Roaring Forties which, after crossing several thousand miles of the Southern Ocean, dump 200 inches of rain, sleet, and snow annually on Tasmania's shores and mountains. Then, at almost any time of year, icy winds blow straight out of Antarctica and as if this were not enough, its summers can desiccate by drought and/or incinerate by bush fire.

Tasmania's flora and fauna are quintessentially Australasian with few recognisable European equivalents. Its dank forests of primeval tree fern and archaic palm are vegetal relics of the primordial super-continent of Gondwanaland, long dispersed throughout the Southern Hemisphere by continental drift. Its discomforting bush – spiny, prickly and spiky – achieves the ultimate in impenetrability, most particularly in the form of a vigorous creeper whose scientific name *anodopetalum biglandulosum* is as convoluted as the shape it assumes as a matted mesh suspended several metres above the ground. Some of Tasmania's fauna is unique, for in addition to kangaroos and bandicoots, wallabies and wombats, trapdoor and redback spiders (both deadly), Tasmania is also home to the platypus and echidna, tiger snakes, Tasmanian devils, and Tasmanian wolves – the virtually extinct thylacine.

When you touch down in Hobart, a deceptively tranquil town backed by the snow-capped Mount Wellington and a pretty harbour bright with ocean-going yachts, you can readily understand why Tasmania is Australia's top holiday destination for the 'great outdoor experience'. Yet, many official histories of what its seventeenth-century Dutch discoverer Abel Tasman christened 'Van Diemen's Land' concealed some of Australia's darkest secrets. By the early nineteenth century, it was notorious as Britain's principal convict settlement and even after transportation had been abolished, the systemised brutality that had characterised the white man's lifestyle was transmuted into a campaign of ethnic cleansing that effectively wiped out the island's aboriginal peoples. For all its wild beauty, Tasmania remains a land where nature is hostile and where, in the unfamiliarity of its dank, silent forests, the ghosts of Van Diemen's Land – convicts, cannibals, bushrangers and aboriginal spectres – still dwell.

Australians take conservation very seriously and Tasmania's near-inaccessible Wilderness National Park well earns its world heritage listing. For natural scenery, the 1,300-square-kilometre Cradle Mountain National Park which occupies the central core of the island, runs it close with a landscape that was sculptured 20,000 years ago by the ice cap sixty-five kilometres in diameter which crowned the mountain ranges then part of the Australian mainland. It was these ancient glaciers that carved out the arêtes, cirques and headwalls, softened by tarns, lakes, waterfalls and gorges, that offer some of Australia's most spectacular scenery, particularly the igneous, red dolerite rock whose plugs and pinnacles, columnar and hexagonal pillars, fluted cliffs and porcupine ridges offer some of Australia's best rock climbing.

The Cradle National Park which became a reality through the enthusiasm of an Austrian *émigré* Gustav Weindorfer, was created in 1922 and its famous bush-whack, the eighty-five-kilometre Overland Track that runs from Lake St Clair to Cradle Valley with a line of well-maintained huts sited within a day's walk of each other, first opened in 1937. The track traces a fragile thread through the heart of the park linking rain forest and swamp with the hummocky sedge lands, button-grass and soggy peats of its moorlands to an alpine tundra of rare cushion plants. To traverse the park within a week seemed about our mark and although, in summer, professional guides charge track trekkers £450 a throw for the wilderness experience, we had no option but to do it in winter conditions.

To limber up, we walked up Mount Wellington and then tramped out to Cape Hauy to gawp at the spectacular sea stacks that emerge like needles from the roiling surf of the Southern Ocean. After buying a map, guidebook and enough food for seven days, we caught the Tasbus from Hobart on 19 October and disembarked at the Derwent Bridge stop together with a couple of heavily laden Oz Overlanders. It was cold and spitting rain with snow-covered hills occasionally emerging through scudding cloud and lowering skies when, after a brief exchange about the weather, the Australians decided to give it away and returned down the road muttering darkly that a 'monster low' was coming our way. Signing in at the Cynthia Bay rangers' office, we crouched under the veranda to escape the rain and after a quick bite, beat off a crowd of crows and grotesquely jowled wattle birds competing for titbits before pushing through a mob of semi-domesticated wallabies and plunging into the Tasmanian rain forest.

For fifteen kilometres, the track to the Echo Point Hut hugs the shoreline of Lake St Clair, the deepest lake on the Australian continent. The forest merged into its waters which, though barely five metres away, were only occasionally visible as the path tunnelled its way through an opaque, vegetal mass with the carcasses of rotting tree trunks hosting a profusion of multi-hued mosses, fungi, and other parasitic growths. Eighty metres above, giant eucalypts, alpine ash, sassafras, leatherwood and Tasmanian laurel formed a canopy so dense as to create perpetual twilight. Though Tasmania boasts 200 different bird species, apart from brief sightings of wallaby and wombat sidling silently through the bush, no other living thing was either seen or heard on that gloomy afternoon. As dusk was falling, we arrived at the hut sopping wet despite our new Goretex oversuits and only after a third despairing attempt managed to light its standard issue, pot-bellied, coal-burning stove to create a cosy fug and dry out.

My original plan had been to bag three peaks – Olympus, Ossa and Cradle Mountain – en route and when studying the map, had wondered why, in this land where aboriginal myth has been consigned to oblivion, so much of its mountain nomenclature – Olympus, Ossa, Pelion, Acropolis and the rest – derived from classical mythology. Apparently, this vogue was initiated by the nineteenth-century scholar/surveyor General George Frankland and has been followed ever since. The 1,447-metre Tasmanian Olympus, dramatically portrayed across the waters of Lake St Clair by Australia's first home-grown painter Piguenit in 1875, seemed an obvious starter for according to Gloria Barnes, the acknowledged Queen of Hobart's bush-whackers, it could be approached from Echo Point up an 'obvious stream thirty minutes beyond the hut coming off Lake Oenone'. Curiously, the park guidebook made no mention of any route up it.

Next morning brought clear skies and sunshine that lit up the hills gleaming bright with fresh snow. But last night's torrential rain had made Gloria's 'obvious' stream indistinguishable from countless others that were cascading down the mountainside into the lake. After forty minutes, we struck off to the west from the track hoping that something of the nymph Oenone's gift of prophecy might have rubbed off. Yet not a vestige of path was visible as we climbed steeply through dense undergrowth past groves of towering Antarctic myrtle. A near-vertical rock staircase, only scaled by clinging on to roots and lianas, took us to the upper forest zone and our first brush with the bovver boy of the bush *richea pandanifolia* or pandani. This twelve-metre-high grass tree resembles a cross between a giant groundsel and a superannuated palm. Like its smaller, but equally vicious relative *scorparia*, it represents yet another Antipodean growth adept at inflicting grievous bodily harm through serrated fronds which can gash your hands at a touch. By the time we reached the snow line, both mine were lacerated.

On emerging from the forest, the pillared buttresses of the Tasmanian Olympus became visible for the first time beyond the uncompromisingly black waters of Lake Oenone. Bashing on through thigh-deep, crusted snow, we clambered up a broad couloir choked with titanic blocks of red dolerite that eventually debouched us on to the flattened summit of the Seven Apostles of Olympus. From this bleak belvedere the secret heart of Tasmania revealed itself as a whitened tableland whose sullen uniformity was broken only by dark-blue troughs marking the forest, a clutch of black outcrops and a line of snow-capped bluffs studding a grey horizon. Away to the north-west, the unmistakable profile of Frenchman's Cap protruded like a thumb's top digit. The sun was still shining, but there was no warmth in it and a chill wind hastened our return to Echo Point, reached nine hours after setting out. As dusk fell, a lone walker hurried by without exchanging a word and heading, we assumed, for the Narcissus Hut – our next stop along the track.

That night, another violent storm battered Echo Point. At dawn, the currawongs' raucous cry was the harbinger of more bad weather to come and cast doubts about our reaching Pine Valley that day via Harrison's Crossing, the Narcissus Hut and Cephissus Creek. The track tunnelled remorselessly through dripping ferns under the canopy of enormous trees whose roots criss-crossed the ground and then along metre-high boardwalks. At first, we scorned these aids which must have taken months of mind-boggling labour to construct, yet without them Harrison's Crossing would have involved a 400-metre swim and was only just fordable with them in thigh-deep water. The hut itself was empty, though according to the hut book a large school party bound for Pine Valley had left only a few hours before us. Later, we learned that they had been marooned there for days and had to be rescued by helicopter. The whole valley seemed to be filling up with water and when, after wading waist-high for fifty metres across Cephissus Creek, the sight of a metre-high bore powering over the boardwalk sent us scurrying back to the main track, all thoughts of reaching Pine Valley abandoned. That night, we squelched into the Windy Ridge Hut shivering convulsively and immediately set to getting rid of the leeches that festooned our necks and arms.

The hut was already occupied by a dull-eyed pair of pot-smoking locals ostensibly employed on its maintenance and a young Swiss who turned out to be the lone walker of the previous night. His name was Didier and his combi-sac/suitcase contained a large Swiss cheese that Georgina reckoned was the best possible reason for teaming-up with him. Friendly enough, but when he baulked at my suggestion that the three of us might make a detour the following day to climb Mount Ossa, Tasmania's highest peak, I doubted that we would see him again for he left Windy Ridge long before us next morning.

Back on the track, Georgina and I broke cover after a five-hour struggle through a Jabberwocky-like forest only to be confronted by windswept moorland thickly covered in snow. Faintly visible at the end of it through veils of driving snow, lay the Pelion Gap flanked by a storm-bound Mount Ossa from whose serrated south ridge spindrift streamed off in tattered banners. Forcing the gap was critical to reach the Pelion Hut, but the moorland turned out to be a glutinous bog, ribboned with concealed trenches and fast flowing melt streams. While trying to jump across one of them, Georgina became unsighted by the stinging snow, slipped and fell in. As the torrent ripped her legs from under her, I grabbed the back of her rucksack and hauled her on to the bank. With Georgina soaked through, there could be no question now of attempting Mount Ossa for the trek had become a matter of survival. To avoid hypothermia, I kept forcing the pace through the skeletal remnants of a fire-scarred forest and only after breasting the gap and dropping down into the shelter of the forest did we escape that deathly wind. Outside the Pelion Hut, a mob of snow-encrusted marsupials were sheltering under its eaves. Inside, Didier was cosseting the pot-bellied stove, preparing a cheese fondue.

For most of the following day's yomp to the Windermere Hut it hailed, sleeted and snowed. We were wet to the skin within thirty minutes of leaving the Pelion Hut and for much of that day waded up to our calves along a torrent that had once been the track. Ensconced in the hut was a Tasmanian Highland Tours guide, John Boden and his shapely client Sylvia. Once past the formalities of ritual Pom-bashing, John admitted to being a deconstructed Pom ex-schoolmaster turned Tassy and our relationship blossomed. Attired in denim shorts worn over woollen long-johns, John explained that 'Sylvie and me have had to hunker down here for the past couple of days, no thanks to this bastard weather' and when Georgina pulled off her boots and socks observed solicitously, 'You've got bush-foot there, Georgie. Take an old bush-whacker's advice – wear plastic bags inside your boots!'

That night, a pack of possums tried to break into the hut to escape the cold and when the nighttime temperature inside plummeted to below zero, Boden had to get up twice to keep the stove alight.

In good weather, the overland track is little more than a strenuous hike. But over the past five days, trial by rain, sleet, snow and flood had left the three of us with festering feet, lacerated heels, streaming colds and coal dust 'smoky-eye'.

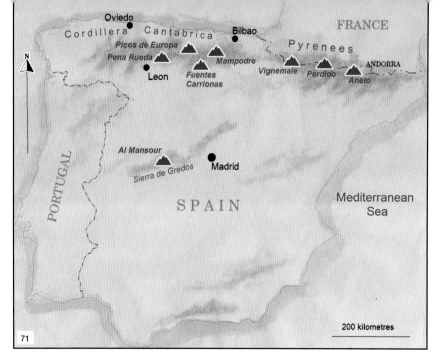

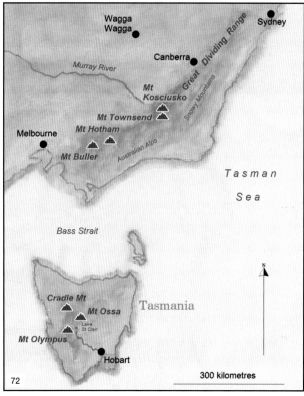

71 Spain.
72 South-East Australia.

73 Tasmania 1988. Mount Olympus.
74 New Zealand 1988. The 'Breakaway' off the Bonar Glacier.
75 Tasmania 1988. The Heart of Tasmania from Mount Olympus.

76 New Zealand 1988. Mount Aspiring.
77 New Zealand 1988. Mount Elie de Beaumont from Mount Broderick.

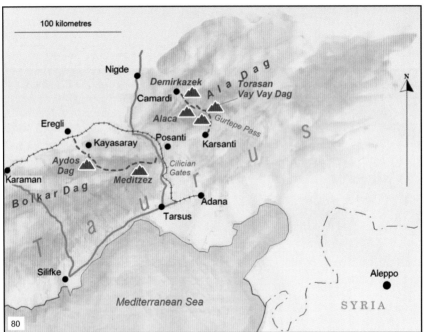

78 New Zealand 1988. Above the Murchison Glacier headwall. Shaun Norman.
79 New Zealand 1988. Mount Broderick.
80 Taurus Range, Turkey.

81 Ala Dag Taurus 1986. Ala Dag. Sundowners at Narpiz Camp. L–R: Georgina, Randall MacDonnell, Francis Meynell, David Wrightson, John Blacker, Liz MacDonnell, Cecily Van Moyland, Sidney Nowill.
82 Ala Dag Taurus 1986. Ibrahim at Emli Gorge camp.
83 Ala Dag Taurus 1986. Exit from Emli Bashi. L–R: Randall, Liz, John.
84 Taurus Traverse 1990. At Adana railway station. L–R: Simon Kirk, David Seddon, Anna Williams, Ronnie Wathen and David Williams.

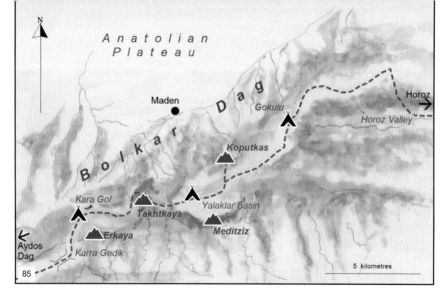

85 Bolkar Dag Taurus.
86 Taurus Traverse 1990. Southern gorges of the Bolkar Dag.
87 Taurus Traverse 1990. En route to Gurtepe Col.

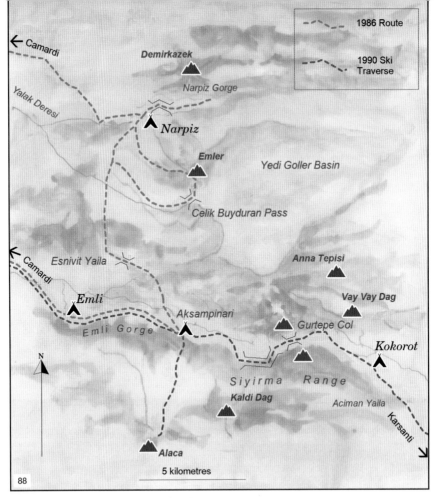

88 Ala Dag Taurus.
89 Taurus Traverse 1990. Eagle's Nest bivouac below Gurtepe Col.

90 Taurus Traverse 1990. Gurtepe Col. The final section.
91 Taurus Traverse 1990. Dolomitic peaks of the Ala Dag.
92 Kackar Dag 1987. The first day. L–R: Georgina, Susan and Robert Sykes.

93 Kackar Dag 1987. *Rhododendron* and *Azalea Ponticum*.
94 Kackar Dag 1987. Camp 3. Georgina and Susan.
95 Kackar Dag 1987. The view westwards from Nanatleme Tepese.

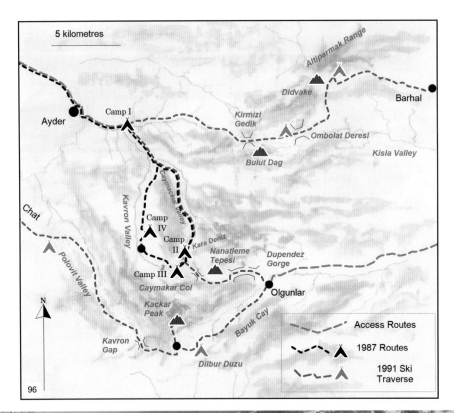

Map labels:
5 kilometres
Altiparmak Range
Didvake
Barhal
Camp I
Kirmizi Gedik
Ayder
Ombolat Deresi
Kisla Valley
Bulut Dag
Caymachin Valley
Kavron Valley
Chat
Camp IV
Camp II
Kara Deniz
Nanatleme Tepesi
Dupendez Gorge
Polovit Valley
Camp III
Caymakar Col
Olgunlar
N
Kackar Peak
Bayuk Cay
Kavron Gap
Dilbur Duzu

Access Routes
1987 Routes
1991 Ski Traverse

97

96 Kackar Dag.
97 Kackar ski traverse 1991. Chalets in lower Kisla Valley.
98 Kackar ski traverse 1991. En route to the Kirmizi Gedik.

98

99 Kackar ski traverse 1991. Escape from the Ombolat Deresi.
100 Kackar ski traverse 1991. Head of Avucar Valley.

101 Kackar ski traverse 1991. Caymakeur Valley, Nanatleme Tepesi on skyline.
102 Kackar ski traverse 1991. Descent into Dupendez Gorge. David and Anna.

103

104

103 Kackar ski traverse 1991. Anglo-Dutch rendezvous. L–R: Kemal, Ronald Naar, Hank, Steven,
    Bas, local Laze, Anna, David.
104 Kackar ski traverse 1991. Before the key passage.

105 Kackar ski traverse 1991. Avalanche debris, Kormik Valley. David and Steven.
106 Kackar ski traverse 1991. Verchenik. Upper Firtina Valley.

107 Turkey 1983. The Lycian Alps. Lolly on *Foresight*.
108 Greece 1985. En route to Olympus. L–R: John, Liz and Georgina.

Georgina had also strained a muscle and sustained a septic toe. Next morning, I stared warily with glued-up eyelids through the hut's frosted windows to see that last night's blizzard had left the ground covered in a metre of fresh snow. John, busily scouring out his billycans with tea-tree leafs announced: 'Sorry mateys, we're going to desert you as we've got to bash on to the Cirque Hut now whatever the weather. We're already two days overdue at Cradle Valley.'

We elected to stay put that day for a break and enjoy the last of Didier's cheese. My only serious excursion was to venture out to visit the composting lavatory sited the statutory 150 metres away from the hut. Within was pinned a notice warning that one puff of a fag could detonate the whole shebang. Setting about my business, I reflected that this must be one of the few instances when the natural functions of a nicotine addict could make mockery of minimal-impact bush-whacking. Tomorrow would be another day, but with time and food running out I was determined that it would bring down the curtain on our overland trek.

It continued to snow that night and on quitting the hut next morning, we were hit by a blanket of horizontal sleet. The track had been completely obliterated by knee-deep snow and after two and a half hours we lost sight of the marker poles. I sounded a lame retreat and back at the hut, cold, wet and dispirited, morale hit a low. But the prospect of being kippered alive for another night steeled common resolve and so, after finishing the last scraps of food, I took a fresh compass bearing and once again we marched out into weather reminiscent of a bad day in the Scottish Highlands. This time, after hitting off the critical col that marked the transition between forest and moorland, the tension eased and we made the Cirque Hut in three hours. It was deserted save for one lone Brit, Richard Bryan, still recumbent in his sleeping bag having spent the past two days waiting for the weather to clear. His overland track was over leaving us feeling a touch smug particularly as John and Sylvia had taken six hours to reach this hut the previous day.

By next morning, the wind had dropped to a murmur leaving the branches of the trees bowed down with snow. Moving fast while the weather held, we skirted the dolerite plug of Barn Bluff as the sun peeped through the thinning clouds for the first time in a week. Two hours on, the unmistakeable porcupine-spine of Cradle Mountain, Australia's most photographed peak, hove into sight. Its red rock was warm to the touch and rough to the hold and an hour of scrambling was enough to reach its summit where Gustaf Weindorfer had once proclaimed, 'this must be a national park for all time!' With the snows of Pelion and Ossa luminescent in the sun, I gazed back almost fondly over the forests and snow-streaked moorlands that had been our penance for the past week. Yet even as we began our descent to Dove Lake, an armada of black clouds came racing in from the west pitching, dipping and accompanied by a gusting wind so strong that it hurled us to the ground. The lake's waters had become choppy with white-topped waves and a skein of waterfalls were being blown upwards in fountains of spray as we raced down to Cradle Lodge. Here, a man with a knowing-look and snake-skin-banded hat, offered us a lift to Devonport in a government truck. Just short of the town, he exchanged this for one bearing the marque 'Proud to be Tasmanian' and then relieved each of us $25 by way of surcharge. This brush with a genuine Van Diemonian left as sharp a taste as had the Overland Track.

NEW ZEALAND MARK II

New Zealand's Southern Alps have everything that a mountaineer could ask for and more. When Georgina and I flew into Christchurch on 20 October for a three-week round tour to visit friends and relatives, I had already set aside a ten-day slot to climb Mount Aspiring and revisit the Mount Cook National Park. Timing was not ideal for either climbing (too early) or ski mountaineering (too late), particularly as the weather at this time of year is unsettled. In 1970, I had been lucky both with the weather and in finding three very competent New Zealanders to climb with. This time, I took Hamish Nichol's advice to hire a guide.

This wise counsel was reinforced by Carl 'Thomo' Thompson, a veteran of eight Antarctic expeditions, who recommended that my man for Mount Aspiring was Nick ('guide anywhere anything') Craddock, recently voted New Zealand's 'mountaineer of the year'. Lean, laconic and aged thirty, Nick had previously been Alpine Guides Mount Cook's chief instructor, but was now doing his own thing. When we met up in Christchurch on 6 November and I told him that I wanted to climb Mount Aspiring, he looked me up and down warily; asked me my age, and then pronounced.

'Yer know mate, I've never climbed with anyone as old as you before and yer better know that we've been having lousy weather for months. We might not even get off the ground, let alone top-out on Aspiring unless it clears pretty damned soon.'

After negotiating unreasonable terms of engagement with Nick, he brightened up: 'Okay then, it's a deal. Anyway, the latest forecast is for a change to the southerlies which normally bring high pressure.'

Later that day, we drove south to Wanaka in a hired car in heavy rain stopping off en route at Twizel. At this former mining village, now a dormitory for Mount Cook guides, Nick insisted on looking up his old mate Gary Ball, the leader of the controversial 1988 New Zealand/Czech Everest expedition when four Czech climbers had been killed and the Australian Linda Brady broke ranks to summit solo. Ball, sharp-witted with hippie-style blond hair, was about to found Adventure Consultants with fellow New Zealander Rob Hall. Both were to die in the Himalaya within the next eight years. Ball in 1993 from pulmonary oedema on Dhaulagiri. Hall in 1996, trapped alone and dying on Everest's South Summit in a terrible storm where he made his last radio call to his wife Jan telling her 'not to worry'.

Wanaka was an unpretentious ski resort in the heart of the 288,000 hectare Mount Aspiring National Park. Rather than stop over for a night in Nick's lorry/cabin convertible, he insisted on driving straight through to the New Zealand Alpine Club's Cascade Hut. After signing in, we spent the next hour bumping along the bottom of the Matukituki Valley by a dirt road in ever-deepening gloom as glistening white ribbons of water cascaded down the mountainside. The whole valley seemed to be awash and the car had to ford a succession of fast-running streams up to its hubcaps. The sheer wildness of the place was overwhelming. As flights of seagulls wheeled and swooped, Craddock, who had scarcely uttered a word since leaving Twizel, now pronounced, 'Seagulls on a south wind! That's a good sign. We're going to leave the car here and walk to the hut.' Two hours later, we reached the Cascade Hut long after dark.

Craddock's forecast was spot on. By the following morning, sunlight bathed a swathe of hoar-frosted meadows running to the fringes of a matt-green forest of southern beech. Far away at the valley's head, the snow cone of Mount Bevan gleamed like a beacon. Were the European Alps ever as green as this or its snows so bright? From here, Mount Aspiring, the 3,093-metre peak for which I was paying Craddock good money to climb, was still invisible. Tucked away, high above a forest wilderness surrounded by a glacial moat, its inaccessibility goes far to explain why it was only climbed in 1909, fifteen years after Mount Cook, by Captain Bernard Head (AC) and the New Zealand guides Jack Clarke and Alex Graham. Two years later, Head was to pioneer skiing in New Zealand with another Englishman, Lawrence Earle, but in 1915 was killed at Gallipoli with many brave Anzacs.

Despite Aspiring's reputation, I found it hard to understand the logic of

Craddock's schedule which allowed a full day to reach the intermediate Lucas Trotter Hut, only 1,000 metres higher than the Cascade Hut, and then another half-day to get to the Colin Todd Hut barely 335 metres higher again. His insistence that we carry a fortnight's food 'just in case we get stuck' carried a message.

I had never previously hired a guide to climb a mountain and was finding it difficult to get through to the taciturn, monosyllabic Nick. Long before reaching the Lucas Trotter Memorial Hut, I had twigged that this particular hut march was unlike anything of my previous experience. After wading a mile or so up the River Matukituki and twice crossing it by rackety suspension bridges, parts of the route up the French Ridge were more by root-ladder than footpath and soon I was bitterly regretting my having volunteered to carry most of the food. It was difficult to sleep that night at the Lucas Trotter Hut thanks to an unholy racket made by a brace of keas who repeatedly slid off its tin roof as if deliberately to annoy. This iron-beaked bird, one of New Zealand's few indigenous species to have survived, is curious, fearless and destructive. Capable of killing a sheep, it is persecuted remorselessly by farmers, but has become a cult bird for Kiwi mountaineers.

Next morning, Craddock pronounced, 'Weather's looking pretty settled today, so we'll head for the Colin Todd by the breakaway.'

'What's the breakaway, Nick?'

'It's what we have to cross under those effing ice cliffs coming off the Bonar Glacier's snout. It's by far the fastest route to get to the hut, but you should know, mate, that there's a darn great risk involved. That icefall can be a real bugger, so be bloody careful how you go. Lucas and his girlfriend Trotter were killed there by an ice avalanche.'

After roping up, we threaded a tenuous line through the debris of recently collapsed séracs under the breakaway's teetering ice cliffs. Two and a half nerve-twitching hours later, we breasted the lip of the Bonar Glacier's ice plateau. Three-kilometres dead-ahead, Mount Aspiring's dazzling white pyramid rose up before us 1,200 metres clear of the glacier. The highest mountain in New Zealand outside the Mount Cook National Park and arguably the most beautiful, its Maori name 'Titita', the 'Uprising Glittering Peak', is at least as evocative as that given it by John Thompson, New Zealand's first surveyor general. The sky was cloudless and in retrospect, we might have gone for it there and then. But I was not psyched-up enough for such a challenge and neither, no doubt, was Craddock who didn't know what sort of Pommie bastard he was taking on. That evening at the Colin Todd Hut, the ice cliffs of

Aspiring's north-west face looked daunting, yet the easier angled north-west ridge gave me a glimmer of confidence for tomorrow's climb.

In the New Zealand Alps, you are always looking over your shoulder to the north-west from where the hogs-back clouds, certain harbingers of bad weather, come from. None were visible when we first arrived, though a fresh wind got up later that afternoon. It was still blowing strongly next morning when we made two abortive starts at 4 a.m. and 6 a.m. before finally leaving the hut at 8.45 a.m. This seemed ludicrously late by alpine standards, particularly as the guidebook advised ten hours for the climb, though the bombastic Samuel Turner's epic ascent in 1913 took sixty. Heading into an icy wind blowing across the Bonar Glacier, I was thankful to be wearing over-trousers over my salopettes and long johns.

To gain the crest of the north-west ridge, Craddock festooned the ice ramp leading up to it with a line of ice screws. I followed behind, held tight like a puppet on a string, feeling faintly ridiculous. The ice-cornices on the ridge above looked menacing, but after half a dozen pitches the crest seemed to be within our grasp. On joining Craddock at the end of yet another pitch, he spoke for the first time since we had left the hut.

'Sorry mate, that bloody wind up there's a bastard. If we get on to the crest now, it'll blow us clean off the mountain. We're going to have to give this one away, so best to get ourselves off pretty damned quick.'

Bursts of spindrift were spiralling off the ridge above, yet most of the technical difficulties were already behind us. Craddock's decision had created an inner conflict in me at having to yield ground so hardly won. Nonetheless, you need a special confidence to gainsay New Zealand's 'climber of the year' so, with an effort, I muttered: 'Okay, if you say so, Nick.'

Once down on the glacier, Craddock suggested that we salvage something of the day by knocking off Rolling Pin, the most southerly peak of the Haast Range and climbed for the first time in 1948. Its jagged summit ridge, suspended over a 1,000-metre dead-drop to the Therma Glacier, was encrusted with double cornices that billowed out like a square-rigger's topsails. It looked a lot harder than anything we had done so far that day, yet yielded with grace. Back at the hut, now besieged by a brace of keas, the sun beamed down and the wind dropped to a murmur as I stared across to Mount Aspiring musing on what might have been, before wandering over to the outside privy accompanied by those same keas who tried to nick my boots. After a hearty Kiwi tea of cereal, sausages and bacon, Nick and I braced ourselves for our second crack at Aspiring the following morning.

Long before the 4 a.m. reveille, the nor'westerlies were rattling the windows and threatening to tear the tiny hut off its wire stanchions.

'We've got to get out of this bummer – fast', Nick announced with unusual animation. 'This bloody weather could last for days.'

As I cast my eye over the mountain of food we had lugged up, he seemed to read my thoughts.

'Yeah, pity about the food. We'll leave most of it here just in case we have to come back. Anyway, some other poor bugger may be thankful for it. The break-away's a no-no in these conditions, so we'll have get down by the Bevan and Hector cols. Look mate, it's only fair to tell you that in bad visibility that route can be effing dangerous. We've just got to hit off both cols dead right.'

After this comforting news, we mooched around for a couple of hours hoping that the storm might ease. It never did. We both had deadlines to meet and so at 10.15 a.m. we quit the hut and walked out into the face of a blizzard. For the next one and a half hours, Nick and I marched across the Bonar Glacier in a near whiteout on a 220-degree compass bearing. I went out in front, rope length after rope length for forty-five metres. Nick would then semaphore 'left' or 'right' for me to maintain dead reckoning when I would mark a large cross in the snow after which he would bring up the rear and we'd repeat the exercise. We hit off the Bevan Col exactly as planned and now began a dodgy diagonal traverse across the glaciated south face of Mount Bevan to the Hector Col. Everything now hinged on Nick's navigation. To wander off east into the upper Waipara Gorge would mean a three-day walkout to the coast while any deviation to the west could precipitate a free-fall off the 1,000-metre high bluffs that overhung the upper Matukituki Valley.

We had closed up together to do this critical passage when, at 12.30 p.m. Nick suddenly sat down in the snow.

'Yer know mate, we're buggered. We're effing lost and this is effing serious.'

'Let's have a look at the map with the altimeter' I suggested brightly.

'I haven't brought an effing altimeter! Nick shouted back.

I obliged with mine. As we pored over the map, I noticed out of the corner of my eye Nick's rucksack moving very fast down the slope unassisted. It then became airborne and after a couple of cartwheels disappeared into the void. Nick moved faster than I had ever seen anyone move on a mountain before. But from a standing start, in no way was he going to catch that rucksack. The air turned blue with Nick's effing and blinding and then, with his normally expressionless face contorted with fury, he turned on me.

'D'yer know what's gone down into that effing gorge with my effing rucksack?

My bivvy bag, sleeping bag, snow shovel, stove and all my ironmongery! That lot's worth a bloody fortune and none of it's insured! Now, we're really up the creek!'

After this *moment critique*, Nick raised his game. Another half hour's frenzied activity saw us through to the Hector Col and by 1.40 p.m. we were steamrolling down the upper Matukituki Gorge through sleet, rain and a stubbornly thick undergrowth occasionally relieved by white splashes of the exquisite Mount Cook Lily. Wading knee-deep down the swollen Matukituki river, we reached the car exactly ten hours after quitting the Colin Todd Hut. Nick's 'Well done mate!' was intended as a compliment and back at Wanaka later that night we sank a number of beers together before dossing down in Nick's convertible caravan.

On 14 November, after three days in Christchurch juggling flight schedules for the next leg of our world tour, I caught the Mount Cook National Park bus stuffed with American and Japanese tourists bound for the Hermitage. It was here that I had arranged to meet Shaun Norman of Alpine Guides Mount Cook for four days ski mountaineering before Georgina came down to join me. Once again, I was chancing my luck with the weather, but not in my choice of guide. Shaun, a Brit, had spent three winter and seven summer seasons in the Antarctic; been on two Everest expeditions, and had guided Hamish Nicoll up Mount Tasman the previous year. Powerfully built, outgoing, with dry Yorkshire wit, he was married and much closer to my own age and temperament than Craddock.

Shaun confirmed that the weather for the past two months had been 'appalling'. However, as a short break was forecast, he suggested that we had better get up to the Tasman Saddle Hut that same afternoon. The scope for ski mountaineering in the southern Alps might seem limitless, but the very wildness, remoteness and steepness of the mountains; the heavily crevassed glaciers; frequent icefalls; paucity of huts and, above all, the violence and unpredictability of the weather, make any ski mountaineering venture a serious undertaking. New Zealand guides have come to regard ski mountaineering as an indispensable skill, yet although the first stirrings of New Zealand skiing pre-date the First World War, its ski mountaineering history really begins in 1936 when the New Zealand government invited an Englishman, Colin Wyatt, to advise on winter sports development. Author, photographer and passionate naturalist, Wyatt had already represented Great Britain at both downhill racing and ski jumping, but was pre-eminently a ski mountaineer who pioneered expeditions to unusual places from the Arctic to the Antipodes. That same September, he teamed up with the famous Hermitage guide Mike Bowie and after making some first ski ascents in the Mount Cook area, they completed the first double ski crossing of the Main Divide via the Franz Joseph and Fox Glaciers. Wyatt's exceptional ski mountaineering achievements have all but been forgotten. For reasons he was unwilling to discuss, the distinguished New Zealand scientist Professor Roland Rodda who knew Bowie well and was himself an outstanding mountaineer and ski mountaineer besides being a very supportive Alpine Ski Club vice-president, could not abide him.

After settling a plan of action, Shaun rustled me up a hired-equipment package of iron-age crampons and some Salomon downhill boots, the only pair in stock. Since my last visit eighteen years before, the Ball Hut had been destroyed by an avalanche and the Tasman Glacier's inexorable retreat had exposed ever more miles of boulder-strewn moraine. This meant that it now took at least two days to reach the Tasman Saddle Hut, forty-eight kilometres further up the glacier from the Hermitage and to save time and trouble, most climbers and all skiers and tourists took the plane.

A dozen light aircraft sat around on the airstrip with a long queue of frustrated sightseers waiting for the gusty wind to drop. When it did so in late afternoon, everyone except Shaun and I had given up. Cramming the rucksacks and food into the plane's tiny cockpit, we strapped our skis under its wings and squeezed inside. Two dummy runs later the plane landed on the upper Tasman Glacier. It was already 5.30 p.m. but without drawing breath, we dumped our kit in the snow and I followed Shaun up to the Aylmer Col on skins just as the sun sank into the Tasman Sea. Unfamiliar skis and boots; breakable crust and altitude lethargy exposed my more obvious technical failings. When I apologised to Shaun for my dismal performance, his only comment was 'Not to worry. At least you've got a good survival technique.'

The Tasman Saddle Hut, perched on a spur overlooking the upper Tasman Glacier, was not the sort of place to have the squitters. Its 100-metre long drop could only be reached by a death-defying, unprotected passage over black ice. Already in occupation was a pair of hard-eyed Yankee girls with their two guides, noisily celebrating their ascent of Elie de Beaumont earlier that day. Named after a nineteenth-century French geologist who never actually visited New Zealand, this most northerly 3,000-metre peak in the Southern Alps dominates the head of the Tasman Glacier with its ice-domed summit and the heavily crevassed Anna Glacier clearly visible from the hut.

'That's where we're heading tomorrow, John,' said Shaun. 'Weather permitting.'

I took this caveat for real after reading the hut book's breathless ten-page account of how, only six weeks before, the Keen Brothers had survived an eleven-day blizzard confined to this same hut.

At 5.45 the next morning 15 November, Shaun and I were making tracks for Elie de Beaumont's south face. To spare me the pain of climbing in the heavy Salomon downhill boots, Shaun suggested that I wear my own mountaineering boots in ascent carrying the Salomons in my rucksack. In descent, we'd do a swap with him skiing in the Salomons and me in his much lighter Dynafit 'Tourlites'. On the steep, icy approaches to the base of Elie de Beaumont *harsheisen* would have come in handy, but these were evidently regarded as pansy by Kiwis. At 7 a.m. we dumped our skis under a sérac, donned crampons, and after negotiating a succession of bergschrunds and ice pitches up the Anna Glacier reached the summit at 9.30 a.m.

'That's the fastest time I've ever done on Elie!' said Shaun delightedly.

'We've been darn lucky. Later on in the season the crevasses and bergschrunds open up to make this route damn near impossible.'

Perched on the backbone of New Zealand, the peaks and snowfields of the southern Alps stretched away north and south: cold, remote and seemingly inaccessible.

Back at the now-deserted hut, Shaun suggested that we climb Mount Mannering the following day.

'What am I letting myself in for?' I asked him warily.

'Just one mighty fine peak on the Main Divide about eight kilometres away to the north-west. I haven't climbed it myself, but conditions are looking good. However, be prepared for a longish day because we've first got to get down the Murchison headwall and then cross both the Tasman and Classen Saddles to reach its base.'

I would happily have settled for something less challenging and already had bad vibes about the glaciated Murchison headwall which closes the eighteen-mile-long Murchison Glacier, the second biggest in New Zealand. But nothing ventured and so, at 5 a.m. next morning we were bumbling around the hut sipping tea by the light of a single candle as the first rays of the sun lit up the ice dome of Elie de Beaumont. On reaching the lip of the Murchison headwall my worst fears were realised. Was Shaun seriously proposing that we ski down 750 metres of near-vertical ice?

'Is this really the route Shaun? It looks horrendous!'

'No worries John!' he replied with a grin. 'She'll go all right. Just relax. All ready now?'

I wasn't in the least bit ready. The headwall was embedded with rocks and riven by small bergschrunds. Hadn't I been to places like this before? Maybe once, or even twice, but long ago. Past resolutions raced through my mind. But if Shaun thought I could get down this suicidal wall in one piece, it was he who would have to pick up the bits if I didn't. Anyway, I couldn't chicken out now, so I bit my lip, braced myself and mouthed a silent prayer.

'Okay then Shaun, let's go!'

On ice, it's the first turn that matters. This one was going to be critical. Above all, you must try to relax: difficult enough when you know the consequences of getting it wrong. Coming into the turn, I flexed my knees for the skis to cut into a rock-hard ice and then, with a touch of my ski pole on the upward movement, torqued them round. One tight turn followed another as we sped on downwards with my mouth dry, my heart pounding and my thighs tightening. The skis were clattering on the ice, yet within seconds I was running fast and free, deeper and deeper into the shadowed depths of the Murchison Glacier. When we stopped at the bottom, I would have shouted out loud with relief if I hadn't been gasping for breath. Shaun just grinned, yet even he must have given some thought to that terrific descent.

A meandering climb led through a maze of crevasses to the Classen Saddle from where Mount Mannering took shape as a spiralling snow cone surmounted by a vertical pyramid of pure ice. It looked very difficult and hours away. Somewhat nearer rose another fine mountain of exactly the same height, Mount Brodrick. I had noticed its cascading ice cliffs on the way down, but never given it another thought.

'I can't see us making Mannering today,' I said stiffly to Shaun. And then, not wanting to appear a wimp, added on impulse, 'But what about Brodrick?'

He looked a bit dubious. 'Okay. Brodrick's quite a tough call. I've never been up it either, but let's give it a go!'

For the next five hours, I kept wishing we hadn't. After dumping our skis at the base of Brodrick's south-east face, we climbed without a break front-pointing all the way, up and around a maze of gaping bergschrunds to a high brèche. From here, the mountain's true summit lay at the far end of a shark's fin of snow with a free fall of 1,300 metres to the Whymper Glacier below.

'Christ Shaun! How the hell do we get across to it? It'll take at least an hour to get there and back. I really don't think I'm on for it.'

'Nonsense,' grinned Shaun. 'We'll be there in a few minutes!'

For the second time that day, more than my nerve was tested. When you're young, you revel in danger. When you're older, you've got more imagination. And what to one may seem a dawdle, will scare the living daylights out of another. The rope wouldn't have given any protection on that wafer of snow so I gritted my teeth, almost paralysed with vertigo, and followed Shaun. It felt like walking a tightrope yet, as he had predicted, it only took eight minutes to reach the summit. Five kilometres away, across the sensational gulf of the Whataroa Gorge, the east face of Elie de Beaumont rose 2,000 metres clear from the Whymper Glacier. Had we really stood on that shining summit only yesterday?

'Better get down fast before the snow gets too soft,' said Shaun, interrupting my reverie.

Front-pointing inwards all the way down Brodrick's face, I twice slipped before reaching the bottom, but was held firm. Slaloming around the gaping crevasses of the Classen Glacier, we dropped down into the Murchison's trough, now become a burning cauldron in the mid-afternoon sun, and then began a long slog up the glacier. But success was the spur and I barely noticed the effort of front-pointing non-stop up the headwall. We reached the hut at 4 p.m. exactly ten hours after leaving it. Brodrick had been one of the most testing climbs of my life. Shaun seemed almost as pleased as I was to have done it.

Next day, the hut's wireless forecasting the onset of the dreaded northwesterlies speeded our eight-hour descent down the Tasman Glacier. Coasting down its upper reaches, I marvelled at the soaring ice peaks that delineate the galactic skyline of the Main Divide and wondered how this twenty-nine-kilometre-long, restless river of ice could exist in the middle of a Pacific island. Any ski descent down the Tasman Glacier will always be an unforgettable experience for it is here, under the shadow of Mount Cook 'the Cloud Piercer', that all journeys in the southern Alps should end.

Brodrick was not quite my last brush with New Zealand's mountains. Before we left South Island, Georgina bussed down from Christchurch to join me at the Hermitage with the idea that we walk the famous Copland Track to cross the Main Divide into Westland. The original Hermitage had been as close to a Highland shooting lodge as exists in the Antipodes, but the modern hotel, seething with Japanese honeymooners and portly Americans, was like any other and the fading photographs of New Zealand's mountaineering heroes, Mannering and Fyfe, Bowie and Hillary, had been relegated to dim corridors. One night there was enough, and as Shaun Norman had predicted, foul weather scuppered our Copland tramp. We retreated to Christchurch; took lunch off Everest-veteran Norman Hardie and then flew on to the North Island.

Before European settlers clear-felled most of North Island's indigenous forests for sheep runs, groves of the giant kauri tree had been its grandest natural wonder. Protected patches of this magnificent tree still exist, but the island's most impressive scenery is to be found in the Tongariro National Park where erupting geysers pose as great a hazard as the ice avalanches that occasionally peel off its glaciated volcanoes. Tongariro's summer landscape of ashen slopes and black basalt ridges was disappointing, but we did climb its distant neighbour Mount Egmont, the elegant 2,517-metre dormant volcano that the Maoris call Taranaki and which, like Japan's Mount Fuji, forms a near-perfect cone, snow-clad throughout the year. Surrounding Egmont's base is a primordial forest of dense undergrowth, tree ferns and huge Rimu and Rata trees whose boles are encased in moss with lianas and creepers dangling from their boughs. The solemn advice of the proprietor of the Mountain House Motor Lodge that a rope, ice axes and crampons were 'indispensible' for Egmont's ascent seemed ludicrous as we elbowed our way through its dense thickets enveloped in the mist for which the mountain is renowned. Eventually, this overwhelming vegetal mass gave way to a sub-alpine zone of tussock grass leading on to bare ridges of pumice and upper snowfields. Near the summit, the clouds parted momentarily and now, for the first time that day a faint patchwork of green fields became visible 2,000 metres below. Breakfasting alfresco on the lodge's wide verandah the following morning in warm sunshine, Taranaki's snow cone gleamed bright as a virgin summit and yesterday's climb might well have been a dream.

Georgina and I made several subsequent visits to the Australia, but never again to New Zealand. The unique land forms, eroded remnants of ancient mountains and subtle vegetation of Australia's wide brown land have left as lasting an imprint on my imagination as the grandeur of New Zealand's Southern Alps. Yet I count myself lucky to have climbed some of New Zealand's great mountains as the summation of my Antipodean ventures.

13

THE TAURUS

SPRINGTIME

Ski mountaineering in the Southern Alps had opened new horizons, yet more
familiar ranges closer to home promised equally exciting challenges. One of
these was Turkey's Ala Daghi Taurus, which I had first visited in December
1961. I did so again in 1986 for a trip that has special memories, as it was the last
time I went to the mountains with Sidney Nowill, my old Turkish mentor.
That visit also sowed the seeds of an altogether more ambitious trans-Taurus
ski mountaineering venture which I undertook four years later in 1990, but
first I shall recall what happened in that Ala Daghi spring of 1986.

Sidney was then sixty-seven though his enthusiasm for mountain travel was
undiminished. Since our 1965 Hakkiari expedition, he had chalked up some
fine routes in the Alps including the *Peuterey Ridge* and *Marinelli Couloir* and
had spent the intervening years roaming the world with his indomitable wife
Hilary. What Sidney grandly called his *Expedition to the Ala Daghi Taurus 1986*
was intended to be light on climbing, but heavy on botanising and bird-
watching as a lure to snare Georgina. It was agreed that responsibility for the
expedition's itinerary, logistics and overall organisation would be his, while
team selection – save for the inclusion of his old chum Francis Meynell
RN (retired) and ex-Turkish Navy – would be mine. Accordingly, I enrolled
John Blacker, Randal and Liz MacDonnell as climbers with Georgina and
old friends David and Jill Wrightson and Cecily Van Moyland as naturalists.
Sidney had assured Georgina – and she in turn the naturalists – that May
would be 'the ideal time of year to enjoy the Ala Daghi's exceptional flora

and that this year there is very little snow so the flowers will be earlier.'

Sidney's lists for 'Phases I, II, III and IV' of the trip would have done credit to a Himalayan expedition. They covered every detail about the party, its objectives, itinerary, motorised and animal transport, weather projections, finance and health. Thirty-one different foodstuffs were itemised down to a single tube of mustard, as were ninety-four articles of kitchen equipment. Sidney's estimate that 'a dozen donkeys (at least) will be required', brought to mind John Hunt's strictures about the Persian Expedition's porterage requirements. Each member was enjoined to take up their five-litre duty-free spirits allowance to supplement Sidney's 'dozen-bottles of good Turkish red wine'. He also spelled out what were 'appropriate ladies items', but left the choice of personal climbing and camping equipment to 'the presumed experience of all members of the party – though ice axes and crampons are essential.' Some participants had never camped before and wouldn't have known a crampon from a karabiner.

On 3 May 1986, the UK contingent flew out to Istanbul and on landing were each presented with a copy of *The Expedition's Current and Projected Expenses to Date*. That night, Hilary produced a delicious alfresco 'light supper' of hors d'oeuvres, smoked sturgeon, strawberries and white wine on the terrace of the Nowills' apartment in Moda while Sidney entertained us with tales of Turkish mores and morales. At 5 a.m. next day, a forty-seater Mercedes '302' bus arrived at our hotel with a crew of three who lost no time stowing a mountain of baggage in the heavy-duty, donkey-friendly, orange kit-bags that Sidney had had specially made for each of us in Istanbul. That night at Nevshehir, he catalogued our hotel's shortcomings with the first of his *Turkish quotes of the day*, 'Do not burn the coverlet on the bed in order to kill the flea', and that '*Datur, Datur!*' means, 'The sound of bed-bugs falling off the ceiling.' After a sightseeing tour of Urgup and Goreme, the charabanc rolled majestically on across the Anatolian Plateau to Camardi.

Sidney had already made a four-day Camardi recce the previous month to ensure that there would be enough donkeys to carry the party's baggage mountain. Also, that his faithful muleteer, Ibrahim Safak, would still be on hand. Ibrahim was there all right, ever ready and willing, but it was his more worldly son Ali, now married and teaching science at a local secondary school, who laid on the yoghurt, boiled eggs and flat bread 'feast' that welcomed the expedition. Sidney took objection to 'that rascally good-for-nothing Ali' as representing everything he disliked about modern Turkey and much preferred his father as the embodiment of the deferential traditions of the old. Propped up in a corner in Ali's tiny living room were a pair of Fischer touring skis. When I asked him how they came to be there, he explained that ski mountaineering was now 'his sport', and let slip that a group of French ski mountaineers had been investigating the area only a fortnight before.

Ever impatient of delay, Sidney left it to Ibrahim to organise the irksome business of loading up our ten donkeys and then personally led the way through the village's blossoming cherry orchards towards the Ala Daghi's cloud-capped peaks. The snow-level was looking ominously low, but the skies had cleared by evening when Sidney selected 'Camp One' high up the Narpiz Gorge in a *yaila* enclosed on three sides by vertical limestone cliffs. After cack-handedly unloading the donkeys, their charges beat a swift retreat back to Camardi leaving expedition members to struggle with what, for some, was the novel experience of erecting a tent. Morale was restored when Ibrahim set up the camp chairs and tables on which Sidney laid out whiskey, gin and wine to which everyone (now heavily muffled-up in anoraks, sweaters and woolly hats) was invited to help themselves. This arrangement worked well enough on the first night, but thereafter the weather was so bad that the MacDonnells' superior tent became a more congenial venue. For reasons best known to himself, Sidney had decided that a communal mess tent would not be necessary.

The thrilling, four-note call of the Caspian snow partridge answered by its partner's trilling reply woke me early next morning. Over breakfast, Sidney congratulated Ibrahim for having driven off a herd of foraging moufflon during the night.

'Those hardy animals were after our precious food,' explained Sidney. 'They've been forced from the heights by unseasonably heavy snow so we may be in for some bad weather.'

His forecast proved correct. The Ala Daghi was about to experience the heaviest snow in May in living memory.

Sidney's six-hour 'training walk' up the Narpiz Valley the following day in sleet and snow left the party sodden, cold and miserable. That evening, Ibrahim announced that he had to return to Camardi to settle a lawsuit and would not be back for a couple of days. This left Georgina and Jill to take over the cooking, crouched double in the lea of an over-hanging boulder. Next day, as the rain pounded down and mist choked the lower valleys, the MacDonnells' tent became a focus of low-life activity while Blacker and I decided to recce conditions on the Demirkazik with the unfocused aim of attempting the Hodgkin-Peck Couloir the following day. The Demirkazik's multi-tiered flanks were smothered in fresh snow and looked little different from when I had first seen it in mid-winter twenty-three years before. We agreed to leave that mountain for another day. A year later, Harding family honour was salved when our eldest daughter Emma climbed the Demirkazik as one of her haul of eight Mount Olympuses. Her guide on that occasion was Ali Safak.

At Sidney's suggestion, Blacker, the MacDonnells and I settled for what he assured us was the less challenging peak of Emler Bashi. His recommended approach route up the 'Black Waterfall Gully', involved a forty-metre ice pitch which dramatically accelerated Liz's apprenticeship in the use of crampons and eventually took us to Emler's dangerously exposed west ridge which was mainly composed of rotten rock. Four hundred metres short of its summit, progress ground to a halt below an impassable gendarme. We then retreated down the steep snow slopes of the Yalak Deresi, an immense glacial valley whose only obvious exit went down a steep snow couloir flanked by blank rock walls. It had no visible run-out so we took on spec the 300-metre glissade into its hitherto unknown depths, mostly on our bottoms. It was the most ex-hilarating descent I ever made and back in camp Sidney pronounced that our route was almost certainly a 'first'. But celebrations were muted, for although Ibrahim had returned triumphant after winning his lawsuit (thanks to a generous Sidney loan), the start of Ramadan prohibited him from cooking between dawn and dusk. Ibrahim's religious dawn rite of washing his hands and feet in our precious hot water now took priority over our early-morning tea. Georgina economised by using the same water to make the breakfast porridge.

To date, bad weather had confined most of the party to camp. To boost morale, Sidney suggested that we all trek together up to the Celikbuyduran Pass, 'to enjoy the spectacular view into Yedi Golu, the Seven Lakes Basin'. The 1,500-metre climb through knee-deep snow that at one stage involved a forty-minute stretch of step cutting, was certainly not the *route de grande-mère*' that Sidney had promised and on reaching the pass, dense cloud blanketed out the view. To save something of a bad day, Blacker, the MacDonnells and I bashed on to Emler's summit by the easy way. That night it again snowed heavily and when thick mist the following day ensured that the long-anticipated botanical excursion to the 'Cathedral Gorge' would be another non-event, the MacDonnells decided that they'd had enough and went home. The Wrightsons too were forced to retreat to the lower valleys because Jill was suffering from severe anoxia.

Now reduced to six, Sidney's decision to move camp from Narpiz Yaila to the Emli Gorge was conditional on the donkeys being able to get across the snow-covered Esnevit Ridge. There was no sign of them next morning so John Blacker began to mutter about his leaving early to rejoin his yacht at Kushadasi. When he complained to Sidney, 'Some of these blokes want to buy my boots. They say their feet are so bad that they can't walk without proper boots.'

Sidney's curt retort: 'To discuss this nonsense any further would be bad policy' closed the matter and the donkeys did turn up eventually. However, the only sign of animal life at Esnevit Yaila, normally thronged with grazing sheep and cattle at this time of year, was wolf spoor in the snow.

'A bad sign,' observed Sidney gravely.

The spring at Sigurmalik in the Emli Gorge was normally Sidney's favourite campsite. Yet despite the snow, it was now bone dry so we had to trudge another one and a half hours further down the gorge to camp at Emli Yaila. Set at the confluence of side valleys, it occupied a broad, grassy meadow around which were dotted scattered clumps of cypresses, dwarf pine, juniper and erratic boulders, which reminded Francis Meynell of the Yellowstone National Park. After unceremoniously dumping the baggage, the donkey men shot off down the valley leaving only Ibrahim and one donkey behind. That evening, the skies cleared for the first time in a week, enabling us to dry out sodden sleeping bags in the sun after which we repaired to the comparative comforts of a nearby cave whose inner walls were soot-blackened from a thousand shepherds' fires. It made an ideal communal mess and with cooking duties now shared out equitably, my *Dauphinoise a la Turque* won plaudits from even John Blacker.

Next day, the cloud level was again ominously low and by midday it was snowing so hard that both Cecily and Francis's tents collapsed the weight. Yesterday's greensward had become a Siberian snowscape and Ibrahim, whose Ataturk flat cap now bore an inch of snow, had to plead with Sidney.

'The state of the snow is such that the state of my donkey is such that my footwear is not adequate for the snow so I need your boots – please!'

Sidney obliged and then retired to his tent leaving the rest of us to hunker down in the cave and watch the snowflakes pirouetting gently outside as we read our books. Georgina chose Newby's *Love and War in the Apennines*, Cecily *The Princess from Siberia* while John sat morose and silent in his orange donkey-bag glued to *Out of Africa* dreaming, no doubt, of bygone Kenyan days and nights. Time passed all too slowly with the life-giving fire fed with clumps of

Berberus, which we foraged from beneath the snow. When this fuel ran out, Sidney bestirred himself and lopped off the lower branches of a nearby cupressus.

Things were not going to plan and to raise our game Sidney suggested that John and I have a tilt at Torasan (aka Vay Vay Dag), a remote peak that lay over a high pass at the end of the Emli Gorge in the least accessible part of the Ala Daghi. Sidney had already made two attempts to reach its summit. The first, in 1963, from the Emli Gorge and then again in 1980 by a much longer and more difficult southern approach from Karsanti on the far side of the range. Sidney called it his 'mystery mountain' though in fact, it had already been climbed in 1965 by Belfast and Cambridge parties. However, their rough sketch maps and Sidney's directions didn't tally. We decided to give it a go anyway and on 14 May, after another extremely cold night, set off up the Emli Gorge with two days' food and my bivouac sac. At first light, the skies had been clear but soon clouded over. As the valley narrowed into the Siyirma Bogazi gorge, the roots of the red limestone towers of Kaldi Dag, the Ala Daghi's second summit, emerged through swirling mist like the pillars of a Gothic cathedral.

Progress stuttered to a halt at 1.30 p.m. Blinding spindrift was whipping our faces as I turned to John and shouted in his ear: 'I don't see any future in this. My altimeter is showing 2,820 metres but Sidney's pass must be at least another 500 metres higher. We haven't got a proper map; we haven't a clue where we are and the snow's getting deeper all the time creating perfect avalanche conditions.'

When the avalanches began to crash around and the thunder rumbled, we scurried back down the valley. Lying in my sleeping bag that night listening to the rain pounding down on our tent, I could only imagine what it might have been like high up in the Siyirma Bogazi caught in that raging blizzard.

It continued to rain, sleet and snow throughout the following day. Sidney had underestimated Blacker's insatiable appetite for *Dauphinoise a la Turque* and when the food ran out, Cecily's 'But we still have the donkey!' didn't go down well with Ibrahim. Sidney despatched the poor man twice down to Camardi to bring up more potatoes. But two more days of bad weather made evacuation inevitable and this decision was hastened by the arrival of a couple of forest guards who poked around the campfire suspiciously. Luckily, the hefty pine bough Sidney had sawn off had burned to ash.

'Definitely looking for trouble,' pronounced Sidney after they'd gone. 'Unauthorised wood-cutting can land us all in gaol.'

Not long after, four hard-eyed moufflon hunters casually dropped by and commandeered both the fire and cave without a word of 'by your leave' or greeting. Sidney told the girls to retire to their tents, and after the hunters had sloped off muttering, convened a brief meeting.

'I don't trust those rascals one little bit. You can be sure they're up to no good. We'd best be off first thing tomorrow.'

That night, I was woken by the howling of wolves higher up the valley. A sinister, eerie sound that made Cecily cry out from her adjacent tent, 'What on earth was that?' Sidney's tales of women being eaten alive by wolf packs didn't now seem so fanciful. Not wanting to alarm her, I didn't reply and when the wolves' cries became fainter, I turned over and unchivalrously went off to sleep.

It was still snowing when the donkey-train arrived the following morning. As we made our way down the Emli Gorge I reflected that in eleven days, only one had been fine. Before boarding the Mercedes bus, Ibrahim kissed me on both cheeks as he pumped his dry, strong hand in mine. A fine man in the best Turkish traditions, I wondered sadly if I would ever see him again. As we began the long journey back to Istanbul, I glanced back for a last nostalgic look at the peaks of the Ala Daghi, but they were shrouded in cloud and no longer visible.

THE TAURUS SKI TRAVERSE

I never forgot the sight of Ali Safak's skis propped up in a corner of his tiny living room, though it was another four years before I returned to the Ala Daghi. Meantime, my mountain world had become embroiled in climbing politics. This is seldom a happy mix, yet the cautionary tale of the Alpine Club's premises merits brief mention for its outcome was to influence the very nature of the club. Briefly, in 1989 the AC's committee took advantage of London's property boom and traded in what remained of the lease of the club's old premises at 74 South Audley Street, Mayfair. In lieu, it was proposed to purchase a 125-year £650,000 lease from the Royal Geographical Society (RGS) to build new underground premises in the society's garden at Lowther Lodge and thereby strengthen the historic links that already existed between the two organisations. Many AC members, including Mike Banks who resigned from the committee in protest, were strongly opposed to what became known at the 'bunker scheme'.

Ever since 1980, I had been one of the Alpine Club's three trustees and although under the club's rules, we had no formal advisory powers, trustees generally have an overriding legal duty to protect trust property. The concept of burrowing underground to house the Alpine Club premises, archives, pictures and library rang warning bells, particularly when the club's surveyors advised that the future sale value of the lease would be barely half that of the proposed purchase price. And when selected 'senior members' were invited to pledge £50,000 (subsequently raised to £150,000) to underwrite the antici- pated loss of income following the proposed premises exchange, I felt sure that we were digging ourselves into a black hole and so expressed my concerns in a lengthy correspondence with the club's honorary secretary.

After two years of protracted negotiations, during which time the Ski Club of Great Britain generously allowed AC members the use of its Eaton Square clubhouse, the premises debate reached a bizarre climax at the club's AGM on 30 November 1990. Although the president maintained that that the site still retained its attractions, George Band had let slip that there might be a 'geology problem'. As almost the only dissenting voice at that meeting, I urged that a fresh vote on the scheme should be taken. By January 1991 negotiations had stalled and professional agents been given belated instructions to find suitable alternative premises. That April, an AC circular captioned 'Premises: A Winner?' triumphantly announced details of the intended purchase of the freehold of 55 Charlotte Road, a converted warehouse north of the city for £635,000 with twice the floor space of the bunker and ample scope for commercial sub-let- tings. The 'geology problem' turned out to be a severe threat from flooding; the bunker was never built, and the developers went bust. The RGS and AC link-up was never seriously pursued and the RGS subsequently merged with the Institute of British Geographers, thereby irrevocably changing the character of both institutions.

Back in the real world of mountains, I had received in June 1989 a letter from the Dutch mountaineer Ronald Naar, whom I had first met some years earlier, describing a ski tour that he had made earlier that year in the Ala Daghi. Apparently, his tour had been 'fantastic as well as bad due to a terrible snow blizzard' which had almost overwhelmed his party on Emler Bashi and precip- itated their premature withdrawal from the area. Nonetheless, Naar had been so impressed by the mountains of Turkey that he was determined to go there again. This unexpected news came as a wake-up call and settled a plan that had been germinating ever since I had spotted Ali Safak's skis: namely, a ski traverse of the central Taurus.

The Taurus, Turkey's principal mountain range, sweeps round its southern rim in a 400-kilometre arc from the Gulf of Antalya to Iskenderun before merging into the Anti-Taurus. In ancient times, it had marked the physical and cultural frontiers of the classical world taking its name from the zodiacal sign that represented Jupiter, the white bull who bore Princess Europa across the sea to found the continent that bears her name. Of the Taurus's two dominant massifs, the Ala Daghi and Bolkar Dag, the former I knew, but the latter was effectively *terra incognita*. I had, however, once caught tantalising glimpses of this mysterious range's precipitous southern scarp when returning to Istanbul with Sidney Nowill and Nigella Blandy after our abortive Ala Daghi trip in 1961. After driving along the coast parallel to the range for a hundred miles, I was so impressed that I had asked Sidney.

'What is this range?'

'It is the Bolkar Dag,' he replied portentously. 'And I have never yet been there.'

That there was *any* mountain range in Turkey that Sidney had never been to was reason enough to go there and the prospect of Naar beating me to it clinched the matter. Detailed descriptions of the Bolkar were hard to come by though it became clear that the range had always presented a formidable physical barrier between the Anatolian Plateau and the Mediterranean. The only record of any ski tour I could find was an undated account of a partial east to west traverse by the *grand raid* specialist Michel Parmentier. Apparently, Parmentier's team (probably Ali's French party) had driven from Camardi to the village of Maden on the northern lee of the Bolkar and thence gained its high plateau. Thereafter, they had pushed on westwards to climb the prominent peak of Aydos Dag before descending the village of Kalameindos to finish their tour.

The undulating Bolkar plateau had enabled Parmentier to make a partial traverse of the range, but he had not attempted to cross its rugged eastern quarter. To gauge what this might involve, I tried to get hold of a reliable map of the area, only to have it confirmed by Patrick Fagan, the British Army's Surveyor General, that the Turks never made theirs available even to their NATO allies. Aerial maps were too imprecise, so I based our itinerary on the Lascelles *Turkey East* 1:800,000 road map and the sketch map in Lonely Planet's *Trekking in Turkey*. I also decided that the Taurus traverse would have to be done in two separate stages, each of approximately seven days in length. The Bolkar Dag leg would start at Kalameindos and end at Posanti at the northern entrance to the Cilician Gates while the Ala Daghi leg would begin at Camardi and end up at Karsanti, some seventy kilometres away to the south-east. Parmentier's 'Kalameindos' turned out to be the same village as 'Kayasary', which was accessible by road from the town of Eregli, a stop on the old Berlin to Baghdad railway. Incredibly, this section of the line was still running and so, by flying to Adana it looked as if it should be possible to catch the train from there to Eregli and then drive on to Kayasary by road.

Yet, nothing is for certain in Turkey and once beyond the comfort zone of the Mediterranean seaboard, rudimentary Turkish will only get you so far despite the innate friendliness of the people. Moreover, neither mountain huts nor rescue facilities existed in the Taurus and food and fuel (not easily available) as well as camping equipment would have to be carried all the way. A dozen would-be participants boiled down to six, three of whom were self-selecting: my Pyrenean traverse veteran David Williams and his dauntless wife Anna, forged from Swedish steel, and David Seddon, a weatherproof medic of the 'patient heal thyself' persuasion. A fourth, Simon Kirk, was an aspirational business executive who had proved himself on my last Pyrenean ski tour and a fifth, though only prospective at that stage, was Ronnie Wathen.

Ronnie was a name to conjure with in mountaineering circles. He had been a member of the 1957 Pumasillo expedition and had climbed with both Chris Bonington and Don Whillans. After school at Marlborough, he had done national service in his father's smart cavalry regiment and then discovered his true metier at Trinity College, Dublin where he developed his musical and poetic tastes and had confirmed his Republican leanings. After introducing himself to me after a lecture I had given to the Alpine Club on *Climbing in Turkey*, Ronnie, unkempt in flower-power dress, professed his love for everything Turkish and cross-country skiing. He then gave an impromptu yoga demonstration on the lecture theatre's floor.

In the course of a lengthy correspondence that followed, Ronnie reported that he had *'been flogging up and down artificial ski slopes and humping great weights on my back to get fit … but needed experience on turns in deep, crusted or wet snow that do not tire the legs'*. David Williams offered him some off-piste ski coaching and although nothing came of this, Ronnie agreed to join me for a trial run at an Eagle Ski Club meet at Fort William. He arrived wearing a Michelin-Man suit of 'Polarfill' with his other equipment stuffed into a cloth bundle slung over his shoulder. Our first day on the piste in good weather went well enough and when the lift broke down, Ronnie entertained the ski queue with a selection of Irish jigs on his tin whistle. His skiing in variable snow was less successful and I recorded in my diary that his performance *'puts a big question mark over his ability … I shall have to take a tough decision over this. Ronnie is a splendid man and great fun'*. I never took that 'tough decision' for

Ronnie had already embarked on his own extensive programme of research and correspondence with Turkish pundits and the British Ala Daghi pioneer Sir Edward Peck.

A sleepless night on the marble floor of Istanbul's international airport was *not* the best way to start the Taurus traverse. However, as our Turkish Airlines plane flew eastwards into a purple dawn on 4 April 1990, my worries that there might not be enough snow faded as its first spidery threads creased the gullies of Anatolia's skeletal hills. Soon, a panorama of snow-clad ranges stretched to every horizon with the volcanic cones of Hasan Dag and Erciyes Dag thrusting up from the Plateau-like giant, blanched molehills. As the plane approached Adana, the Bolkar Dag came into focus as an immense V-shaped upland plateau, open at its south-west end and bounded to the north and south by containing ridges with a knot of shapely peaks at the north-east corner marking its apex.

Ronnie, now living temporarily in Turkey, was waiting at Adana airport to whisk us off to the railway station in two taxis just in time to board the 9.48 a.m. 'Taurus Express'. The 200-kilometre ride to Eregli cost £1.50 a head with our own compartment thrown in. The train's steam engine and carriages were genuine relics of the original Berlin to Baghdad Railway, that heroically ambitious project which had cost German banks alone the equivalent of $125 billion. The Kaiser had originally intended this railway as his military master-stroke to strengthen Germany's bid for world domination by transporting troops to the Middle East and thus cut the Suez Canal and British links with India. Had it been completed in 1915 rather than in 1918, it might even have influenced the outcome of the Great War. The engineers' main stumbling block had been the sixty-eight-mile stretch through the rocky heart of the Taurus between Belemedik and Durak, which involves a vertical ascent of 1,432 metres. Grinding up its labyrinth of thirty-seven separate tunnels, I caught occasional glimpses of giddying drops into chasmic depths and marvelled at this astonishing feat of engineering.

The railway stop at Posanti was always going to be the key to the expedition's success for it marked the halfway point of the traverse. It was where I was banking on dumping a ten-kilo cache of AFD food (then unobtainable in Turkey) with its stationmaster as essential rations for the Ala Daghi stage, and which could be picked up after we had come off the Bolkar Dag. Only when the Taurus Express came to a hissing halt, did the full absurdity of this plan hit me. For how could I possibly explain in execrable Turkish the intricacies of so delicate an operation?

The station looked deserted. Not a single passenger got either off or on. Clutching the food bag, I ran into the stationmaster's office only to find it empty, so raced back on to the platform shouting, *'Istasyon Muduru, Istasyon Muduru!'* – 'Stationmaster, stationmaster!'

A small knot of Turks emerged from nowhere.

'Deutsch?' asked a young man.

'Nein – English'

'Where you go?'

'Eregli, Eregli – *Istasyon muduru, Istasyon muduru, lutfen, lutfen!'*

'No stationmaster here today,' he said shaking his head.

As I pointed despairingly to the bag trying to explain the situation, the train emitted a warning whistle and a chorus of voices yelled out: 'For God's sake John, get back on board!'

And now, as if on cue, one man stepped forward.

'Give me the bag *Effendi*. I will look after it until you return.'

'But what is your name?'

'Akdemir Mehmet,' he replied. 'Just ask for me when you get back.'

As the train drew away, my eyes never left that dignified figure gently waving his hand until we swung sharply round a bend westwards and Pozanti disappeared from sight.

Five hours after leaving Adana, the train chugged into Eregli's stolid, German-built station. The modern town, built on a site continuously inhabited since Hittite times had once enjoyed some fame as the classical Heraclea-Cybistra. It was now a dump. Despite Ronnie's befriending a handy schoolmaster who claimed we were the first British he had ever seen in Eregli, a two and a half hour wild-goose chase round the town failed to find a sniff of paraffin for our two cooking stoves. We settled for high-octane petrol, which worked well enough when tested in the bathroom of the Koch Oteli.

Yesterday, that first sight of the immense north wall of the Bolkar Dag had left me wondering how we would ever climb up to the plateau, two-kilometres higher. However, when viewed from Eregli the range had settled back to look much less intimidating. Our jeep driver Yusuf had never heard of Kalameindos, but knew Kayasaray and after a two-hour joint-loosening jolt along a rutted track, I recognised the squat, flat-roofed houses clustering around the foot of an enormous monolith as the same village that had featured in a Parmentier photograph.

A brisk half-hour's walk towards an outlying spur of Aydos Dag gave access to a steep, open couloir covered with spring snow. The next ten hours involved a seemingly endless 1,700-metre climb mainly carrying skis, which took us to within a hundred metres of Aydos Dag's summit. Sheer exhaustion and deteriorating weather persuaded me to go no further so we ended the day with a ski descent through gently falling snow to a patch of level ground where Bolkar Camp I was established. That grinding slog had been worth it, for we had attained the Bolkar's plateau in a single day.

But elation soon turned to desperation. Both stoves had worked well enough at Eregli, but at 2,750 metres they spluttered to a sulphurated stop within minutes of starting. This was potentially disastrous, for without being able to melt snow for drinking water, the traverse would have to be abandoned. After three hours of coaxing and wheedling by torchlight, the two Davids managed to get one stove working to make a tepid brew. We sat on our rucksacks, huddled together for warmth amidst flurries of snow and then broke into the emergency rations wondering how to carry on.

Heavy snow, unaccustomed cold, cramp and lack of space tested sleeping arrangements and temperaments to the limit on that first night. David and Anna shared one tent and Ronnie and David Seddon another. But Simon and I had to make do with my one-man Phoenix 'Phreerunner' bivouac tent. This meant lying head to toe, with whoever occupied the 'inner berth' having to climb over the other to get outside to relieve himself. By the following morning, my camera shutter had frozen solid yet when the sun came up, the heat inside the tent became unbearable. Patience and a degree of familiarity got the stoves working again, so we pressed on.

The aerial view of the Bolkar Dag had given us a general idea of the topography of its 2,800-metre high, thirty-kilometre-long triangular-shaped plateau. Now, at ground level it resembled a gently undulating polar waste. But at least there was no wind and for twenty kilometres, we poled along eastwards, langlauf style, with the snow a blinding sheet of skin-searing white. Bolkar Camp 2 was pitched at mid-afternoon just as it began to snow in earnest – a weather pattern that repeated itself almost every day.

The following morning, with the stoves just about under control, we made tracks for the Kara Gedic, the only summer mule pass across the Bolkar that links the Anatolian Plateau to the coast. An awkward traverse led to an airy belvedere overlooking the beetling cliffs and tangled gorges of its southern scarp, which merged imperceptibly into the Mediterranean littoral. From the Kara Gedic, a spiralling ski run on perfect snow down the Bolkar's northern versant led through the Cini Gol's grey-pink limestone slabs to the frozen Kara Golu, a secure campsite beneath the ice-encrusted north face of Erkaya.

This lake had been Parmentier's first staging post after he had climbed up from the plain and thus avoided the direct passage across the three high ridges that now separated us from the Yalaklar Basin, our next destination. *Lonely Planet* had described this passage as 'virtually impossible' even in summer. However, to bypass it would have involved a 2,000-metre descent to the plain followed by an equally long climb up to the basin. This would have lost two days and with it the point of the venture so that option was never seriously discussed though everyone knew that success was going to depend on the weather, some ingenious route finding and a dollop of luck.

At dawn on the 8 of April, a clear-washed blue sky augured well for this key passage. A punishing three-hour climb led to a high col north-west of Takhtakaya. From here, the dun steppes of Anatolia rolled effortlessly away to the north, the peaks of the Ala Daghi gleamed faintly in the sun and we found ourselves staring down into the depths of a gloomy amphitheatre ringed by cliffs encased in snow and ice. The direct traverse line eastwards was now barred by Tahtakaya's serrated north ridge and the only way around it would be to ski down into the yawning gulf at our feet hoping that some way could be found around its base. I turned to David Williams, 'Damned if I can see what happens at the bottom of this lot. To ski into that abyss could be a one-way ticket.'

'I'm sure there's some way through,' he replied prodding the snow with his ski pole. 'Anyway, this snow feels mighty good!'

Williams could ski any sort of snow in any conditions with or without a fifty-pound pack on his back and Anna was not far behind. But we weren't all like that. I glanced anxiously across to Ronnie. So far, he'd been going without a tremor but this descent was going to be a real test.

'You okay about this one Ronnie?' I asked him.

'Don't give it thought,' he grinned. 'Just a dawdle.'

And then, with the all-too-familiar Williams' battle cry of, 'Well, here goes then!' he snaked away with Anna at his heels. The rest of us followed like a flight of startled choughs, down and down, faster and faster, deeper and deeper into the amphitheatre's unplumbed depths with no way of knowing where this crazy run would end.

We all reached the bottom by various ways. At first glance, the only exit appeared to be by para-punting over a terminal cliff. However, on closer inspection, David Williams discovered an improbable passage which inched around the roots of Takhtakaya's ridge and which, in turn, gave access to a broad cwm leading up to the Kizil Dokat col. On breasting this col, I imagined that we were home and dry until I peered over the edge into the Yalaklar Basin. This, the Bolkar Dag's most dramatic natural feature, took the form of a colossal bowl enclosed on all sides save to the north by 200-metre sheer rock bluffs fringed with snow cornices. Late afternoon clouds were darkening the sky as we tramped up and down the basin's rim, searching ever more desperately for a way down. I was preparing myself for a very uncomfortable night when David Williams suddenly launched himself through a rock defile barely wide enough to take the length of his skis. We held our collective breaths as he corkscrewed down a near-vertical gulley taking great wedges of wet snow with him. On reaching the bottom, we shouted and cheered out loud and then – with or without skis, according to nerve and technique – followed him down. Barely fifteen minutes later, we were erecting the tents in a raging blizzard. But nothing seemed to matter now. Thanks to David's verve and inspired navigation we had cracked the key passage of the Bolkar Dag.

The following morning, the clouds parted to reveal the 600-metre north face of Medetsiz (3,585 metres) the culminating peak of the Bolkar. Its beetling cornices seemed to threaten the camp like some incipient tsunami and although its ascent had originally been high on the agenda, the accumulations of fresh snow left by yesterday's storm posed an unacceptable avalanche hazard. Instead, we skinned up the nearby peak of Kopuktas Teppi to be rewarded with panoramic views followed by a glorious *wedelning* descent through deep powder snow. Late that afternoon, beyond a rampart of unsullied limestone cliffs buttressing a string of unnamed peaks, we made our last Bolkar camp at Gucuklu.

Early next morning, the *equipe* swooped down to the treeline before following a zigzag shepherd's path carpeted with blue gentians and campanulas that led through a pine and cedar forest scented with juniper. The Horoz Valley that had first appeared from on high as a patchwork of reds, ochres and browns, now took shape as a pattern of vineyards, orchards, and fields where gaily-dressed women broke off from their tilling to offer us crystal-clear water from a spring. That same evening at Pozanti, I recovered the precious food cache from Akdemir ('White-Iron') Mehmet after he had insisted that I take coffee with him and the women of his house.

Our leap in the dark had landed on firm ground. The Bolkar traverse had taken exactly six days and for once, all the pieces – timing, party, route, snow conditions and even the weather when it mattered – had fitted perfectly. Anna's deep sunburn and sprained ankle; David Williams's sore throat and

Simon's battered 'Koflack boot' toes were dismissed as 'bagatelles' by Doctor David. Best of all, my earlier worries about Ronnie's ability to cope had been wholly misplaced.

Waiting at Pozanti's bus stop next morning to catch the 'Camardi Express', our garish ski clothes made a bizarre contrast with those of a fellow passenger whose dun, baggy-trousers sported a messianic rear pouch. Since my last visit, Camardi had got itself the Ipec Palace Hotel but we would have swapped it for our tents any day. Foul tobacco smoke from the hotel's combination reception room/kitchen and the stench from its one privy permeated our overheated bedroom and made sleep impossible. Such things would not normally have worried Ronnie, but when during supper he began talking about moving on to Greece and then wandered off with Ali Safak's brother to see what Camardi's nightlife had to offer, I wondered what was bugging him.

The municipality bus dropped us off within easy reach of the Emli Gorge next morning and here, like some conjurer, Ronnie produced a pair of snow-shoes from his battered rucksack and insisted on wearing these instead of his skis. Inevitably, he was soon lagging behind the rest of us. After waiting for him to catch up, he eventually came clumping in without his rucksack.

'What's the problem, Ronnie?' I asked him.

'That damned thing's totally disintegrated. It was never intended to carry skis on top of all this other stuff. It's like some broken-down car and I need someone to come down to repair it.'

Although she had never complained, Anna was still limping with pain from her sprained ankle. David Williams, still ailing himself, had taken over most of her load. I couldn't understand what had got into Ronnie.

'Surely Ronnie, you can nip down to get it yourself. We'll wait for you here,' I told him.

He did so, gracelessly. On his return, David Williams spent twenty minutes repairing his rucksack with needle and thread and when the job was finished I said, somewhat impatiently, 'We really must push on now.'

At this, Ronnie turned on me: 'John – I've no idea what you're trying to achieve; what pass we're heading for or how we're supposed to exit at the end of it. You've never made this clear and you never replied to all those letters I sent you!'

At first, I couldn't think what to say. Ronnie *had* bombarded me with letters, but I had answered most of them and weeks before leaving had sent everyone explicit details about the expedition's proposed itinerary.

'Sorry Ronnie, but I've already given you all the information I had available,'

I replied tersely. 'We've crossed the Bolkar Dag without a hitch and I can see no reason for not sticking to the Ala Daghi route as originally agreed.'

Ronnie gave me a belligerent stare and after a mock salute said: 'Okay, Major!'

The last seven days had been hard graft and we were all tired. Even so, I should have been more accommodating. In Ronnie's *The Unwritten Mountains* (Es Clot Press, 1990) he recorded our spat in verse:

> *'John Harding is the head of the whole.*
> *It's his idea, his lifelong goal*
> *To traverse Ranges which are off-piste*
> *Toros is one of the last on his list.*
> *What happened was briefly this:*
> *our characters had clashed with a hiss*
> *like hot metal hitting on frozen ice*
> *'You should have slugged him,' says Mike Banks*
> *'A hard manoeuvre,' I counter, 'thanks*
> *To my feet planted on wooden planks.'*

We were both upset, but by the time tents had been pitched in thick snow at Aksampinari, the 'Evening Spring', I was more focused on the weather and our chances of climbing the peak of Alaca tomorrow. During a night of sleet, snow, thunder and lightning this had seemed improbable, but by the early hours the storm had passed. It was 4.30 a.m. when Ronnie called out from his tent: 'Sorry John, some bad news.'

'What's the problem, Ronnie?'

'I've decided to call this whole Ala Daghi thing off. I'm making tracks for Greece today.'

I was completely stunned. Ronnie had been going so well and the potential consequences of him pulling out at this stage were bound to upset the finely balanced distribution of food and equipment. Eventually, I blurted out: 'I'm very sorry indeed to hear this Ronnie. However, if that's your decision you must stick to it.'

Breakfast was a muted affair, which I should have used as an opportunity to talk him out of it. As his sad, solitary figure wandered off down the Emli Gorge I wanted to shout after him, 'For God's sake Ronnie, come back!'

I should have done, but I didn't and lived to regret it. Later, when we all got home, Ronnie wrote to me: 'The Bolkar traverse was one of my greatest experiences in the mountains.'

The tragedy was that in ski mountaineering Ronnie had found a new métier. After the Taurus, he became an enthusiastic member of the Eagle Ski Club enlivening its Scottish meets with anecdote, verse and airs on his Irish pipes. Three years on, he died from a brain tumour aged fifty-nine, leaving his wife Asta and young family. Iconoclastic, argumentative and articulate, Ronnie was a brave and lovable man and a true scholar gypsy.

The glorious four-note call of the Caspian snow partridge heralding the start of a brilliantly fine day should have lifted our hearts, but Ronnie's departure had put paid my enthusiasm for climbing Alaca. We set off anyway, spurred by the sight of Parmakayya's limestone monolith glowing like a red candle up the valley. At the Auceveli col, Dr David and Simon took a well-earned break while David, Anna and I pushed on to Alaca's summit. Back in camp, we discussed the consequences of Ronnie's exit but decided to keep going, confident that Alaca's 1,500 metres of ascent and descent had been a useful dress rehearsal for tomorrow's key passage across the Gurtepe Col to the Kokorot Valley. Closing the head of the Emli Gorge, this was the very col that John Blacker and I had failed to reach four years earlier.

It snowed heavily for a third successive night and was still snowing when we made a late start up the valley. The peaks were shrouded in cloud and with no let-up in the weather, I called a halt after two hours to discuss whether we should continue. When the clouds lifted slightly we pressed on into the Siyirma Gorge where the angle of the slope suddenly steepened. Persistent snow showers and thick mist were making it difficult to judge the gradient and see exactly where we were heading. For the next three hours David Williams and I swapped leads to break the trail with tight zigzag traverses and inverted ski-turns in knee-deep snow which kept balling up under the skis. It was taxing physically and mentally and when the angle of the slope sharpened to forty degrees and a vertical rock buttress emerged like a ship's prow out of the murk, I turned to David.

'It's 3 p.m. and the weather's worsening. My altimeter's registering 3,240 metres. The Gurtepe Col can't be much more than a hundred metres above us but the real climbing's about to begin and we can't see what we'll be taking on. I vote we camp here tonight under this rock buttress which will at least give some protection from whatever's coming down.'

We set about excavating a platform recess for two tents in the hard-packed névé backing the buttress. After an hour, David W. threw down his snow shovel and turned to me.

'John, I want to make a recce to make sure we can reach that col tomorrow.'

'You can't go on your own,' I protested weakly. 'I'd better come along too.'

Digging like an automaton, he ploughed a waist-deep furrow up a near-vertical wall of snow, which had the consistency of castor sugar. When my legs gave out, I told him to carry on. After another half hour he returned looking pleased with himself.

'That's the col all right. I reckon it should go tomorrow, provided there's no more snow tonight.'

The col might well be within our grasp, but to get there posed a horrendous avalanche risk, particularly if it kept on snowing. Yet the alternative of retreating 800 metres down into the perilous Siyirma Gorge was equally unattractive. I put the final decision on hold until morning. Back at the eyrie, it needed a couple more hours to hack out a recess big enough to fit in our two tents with me moved in with David and Anna. When the weight of spindrift pouring off a gulley above threatened to crush all five of us, we had to get out to excavate an even deeper platform while buffeted by driven snow. The job was only finished three hours later by torchlight. Squashed together, with spindrift constantly sweeping over the tent, I kept thinking of my family safely tucked up in bed and wondering what the hell I was doing here.

No one slept much that night, but by dawn it had stopped snowing. An eerie silence had descended when I shook a thick layer of snow off the tent and poked my head out. Halfway down the Emli Gorge, Alaca was emerging like a pink pyramid from out of a rapidly dissolving cloud sea. The Gurtepe Col above was still invisible and the only way of reaching it was up the near-vertical couloir flanked by rock buttresses encased in ice that David and I had struggled up yesterday. It took two hours to thaw out, pack up and steel ourselves for the ascent. David W. led with me following behind and Anna, Doctor David and Simon bringing up the rear. The metre-deep channel dug out yesterday evening had been obliterated. In David's wake I shovelled out another passage through seemingly bottomless powder snow which, towards the top, turned to hard névé so steep that the ski tips atop my rucksack kept butting into it.

That eighty-metre climb to the Gurtepe Col was one of the most nerve-wracking hours of my life. On breasting the col, I stood there transfixed as I watched the three figures below me glued to that awesome slope willing them to inch their way up it. I prayed that the dreaded roar from ten thousand tons of snow and ice that would take their mangled bodies to the bottom would never come. It never did and when Simon at last joined us we all clustered round him, hugging and embracing each other.

And now, for the first time, I felt relaxed enough to take in the panorama of unclimbed peaks and pinnacles festooned in a fantastic confectionary of ice and rime that surrounded us and take a look into the Kokorot Valley. Its versant was not steep, but the stresses and strains of the past forty-eight hours had drained me, and during the descent to the prow of rock that became our last camp I could barely turn my skis. The dark, densely forested ridges that rolled away eastwards revealed a very different world from that of the stark limestone peaks that had marked our passage over the past fortnight. They represented the outer limits of the Ala Daghi and the end of our voyage.

On our last full day, David Williams nonchalantly soloed Vay Vay Dag's north-west face, leaving the rest of us to bag a subsidiary 3,510-metre peak which we christened Anna Tepesi. The following morning, with the weather closing in, our final ski descent ended at the tumbled-down remnants of Aciman Yaila occupied by a single shepherd. Simon's ingenious quiz game 'Boticelli' helped pass the tedium of the forty-kilometre walk-out to Karsanti and a lucky lift from a forestry truck saved our feet from complete disintegration. The Forestry Department also offered us warm beds for that night and at 6 a.m. next day, 18 April, we caught the bus to Adana from where we had started sixteen days before. Luck had been with us in the Taurus, for any injury would have been serious and continuous bad weather made progress virtually impossible. The Bolkar Dag had given some exceptional skiing and the Emli-Kokorot crossing a *grand raid*. Best of all was to have made a magical journey across the White Bull's back riding the sky's chariot along the way.

14

THE PONTIC ALPS

THE LITTLE CAUCASUS

The year of the Taurus traverse coincided with my becoming president of the Alpine Ski Club (ASC), the world's first ski-mountaineering club, founded in 1908 by Arnold Lunn. This was only one of half a dozen mountain clubs (including the Oxford University Mountaineering Club) that owe their existence to Lunn, but the ASC was his most cherished creation with its primary object 'To encourage mountaineering expeditions on ski throughout the world'. Another of Lunn's aims was to unite both skiers and climbers to become *complete mountaineers* by forging close ties with the Alpine Club. This he never achieved, yet his contributions to the development of skiing and ski mountaineering were exceptional and I took it as a great privilege to have become president of his club.

The immediate post-Second World War years had seen the nadir of both British ski mountaineering clubs, the ASC and the Eagle Ski Club. By 1990, the ASC was making a slow recovery but its reputation was more for hosting convivial annual dinners than pushing the boundaries of ski mountaineering. Membership was static and a change of direction was needed to restore its pioneering role. To honour Lunn's original intentions, my solution was to propose a merger with the Alpine Club in order to attract new members and promote ski mountaineering as an integral part of the AC's activities. Initially, the prospects of achieving such a merger seemed propitious. A joint working party was established and to ensure that the ASC's membership standards should be broadly comparable with those of the AC, we upgraded our membership qualifications and revised the ASC rules, which had been un-changed since 1958. Lunn had specifically prescribed that women should not become ASC members and I was determined to scrap this archaic rule. The motion I proposed for doing so was passed unanimously at a general meeting with only one abstention.

The merger negotiations dragged on into 1991 and then broke down. Ostensibly, because no acceptable formula could be agreed that would ensure that the ASC retained a degree of administrative and financial autonomy. More likely, because of politics and personalities reflecting, in part, the AC's traditional antipathy towards ski mountaineering. Nonetheless, one positive result of the merger negotiations was the establishment of closer relations with the Alpine Club enabling ASC members to attend AC lectures and make use of the AC's premises and library. In reciprocation, AC members were given access to the ASC's avalanche rescue transceiver scheme and I transferred to the Alpine Club library, the remnants of Lunn's joint ASC/SCGB ski-mountain-eering library which the SCGB had been in the process of selling off without prior consultation with the ASC, together with a full run of the *British Ski Yearbook* which Lunn had edited for fifty years and which remains the source book for the ASC's early history. Happily, a reinvigorated ASC now goes from strength to strength producing its own annual record and a fine centenary history of the club entitled *Explore, Climb, Ski.*

These merger negotiations had been time consuming and ultimately frustrat-ing. However, the success of the Taurus traverse encouraged me to plan a second Turkish ski mountaineering traverse the following year. My objective this time was the Kackar Dag, a range of granite peaks and small glaciers in north-east Turkey, which form the culmination of the 500-kilometre-long mountain chain that delineates its northern approaches. Known to the Romans as the Pontic Alps, after the Kingdom of Pontus and realm of Mithridates the Great, the eponymous hero of the fourteen-year-old Mozart's first *opera seria,* their wider fame derives from the Athenian general Xenophon's epic crossing during the winter of 401 BC with the remnants of his 10,000 Greek mercenaries.

Schoolboy memories of translating Xenophon's *Anabasis* were revived in 1963 when, while serving in Aden, two articles in *The Times* by Robin Fedden described a mountaineering expedition that he had made to the Kackar earlier that year with Basil Goodfellow, a former AC honorary secretary who had once been despatched to Zurich by the Himalayan committee to persuade the Swiss to abandon their 1952 attempt on Everest. Fedden's account of the

Kackar's giant forests rising above Black Sea mists surmounted by alpine peaks and glaciers, gave the range a comforting sense of geographical familiarity with the Elburz. His references to rainbow-skirted Laze ladies and intoxicating honey added fascination to a range that I promised myself I would visit one day.

The choice of the Kackars as a 1991 ski-touring venue was also the direct result of a summer recce to the range that Georgina and I had made five years earlier. The Kackar's outstanding natural beauty and exceptional flora have made it a popular trekking destination today, yet until 1959, when the dauntless Cecil Denis Hills, once acclaimed by *The Spectator* as 'A Hero of our Times' for defying the Ugandan tyrant Idi Amin, rediscovered its long forgotten Georgina churches in what he described as 'a botanist's and climber's paradise', it was virtually unknown. Times change for in the late nineteenth century, British consuls based on Trebizond (modern Trabzon) would have taken more than a keen interest in these 'Little Caucasus', which bordered on Russia's ever expanding empire. In 1901, the British scholar H.B. Lynch wrote his two-volume *Armenia* as the definitive history of the area, but once more it was a German, the redoubtable Rickmer Rickmers, an RGS Gold Medallist for his pioneer expeditions to Central Asian and the Caucasus, who undertook the first exploratory mountaineering in the Kackars at the turn of the twentieth century. Austrian and German expeditions followed his lead in the 1930s and picked its choicest plums.

Fedden and Goodfellow were the first British mountaineers to climb the eponymous Kackar Peak (3,932 metres), the highest in the range. Thirteen years later, Sidney Nowill made the first of his three attempts to climb the mountain and like his predecessors was plagued by bad weather throughout. On his last sortie in 1980, he fell thirty metres; suffered multiple injuries and without the ministrations of a local peasant, who applied a mixture of eggs and soap to relieve the pressure on his fractured rib cage, might have lost his life.

When I first suggested to Sidney in early 1987 that we might visit the Kackar together, his reply was not encouraging: 'Sorry, but simply can't do. I'm currently mixed up with a Peter Holmes project involving Turkey, London, Washington and New York. The Kackar are a magnificent environment, unique in Turkey, but neither proper maps nor mule transport are available and the magnetic rock throws any accurate compass readings. The logistics are *formidable* and you'll need at least three weeks to get to grips with the area. The weather is like the Ruwenzori: rain, mist or snow (depending on your altitude). This apart, kidnapping, robbery and molestation by the local inhabitants are endemic. It's not a bit like the Ala Dag!'

The gloomy tenor of Sidney's letter might well have reflected our previous year's experiences in the Ala Dag. Nonetheless, Georgina and I allocated a week that summer to make a Kackar reconnaissance after persuading Robert and Susan Sykes to join us. Common threads were that Robert and I had both served in the Colonial Service and had ski toured together in Scotland. Less common were that both the Sykeses were vegetarians with pronounced political views. Susan, a child psychologist, also held to the theory that a principal motivation of mountaineers who push themselves to extremes, could often be attributed to some childhood trauma, illness, deprivation or bereavement. We never explored this in depth, but from my own observations and experience there may be something in it. I never willingly pushed myself thus, but mountaineering aspirations can have curious origins. During my early childhood I had been bedridden for weeks with TB and up to the age of nine, had attended six separate schools in widely different locations seeing all too little of my parents.

On 3 June 1987, the four of us flew out to Ankara to spend a night at the British Embassy as guests of the British Ambassador Timothy Daunt and his wife Patricia. Dinner of fish mousse, beef Wellington and raspberry sorbet was the last civilised meal we had for the next ten days. Flying on to Trabzon, visions of Rose Macaulay's dreaming towers were quickly dispelled by the slew of ugly concrete buildings that had all but obliterated the old town. Our visit in heavy rain to the cliff-hanging Sumela Monastery was ruined by a busload of obstreperous German tourists. Trabzon's Oteli Ozgur was also the dirtiest and most unwelcoming hotel I ever stayed at in Turkey. The mewing of stray cats, cockerel calls and ear-splitting dawn summons to prayer from the town's several dozen muezzins made one night in that city more than enough. The following day we hired a taxi to Ayder (Ilica) by a bumpy road that hugged the Black Sea coast. Formerly the land of Colchis, to which Jason had sailed in 1,263 BC in search of the golden fleece, the forested mosaic that lapped the sea's edge, displaying every imaginable shade of viridescent green, was occasionally interspersed by neat tea plantations and the hazelnut groves that make that irresistible chocolate spread Nutella. Disappointingly, the coastline itself lacked either sandy beaches or picturesque harbours and I sensed something curiously disturbing about this tideless inland ocean. Its original Greek name 'Inhospitable', allegedly reflecting the savagery of its coastal peoples, had been softened over time to *Euxinus* or 'Hospitable'. Yet, it was only after reading Neal Ascherson's *Black Sea* that I understood why its dark waters should have stirred in me such uneasy feelings. Apparently, its depths harbour a terrifying and little-known secret caused by the overwhelming inrush of organic matter into a relatively confined space from the combined waters of the Kuban, Don, Dneiper, Dneister and Danube rivers. As a result, the normal bacterial process of decomposition is prevented from operating, thus converting the Black Sea's waters below a depth of 200 metres into a residual gas, hydrogen sulphide, which is one of the deadliest natural substances known to man. If ever some cataclysmic eruption were to bring these anoxic waters to the surface, the consequences could be catastrophic.

Swinging inland, we drove up the lower Buyuk Valley through groves of chestnut, alder, walnut, hornbeam, oak and spruce, oversized variants of our European familiars, whose canopy overlaid a dense undergrowth of blackberry, bay, laurel, holly, cotoneaster, privet, ivy, clematis and fern. Higher up the valley, the road climbed through impenetrable thickets of *Rhododendron ponticum* which left drifts of petals piled up on either side. In Britain this exotic shrub grows like a weed. Here, in its native habitat, it covers whole mountainsides in livid pink. Save for the Kackar's characteristic humpback pack bridges, its four-storey, half-timbered chalets perched like eyries on the hillsides and linked to the valley bottoms by primitive *téléfériques,* one might have been in nineteenth century Switzerland.

Six bone-rattling hours after leaving Trabzon, we arrived at the village of Ayder, famous locally for its hot sulphur springs and chosen as a road-head by both Fedden and Nowill. I had taken to heart Sidney's strictures about not wasting time here in trying to engage pack animals to get up to his upper Kavron Valley base camp. Sidney had experienced such problems over this that he compared the local Lazes very unfavourably to either the Turks or Kurds. This was unfair to the Lazes, a curious ethnic remnant of Caucasian stock related to the same peoples who inhabited Colchis in Jason's time and whose unwritten language is akin to Georgian. Despite their skills as mariners and pastry cooks, they are butts for Turkish wit even though we found them willing and friendly and were neither kidnapped, molested nor robbed. However, by deciding against the mule option, we not only lumbered ourselves with outsize packs but also denied ourselves the benefits of a local guide. This was a bad mistake for with only a rough sketch map to hand, we found the Kavron Valley difficult to identify particularly as the surrounding deciduous forest was so dense that the mountains above were invisible.

After scouting around in the grilling heat of mid-afternoon, we eventually plumped for a likely looking track leading up the main valley. Robert and I were shouldering sixty-pound rucksacks and the girls not much less, which had seemed ridiculously heavy until we passed two local women bent double under immense piles of brushwood and laurel. Three hours on, hot, bad tempered and exhausted, we camped by a foaming torrent. Conversation was stilted and Georgina had developed a raging migraine.

Contrary to Sidney's dire prophecies, the sun was still shining next morning as we strode out with somewhat lighter hearts until the path divided. The left fork, which seemed more likely to lead to the Kavron Valley, in fact led to the adjacent Kaymakcur Valley, another fatal mistake that was to dictate the course of events thereafter. Beyond a tumbling torrent, a pinnacled peak framed by a gap in the thinning pine forest closed the head of a beautiful alpine valley. Clouds of butterflies fluttered and fell as we wandered through meadows ablaze with blue gentians, yellow anemones and purple primulas, which vied for colour with clumps of red azaleas and wave-tossed tracts of white-blossomed *Rhododendron caucasicum*. I had half hoped that the shining mountain directly ahead might be Kackar Peak itself so we pitched our tents in the snow by a frozen lake and ate the first of the Sykes's spartan suppers al fresco.

On waking to the four-note trill of the Caspian snow partridge, there was still no sign of Sidney's 'Ruwenzori Weather' so Robert and I took this as an opportunity to shin up the shattered rocks and snow gullies of the north face of our mystery mountain. My summit altimeter reading of 3,400 metres confirmed that this could not possibly be the 3,932-metre Kackar Peak and I subsequently identified it as Nanetleme Tepesi. However, as no summit cairn was visible, we were happy to claim it as a 'first'. Kackar Peak itself remained hidden by intervening ridges, but from this fine belvedere a panorama of snow-filled cwms and crenelated peaks stretched for over a hundred miles and promised future adventure.

Back in camp, the weather finally broke and the Black Sea mist that swept in that afternoon never left us thereafter. By evening, heavy rain and sleet had turned to snow which drove straight through the walls of our tiny Phoenix bivouac tent. That night, a monumental thunderstorm rolled around shaking the tent like a leaf and nearly collapsing it under the weight of snow. Next morning, Nanetleme Camp was hastily abandoned for Camp 3, an altogether better site on the other side of a high ridge beside a small lake set in a meadow of ravishingly beautiful wild flowers.

Over the next two days, Robert and I made a series of abortive recces to locate the Kavron Valley. The swirling mists never lifted; our compasses swung wildly out of true and, apart from climbing one minor aiguille, we invariably returned to camp sodden, dispirited and none the wiser. After a third night's buffeting, we packed up Camp 3 and struck out westwards in driving snow, relying more on instinct than compass bearing to reach the elusive Kavron Valley. Another wearisome ridge crossing followed by a vertiginous descent down a hillside covered in *Rhododendron caucasicum*, yellow azalea and pink raspberry bushes, ended up at what could only be Kavron Yaila. More like a mountain hamlet, with paved pathways flanked by two-storey chalets built of dressed granite blocks, the place was completely deserted. Had we arrived only a couple of days later, the place would have been seething with women dressed like peacocks and men be-hatted in black bearskins settling in for the summer.

With time running out, we made our last camp further down the valley by a lively stream to make a quick exit to Ayder the following day. Any chances of climbing Kackar Peak were long gone, but when the dawn sky came up clean-washed blue I raced up to the nearest ridge to get a glimpse of the elusive Kackar Peak before the Black Sea mists closed in. For brief seconds, the clouds parted to reveal its satellites glittering in the sun and for days I clung to the illusion that I had seen Kackar itself.

We missed the daily bus down to Trabzon, so booked into the Ayder Hilton Oteli for the night. Though definitely not part of Conrad Hilton's chain, it was good value at £2.40 a head for supper, bread and breakfast. Georgina spent a happy afternoon in the sulphur baths talking knitting and embroidery with a group of Turkish ladies up from the coast and early next morning we joined them on the downward run to Trabzon. Dressed up to the nines in rainbow shawls and stockings of red, blue, brown, purple, orange, green and black, they filled the bus with laughter. At Pazar, everyone trooped out for coffee and to watch a bear climbing a 150-foot tree to get at a barrel-shaped beehive lodged in its upper branches.

Our Kackar venture might not have been a laugh-a-minute for al fresco meals in sleet and snow don't do much for conviviality. But the Sykes's regime of muesli for breakfast, oatcake with vegetable spread and soup, cheese, dried peas and lentils for supper kept us healthy throughout. I also promised myself that the fleeting view of the Pontic Alps from Nanetleme Tepesi would eventually translate itself into something more ambitious.

KACKAR CHARIOT

'There are no bears in Kackar Dag and no wolves either – but our butterflies are very beautiful!'

Ozkan was doing his best to reassure us for, as folk do in Turkey, he had seen us coming, incongruous in bright anoraks wandering through the dusty, main street of Yusufeli in search of a taxi. Our self-appointed 'Treking Mauntainer Guy' (as his calling card pronounced) was only anxious to have a chat and quick to point out that he was strictly a summer-season guide. 'Kackar Dag', he declared 'should definitely be avoided in winter when it is dangerous with too much snow.'

Five years on from that 1987 summer visit, I was back in the Kackar Dag but this time with the aim of completing an east to west ski traverse of the range. No one, to my knowledge, had previously attempted this, so it had come as a shock to have received another letter from Ronald Naar in December 1990 to say that he was intending to do precisely that the following April. Naar again in the field! Ever since a chance meeting on Mount Olympus in 1985, our friend-ship had blossomed and earlier in the year, he had accepted my invitation to lecture to the Alpine Ski Club and become an honorary member. Both his mountaineering and ski mountaineering achievements were exceptional so his entry to the lists added a *frisson* to my own Kackar challenge. At first blush, our dates seemed to clash, but on comparing itineraries I was relieved to note that his proposed route from Yaylakar to Pokut was more a diagonal crossing of the range rather than my proposed east-west traverse from Barhal to Chemlihensin.

My original aim had been to achieve ski mountaineering priority. However, I was also tempted to solve the mystery of where exactly Xenophon had crossed it. His fighting retreat through Kurdistan and Armenia after the battle of Cunaxa in Mesopotamia was not only one of history's greatest military adventures, but his crossing of the Pontic Alps in winter an exceptional feat that pre-dated Hannibal's crossing of the Alps by 182 years. However, as prepa-rations took shape, I became preoccupied with more important issues. The first Gulf War, launched in August 1990, had created security concerns and travel uncertainties. And then, in early 1991, my father died after a long illness in his ninetieth year. He had led a full and successful life, but few of us are fully prepared for the reality of a parent's death. Preoccupied with the trauma of bereavement and the mournful business of making the necessary funeral and probate arrangements, I was minded to call the whole thing off. However, as I had already committed four others to some expense and despite misgivings, I reverted to the original Kackar plan when the Gulf War ended.

On 19 March 1991, David and Anna Williams, David Seddon, Stephen Baker and I flew out to Istanbul to be welcomed there with typically generous Nowill hospitality. That night, the sound of honking foghorns floating across the misty Bosphorus set my mind racing back to the excitement of my first Turkish mountaineering venture with Sidney and Nigella thirty years before. This ski tour also had its uncertainties for bad weather had disrupted Turkish Airlines's flight schedules and resulted in our having to spend an extra day and night in Ankara. Flying on to Erzurum, the aerial view of the Anatolian Plateau, blanketed in snow with its towns and villages showing up as black smudges against a dead-white backcloth, only confirmed reports that fifty metres of it had already fallen in the Kackar that winter.

From Erzurum, the 150-kilometre bus drive through the Kackar's bleak southern foothills led through ever wilder and wilder country before ending up at the Celik Palas Hotel, Yusufeli where snow-capped peaks lining the northern horizon confirmed that we had reached our intended destination. My basic plan for the twelve-day Kackar traverse was to split it into three phases: Barhal to Ayder; Ayder to Chat; and Chat to Chemlihensin. This schedule was intended to take in the minor massifs of Altiparmak, Bulut and Kackar, yet allowing time to climb both Kackar and Verchenick peaks en route. Ayder was earmarked as a critical reprovisioning stop, though the key to success was likely to be the weather for we had nothing to guide us save Lonely Planet's sketch map.

Our butterfly-fancier Ozkan had been true to his word when the two taxis he had ordered last night arrived on time next morning. Without a shred of tyre tread between them, their drivers raced up the Altiparmak Valley in a wild, thirty-two kilometre slalom to Barhal from where we headed up the valley under a broiling sun, which seemed to promise settled weather. The first day of any tour is always a trial, but this time my rucksack seemed unconscionably heavy and old hip and shoulder injuries were playing up. Besides the frozen Karagol Lake, eight hours on and 1,300 metres higher, I was so tired that I collapsed into my tent and went straight to sleep without supper. Next morning, a cold, clammy mist enveloped the camp and three hours on, a Black Sea blizzard stopped us in our tracks below the coal-black cliffs of Didvake. Snow holes can give better protection from cold weather than tents. On this occasion, ninety minutes of excavation generated much heat, but then left us sopping wet and cold. After a spell of deep-freeze refrigeration huddled together in semi-darkness, tents were voted the better option.

It was still snowing hard the following morning and I was worried that this might be the pattern of things to come. Warm air and heavy precipitation coming off the Black Sea produces soggy, unstable snow liable to slide at a touch. In the summer, we never worried overmuch about avalanches in the Kackar, but now they became a constant preoccupation. David Williams's uncanny navigational skills shepherded the party up to a windswept col above the Percha Valley, but the 800-metre descent down the other side through crust, crud and slush in thick mist saw my skiing technique and morale disintegrate. 'Am I getting too old for this sort of thing?' I kept asking myself. The answer was almost certainly 'Yes!'

Near the end of that helter-skelter run of thrills and spills, the sight of fresh bear-claw prints the size of dinner plates in the snow brought us up short. Black, brown, or grizzly? Irrespective of species, if confronted should one stand one's ground, go to ground or simply grovel? A diagonal descending traverse through thick forest led gently down to the bottom of the Kisla Valley where the clouds lifted and there was shelter from the wind. Gliding on past clusters of deserted chalets with their roofs capped by foot-deep snow, we might have been in the European Alps.

Once above the treeline, the ground steepened and avalanche debris forced us to take an uncomfortably higher route above the ever-narrowing Ombolat Deresi gorge. Here, the only available campsite was marked by a solitary pine perched on an isolated rock bluff overlooking a fifty-metres-deep gulch whose trough was buried under another fifteen metres of consolidated avalanche debris. Cushioned by a mattress of *Rhododendron caucasicum,* this site was safe enough, but yesterday's fresh snow posed a serious avalanche threat and tomorrow's crossing of Kirmizi Gedici, a 3,100-metre double col at the head of the valley, might even decide the outcome of the expedition.

That evening, crystal-clear skies presaged a cold night. A 4 a.m. reveille sped our passage over hard-frozen snow and a succession of avalanche cones that littered the upper Kisla valley. Above its tightening jaws, the sun lit up a saw-toothed, skyline ridge framing the Kirmizi Gedici luminous pink. During that long climb, I had fallen some way behind the others but on joining them on the col we stared together north-eastwards beyond the lazy mass of Karchal Dag to the dim outlines of the frosty Caucasus. And might not this, I wondered, have been the belvedere, called Thekes from which Xenophon and his weary, homesick mercenaries had first seen the Black Sea and passed down the ranks the famous cry *'Thalassa, thalassa!'* – *'The sea, the sea!'*

No chance of that. Although the sea was no more than fifty kilometres away, it was masked by intervening ridges with its presence only betrayed by a swelling bank of cumulus cloud. And difficult as it would have been for sandal-shod soldiers to climb up to the Kirmizi Gedici, to have descended the other side by the icy couloir that guarded its western approaches, a Peltast would have had to ski like a Williams. Doctor David and I tackled this tricky passage with crampons, but once past it the pressure eased and with the sun warming our backs, we slalomed down the fourteen kilometres to Ayder stopping only once for a breather. That glorious run of 1,800 metres vertical descent had cracked the first critical stage of the Kackar Traverse. But at a cost – Doctor David had twisted his knee during its final stages and as we trudged through ankle-deep slush down Ayder's solitary street he could only hobble. And what I remembered as a bustling summer resort was now deserted save for the proprietor of the Hilton Oteli who was just about to leave for Çamlihemşin. Without demur, he opened the place up and gave us a room for the night. He then produced olives, cheese, scrambled eggs, rice, bread and butter in the warmth of his kitchen. It was a kind gesture, but with all the village shops shut there was no question now of being able to reprovision at Ayder to see us through the next five-day stage to Chat. Disconcerted, I took little comfort from David Williams's aside, 'We've still got emergency AFD rations plus Anna's porridge cake and can always live off our fat for at least a week!'

Anticipating leaner times ahead, we ate to bust.

More serious was Doctor David's injury. This was definitely not a case of 'doctor heal thyself' and by the following morning he had decided to catch the next bus to Trabzon and fly home. After diagnosing David and Anna's 'spotty dick' appearance as nothing more than bedbugs, he handed over the expedition's medical kit in a single Kodachrome film canister, wished us luck and waved goodbye. Skinning southwards through the dark pine forests of the Kale Duzu frequently crossing the spoor of wolf and bear, the loss of Doctor David preyed on my mind. Apart from his daily malingerer's dispensary, we would miss his mordant rebuffs to our childish efforts to rag him with facetious questions about prostheses, prophylactics and plastic surgery.

Once beyond the forest, a tableau of glittering snowfields and crenelated peaks opened up. Preoccupied with gloomy thoughts, it suddenly dawned on me that beneath the snow lay the same meadows of yellow peonies and blue gentians through which Georgina and I had wandered five years before. The hot sun made for heavy going through deep, avalanche-prone snow and when we eventually pitched our tents besides that same frozen lake, I was not surprised that it had taken over nine hours to get here. That night marked my Kackar nadir. Doctor David's demise; concerns about food, the weather and avalanches; nausea and sheer physical exhaustion were a bad recipe for tackling tomorrow's key passage across the 3,201-metre Kaymakcur Col that marked the watershed. It lay just to the west of Nanetleme Tepesi, the peak that Sykes and I had climbed, but there was no way of knowing whether the descent down its far side into the Bukuk Chay would be skiable.

A wakeful night followed by a bleary-eyed, pre-dawn start and a tiring slog to the col drained me. But once out of the shadows, bright sunshine steeled my resolve. The first part of the descent looked easy enough, but beyond the upper basin's convex snow-lip, it swung sharply to the left before disappearing into the black void of the Dupendez Gorge. This was going to be another of those jaw-clenching, stomach-tightening, adrenaline-pumping challenges. I took a deep breath and swallowed when Williams let out his familiar 'Ready to go?' On that, he and Anna swung away as a synchronised duo with the stylish Steve following close behind. Taking up the rear, I faced down to the fall line; launched myself off and found myself skiing on perfect 'spring' snow. After a couple of turns, I too mounted my Kackar chariot hot on the heels of the others and swept down a thousand metres on a lung-bursting run which, for its nail-biting uncertainty, even rivalled that leap into the unknown on the Bolkar Dag.

On a spur overlooking the Buyuk Chay, we paused for breath. Far below, just visible through a gap, I spotted a figure moving purposefully upwards with a skier's gliding stride. Preoccupied with our own problems, I had completely forgotten about our promised tryst with Ronald Naar. Yet on this very day, 27 March, had we not surmised that our paths might cross at Olgunlar? Swooping on down past a cluster of startled shepherdesses raking dung, we reached the valley bottom in concert and within minutes had become a happy group of laughing, hand-shaking, back-slapping Brits mixing it with the three Dutchmen – Ronald, Bas, Hank – and their Turkish guide Cemal.

'We spent last night at our roadhead Yalaklar.' explained Ronald.

'We're now heading up the valley to make our high camp at Dilber Duzu below Kackar Peak.'

'That just where we're going' I said, glancing sidelong at their enormous rucksacks.

'Oh those!' exclaimed Ronald. 'We may be a bit slower than you. Stupidly, we've doubled up on food!'

Our meeting was to prove a lifesaver for we were almost running on empty.

Leaving them to a hearty breakfast, we pressed on up the airless corridor of the Buyuk Chay, passing en route a trio of local shepherds wearing straw hats, smelling as high as badgers and skiing on rough wooden boards. Pitching our tents at Dilber Duzu opposite the black, pillared buttresses of the Devil's Rocks, the Dutch party rolled in late that afternoon. Methodically levelling the snow into a platform, they then built a circular snow-wall around it to act as a windshield and cooking area. Later that evening, the admirable Cemal brought us a container of delicious curried rice to soften the impact of our indigestible AFD *boeuf bourguignon*.

Somewhere up in the clouds, another thousand metres above, lay the 3,932-metre summit of Kackar Peak. A 5.30 a.m. start stole a march on the Dutch though I took Ronald's cheery 'Goodbye, see you later for supper' as a genuine invitation. Beyond the mountain's rock-ribbed face, I looked down on a maze of snow peaks and receding ridges suffused in an ethereal light as we climbed on to the summit. On the way down, we met the Dutch coming up with Ronald in the lead and the lion-hearted Cemal bringing up the rear in snowshoes. That evening's celebratory supper in the Dutch tent filled British bellies, but left me with a disquieting note. Cemal, having humped up a Herculean load including a large tin of honey, was now sitting snow-blind and miserable on his own in a corner of the tent, the butt of Dutch humour for forgetting his snow-goggles. Naar described him as 'an excellent guide and an exceptional organiser' and as the owner of five *yailas* had given his clients the entrée to lavish local hospitality and 'marvellous photo opportunities'. Yet their treatment of him in his distress was less than sensitive.

Ronald's lieutenants, Bas and Henk, were both big, powerful men, but there was no doubt who was boss. Tough and combative, charismatic and charming, Ronald Naar had marked himself out as a highly ambitious mountaineer after climbing many of the great north face routes in the Alps before the age of twenty. Since then, he had made a solo ascent of Nanga Parbat and chalked up several notable firsts. He had also led mountaineering expeditions far and wide and become one of the world's foremost ski mountaineers. The year after our Kackar encounter, he guided a fourteen-man Dutch expedition on Everest and was severely criticised by Joe Simpson allegedly for failing to aid an Indian climber who lay dying on the South Col. On this account, several members of the Alpine Ski Club wanted to withdraw his honorary membership. Ronald certainly had a ruthless streak, but I resisted this censure for without knowing all the facts we were in no position to pass judgment. After Kackar, we often corresponded, but never met again. Holland's most outstanding mountaineer and ski mountaineer died on Cho Oyu on 22 May 2011 aged fifty-six. I shall always remember him for his humour, elan and buccaneering spirit.

Cemal, who knew the Kackar better than anyone, warned us that the next stage of the traverse was going to be the most difficult and dangerous. For from here, the only feasible way to get back over the watershed was across the

Kavron Gap, which could only be reached by traversing the four high cols that linked the radiating ridges of Kackar Peak's massively exposed southern flank. From there, descent down the Polovit and Kormik valleys should get us down to our next destination, Chat. The Dutch too were bound for the Kavron Gap, but thereafter our paths would divide.

The weather had held fine for the past six days, but on Good Friday high winds, low cloud and driving snow threatened to trigger the avalanches that are the ski mountaineer's most feared and unpredictable hazard. However carefully you exercise judgement, timing and caution, they will always pose an unquantifiable danger especially in an unfamiliar range with capricious weather and unstable snow. Nonetheless, if we didn't break out now, a prolonged period of bad weather would make a delayed exit even more hazardous.

Striking camp well ahead of the Dutch, we got our first proper sighting of Kackar Peak's south face from the col above the Deniz Golu lake. On seeing its discoloured flanks, deeply furrowed by rock, snow and ice avalanches my heart sank. Visibility was deteriorating and the snow falling fast when I turned, grim faced, to David.

'Sorry, but I don't think that we should even think of crossing that face. It looks horrendous. Those south-facing slopes could set off avalanches at any time.'

'At least there's no sun today,' he replied quietly. 'Otherwise, I certainly wouldn't risk it. But I don't see any alternative unless we retreat all the way we've come and that would mean the end of the traverse. Let me go on ahead to see how it looks. I'll keep as high up the slope as possible.'

The logic was unanswerable, but the risks were imponderable.

'Okay,' I said. 'But let's all make sure that our autophons are set correctly, avalanche spades accessible and waist straps undone.'

With that, David shot away like a bullet, steering an unerring line across that baleful face. We watched in awed silence at his flying figure until he became a dim spec on a distant ridgeline. This time, we didn't clap or cheer but just followed on in silence, singly and leaving big gaps between us always waiting for the dreaded roar that would mark the end. But it never came. David's was the boldest ski-mountaineering lead I ever witnessed.

Although it had seemed endless, that trapeze-like crossing of Kackar's four southern cols had taken barely three hours. But the nervous strain had taken its toll, and we all struggled to reach the Kavron Gap. From here, the 700-metre descent down the Polovit Valley should have come as light relief, but the snow changed in rapid succession from breakable crust to a crumble so rotten that you could drop through a metre of it as if a trapdoor had opened underneath. With everyone tiring, the cloud lifted just long enough to identify the critical col that led over the fifth and final ridge of the day. As dusk fell, we cruised gently down the upper Kormik Valley and pitched the tents beside the deserted chalets of Karam Yaila. Exhausted but exhilarated, it was still difficult to believe that we had just completed the most testing passage of the Kackar Traverse.

But where now? Those two lost days on the outward journey and at the Didvake had thrown my schedule. With time running out, David came up with his own solution.

'Why not give Chat a miss and strike due west towards Verchenik?'

David was always hard to gainsay, but not this time.

'Sorry David, I just don't think that's on. We'd have to cross at least another two big ridges without knowing whether that's possible or where it might lead. Besides, there's nothing left to eat whereas I'm sure we'll find something in Chat so let's stick to the original plan.'

We did just that, but the descent to Chat down the gun-barrel Kormik Valley was another nerve shredder. The valley's sides were scarred by huge avalanches and its trough choked in metres-deep debris. The knee-breaking snow reduced even David to the odd kick-turn before it began to thin and the valley widened to reveal clumps of snowdrops, gentians and primulas lining the path.

Set in a confluence of several deep valleys, Chat was deserted save for the Oteli Chanik guarded by its proprietor Rasim's monstrous dog 'Arslan', Turkey's answer to the Japanese Tosa. Avoiding the beast's wicked intentions with an outflanking movement, we dumped skis and rucksacks outside and flung ourselves over the threshold into the arms of Rasim. Somewhat grudgingly, he produced boiled eggs, sardines, bread and butter for an extortionate price plus a large pot of Pontic honey. Xenophon's soldiers had so gorged themselves on this stuff that some had died of a surfeit. Its intoxicating properties derive from the pollen of the yellow azalea. We too gorged ourselves, but suffered no ill effects.

The 1,350-metre descent to Chat had taken four and a half hours. The sensible thing would have been to stop here overnight, as our chances of climbing Verchenik, another fifteen kilometres away at the head of the Firtina Valley, were virtually nil. And when Rasim assured me that at this time of year, neither public transport nor taxis were running to Chemlihensin, the timetabling for catching the plane home from Trabzon was looking uncomfortably tight.

And yet, and yet … a full belly and even the faintest prospect of bagging a rare mountain can confound common sense. After dumping all the surplus kit, we headed up the Firtina Valley and five hours later reached its lower snow-fields shrouded in Black Sea mist. I had lost all sense of place and time when two enormous guard dogs came racing down the hill barking and snarling. Things were looking nasty until a spectral figure emerged through the murk and after calling his dogs off, escorted us to a chalet. Thus began a fairy tale ending to our Kackar venture.

Our rescuer, Barki Kasholi, the winter guardian of Ortakoy Yaila took us to his bosom to share hearth and home with his wife, two daughters, son Ali and the 150 sheep and ten cows that occupied his chalet's basement. On that stormy night, we slept not in the snow but in a pine-walled bedroom under hand-embroidered linen sheets scented with lavender. The following morning, Easter Day, we breakfasted off eggs with golden yolks and bread smothered with orange and raisin jam while Barki's two daughters suckled their pet lamb from a milk bottle. Before setting off up the narrowing Firtina Valley for Verchenik, David gave young Ali a skiing lesson and I gave Barki my Swiss penknife.

As the morning mists cleared, the pyramid of Verchenik, Queen of the Kackar Dag, emerged like some vision at the valley's head. Accepting reluctantly, that it was a peak too far, we made our last camp not that far from its base at Ovit Yaila in the afternoon sun. After returning to Chat next day, I took my first shower for a fortnight in Rasim's rude hamam, emptied a jug of paraffin over my head assuming it was water and only then remembered that it was April Fool's Day. A chance lift from a passing lorry on the dusty road down the Firtina Valley to Chemlihensin ensured that we would catch the homeward flight from Trabzon, and as we had trudged down that long valley, it occurred to me that Xenophon might well have taken this same route to the coast 2,392 years before. Fanciful maybe, but it was in the spirit of Xenophon that we had made the first ski traverse of the Kackar Dag, just as the kindness and hospitality of those we met along that challenging way had buoyed our passage.

15

MEDITERRANEAN SNOW
TO ARCTIC ICE

THE BITHYNIAN AND THRACIAN OLYMPUSES

It was fitting that two of my most ambitious ski mountaineering expeditions should have been in Turkey, the country that had set the scene for some of my earliest mountain ventures. Yet although the climate and character of both the Taurus and Pontic Alps are significantly affected by their proximity to historic seas, the most perfect symbiosis between mountains and the sea is realised in ranges that skirt the northern shores of the Mediterranean. Mount Etna apart, my first experiences of climbing any sea-girt Mediterranean mountains had been the Thessalian and Bithynian Olympuses. And so it was, many years later, that when Sidney Nowill told me about another little known Mount Olympus on Turkey's Lycian coast, I felt impelled to visit it particularly as its modern Turkish name, Takhtali Dag 'The Throne of Ali', resonated with that of Takht–i Sulaiman in the Elburz.

There were as many Olympuses in the classical world as there are Thrones of Ali in the lands of Islam. The Lycian Olympus took its name from ancient Lycia, the 'Land of the Tombs', once a prosperous member of the Delian League whose past glories can still be seen in the ruins that bestrew the mountain's base and whose ancient myths survive at the nearby village of Olympos where a natural combustion of methane gas issuing from a rock vent preserves the memory of the Chimaera, the fire-breathing monster with the triple heads of lion, goat and dragon that Bellerophon slew on his winged steed Pegasus. The Turkish government, zealous and imaginative in its efforts to preserve the monuments of past civilisations, has designated the entire area as the Olympus Beydagli National Park.

Long before its discovery by charter yachtsmen, Sidney had sailed this Lycian coast with a Turkish crew for its scenery of limestone cliffs rising sheer from the sea and incised by hidden inlets whose forests run to the waters' edge, is unrivalled in the Mediterranean. These same inlets were once the hideouts of the pirates who threatened even the *Pax Romana* until Pompey swept them from the Mediterranean during his forty-day purge in 67 BC. Well known anchorages such as Genoese Harbour recall a prosperous medieval mercantile age and these, in turn, became the lairs of Barbarossa's corsairs. Dominating this peerless stretch of coast is Takhtali Dag whose summit dome of bleached limestone shines as brightly in summer as it does when snow-capped in winter and presents an unmistakeable landmark for modern sailors rounding the Chelidonian Peninsula as it did in Phoenician times.

In 1983, John Blacker, a modern Argonaut with a passion for climbing mountains in the style of Bill Tilman, happened to be wintering his yacht *Foresight* at Kushadasi on Turkey's Aegean coast. This offered a rare opportunity for the two of us to climb Takhtali Dag from its seaward side after making landfall at the ancient port of Phaselis. The plan was that he and Janet Macrae would sail the 300 miles from Kushadasi to Antalya for a rendezvous with crew members Lolly Osmond and me. And so it was that on the 24 September, Lolly and I were breakfasting on the sunlit terrace of the Hotel Talya scanning the horizon for one small sail that might betoken John's plucky little ship, concerned as we were about the sudden storm that had blown up the previous night. From time to time, my gaze shifted westwards across the shimmering waters of the Gulf of Antalya to where a 2,000-metre-high range of mountains, crowned by a line of jagged peaks that displayed every mountain facet that delights the climber's eye, rose from the sea. These were the Lycian Alps, whose climbing history was still unwritten and whose crown, distant but unmistakeable to the south, was Takhtali Dag.

Antalya, founded over 2,200 years ago, has the finest setting of any Turkish city along the Mediterranean coast. Little of the ancient city remains save for Sultan Aladdin's thirteenth century 'Fluted Mosque' whose mellow red brick and blue-green Seljuk tiles, mirroring both the sea and sky, overlooks the old harbour. Here, where garishly painted local fishing craft jostled the sleek gin palaces of the mega-rich, Lolly and I spent much of that day scanning the horizon with binoculars for the comfort of spotting just one small, white sail. We had almost given up hope when, late that afternoon, we bumped into

Blacker at the bar of the Sehir Hotel pre-selected as a 'last-resort' rendezvous.

'Sorry to cause alarm,' said John, quite unconcerned. 'To avoid last night's storm, Janet and I decided to hole up at Kemer's new marina just down the coast and bang opposite Takhtali Dag. I sent several messages up to your hotel, but they must have been lost in transit.'

Reunited late that evening for delayed sundowners in *Foresight's* cockpit with the silky, phosphorescent waters of the Aegean lapping its hull, the night sky was ablaze with stars and our cups were full.

Next morning, the massive bulk of the Lycian Olympus filled the western horizon clean-cut and uncompromising with its bald head luminescent in mellow September sunshine. It didn't look a difficult climb, yet between the seashore and its summit lay eighteen kilometres of tangled forest and 2,375 metres of vertical height. Moreover, with nothing to guide us save for John's nautical maps, we could only guess at what precisely lay ahead. After completing some ponderous customs formalities with the harbour master, John and I picked up a couple of days' food, slipped *Foresight's* comforts and left the girls in command. An itinerant bus dropped us off at the ruins of Phaselis where Alexander had paused in 333 BC before marching along the coast to capture Antalya and where, according to his chronicler, 'the sea bowed low to do him homage'.

At this time, the only practical way of getting within striking distance of Takhtali Dag was by sea. *Foresight* had given us a flying start, but by the time we had entered the coastal pine forest the mountain was enveloped in cloud. Route finding through dense thickets, interspersed with stretches of stubborn *maquis* overlaying jagged limestone scarps that radiated heat, made for slow going. A skein of dried-up watercourses along shallow ravines led to a forestry camp, which we skirted very cautiously. I had taken to heart Sidney Nowill's advice that discovery by Turkish authority of civilians in possession of altimeters and compasses could have unpredictable consequences.

After four and a half hours struggling through successive bands of pine, fir, oriental beech, medlar and juniper, we had climbed a mere 200 metres without even reaching the skirts of the mountain. An unlikely forest track ran steeply to a clearing atop a ridge that overlooked a gaping gorge which brought us face to face for the first time that afternoon with the Lycian Olympus. Rearing up above us like some elemental force of nature, it looked remote, resentful and seemingly inviolable. In winter, these Lycian mountains have abundant rain and snow, but by late September all surface water disappears into the underlying limestone. The undergrowth was tinder-dry, the heat intense and by mid-afternoon our four water bottles were quite empty. Dehydration was crippling our work rate and had we not chanced on a shepherd's wooden water trough, we would have been forced to make a humiliating retreat to *Foresight*. With thirsts slaked, we refilled the bottles and pressed on upwards past a deserted *yaila* and thence up the flanks of a broad ridge shaded by majestic stands of Cedars of Lebanon. By 7 p.m. the temperature had at last dropped and at 1,360 metres John called halt on the crest of the ridge under a huge pine tree whose fallen needles made our bed.

After my years in South Arabia, I was not unused to heat, yet the day's climb had been totally debilitating. Under winking stars, the night passed restfully enough but a purple dawn heralded another desperately hot day. Far below the heavily forested ridge that snaked down in lazy cadences to the sea, Kemer's marina was just visible as a faint smudge tucked into the roots of the Chelidonian Peninsula. High above, Takhtali Dag glowered like an incandescent beacon. Our drinking water had been finished the previous night and without replenishment I wondered how we could possibly climb another thousand metres to Takhtali's summit. The broad ridge now contracted into a narrow causeway of white limestone that spanned a dizzying chasm that dropped plumb to the plain. This, the Bridge of Ali, would lead either to paradise or perdition. To postpone full exposure to the sun we kept to partial shade offered by an ever-thinning line of trees, which gave out after two and a half hours. Once in the open, the heat took my breath away and the sun's glare was blinding even through snow goggles. John, now stumbling around like a drunken man, called a halt.

'Sorry John, but I'm totally dehydrated. It would be crazy for me to carry on in this state. But don't let me stop you if you feel up to it. I'll stay here and wait for you.'

I didn't feel in the least up to it and we should have gone down. But having got so far, I wasn't finished yet and surely, the top couldn't be that far away? I didn't dare look at my altimeter for fear of disillusionment and scrambled up and over an awkward band of white-hot limestone that gave way to easier ground where virgin scree was studded with cushion-shaped xerophytes and helicrysum. The next hour passed as in a dream before I was brought up short by a steep rock barrier. Alone on that silent, shimmering slope I was overcome by lassitude and nausea. The summit was less than 200 metres higher, but it might have been a mile and when my vision began to blur I knew that this was no time for solo heroics.

The descent to Kemer took another seven hours. Once again, a providential water trough saved us from serious dehydration for we found no other water that day. Back on board *Foresight,* with iced beers to hand, John attributed our feeble showing to middle age 'mountaineer's foot'. Actually, it was a simple case of dehydration, that most insidious mountain threat. Youth steers a surer course and the following year our eldest daughter Emma breezed up Takhtali Dag to add to her tally of Mount Olympuses.

I slept well that night and the following morning, after John had insisted on a regulation skinny dip, we hauled up the anchor and sailed on westwards under his unflurried helmsmanship in sight of Takhtali's white beacon for another two days. Odysseus too had once passed this way on his return to Ithaca having at last broken the seven-year spell cast upon him by the enchantress Calypso. For me, the Lycian Olympus also casts a spell still unbroken.

Two years on, the Lycian Olympus rebuff spurred me to have another shot at climbing its more famous Thessalian namesake. Breakfasting in Litochoro's square on a bright morning in May 1985 with John Blacker, Georgina and Liz MacDonnell, I marvelled that the gloomy village I remembered as one haunted by the ghosts of bloody civil war, had now become a bustling tourist resort with a host of tavernas and four international hotels. Yesterday's scudding clouds had given way to sunshine lancing its shining rods through the swathes of yellow broom that covered the hillsides. Thanks to a newly built road to Prionia, the trek to the Agipitos Hut that had taken me nine excruciating hours in 1961, now took only three. At the hut's threshold stood a beaming man his arms akimbo. Climber, visionary and conservationist, it was the Greek mountain Zorba himself – Costas Zelotas!

'You are very lucky to find me here, my friends!' said Costas. 'The hut is not yet officially open and I was just about to go down to Litochoro after taking stock of the supplies I shall need for the forthcoming season.'

'You couldn't possibly remember,' I chipped in, 'but I came here back in November 1961 after being recommended to climb with you by Athanos Tzartzanos. Unfortunately, you were then away in Munich.'

'Yes, indeed,' he replied. 'I vaguely remember Athanos telling me about some crazy Englishman coming here to climb Olympus in the middle of winter. We had very few visitors in those days, but times have changed. Last year over 7,000 people stayed at our huts. This year, I'm expecting 10,000 as the whole area is about to be designated a national park. My own climbing days are over as I'm now fifty-one and have joined the "Old Boys", though I still keep an eye on everything going on here. You and your friends are doubly welcome. However, I can't yet open up the main hut so I'm going to leave you with the keys to the winter quarters. Make yourselves at home and when you get back to Litochoro, tell me how you got on!'

Before parting, Zolotas broached the hut's cellar and left us with a complimentary crate of beer.

The following day, after we had all climbed Skolio, John, Liz and I went on to Mytikas. Sunshine and dry rock reduced the passage that had looked so daunting in winter to a scramble. Now it was spring and the hills rejoiced. On the way down, we met a young couple. She, a fresh-faced, willowy blonde with a winning smile. He, tall, dark and handsome, toting a pair of miniature skis.

'Ronald Naar's the name,' he said, grinning broadly. 'And this is Tilleke. We're both from the Netherlands.'

At that time, I had never heard of Ronald Naar, the flying Dutch seven-summiteer, though our paths were to cross often in later years. For a couple of nights all five of us shared the hut's winter quarters drinking, laughing and swapping yarns together. Tilleke, an artist, judged our painting competition. Modesty forbids me to name the winner.

The British quartet climbed Pagos, the highest peak in the Kalogeros Group which gave a magical eight-hour trek around the massif's winter-worn upper pastures as diaphanous wreaths of mist closed and parted and explosions of swelling cumulus bubbled up from the Thessalian plain. The fast-melting snowfields were giving way to carpets of *Crocus sieberi* and when we left for Litochoro the following morning by a spiralling path down the Enipeus Gorge, the mountain's upper reaches had been transformed by the onrush of spring with a mosaic of alyssum, rose, cowslip, scilla, hyacinth, snowdrop, lily and fritillary confirming the Greek adage that when God created the world he forgot about Greece, but then made good his omission by scattering every flower left over about its face.

The half-ruined monastery of Saint Dionysius of Alexandria, built on the site of more ancient shrines and used as a refuge by patriots during the Greek War of Independence and partisans during the Second World War, was now occupied by a trio of hirsute hippies and a gigantic Salonikan, who claimed to be its guardian and who was wearing a pair of dirty pyjamas. On emerging from a dome-shaped cell set in the courtyard's vaulted colonnades, he bent our collective ears with 'Dionysius lived here 1,700 years ago. He very strong man. You lucky to see this place of magic'. Apart from icons in the chapel depicting the agony of Christ, little of that magic remained, but at least the plan to make it into a hotel has lapsed.

The genius of the place was in nature itself for by now the Enipeus river, so furious in its upper reaches, had slowed to tumble down polished boulders into a limpid pool that reflected the beech thickets, intertwined with the wild vines that lined its banks. We swam naked descried only by Dionysius, the scion of Zeus. And then, with the gorge ever narrowing, tier upon tier of beetling cliffs stretched up to the sky as the path swooped down and up, crossing and recrossing its trough by an ingenious network of bridges. John reckoned it even finer than Crete's Gorge of Samaria.

Eight hours after leaving the Agipitos Hut, we slaked our thirst at a taverna on the outskirts of Litochoro before dining with Zolotas at the Hotel Myrto.

'And how did you like my path down the gorge?' the great man asked, now immaculate in khaki uniform.

'It's only just been finished and I've smartened up the ancient track to the monastery by adding in a few bits here and there to link the past with the present.'

Zolotas's Olympus will always retain pride of place in my Olympic pantheon.

CORSICA

Some of that same Mediterranean magic prompted our return to the Turkish coast later that summer for a family holiday at Bodrum, from where the girls and I made an abortive attempt to climb Beshparmak in whose secret cave the shepherd Endymion still slumbers in eternal youth. In August the following year, we took another Mediterranean summer holiday with the combined Band and Chorley families plus boyfriends for a week's walking in Corsica, the 'Granite Island' that rises like Venus from the sea to its 2,706-metre culmination in Monte Cinto. Few travellers have not succumbed to the island's potent charms and the 'grave hard splendour of wooded landscapes and brooding heights of rock and snow' that are so faithfully conveyed in Edward Lear's engravings. Its white-sand beaches, coves and anchorages are the stuff of sailors' dreams and its forests contain the monarch of all European trees, the transcendental Corsican pine that can attain 700 years in age and over fifty metres in height. For the mountaineer, trekker or walker the island's mountain backbone, a twisting snake of granite and gabbro, crossed and recrossed by multiple transverse ridges and crowned with peaks, aiguilles and obelisks, makes Corsica *the* Mediterranean playground for all seasons. Douglas Freshfield professed that he knew of 'no region in Europe where within so small a space nature takes on so many different sublime or exquisite aspects.' Yet another contemporary Alpine Club member, T.G. Ouston, likened it to 'a woman with a past ... fascinating, romantic and beautiful but otherwise to be left severely alone,' perhaps because what the French call the Île de Beauté has a tough inner core. Its high valleys are choked in *maquis* – a near-impenetrable wilderness of aromatic shrubs and plants interlaced with arbutus, myrtle, cistus, rosemary, lavender and thyme – which was once a refuge for bandits, outlaws and wartime resistance fighters and remains a challenge for all who stray off the beaten track.

The thread which binds together so many of Corsica's component parts is the GR20 High Level Walking Route, one of the most popular and famous of its kind. *Gruppen Fuhrer Band* lost no time in mobilising all thirteen members of the 1986 family party to walk the Bonifato to Calenzana stage of the GR20 before collectively shinning up the Paglia Orba. A splinter group bivouacked under the stars at the Bergerie de Ballone before completing the GR20's final stages via its most dramatic natural feature, the gloomy Cirque de Solitude. En route, I bumped into Ronald Naar's partner Tilleke Lippman who was shepherding an elongated group of fifteen Dutch men and women along the GR20. When she told me that Ronald had traversed Corsica on ski earlier that year, I simply didn't believe her. The terrain looked quite un-skiable. And what about snow? On our first day's trek, one of the boyfriends had succumbed to heat stroke.

After getting home, I received by post a brief account of Ronald's traverse of the Haute Route de Corse and hurriedly consulted Parmentier's oracular *Les Grandes Raids à Ski* for further elucidation. It transpired that Parmentier had already done this most unusual ski traverse some years before, following the most spectacular section of the GR20 from Battelica to Asco despite bad weather and a near-fatal avalanche incident. Ronald's party, following this same route, had found it 'extremely challenging' with high avalanche risk and with weather so unpredictable that for a day and a half they had been marooned by floods at the Onda Refuge when torrential rain, mixed with red sand, had blown in from the Sahara by the *Sirocco*. Overall, he rated the Haute Route de Corse as 'the most difficult traverse in Europe ... with passages which challenge the skier's technique to the limit'.

I never forgot the Corsican ski challenge, but for the next eight years had to consign it to the back-burner. And after completing the 1991 Kackar Traverse, I even wondered whether I was up to it. However, in 1992 I went as far as to prepare a draft Haute Route de Corse itinerary only to abandon the project for lack of snow. Instead, to stay in the game, I joined Major Alun Davies's British Army expedition Golden Road, which was to spend a week in the Vanoise prior to making a ski ascent of Mont Blanc. This expedition was not only sponsored by the Ministry of Defence, but also 'approved' by the French government and when a succession of *warning orders* and *general instructions* from headquarters 160 (Wales) Brigade came thudding through our letterbox, I imagined myself recalled to the colours.

With Alun as team leader, the party's other members were Malcolm Gilbertson, a retired brigadier; Lieutenant Colonel John Newman-Carter, then responsible for the British Army's adventure training, and Jon Ellis-Roberts, the head warden of the Snowdonia National Park, as guide. Support staff included two warrant officers, one as base camp manager and the other as the driver of the MOD long-wheelbase Land Rover that was to ferry us to and from our various entry and exit points between valley stopovers at the French Army's *Chasseurs Alpines* barracks at Bourg St Maurice, Modane and Chamonix. Here, we were fed like fighting cocks by young French national servicemen waiters who discharged their mess duties with *élan* and *politesse*. It was a very different type of ski mountaineering to what I was used to.

Due to holiday constraints, I could only manage the first week. We climbed Pointe Mean de Martin but failed to achieve Alun's long-cherished ambition of completing the fourteen-kilometre crossing of the Vanoise Glacier, which we abandoned after reaching the upper glacier L'Arport due to deteriorating weather and avalanche risk. This particular passage had qualified the army contingent for the 'arctic allowance' and left me to ponder at the Bourg St Maurice mess that evening whether we might not have pushed our luck. But as is so often the case, the harder course is to turn back to fight another day and next morning, a terrific storm fully justified that decision. Frustratingly, I then had to return home while the rest of the team went on to Chamonix and successfully climbed Mont Blanc. I was to see a lot of Alun after he retired from the army and went on to organise a number of imaginative ski tours with a military flavour including a crossing of Crete to emulate Patrick Leigh Fermor's and an Arctic trek in the steps of the Norwegian war hero Jan Baalstrud.

Save for a couple of Highland weekends with the Eagles, 1993 was a barren ski mountaineering year for me, due in part to the IRA bomb that exploded fifty metres from Norton Rose's Bishopsgate offices forcing us to find new accommodation and relocate 950 staff within a matter of days. The following year, Edward Whymper's maxim that 'a man does not climb mountains after his sixtieth year' reminded me that mine was due that August and that if I didn't attempt the Haute Route de Corse soon, it would be too late. Fortunately, the well-tested trio of David Williams, Rupert Hoare and Steven Baker were all available plus Rodney Franklin whose impressive ski-mountaineering CV included expeditions to the Himalaya and an ascent of British Columbia's Mount Waddington. As a distinguished paediatrician, Rodney was well qualified to deal with his charges' infantile banter, something I had missed on expedition Golden Road. For someone nearer my own age, I recruited Patrick Fagan whom I had first met on the 1974 Eagle Ski Club Pyrenean tour twenty years before.

Both Parmentier and Naar had begun their Corsican traverses at Batellica and finished with ascents of Monte Cinto, the island's highest peak. Parmentier's account was short on detail and Naar had questioned how the Frenchmen could possibly have completed the Batellica to Vizzavona stage in four to six hours when this same section had taken his Dutch team two and a half days battling through forest and *maquis*. We could only afford ten days for our own trip, so I decided to drop their first stage and start from Vizzavona, a convenient stop on the Ajaccio to Corte railway line.

We flew to Ajaccio on 25 February 1994 and the following morning waved-down the incredulous but indulgent driver of the 8 a.m. Corte Express with ski sticks as it passed our hotel. Alighting at Vizzavona, we left behind the sad, shuttered hotels that had once welcomed Corsica's fashionable nineteenth century British community for winter holidays with log fires and ballroom dancing. Striking up a mountain track fringed with clusters of the delicate blue *Veronica repens*, the harbingers of spring, we climbed on through the beech, oak, chestnut and pine forests that had so impressed James Boswell during his 1768 tour. Skis were first donned at the spirited *Cascade des Anglais* waterfall and for the next five hours, my principal preoccupation, and that of Patrick, was how to survive the 1,000-metre climb to the head of the Agnone Valley in the heat of the midday sun. We both made it after much huffing and puffing but any hopes of an easy descent to the Onda Hut were dashed when Williams insisted that we should ski the fall line down Muratello's north ridge, a testing passage through lumpy snow which was accomplished at variable speeds and different levels of proficiency. All eventually regrouped at the Onda Hut where Rodney administered potions to ameliorate a vicious attack of gout that my unyielding plastic ski boots had exacerbated.

During the small hours, with my hip playing up and my gouty toe throbbing, I wondered what had possessed me to embark on the Haute Route de Corse particularly as tomorrow's stage to the Pietra Piana Hut along the crests of the Serras di Tenda and Bianca was an inducement for peak-baggers but took in the very passage where Parmentier had been avalanched. It would have been possible to avoid this section by sticking to the standard GR20 route which ran along the valley bottom, but this would have meant descending 500 metres and then climbing another 900 metres to regain the ridge. In the event, it was never put to the vote, for to prevent any backsliding Williams and Hoare raced up the Capu di Meta immediately after breakfast, thereby committing everyone to the high route.

For one kilometre, it was just possible to continue along the crest of the Serra di Tenda on ski before the way ahead became blocked by a line of gendarmes. Until then, I had been blindly following Hoare, but his attempts to surmount an intractable tower were doomed from the start. As a result, we had to retrace our steps along the ridge to rejoin the others only to find that three of them appeared to have base-jumped off a malign nick and were already halfway across the steeply shelving snow slopes suspended above the Manca Ravine which the map dignified with the dotted lines to signify a dangerous passage. Patrick was still cogitating how best to tackle this *mauvais pas,* which I now recognised as the very place where Parmentier's party had narrowly escaped their avalanche near-disaster. When Rupert and I joined Patrick, each of us traversed the slope with extreme caution one by one well spaced out. Both nerve and snow held firm despite some wobbles, though once on the other side Rupert confessed that he thought it might have been our last. On the summit of the Pinzi Corbini, Ajaccio flashed white against a backcloth of Tyrian blue. To the east, the cloud-sea that had settled over much of the island stayed firmly put for the next four days.

The empty Pietra Piana Hut was ideally placed for the ascent of Monte Rotondo, once thought to be Corsica's highest peak. The 800-metre ski descent on south-facing snow, hardened to perfection by Mediterranean freeze-thaw, boosted team morale for tomorrow's passage to the Manganu Hut. Both Parmentier and Naar had marked this as the crux of the Haute Route de Corse with warnings that it should only be attempted under safe snow conditions and in good weather. Rodney's pills had done wonders for my gout, but a dramatic drop in barometric pressure that evening left me with bad vibes.

At 6.25 a.m. the following morning, appropriately 1st of March, Saint David's Day, a fish-scaled sky displayed sinister hues of salmon pink shot through with vermillion. Stick or bust? We were cosily ensconced in a dry, warm hut with plenty of food and could have stuck it out for days if necessary. But to have lost even a single day at this stage of the traverse would have forfeited the venture, so we chanced it and for the next two hours never once took off our *harscheisen* during a crab-like, diagonal traverse to the Col de la Haute Route. From here, a steep descent ended at the Col Rinoso where the weather finally broke. Another awkward traverse led on to the Bocca a Soglia to be followed by a tricky descent to the base of the Punta alle Porta's south-west ridge. This place marked the start of the key passage. We were now committed.

Before everything faded into a grey obscurity of swirling mist and driving snow, I glimpsed a staircase of gendarmes disappearing into the clouds above. With skis strapped to rucksacks, Williams led the way in crampons, weaving through ice-encrusted rocks choked in avalanche-prone snow with the ground on either side falling away to soundless depths. Four and a half hours later we breasted the Breche Capitello and completed the key passage of the Haute Route de Corse that had taken Parmentier seven hours. It was a sweet moment and another Williams *tour de force.*

But there was still a sting in the Corsican tail. The climb to the Breche had almost exhausted my physical reserves and I now found myself shivering uncontrollably. Even so, as I slipped comfortably into the rear as Tail End Charlie, I didn't give a thought about what should have been a simple enough descent to the Manganu Hut. But the late afternoon snow was heavy and a bungled turn saw me doing the splits in slow motion before landing headfirst in the snow and wrenching both my left leg and buttock muscles in the process. The bindings didn't break, I couldn't move and the pain was so excruciating that I yelled out uncontrollably. In less than a minute, David was at my side breaking the bindings, easing me out of the snow, sharing out the contents of my rucksack and then shepherding me down to the hut where Rodney stuffed me with painkillers.

I felt a complete wreck and was furious with myself for such an elementary fall. After Rodney had administered a vigorous massage, I fell sound asleep and on waking felt much better to find that a newcomer had joined us. This was Laurent Hemmerle, a young Frenchman bent on skiing the last stages of the GR20 solo. He had brought with him a three-day food cache that included paté, chocolate and cherry liqueur and when he took to Liar Dice and Hearts like a natural, we invited him to join the club. That night, I mused that things might have been worse but doubted that I would be able to carry on and agonised that I had landed the others with a casualty and the prospect of an expensive helicopter rescue just when the traverse seemed to be in the bag. Verghio, the nearest GR20 breakpoint with a roadhead and hotel, was still a full day's skiing away and the potential consequences of having another fall while getting there were daunting.

By the following morning the pain had eased. With some trepidation I followed the others gingerly down into the Pianu di Campolite basin closely shadowed by Rodney. The strained muscles felt very tender, but as the clouds melted away and the sun warmed our backs, I loosened up and, wonder of wonders, found I could still ski. Once across the Pianu's frozen lake, I felt confident enough to take the lead through an ancient beech grove that merged into the Tavignano Valley before climbing past monumental boulders of polished granite to the Capu a u Tozzu from where the sprawling mass of Monte Cinto first hove in sight and the porcupine ridge that had given so much trouble yesterday settled back into the landscape. During a long, steady descent through giant stands of chestnut and Corsican pine, Steven demonstrated his elegant Telemark technique before we reached a path to shed our skis and walk in boots for the first time in six days.

Carefree and still congratulating ourselves on having cracked the key passage, Steven stumbled just short of Verghio, swore and stopped dead in his tracks. 'Bloody hell! I can't move,' he groaned. 'Something's gone in my knee!'

Steve was young, fit and a very strong skier. Yet a single misplaced footstep on a loose stone had snapped a ligament. Supported between Patrick and me, he hopped one-legged the rest of the way to Verghio where we were met and then questioned by a suspicious member of the Mountain Gendarmerie. The hotel was full, but after a robust verbal exchange with 'Peppery Jo', a Brit-bashing Bonaparte-loving ski-pioneer, cordial relations were established and after putting us up at the Ajaccio Post Office Union's ski chalet for free, he numbed Steven's pain and disappointment somewhat with an eighty per cent proof local *marc*.

By rights, I should have been the casualty not Steven and during the night, I wondered whether to call the whole thing off. But next morning, I didn't bother to take a vote for David Williams was wearing that fixed, determined expression I knew so well. Beneath his boyish exterior was a will of iron and in no way was he going to give away the Haute Route de Corse. After Steven had been bundled into an ambulance with the promise that we'd meet up at Ajaccio in three days' time, we walked pensively up to the Mori Hut to find its roof disintegrating under the weight of snow. I was feeling immensely depressed at this latest turn of events, but Rupert was more sanguine and took the break as an opportunity to shin up Tofanata with David and Laurent, it being 'the sort of thing that makes a trip like this worthwhile.'

Darkness frustrated his attempt to complete the Tofanata traverse and a majority vote dissuaded him from making a solo sally up the Paglia Orba's historic *Finch Route* the following day. The compromise route on the Paglia was less challenging, though Rupert's abortive confrontation with a Grade VI diedre produced a shower of crampon sparks and brought to mind that lost Lear limerick:

> *A cheeky young ski mountaineer*
> *Who thought he had nothing to fear*
> *Stormed the Paglia Orba*
> *With no inkling of trauma*
> *And then fell headfirst through thin air.*

That same evening, relaxing in the luxurious, solar-panel heated Tighiettu Hut that overlooks the sinister Strancione Ravine, the scene was set for what Ronald Naar had described as 'one of the great ski climbs of Europe'. At 6.25 a.m. on 5 March, we slipped the hut and for the next two hours cramponed up the shadowed Stagni Ravine, hemmed in on either side by boiler-plate granite slabs, to the Col Vallon. Behind to the west, the great tooth of the Paglia Orba glowed red in the rising sun as we part-skied, part-cramponed along a two-kilometre twist of rock and ice that led inexorably to Cinto's summit. Here, at exactly 11 a.m. the whole team assembled to shake hands and take in the panorama of Corsica with the peaks of the past week becoming indistinct clusters on the horizon. Far across the Ligurian Sea, the luminescent arc of the Alps was faintly visible.

Setting our skis in the direction of Catacuccia, a grey smudge below the skein of bleached granite ridges that stretched down to the Erco Valley, we flighted across its backwall before launching off on a non-stop 1,600-metre vertical descent to an icy pool beneath a waterfall. Here, the hearties took a skinny dip leaving the weeds to gawp at our hardihood. By now, we were hours ahead of Parmentier's time, but the final walkout to Catacuccia became a trial of will as an accumulation of strains and pains finally caught up with me. Only at our celebratory supper at Francardo's Auberge Casimir with its walls decorated not with pictures of Napoleon Bonaparte but with those of the Corsican patriot Paoli and the bandit Bellacoscia, did it dawn on me that we had just completed the first British Haute Route de Corsica.

ARCTIC ICE: SVALBARD 1994

It would be hard to imagine anywhere less like Corsica than Svalbard, the Arctic Archipelago encased in ice that is as close to the North Pole as the northern coast of Greenland. Like many other schoolboys, I had been inspired by the feats of the early polar explorers and when, at Stowe, my housemaster inexplicably sold off our house library, I bought first editions of Scott's two Antarctic expeditions for the princely sum of five shillings. Polar exploration still retained its hold on me at Cambridge and after graduation I applied to join the British Antarctic Survey. The outcome of my application was decided by the hip operation that put me out of contention for any form of employment for the next twelve months. Thirty-seven years on, Derek Fordham's invitation to join his 1994 Eagle Ski Club Svalbard expedition promised the fulfilment of a boyhood dream.

Svalbard's main island Spitsbergen is peppered with spiky peaks and topped by the 1,717-metre Newtontoppen named after Sir Isaac. Derek, a veteran of twenty Arctic expeditions, was determined to make its first British ski ascent that April, a time of year when Svalbard enjoys almost twenty-four hours of daylight and when its ferociously cold winters are tempered by the Gulf Stream. Incredibly, while Svalbard's capital Longyearbyen can now be reached within a day's flight from Heathrow, its archipelago was only discovered in 1596 when the Dutch explorer Barentsz accidentally came across it during his abortive attempt to discover a polar route to China. Russian fur trappers were closely followed by British, Dutch and Basque fishermen bent on hunting Svalbard's prolific population of walruses, whales and seals to near-extinction. By the eighteenth century, its wider strategic importance had been recognised by both Britain and Russia, and when the Russian explorer Mikhail Lomonosov urged Catherine the Great to secure Svalbard as a base to force the Northeast Passage, Britain responded by despatching Captain Phipps's 1773 naval expedition. Trapped in the ice at latitude eighty-degrees north, a fourteen-year-old midshipman called Horatio Nelson took this opportunity to embark on the solo polar bear hunt which would have been his last had he not managed to beat off his intended quarry with the butt of his musket.

Sir Martin Conway, the first president of the Alpine Ski Club, had made the first crossing of Spitsbergen in 1896 and Russian scientists the first ascent of Newtontoppen in 1900. From available photographs, the mountain's ascent did not look difficult, but it lies ninety kilometres north of Svalbard's capital Longyearbyen surrounded by a glacial wilderness. Derek reckoned that we would need a week either way to get there and back using *langlauf* skis and pulling miniature sledges or *pulks*. His team, whose ages averaged fifty-one, included some genuine Nordic skiers – Andy Roberts, Patrick Fagan and David Hall – and three others – Paddy O'Neill, Andrew Coatsworth and David Seddon – who claimed some acquaintance with the technique. Roger Childs and I had virtually none.

On 21 April 1994, the party flew from Heathrow and reached Longyearbyen that same evening. My flight was enlivened by an attractive, cherry-brandy-swigging, divorced lady barrister, who was heading to a weekend law seminar with forty Oslo lawyers. Longyearbyen, lying 2,046 kilometres north of Oslo at 78:30 degrees north shares the same latitude as Scott's Antarctic base at Camp Evans and would probably have remained an abandoned whaling station had it not been for the discovery of coal at the end of the nineteenth century when the American entrepreneur John Longyear purchased all Svalbard's mining claims and proceeded to transform its economy. In 1925, the Norwegian government bought the claims back and declared Svalbard Norwegian sovereign territory in the face of vigorous Russian objections.

This most unusual capital city also occupies a special place in the history of Arctic exploration as the setting for the dramatic confrontation between the veteran Norwegian explorer Roald Amundsen and a dashing young American naval officer, Richard Byrd. In 1926, both men had chosen Longyearbyen as their base from which to be first to fly across the North Pole. Byrd was backed by the might of the US government and the Ford Motor Company. Amundsen, aged fifty-four and desperate to restore his fading reputation, was near destitute. Byrd's claim to have done the first crossing made him an all-American hero. Yet, like his compatriot Peary who had claimed to be the first to reach the Pole, Byrd's bid for glory later proved false and it was Amundsen who completed the first crossing on 12 May 1926 in the airship *Norge*. Two years later, this greatest of polar explorers perished in the Arctic Ocean on a mission to rescue his erstwhile Italian companion Nobile, reported lost in the Arctic ice in his airship *Italia*.

At 9 p.m. Longyearbyen was still bathed in an ethereal light. The simple wooden bungalows which housed us were painted in vivid reds, ochres and greens as if to relieve the bleakness of the monochrome mountains overlooking the town and which had originally been built for the mining company's employees. They were fitted with all mod cons. Perpetual twilight made sleep difficult, but when the sun peeped over the horizon next day, I lifted my eyes to the north and beheld a dazzling array of snow mountains that seemed to stretch to infinity.

109 Corsica 1986. On the Paglia Orba. L–R: Emma, Victoria and Joanna.
110 Corsican High Route 1994. David Williams.
111 Corsican High Route 1994. L–R: David Williams, Rupert Hoare and Stephen Baker on Muratello.

112 Corsican High Route 1994. At the Manganu Hut. L–R: David Williams, Rodney Franklin,
Patrick Fagan, Rupert Hoare, Steven Baker and author (sitting).
113 Corsican High Route 1994. Sierra di Tenda passage above the Manca Ravine.
114 Corsican High Route 1994. Paglia Orba from Monte Cinto. L–R: Patrick, Rupert,
David, Rodney, Laurent Hemmerle.

115 Svalbard 1994. Templefiord. The first day out.
116 Svalbard 1994. Camp at Bromsfjellet.

117 Svalbard 1994. The interior of Spitsbergen.

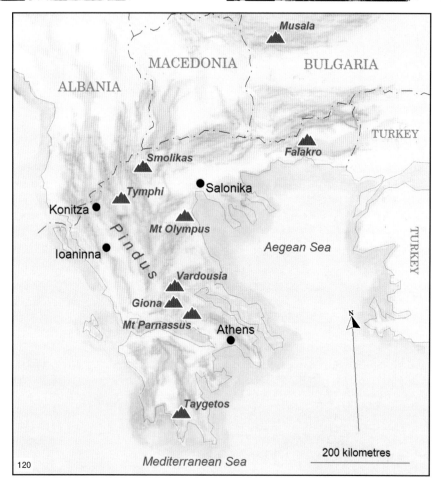

118 Svalbard 1994. Journey's end. L–R: David Seddon, Roger Childs and David Hall.
119 Greece 1995. Mount Parnassus. Upper Velitza Gorge.
120 Greece.

121 Greece 1995. Parnassus Camp 3 after the storm. **Photo**: David Williams.
122 Greece 1995. Korakas Peak. Richard Cooper.
123 Greece 1995. Ghiona Massif, Sterea. David Williams.

124 Greece 2000. Metsovo, Northern Pindus.
125 Greece 2000. En route to Smolikas. Tymphi north face.

126 Cairngorm ski tour 1980. The young idea. Emma and Victoria.
127 The Julian Alps 1995.
128 The Julian Alps. Triglav north face. Rose and Joanna.

129 Mont Blanc 1999. North face with Bossons Glacier.

130 Mont Blanc 1999. Descent of Bossons Glacier. Joanna.
131 Monte Viso 2001. En route to Sella Hut. Rupert Hoare.
132 Kyrgyzstan 2004. Lunch on the Inylchyk Glacier.

133 Kyrgyzstan 2004. Tien Shan. Trek up the Inylchyk Glacier.
134 Kyrgyzstan 2004. Camp 3 on the Upper Inylchyk Glacier.

135 Kyrgyzstan 2004. Tien Shan Base Camp. Khan Tengri.
136 Kyrgyzstan 2004. Author at Khan Tengri Base Camp.
137 Kyrgyzstan 2004. At Tosor Camp. L–R: Peter Christie, Neil Macpherson and Bill Heber-Percy.

138 Tajikistan 2012. Kyrgyz family on Sandal Plateau.
139 Tajikistan 2012. Camp at Maida Kul.

140

141

140 Tajikistan 2012. Bill Blackburne fords the Karashura Valley. Peter the Great Range in background.
141 Tajikistan 2012. Tipchak Plateau. Rickmer Rickmers Camp.

Derek and his wife Jennie had spend long months meticulously organising the expedition's food and equipment. However, when everything was unpacked, only four of the seventy-six steel tent pegs essential for securing our five tents in the ice could be found. Within a couple of hours, a nonchalant lady carpenter obligingly knocked-up the missing pegs from imported birch wood. By law, no one may travel outside Longyearbyen without a rifle as a precaution against polar bears. Horatio Nelson might have got away with it, but in 2013 the hapless Horatio Chapple, a seventeen-year member of a British Schools Exploring Society, was tragically killed when a bear broke through their camp's perimeter fence in a supposedly low-risk location. Polar bears are a protected species and may only be shot *in extremis*. Halberdier Hall, our dauntless ex-SAS member, was entrusted with an antiquated .303 Lee-Enfield rifle and left to decide, in the event of an attack, whether to save our skins or face imprisonment.

On 23 April, a tracked 'Weasel' ferried the party to Fredheim, a weathered shack on the edge of the frozen Templefiord, built by the legendary bear hunter Hilmar Nois and now preserved as a national monument. The air was so clear that you imagined you could see to the ends of the earth and the temperature such that once in the open, we had to beat our over-gloved hands furiously into life before strapping ourselves into the harnesses of our fibreglass *fjellpunken*. I had never before pulled one of these mini-sledges, which for the next seventeen days were to carry the sixty kilo individual loads of food, fuel and camping equipment on which life would depend. Mine had a will of its own, but was infinitely more efficient than the cumbersome man-hauling sledges that made the lives of those heroic pioneers of the golden age of polar exploration such a misery. Modern polar travellers think nothing of pulling pulks twice the weight of ours.

With Derek leading the way, the rest of us followed in Indian file across Templefiord's ribbed *sastrugi* surface, already veined with ominous cracks that masked the open sea only metres below. Progress on *langlauf* skis largely depends on the type of wax best suited to the snow conditions and 'expert' advice on the subject was never in short supply. At Camp 2, pitched under the columnar cliffs of Kolonden, the din made by numberless nesting fulmars and my leaking air mattress made sleep impossible. I was never able to repair its defective valve and had to cannibalise discarded cardboard food boxes along the way to fashion a protective underlay to prevent hypothermia. The junction of two enormous glaciers marked the start of a three-day-long haul up to the Lomonosov ice cap by a broad, white highway flanked by brooding snow mountains bearing Nordic and English names and closed a ghostly horizon that never seemed to get any nearer.

Throughout the expedition, I shared a tent with Derek whose calm, un-demonstrative leadership never faltered. Because he was responsible for the expedition's overall management and route finding by GPS, I took over all our tent's domestic duties including the diurnal ritual of pitching and securing it, excavating a cooking pit and collecting sufficient uncontaminated snow to melt water for cooking and keeping our thermos flasks full. These menial but essential tasks could take up two hours both morning and evening. Survival ul-timately depended on the proper functioning of our multi-fuel stoves. Ours turned out to be a dud and had it not been for Paddy O'Neill's expertise, the expedition might have foundered after day one. Delicate coaxing was required to get the thing going and unless the flame was properly controlled, both tent and occupants risked incineration.

I normally enjoy cooking, but not within the confines of a two-man tent. Derek's pre-packed, twenty-man-day food units were designed to give each person 4,234 calories a day. Yet even Escoffier would have been pushed to produce anything palatable from basic ingredients of packet soup, AFD meat-slop, Kraft cheese slices and oatmeal biscuits. Derek assured me that this 'was a lot better than pemmican'. Nonetheless, the cheese slices so affected my bowels that I had to crawl out of the tent several times every night for relief in temperatures of minus thirty degrees at peril to my manhood.

For four successive days we enjoyed perfect weather. Spitsbergen's peaks and limitless horizons were transcendent, but the marches were monotonous and during the brief halts the cold was too intense to encourage either conver-sation or photography. On reaching the Lomonosov ice cap on 26 April, dense cloud made it impossible to see anything beyond the back of the *pulk* immedi-ately in front, leaving my benumbed mind to do nothing more constructive than to tease out as many words as I could from *fjellpunken*. A second day's march on compass bearings in a whiteout ended at the totally featureless Lomonosov Camp I.

Given the warnings about bears issued back at base and Derek's long Arctic experience, I was surprised that this should have been the first time he insisted on erecting anti-bear perimeter defences. These consisted of a thick wire strand secured to ski sticks which were stuck into the snow with flares and thunder-flashes attached. Shortly after supper, a loud bang went off which sent everyone scuttling from their tents and Halberdier Hall scrabbling around in the snow to find the precious rifle. A bitter, snow-laden wind froze the eyelids as we scanned the scene for a sight of the world's biggest carnivore. None were visible so Derek ordered a stand-down. Half an hour later, another big bang triggered a second tent evacuation. Once again there was nothing to be seen. Closer examination revealed that a heavy build up of rime had triggered the alarm system and that a flare had burned a chunk out of one of Derek's skis.

We pushed on the Lomonosov Camp 2 in another whiteout and here, for the next two days, remained pinned down by a blizzard. As it hammered away at the walls of our flimsy tent, I was happy enough at first to have a break from life in harness. But whereas in a mountain hut you can sit out bad weather playing silly card games; rolling dice or endlessly comparing the relative permeability of Gore-Tex, Pertex or indeed any other fabric, social life in a small tent is limited. Our conversations seldom strayed beyond the weather, navigation or the fuel situation and when supper was finished, we simply snuggled down into our sleeping bags and tried to read our books before it became too cold to hold them. My choice was Cellini's swashbuckling autobiographical romp in sixteenth-century Florence. Derek's was Steve Jones's *Language of the Genes*.

By the evening of 29 April, we had experienced four days of continuous bad weather. While Derek was beginning to worry about the expedition's progress, I wondered what madness had induced me to be spending this particular night on an ice cap when I might otherwise have been indulging in the gastronomic delights of Norton Rose's bicentennial celebration dinner at the Guildhall. Early the following morning, the incessant flapping of the tent's outer skin suddenly stopped and in the breathless silence that followed, sunlight shone through its translucent walls. Setting off a mini blizzard from built-up interior condensation, I crawled outside and had to shield my eyes from the snow's dazzling reflection. The sky was cloudless and Spitsbergen's white wonderland had burst back into life.

The rest is short in telling. Thanks to Paddy O'Neill's loan of a spare sleeping mat, I enjoyed my first decent night's sleep in a week before we climbed Newtontoppen two days later. Now at latitude seventy-nine degrees north, the panoramic views from the summit were just about enough to justify Derek's quest and the downhill ski back to camp without the impediment of pulks an expedition highlight. The eight-day return journey to Longyearbyen via the Kvitbreen, Oxfordbreen and Akadamikbreen glaciers opened up a new array of dazzling glacier-scapes resembling wave-tossed seas backed by range upon range of ethereal mountains.

After five successive days of fine weather, another blizzard pinned us down for a day and night on the dreaded Lomonosov. Down at last on Templefiord, the sight of its sea-ice breaking up to form grotesque excrescences signalled that our time was up and safely back at Fredheim, the twittering of snow buntings announced the advent of the Arctic spring. As we relaxed in the sun for the first time in seventeen days, Patrick Fagan set off for a spot of solo seal spotting. We had not yet seen a polar bear, but when our errand general disappeared over the horizon, Halberbier Hall took the opportunity to loose off a couple of warning rounds in his general direction.

While waiting for the plane home at Longyearbyen's airport, I pondered on the pleasures and penances of Arctic travel and concluded that the polar wilderness was better suited to temperaments sterner than mine. Spotting a young Norwegian couple standing alone besides their skis and outsize rucksacks, I wandered over for a chat.

'Been anywhere interesting?' I ventured.

'Thank you for asking' replied the male Viking with piercing blue eyes. 'As a matter of fact, we've just completed a north to south traverse of Svalbard.'

'The whole way?' I gulped, trying to make a quick calculation of the distance involved. 'How long did it take?'

'Exactly twenty-five days, of which three were storm-bound.'

'What about polar bears, weren't they a problem?'

'Yes, of course, and we saw plenty of them. But they only gave us real trouble right at the end of the trip when a big male stalked us for two days and then cornered us at a hut while we were waiting to be taken off by a fishing boat. It smashed down one wall with a single blow of its paw. Luckily, we managed to scare it off with a thunder-flash.'

On the plane home, I calculated that the Norseman and his woman must have covered over 500 kilometres at an average of twenty-two kilometres a day. Our own 178-kilometre journey had taken fourteen marching days at a daily average of less than thirteen.

16

HELLAS REARS ITS MOUNTAINS

In the same year as the Haute Route de Corse and Spitsbergen trips I became president of the Eagle Ski Club (ESC), the club that had first fired my ski mountaineering ambitions thirty years before. When I joined the ESC in 1964, its fortunes were already taking an upward trajectory having sunk to a nadir in 1951 when Gerald Seligman, the eminent avalanche scientist and a future ESC president, had been so concerned about the club's future that he saw no alternative but to either close it down or 'put it into cold storage'. Neil Hogg's inspirational alpine training meets had reinvigorated the club and encouraged members to undertake ambitious guideless tours such as Alan Blackshaw's Alpine and Scandinavian ski traverses during the 1970s. Guy Sheridan's expeditions to Iran, North America, Asia and Africa had also shown what was possible on Nordic skis and during the 1980s and 1990s, ESC members lifted their sights to lead successful expeditions to Greenland, British Columbia, Alaska, Tien Shan, Kulu Himalaya, Caucasus, Nepal and Spitsbergen.

Some statistics tell their own story. In 1965 when ESC membership stood at just over 385, it ran two alpine training meets and four club-supported alpine tours including one to the Atlas. Over the next three decades, the club's open-door policy and training programmes attracted a steady flow of new recruits and by 1995 membership stood at 513 with seven ESC sponsored tours and ten members' tours. Guideless tours were becoming ever more popular and to encourage this trend on becoming president I set myself four objectives. First, to promote training at introductory and intermediate levels by increasing the number of professionally guided alpine tours and to supplement these with

UK weekend meets which would cover technical issues, avalanche rescue and first aid. Secondly, to extend the club's touring programme. Thirdly, to increase membership. Fourthly, to update the club's rules and by limiting office holder's terms – in part a reaction to my having already served six years as a vice-president – and thereby infuse new administrative blood. In implementing this programme, I was fortunate to have the loyal and enthusiastic support of the club's hard working officers and committee. By 1996 membership had been increased to 585 with ten ESC sponsored tours; seventeen members' tours (including those to the Caucasus, Karakorum and New Zealand) and a club expedition to Greenland. A year later, membership had risen to 622. The ESC has since gone from strength to strength. In 2014 membership stood at 1,270 (not far short of the Alpine Club's) with twelve training meets/courses and fifty-six members' ski tours, plus biannual pioneer expeditions ranging from the Arctic to the Antarctic.

Corsica and Spitsbergen had represented the opposite ends of the ski mountaineering spectrum. Thereafter, I decided that I would confine my ambitions to less well-known ranges within Europe which offered scope for exploratory ski mountaineering. Greece – whose mainland is four-fifths mountain and vies with Switzerland as the most mountainous country in Europe, yet still retains the rough edges cherished by mountain travellers – most closely fulfilled this criterion. My fascination for its mountains predated both my 1961 winter and 1985 summer visits to the Thessalian Mount Olympus and probably stemmed from a hardcore classical education at my preparatory school, Summerfields, Oxford, where Latin and Greek were taught daily as alternate lessons to make Olympus and Parnassus at least as familiar as Mont Blanc and Everest. Yet despite Britain's philhellenic traditions and Edward Lear's judgment that they were 'the most beautiful in the world', Greek mountains were never popular with British climbers. Lear was no mean judge for his painting safaris took him to the Abruzzi, Albania, the Alps, Corsica as well as the Himalaya, yet Douglas Freshfield's verdict that the mountains of Greece were 'unpalatable food for the robust appetites of Alpine Clubmen' stuck and is echoed in more modern mountaineering literature. Wilfred Noyce's magisterial *World Atlas of Mountaineering* gave them no mention and in Edward Pyatt's *Guinness Book of Mountains* there is but a bare reference to the monastic sanctuaries of Meteora and Athos.

The first significant Greek mountain I saw close-to was Parnassus from my railway carriage window en route to Olympus in 1961. That Olympus experience had brought home the depth of Greece's winter snow cover, yet its potential for ski mountaineering had not occurred to me until that chance meeting with Ronald Naar on Mount Olympus in 1985. Over the succeeding ten years, more pressing ski mountaineering ventures intervened and it was Lear's dramatic portrayal of Mount Parnassus (1862) – as fine an example of the 'sublime' as his more famous *Kinchinjunga* – that inspired me to choose this fine mountain as my first Greek ski mountaineering objective.

Named after a son of Neptune and linked both geographically and historically with the oracle at Delphi, Parnassus was sacred to Apollo and long revered as the resting place of the ark of Deucalion, the son of Prometheus who dared to steal the secret of the fire of the gods.

Overlooking the Gulf of Corinth, it is more a massif than a single peak for it covers an area the size of the central Cairngorms and seemed to be the ideal launch pad for a Grecian ski tour as being easily accessible from Athens with guaranteed winter snow. By starting from the village of Kato Titherea, a conveniently placed stop on the main Athens-Salonika railway line at the foot of Parnassus's eastern approaches, I reckoned that it should be possible to make an east to west traverse of the massif finishing up at the long-established Athenian ski resort of Arachova above Delphi. Thereafter, we could continue with exploratory tours in Sterea's less-accessible ranges of Vardousia and Ghiona.

Downhill skiing had long been popular in Greece and although in 1945 both John Hunt and Edward Peck made some tentative ski tours, ski mountaineering at this time was virtually unknown in Greece. One reason is that most of the country's bleak limestone ranges are riven by deep gorges that obstruct continuous passages of skiing. Others are that outside the recognised ski resorts mountain huts were few; mountain-rescue facilities virtually non-existent and reliable maps (based on the Greek Army's restricted 1:50,000 series) covered only limited areas.

On 3 February 1995, the well-seasoned trio of David Williams, Rodney Franklin and Derek Fordham plus a new recruit, Richard Cooper, were filing through Heathrow's passport control to catch a BA flight to Athens. When it came to my turn, the passport officer glanced up and asked me, 'And where is *Mrs Harding?*' The saga of how Georgina managed to press-gang a prospective lodger who happened to be waiting to be interviewed on our Putney Heath doorstep into driving her to the airport where she thrust into my sweaty palm my passport within minutes of take-off, has long passed into family legend.

That night, old family friends George and Erica Akrivos had all five of us to stay at their luxurious villa at Kifissia overlooking Athens. The following afternoon, scarcely missing a beat, we alighted from the Athens-Thessaloniki Express at Kato Tithorea and on learning that we were British, a wizened ancient gave me a garlic-ridden bear-hug and then recounted in gory detail how he had single-handedly shot down several German warplanes fifty years before. My basic plan for the Parnassus traverse was that we should camp that first night just above Kato Tithorea and then make a second camp at the head of the Velitza Ravine from which to climb the massif's culminating peak Liahkhoura before descending the twenty kilometres to Arachova on ski.

There was no obvious path out of the village and so, after shouldering skis and rucksacks, we headed straight up the Velitsa Ravine in drizzling rain relying on *Lonely Planet*'s assurance that this gloomy chasm gave easy access to Parnassus. The Velitza Valley, the grandest natural feature on this wild side of Parnassus, gouges its way into the heart of the massif by a limestone gorge that has been thoroughly polished in its lower reaches by repeated spring floods. Struggling through near-impenetrable undergrowth clogging its entrails, we emerged two hours later scratched, bruised and bemused. Only then did I notice the perfectly good track running along one side of the gorge that would have got us to Camp I in forty minutes. At dawn next day, a hazy sun illuminated Parnassus's lofty heights, but by the time the tents had been packed away it had disappeared and was seldom seen again for the next seven days. For once, David Williams's normally impeccable route finding led to an impasse high up the ravine. Extrication involved a near-vertical scramble through thick scrub and densely packed pine trees that kept snagging the skis and severely tested tempers. Megawatts of energy were expended to gain 1,240 metres of height and when Camp 2 was eventually established in a snow-filled sheepfold above the Tsares Spring, a cold, clammy mist descended and blotted out everything around.

Camp 2! It seemed ridiculous that a mere Greek mountain should have involved a Himalayan-style approach march to get barely halfway up it. Sleeping and cooking arrangements in my spacious North Face VE25 tent with Derek Fordham and Richard Cooper were also proving a challenge. Only a year before, Derek and I had spent eighteen successive days cooped up in a tiny tent in Spitsbergen with night-time temperatures plunging to below thirty degrees Celsius yet cohabiting in near-perfect harmony. Life with Richard, whom I had only recently met, was less comfortable. He worked for the *Financial Times*, held forthright views on everything, had climbed hard rock with some of the best and had also been on Everest. From the outset, Richard had insisted on taking charge of our tent's cooking arrangements with a petrol stove that was as combustible as its owner. Initially, this task kept him busy until after supper when his prodigious energies had no proper outlet. But rather than read a book, he then psyched himself up for action by repeatedly zipping and unzipping the tent's entrance flaps as if on the lookout for marauding bears.

Next morning, the snow-charged wind that blasted down the upper Velitza's gun-barrelled couloir added a new dimension to Mediterranean ski touring. Overnight, the couloir's sides had become coated in ice, a phenomenon caused by extreme diurnal temperature variations. Even with *harscheisen,* traction on this surface was difficult and when the ground steepened it became imperative to swap them for crampons. Derek now admitted that he had left his behind. A near-vertical, diagonal traverse on rock-hard ice was more than most ski edges could have managed. Derek's didn't and he fell fifty metres very fast before landing in a crumpled heap at the bottom. Initially, he showed no sign of movement and I feared the worst. However, by the time we had scrambled down to help him, he had managed to get to his feet. The only apparent damage was shock and mild concussion, but the moment he put pressure on his elbow he dropped his ski pole with a cry of pain. For the next three hours Derek was reduced to using only one arm, yet climbed on doggedly with David shadowing his every kick-turn.

It was a gritty performance, but Derek's injury inevitably slowed progress and it was mid-afternoon by the time we breasted the lip of the massive cwm that marks the head of the Velitza Ravine. The wind was rising, visibility deteriorating and the steep snow slopes all around that swept upwards into the clouds were liable to avalanche. To escape the biting wind and get Derek under cover, the four of us began digging into a massive snow bank on the leeside of the cwm's lip to excavate a space large enough to fit in the two tents. Once Derek was tucked up in his sleeping bag, I imagined that the crisis had passed. But spindrift kept piling up so fast that the tent walls were soon sagging under the snow's weight leaving it black as night within.

Richard now seemed to be possessed of St Vitus Dance.

'For God's sake Richard,' I remonstrated. 'Do please calm down!'

'It's okay for you,' he shot back. 'But I'm being squashed by this bloody snow and there's not enough space for all three of us in your damned tent!'

I crawled outside to investigate and found that in the space of only an hour the snow had built up several metres thick over both tents and was now projecting as a metre-wide overhang. In a vortex of blinding spindrift, the four of us began shovelling frantically to hack off great slabs of the stuff from an ever-expanding snow mushroom. The effort left us sopping wet and too tired even to brush the snow off our clothing before crawling back into the tents. For the next five hours, the blizzard showed no signs of slackening and at midnight the same exercise had to be repeated by torchlight.

It seemed bizarre that in Greece, the gift of sun and the sea, we should now be in serious danger of being buried by snow within sight of the Aegean. With Derek injured, I had long abandoned any prospect of climbing Liakoura let alone of reaching Arachova tomorrow. It was going to be difficult enough to reverse the Velitsa Gorge and get him safely down to Kato Titherea. The storm lulled temporarily in the early hours of the morning and at dawn the mountaintops were touched with gold. Hard shovelling cleared a passage from the tents to open ground, but it took three hours to pack up by which time blue skies had been replaced by dark cloud. Derek, drawn and shaky, was obviously in great pain and the eight-hour descent down the Velitza had many fraught moments which were better recalled that evening in the security of Kato Tithorea's Hotel Zaka's cosy bar. Derek caught the train to Athens the following day leaving me to reflect that six days into the tour, we had climbed nothing; got nowhere far and lost a staunch companion.

Vardousia, our next traversing objective, is the remotest range in Greece. To reach a suitable start point for the proposed crossing involved a circuitous sixty-kilometre taxi-ride to the village of Ano Mousinitza. From here, a four-hour slog on foot ended on the windswept Stavros Col where the concrete shell of an abandoned Greek Army lookout post was ready-made to serve both as Camp 4 and a kennel for two stray mongrels, Dave and Rik, which attached themselves to us for the rest of the tour. The screaming blizzard that blew up next day kept Richard intermittently busy with his stove, but his insistence in drawing off water from a stagnant pool to concoct a hooch from AFD tomato soup and dried fruit gave me all-night squitters.

By the following morning the wind had dropped but with thick cloud obscuring the mountains I seriously wondered whether we might be better off returning to Athens. This suggestion was vetoed and after taking precise compass bearings, we located a rough track through a dark pine forest which eventually led to Artotina, a sprawling, once-prosperous village whose ancient field-terracing had long since disintegrated as a result of civil war and rural depopulation. Vardousia's Dolomitic peaks, framed by the eves of the chalet-style houses that fringed its pretty square, gave the place a genuine alpine feel, and when the proprietress of its one open coffee shop produced pickled vegetables, feta cheese, bread, sardines and oranges for tea and dry beds for the night, morale went up several notches. The rite of drying off our sodden clothes around her furnace-like stove was incuriously observed by two old crones dressed overall in black widows' weeds and a cross-eyed shepherd who feverishly fingered his prayer beads while a local bard mouthed a lilting Turkish rune.

On 11 February, the sun shone bright from a cobalt sky for the first time in seven days. This promising start to the Vardousian traverse began well enough as we strolled with the dogs at our heels past ranks of blue-painted beehives before entering a scented forest already greening in the hot sun. But by the time we had fastened our skis at midday, ominous, black clouds were already masking the tops. Afternoon was stealthily merging into early evening when we were confronted by a testing traverse along the precipitous, south-eastern flanks of the Soufles Peaks. At this critical passage the rearguard juddered to an unscheduled stop when one of Richard's skins peeled off. This can happened to anyone and try as he could, Richard could not make his skin stick on again. While he struggled on manfully with only one operational skin, the rest of us waited less than patiently in a piercing wind on a precarious col. On rejoining the rest of the party, Richard turned to me angrily, 'John, I don't know why the hell you haven't brought extra glue with you. It would have saved us all a lot of trouble!'

'Don't be bloody ridiculous, Richard!' snapped David. 'In no way can you make skins stick back on in these conditions. The glue won't hold so you'd better bind that skin on with this tape.' David always seemed to have the right answer and piece of equipment to hand.

The light was fading before we got started again. During the twenty-minute stop, Rodney's skis had frozen solid in the snow and when he tried to move on he overbalanced, broke his bindings and fell headlong down the slope. The closing hours of that seemingly endless day were skied after dark with the moon occasionally breaking through scudding clouds to reveal our ghostly procession moving silently and slowly up and down a succession of parallel ridges back to the cold comfort of Stavros Col.

The challenges of Greek ski touring had come as a surprise to everyone, but for me, this otherwise successful tour ended on a particularly distressing note. The day after the Vardousian traverse, we climbed the range's highest peak Korakas (2,437 metres) with Dave and Rick leading the way along an airy ridge to the summit from where the whole of mainland Greece lay at our feet and the snow-capped heights of Taygetus glinted faintly in distant Peloponnese. It had been an exceptional day's ski mountaineering, and though the 1,450-metre descent to Ano Mousonitza sorely tried my hip, it was on ringing home that evening that I felt something serious was amiss even before Georgina had answered the telephone.

'I'm afraid that Victoria's been very ill,' she said tersely. 'She's just come out of Queen Charlotte's Hospital after an emergency operation.'

After Georgina had explained the problem, I told her that I would fly home immediately after I had worked out the logistics and would ring back later that evening. Victoria had represented Edinburgh University at both skiing and rugby, but had only just recovered from a long, debilitating illness. And now this. Sometimes, you have to make your own private journey into despair but thanks to Rodney's reassuring diagnosis this was not one of them. On ringing home again, both Georgina and Victoria assured me that the crisis was past and urged me to carry on, as 'saving one day is not going to make any difference'. Victoria knew me only too well, but I was drained emotionally and physically by that special form of guilt felt by fathers who go absent when most needed.

The following day, it gave me little pleasure to climb Pyramida, the crown of the Ghiona massif. A breathless, thousand-metre ski descent to our final campsite overlooking the stupendous Rekka Ravine made a fitting end to the tour and next morning we walked out to Delphi. Before catching the bus back to Athens, I wandered alone amongst its ruins still imagining the worst at home. The cherry trees were already white with blossom and I was seized by the genius of the place. Victoria was to make a complete recovery and subsequently completed an Operation Raleigh expedition to Mongolia before getting married and producing four fine children.

For me, the Parnassus tour marked the end of an era for it was the last I ever did with David Williams and Rodney Franklin, both outstanding ski mountaineers and exemplary companions. David had been our spearhead during the later stages of my Pyrenean High Route and a driving force on the two Turkish traverses and the Haute Route de Corse. The brave night-time rescue mission that he and Anna had made in the Cairngorms had certainly saved my right shoulder from permanent damage. David could not only ski with style blindfolded, but was also an all-round mountaineer who had climbed the *Walker Spur* on the Grandes Jorasses on spec. His uncanny instinct for route finding and improvisation were allied to an unflappable temperament, steely determination, and innate self-confidence.

Later that year, my retirement from Norton Rose gave Georgina and I another excuse to embark on a round of adventures that included a three-week cold-water cruise around the snow-covered Lofoten Islands in Kit Power's *Kwai Muli* as well as mountain forays in Scotland, the Julian Alps, Spain, Mount Sinai and the Pyrenees. Yet the mountains of Greece still retained a special fascination and I particularly wanted to visit the Tymphi Massif in Epirus, that remote province in north-west Greece which enjoys heroic status as the birthplace of King Pyrrhus, remembered for his 'Pyrrhic victories' over Imperial Rome. Epirus's wild mountains had been the inspiration for Byron's 'Childe Harold' and some of Edward Lear's most dramatic paintings. Traditionally, a refuge for the oppressed, it remains the homeland of the Klephts, an anarchic race of brigands/patriots who follow no man's writ and who successfully repulsed Mussolini's expeditionary forces in 1940.

For climbing information about the area, I had to turn once again to Robin Fedden who had scaled the north-west face of Astraka in 1972 and compared it to a 'classic Dolomite' route. Although Fedden had not been tempted to take up the challenge of ski touring in Greece, I fancied that the Tymphi might offer precisely this, though after last year's experiences on Parnassus I decided to make a preliminary summer reconnaissance on foot to gauge the lie of the land. On 20 September 1996 I flew out to Corfu with John Blacker, Peter Lowes and David Seddon to do just that. We had all recently trekked together in Bhutan and Sikkim and Peter, now seventy, had spent most of his working life with the United Nations. His insatiable thirst for travel; unbounded intellectual curiosity and an infinite capacity to engage with people from every walk of life for endless chat made him a stimulating, if exhausting companion.

Lonely Planet's Trekking in Greece offers some salutary advice about Epirus's weather and includes a warning that heavy rain will arrive with unswerving regularity on 21 September. Basing ourselves on the Zagorian villages that cling limpet-like to the base of the Tymphi's northern scarp, this advice was to prove entirely accurate. When not otherwise sheltering for cover from the rain in the Byzantine monasteries of Stormiu and Rongavu, traversing the gloomy Vikos and Aoos Gorges, or admiring the hump-back bridges of Piti and Palioyeviro through veils of mist, most of that week-long trek was undertaken in a downpour.

There were many natural and man-made wonders to behold in the Tymphi, yet despite the bustle of Zagoria's many tavernas, the memories of German wartime atrocities and the internecine savagery of the subsequent Greek civil war, so harrowingly described in Nicholas Gage's book *Eleni,* gave the place a hard edge. During the closing stages of that trip, we tramped across the Tymphi Plateau's rolling grasslands, where black-cloaked Vlach shepherds tended their flocks as furtive groups of Albanian migrants stole past, climbing Gamila II in thick mist. On our final trek from Megalo Papingo to Tsepolov, my right hip became so painful that I could only hobble along supported by ski sticks.

Six months later, on 19 March 1997, I was admitted to the King Edward VII Hospital for a total hip replacement. Hamish Nicoll, who had successfully survived this same operation, had warned me that it carried a thirty-percent fatality rate. Mine was complicated by the threat of my childhood TB recurring. Some weeks after the operation, Georgina took me back to my surgeon, Sarah Muirhead-Allwood, for a final check-up. On entering her consulting room, she exclaimed, 'What on earth are you doing with those crutches? Chuck them away!'

I did as bid and then asked her, 'Is there any reason why I should not be able to continue to climb and ski?'

'Why not?' she replied 'Do what you like!'

I took her at her word and two months after my release from hospital, Georgina and I were staying as guests of old friends Konrad and Lisa Schiemann at their Interlaken chalet to test her prognosis. On the first day, we walked from Kleine Scheidegg to Wengenalp and on the second climbed 1,400 metres from Bonigen to Schinge Platte. That autumn, a series of hut-to-hut walks in Haute Savoie confirmed that Miss Muirhead-Allwood's surgical skills were unrivalled. Despite some bumps and falls, my hip has lasted the course to date.

But walking and trekking is one thing, ski mountaineering another. The Tymphi were clearly not suitable ski touring terrain, but other Greek ranges surely were, and after further research I set my sights on Smolikas, the country's second highest mountain just south of the Albanian frontier. In early March 1999, Derek Fordham, Roger Childs, John Ducker and I flew out to Salonika for a preparatory warm-up on Thrace's little known Falakro massif prior to tackling Smolikas. In a hired van, we drove north-east to Volakas, a picture-postcard village cupped in a pretty valley surrounded by ochre fields and overlooked by Falakro's snow-clad heights. The Dhrama Mountain Club's hostel halfway up the mountain was securely locked but Giovanni, the proprietor of the burned-out shed that had once served this improbable resort's solitary draglift, was in the process of repairing it. When I asked him to recommend the best route to Falakro's 2,322-metre summit, he shook his head.

'But no one climbs Falakro! I've never been there myself for it must be at least five hours away!'

On that lovely sunny day, Falakro's giddy limestone precipices and snow-choked sinkholes gave us no trouble and from its summit, a tangle of snow-capped mountains rising from the blue-shadowed Thracian Plain offered the prospect of fresh heights to conquer. That was the last good weather for the next six days. A bone-shaking, ten-hour drive across the length of northern Greece under sullen skies led to safe harbour in the Koygias family's hotel at Konitza, our comfortable base for the next three nights, but the weather was so foul that our time was filled with daytime excursions to the Stromio Monastery, the bazaar at Ioannina and a despairing visit to the oracle at Dodoma for guidance. With time running out we then drove to Paleoselli, the roadhead village for Smolikas, hoping that our luck must surely change.

Once famous for its vineyards, this pretty mountain village was graced by a small church and an enormous plane tree that shaded a tiny square enclosed by squat, stone houses roofed with limestone slabs. The view across the trough of the upper Aoos Gorge, a forested wilderness of black and Balkan pine lapping the Tymphi's northern scarp, is one of the grandest in Greece while the feast served up by Georgio Jimas, the village's publican/postmaster, of wild boar garnished with red peppers, beans and green salad and sluiced down with red wine and a 100 per cent *marc*, was the most delicious I ever ate in that country.

After assuring Georgio that we would have no trouble finding our own way to the Naneh Hut, he entrusted us with its key. Had it not been for two local lads, Zakis and Michael, who Georgio had surreptitiously instructed to shadow us, we might never have got there. After we had battled through sleet, snow and mist making miserably slow progress, the boys took over the bulk of the carry, guided us to the hut and then lit its temperamental stove. Before they left, I promised that we'd be back at Paleoselli the following evening 'after we've climbed Smolikas'. From the look on their faces, I knew they didn't believe me.

The storm that buffeted the hut that night was still blowing strongly next morning. We should have gone down with no more ado, but perversely decided instead to recce the route to Smolikas despite the weather. On attaining a col on its south south-west ridge, the wind had risen to a shriek and visibility dropped to nil. This was sufficient punishment for one day and after sounding the retreat, what remained of it was spent practising avalanche search techniques outside the hut. Meantime, I had clean forgotten my promise to Georgio and when, next morning, the skies were clear for the first time in a week with the pink-tinged northern scarp of the Tymphi framed by snow-encrusted boughs of Balkan pine looking tantalisingly beautiful, there seemed no excuse for not having another crack at Smolikas.

Yesterday's col led up to an awkward rock-step, steep and plastered in unconsolidated snow. It rebuffed all my efforts to surmount it and although the
problem was eventually solved by an out-flanking movement, by then the sun
had long passed its zenith. Smolikas, still another 700 metres higher, remained
out of sight and at least another three hours distant. Once upon a time, I would
have pushed this route. No longer.

On the way down the mountain we were met by an agitated Zackis and
Michael riding tandem on a motorbike. Apparently, when we had failed to
return last night, Georgio had alerted the police and put a helicopter on
standby. Just short of Paleoselli, the man himself was waiting to meet us.
I expected a rocket, but instead he hugged me and then drove us back in his
truck to the village to be feted like heroes.

'But no one, my friends, no one', grinned Georgio as he served up iced beers
from behind his bar, 'has ever before been so crazy as to attempt to climb
Smolikas on ski!'

Before flying home from Salonika, we spent a night at Metsovo, the ancient
Vlach capital at the northern end of the Pindus. Its cobbled streets, dignified
by solid merchant houses, were thronged with tourists and a panoply of
handsome snow peaks broke the southern horizon. These, unlike the Tymphi's
uncompromising cliffs, looked eminently skiable and revived an embryonic
ambition to traverse the Central Pindus on ski before revisiting Smolikas.

This 125-kilometre-long range, which forms the backbone of Greece, is
distinguished by the fifty-five kilometres stretch between Vougareli and
Metsovo that seldom drops below 2,000 metres. In 1963, ten years after Everest,
John Hunt had led an international youth party that walked it from south to
north in summer. In 1984, a strong RAF party skied much of it in the opposite
direction, before being forced off the ridge by difficult weather conditions.
My own plan was to pioneer a south to north ski traverse along the Vougareli/
Metsovo section. It looked quite a tough call for with few natural break points,
tents and food would have to be carried throughout.

When I told Georgina that the nucleus of the party would be Fordham and
Childs, she dismissed it as 'just another gastronomic binge', so David Seddon
was roped in to give geriatric support. A month before our departure, a spell
of Nordic skiing in Ottawa's Gatineau National Park with our *trés sportif*
hostess Veronica Goodenough had persuaded me that I was still in reasonably

good shape, but when I spotted two greying old gents in faded anoraks waiting for me at the Heathrow check-in on 2 March 2000, I wondered what we were trying to prove.

At dusk two days later, we drove into Vougareli and were instantly cowed by the sight of the 1,500-metre-high ice-encrusted buttresses of Tzoumerka, the sentinel peak that overlooks the town and guards the southern approaches of the Central Pindus. After booking in at the Hotel Galini, its comely proprietor Kate asked how long we were intending to stay. When I told her our plans, she stared in disbelief.

'The Pindus? At this time of year? You must be raving mad!'

At this, Derek's chat-up line didn't help.

'How come you speak such good English, Kate?'

'Because I'm a British citizen, born in Cyprus!' she flashed back.

'I suggest that you gentlemen take a stiff drink at the taverna next door and have a rethink. I don't want to be responsible for picking up your pieces.'

I had already made a mental readjustment to our original plans by the time we had seated ourselves at the taverna. When a young man wearing SAS-style combat kit stalked in and plonked down an AK-47 Assault Rifle on the table beside, no one at the bar batted an eyelid. Avoiding eye contact, we busied ourselves scanning the 1:250,000 road map we were using as our guide and then retreated to the hotel.

'D'you know anything about this mountain marked "Astri 1,852 metres"?' I asked Kate.

'Not a thing,' she replied. 'But I strongly advise you to attempt nothing like that without hiring a local guide.'

Next day, we crept out of the hotel carefully avoiding Kate's eagle eye and after a couple of hours' driving reached the end of a track at Astri's base where a sign in Greek pointed to the 'Aeton Hut'. The hut wasn't open, but Astri's sweeping snow slopes, dotted with clumps of dwarf pine and juniper, were reminiscent of the Spanish Pyrenees. A thin ridge led to a shapely summit with fine panoramic views and from here, a swooping descent took us back to the car. Kate, genuinely surprised to see her guests back safe and sound, stood us free drinks to celebrate Astri's first British ascent.

Heavy cloud and continuous rain the following day supported by Kate's warning that all mountain roads would be blocked and all upland villages deserted, stilled any further talk about a Pindus traverse. Instead, it was decided to drive direct to Metsovo and use this as a base for day tours in the northern Pindus in preparation for another assault on Smolikas. The day-long drive through mist and sleet, shadowing the range's deeply incised flanks along treacherous, dirt roads that soared and swooped up and down the sides of dizzying ravines, so alarmed David that he took to running on ahead to clear debris from the track rather than hazard Derek's unnerving habit of feathering every hairpin bend. Save for two near-deserted hilltop villages, no other habitation was visible that day and as dusk fell, the directional plot was so comprehensively lost that the night had to be spent at Ioannina.

Ensconced at Metsovo the following day, an exploratory tour of the bleak, wind-swept tableland north of the town (with a chill factor Derek compared with that of Greenland) revealed the general lie of the land. A shapely peak, identified as Peresteri, looked good for starters, but our feeble recce the following day failed to disentangle the mountain's complex topography and the best way to approach it. A more spirited attempt the day after began badly when Derek took a bad fall while traversing an icy slope studded with dwarf pines and which left him with a half-inch-long wood splinter sticking out of his palm. Derek seemed to be fated by Greece's 'Three Furies' and this latest injury made it difficult for him to grip his ski pole so David and I pressed on to investigate whether a summit bid was still feasible. From a bleak col perched high on its narrow terminal ridge, Peresteri's summit was only another 200 metres higher but only accessible up a steep couloir overhung by cornices and choked in unstable snow. Unsurprisingly, prudence prevailed though a modicum of honour was salved by our spiralling ski descent down Peristeri's northern slopes in a setting that parodied Mont Blanc's Vallée Blanche.

Georgina's earlier prophecy about the likely trajectory of this tour was proving correct. Apart from two comfortable hotel nights at Vougareli, one at Ioannina, three at Metsovo and a seventh in Konitza (with a sprinkling of sight-seeing trips in between) we had nothing to show for it save for Astri and the aborted attempt on Peresteri, so it was time to square-up to Smolikas. At 2,637 metres, this apex of the Pindus would struggle to make mountaineering's fourth division. Yet its size (covering some 400 square kilometres at over 1,700 metres), isolation and the dense forest wilderness that surrounds it and which harbours a menagerie of bears, boars, wolves and lynx, lend it an aloof presence and dignity. Pitching up at Paleoselli early in the morning, I asked Georgio if he would kindly prepare us the fatted boar in anticipation of our conquest of Smolikas. This time, he just gave me an indulgent smile.

Until we reached the Naneh Hut, it had not been necessary to broach the expedition's camping rations, which were strictly Derek's responsibility and had already cost us dear as excess luggage. But when he produced from his rucksack like a conjurer the mildewed remnants of the Kraft cheese slices, AFD potato and Cadbury's Dairy Milk that had made Spitsbergen such a gastronomic trial, my heart sank, and I made do with a mouldy sausage left hanging from the ceiling by a previous party. Early next morning, we reached last year's high point in bright sunshine without a hiccup. Further up the ridge, Smolikas's dome-shaped summit became visible for the first time as the culmination of a long, connecting ridge indented by humps and hollows. To the south, the Tymphi's ten-kilometre-long northern ramparts glittered with fresh snow, while to the north a line of mysterious Balkan ranges melted away into a blurred horizon.

Derek had not forgotten his crampons this time and we jettisoned skis. The first pair reached Smolikas's summit at 11.30 a.m. but it took Roger another forty-five minutes to get there. He hadn't been going well on Peresteri and though never over concerned with the climbers' canon of 'never the wasted minute', was nothing if not competitive. On joining us, the habitual grin was still there but his breathing was laboured and he looked unduly strained. During the descent, we kept closely together as far as the forest where the morning's upward tracks became easy to follow. When a grim-faced Roger got back to the hut long after the rest of us, I realised that something was seriously wrong. He never complained and down at Paleoselli, countless beers later, was back to his old, jokey self, claiming that our Smolikas ski ascent was at least an OAP and British all-comers first. None of us realised that he was already suffering from the debilitating illness that was to end his life prematurely. His gutsy ascent of Smolikas was typical of the man.

17

ALPINE ENVOI

THE JULIAN ALPS

In 1994, the year before I retired from Norton Rose, I was asked by the Longland family to deliver Sir Jack Longland's eulogy at a service of Thanksgiving in Saint Bartholomew's the Great. Longland, who had outlived his elder son John by seventeen years, had been famous as a long-serving chairman of the BBC's *Any Questions?* as a reforming educationalist and iconic inter-war British mountaineer who had presided over the Climbers' Club, British Mountaineering Council and Alpine Club. When preparing myself for this task, I was surprised to discover that Longland had deliberately brought his active mountaineering career to a premature end at the age of thirty-two. In part, this decision was motivated by his experiences amongst the unemployed during the 1930s, which had shaped his radical political leanings and subsequent career. But it also reflected a personal philosophy that had persuaded him to refuse invitations to join both the 1936 and 1938 Everest expeditions notwithstanding his outstanding contributions to the earlier 1933 expedition when he had single-handedly shepherded eight Sherpas down to safety during a blizzard at over 27,000 feet. For his last serious climb, which he did with his young wife Peggy, Longland chose the Matterhorn describing this as 'more completely satisfying than any I can remember'.

I could never have matched Longland's self-denying ordinances, but days in the mountains with my family have given me more pleasure than any others. Skiing is a good introduction to the hills for the young and we started our three daughters early with Cairngorm holidays as guests of the ski-crazy

Macpherson family. For many years thereafter, we skied *en famille* in the Alps and in 1988 bought our own apartment in Saint Gervais Les Bains under the shadow of Mont Blanc. This served the family well until the girls progressed to ski racing for their respective universities. Rock climbing was never taken seriously beyond Sally Westmacott's Climbers' Club family meets at Bosigran and the occasional joint Wedgwood/Harding family holiday around Glen Coe. We also did one Easter week climbing in Torridon and survived that memorable holiday in the Pyrenees. But unquestionably, our daughters' teenage mountaineering highlight was a hut-to-hut traverse in Austria's Stubai Alps with the MacDonnell family in 1983.

After scrambling up the lowly Alp Feuerstein, we moved on to the Nurnberger Hutte as a base from which to climb the 3,418-metre Wilder Freiger. Neither former cavalryman Randall Macdonnell's Wehrmacht impersonations nor daughter Victoria's projectile vomiting in the confines of the hut's *schlafenlager* did much for Anglo-German relations. By the following morning, Victoria had more or less recovered, but all the Teutonic would-be summiteers had left the hut hours before. Given the previous night's alarums, I never thought that we could possibly make the summit. We set off nonetheless and, as the day progressed surprised ourselves by gradually overtaking one party after another. On the Wilder Freiger's glaciated upper slopes we roped up in column, and with Randall humming snatches of the *Horst Wessel* marching song, swept past the last of the opposition to top-out an easy first. Two days later, during a less-focused attempt on the Ost Sneespitze, I fell straight through a crevasse. Randall's strong arms held me tight on the rope and anxious hands hauled me to safety, though at the cost of any remaining *Berg Fuhrer* credibility.

Something of these early adventures must have stuck. Our eldest daughter Emma went on to organise a successful Bristol University expedition to climb all the Mount Olympuses of antiquity and Victoria founded the Adventurous Sports Club at Edinburgh University and joined the ESC. Joanna, our youngest, retained her climbing interest longest, and in the year of my retirement agreed to join me and her godfather John Blacker for a week's climbing in the Julian Alps on condition that her girlfriend Rose Cottam came along too. The Julians, the most easterly extension of the main Alpine chain, were formerly part of the Austro-Hungarian empire before its disintegration after the First World War and conveniently divide into a Western Italian section and an Eastern Slovenian section with Italian, German, Slovenian and Serbo-Croat the most commonly spoken languages. Forever associated with a latter day Julius, the Austrian pioneer mountaineer Julius Kugy (1858–1944) who was also a gifted writer and musician, these mountains offer fine Dolomite-style rock climbing. The fact that they were seldom visited by British climbers particularly appealed to John Blacker.

On 24 August 1995, the girls and I met John off his boat in Trieste before taking the slow train to Chrisaforte from where a taxi driver, who clearly fancied himself for the *Mille Miglia*, dropped us off at the village of Sella Nevea. The quality of the Julian huts is exceptional and none more so than the Rifugio Julia where, for three nights, our two English roses were offered obsequious service by fawning, black-tied waiters. The scenery of the Julians is bleak but grand with the predominant rock a startlingly white limestone which forms soaring pillars and sheer cliffs. Few summits exceed 2,700 metres, but the vertical interval between the valleys and the huts is much the same as in the Western Alps.

Our first foray, a four-hour ascent of Monte Forato, took in the full ambit of Julian scenery which ranged from the lush meadows and fragrant pine forests of the valleys to rough, alpine grasslands that gave way to desiccated 'karst' scenery of exposed rock and desolate screes where surface melt-water vanishes without trace into a subterranean world of sinkholes, caves and caverns. The climb in no way troubled the girls, but left John and me panting. On the way down, so as to avoid the dense pine forest, we made the mistake of choosing an extremely steep, snow-less 'piste from hell' whose polished limestone boulders had the consistency of marbles. Three days of continuous bad weather, apparently typical of the Julians in August when rainstorms can inundate the valleys while blizzards sweep the hills, reduced us to trekking sorties to give the old men a break.

On 28 August, we crossed the border on foot into Slovenia whose Alpine chalets, with their overhanging eves and window boxes filled with geraniums, might have been in neighbouring Austria. By the time we reached Kranjska Gora, the 'Zermatt of Slovenia', John was champing for beer and bed and when a kindly bystander recommended the Pension Saturn as 'good value, though a little way out of town', John insisted that we stop 'mucking around' and settle forthwith for the pretentious Pension Lipa. The girls were soon fixed-up with a spacious bedroom, but the only one left for John and me contained a double bed better suited to a heroic Teutonic honeymoon. On seeing this object of wood and brass, John spluttered, 'Not tonight Carruthers!' and proceeded to sunder the bed apart so as to form two singles. Amazed at this wanton act, Joanna let her godfather have it straight.

'John, I simply don't understand what you're on about. You and Dad must have been sharing tents, bunks and probably beds together for the past thirty years. This charade is just damned ridiculous!'

That squall also passed, but with time running out I was determined to have a crack at Triglav before the generation gap widened too far. At 2,864 metres, this fine, triangular peak is the highest in the Julians and has long featured in Slovene folklore, literature and verse. During the Second World War, it came to symbolise Slovene resistance to German occupation when partisans wore the 'Triglav Cap'. Its first recorded ascent, fired by intense competition between Slovenes and Austrians, was achieved by a Slovene quartet in 1778. Since then, hundreds of Slovene patriots climb it every summer.

A head-on road crash in Kranjska Gora, which killed its driver outright, delayed our bus journey to the Aljavez Hut road-head by several hours. This, coupled with the twelve-kilometre walk to the hut, lost a precious day. Unmistakeable for the partisan war memorial outside it shaped like a gigantic karabiner, the Aljavez comfortably accommodates 180. Yet it worried me that apart from four others, we should be its only occupants and this at the height of the summer season. The following day's trek to the Triglavski Hut confirmed that the locals knew more about Triglav's weather than we did. This hut march, which must be one of the most dramatic in all the Alps, claws its way up the left-hand margin of Triglav's spectacular three-kilometre-long, 1,400-metre-high north face. First climbed in 1906, it was another thirty years before its first British ascent. Even with safety cables, irons pegs and stanchions this veritable *via ferrata* merits a grade in itself for the exposure is terrific. Rose had never climbed before, but never once wobbled.

As we trudged across Triglav's bleak, snow-covered plateau the Triglavski Hut emerged through the mist like some Transylvanian redoubt. Like the Aljavez, it was virtually deserted and colder inside than out. After a snack, I went outside to inspect the mountain's east ridge which is the normal route to the summit. Face on, its snow-plastered rocks looked so intimidating that I asked a member of staff whether there was an easier alternative.

'Not really,' he replied. 'You could always try the southern route, but it's no easier. I've tried it five times over the past few days and have always failed.'

I should have guessed that he was talking nonsense for, as I discovered later, the teeth of the east ridge have long been drawn by climbing aids and artificial steps cut into the rock. However, as none of this was visible from the hut, I spent that night worrying about what we might be letting ourselves in for. Next morning, the sky was still overcast so I plumped for the southern route.

This involved an extra hour's trek to the Planika Hut and by the time we got there, it was already too late to climb Triglav and then get down to the bottom of the Trenta Valley before dark.

It was now that John dropped his bombshell.

'I'm very sorry John, but I just don't feel up to doing this climb. I must leave you to decide what you want to do.'

John and I had trekked together several times in recent years, but it was fourteen since we had been on Mount Kenya and twenty-one since our last serious rock climb in the Pyrenees. No mountain companion was ever more steadfast and reliable than John, but he was sixty-six and had not been moving well over the past few days. Now, he was looking tired and drawn. At that time, I had no idea that he was battling with cancer.

Rose had proved herself a brave performer, but was sensitive to the situation and the dilemma it posed.

'It's just another mountain, Rose,' I told her. 'We're not here to prove anything. You've done jolly well to get this far.'

'I think I'll stay here with John, if you don't mind,' she replied quietly.

In fine weather with dry rock, this would have been an easy climb. But with the clouds thickening and the rocks covered in fresh snow, Triglav looked a real proposition. Joanna was a natural rock climber, but had no experience of snow and ice. Was I mad to even think that she and I might attempt this climb in such conditions? In the event, she took the decision out of my hands.

'Okay Dad, I'm on for it. Let's get going.'

Apart from a steep couloir that required bridging, the route was straightforward enough, but the snow that plastered the rocks overlaid hard ice that needed great care and on the narrow summit ridge exposure and a gusting wind gave the climb a serious character and me an acute sense of isolation. In the event, it took us only an hour and a half to reach the Aljaz Tower, the storm shelter and triangulation point that marks Triglav's summit and which was originally donated to the Slovene Mountaineering Society in 1895 by the eponymous priest who had purchased the entire mountain top from the Austrian government for five Austro-Hungarian florins. As we began to retrace our steps, the sky momentarily cleared and a ghostly figure emerged from the clouds. Before leaving the summit, he insisted on taking a photograph of the two of us that I particularly cherish.

The 2,400-metre descent to the Trenta Valley by a dizzying, corkscrew path, broken by the occasional cable-assisted rock scramble, seemed interminable.

Both of Joanna's knees became badly inflamed and I limped most of the way. Long after dark, we found the Na Logu hut at the bottom of the valley locked. In desperation, I knocked on the door of a nearby house where a kindly woman beckoned us in with the magic word *'schlafen?'* She then produced bowls of hot soup and fussed around the girls like a mother hen. The following day, a combination of walking and hitching got us as far as the statue of Julius Kugy which marks the top of the Vrsic Pass and thence by lift to Kranjska Gora where John decided to stay on awhile. As our bus to Tarvisio drew away from the terminus next morning, the three of us leaned out of the window to wave him goodbye. His sad, lonely figure standing on the curb-side triggered a flood of memories of the adventures we had shared together over the past forty years for I had a presentiment that we might never climb together again. In fact, we nearly did when I drove him out to Saint Gervais the following summer to get him fit enough to repeat Shackleton's 1916 epic crossing of South Georgia. After a couple of stiff training walks, our attempt on Mont Tondu got no further than the upper reaches of the Tré la Tête Glacier and more disappointingly, John's intended South Georgia crossing proved an endeavour too far for his brave spirit.

During the last decade of his life, John confronted his progressive cancer with the same stoicism and courage that had marked both his mountaineering and sailing by offering himself as a guinea pig at the School of Hygiene and Tropical Medicine to test a range of cancer treatments. His professional achievements, dedication, integrity and generosity had been an inspiration to his many devoted friends and professional colleagues. We walked together in the Alps for one last time in 2007 during the Alpine Club 150th anniversary celebrations at Zermatt. He died a year later.

MONT BLANC 1999

Without Joanna's encouragement, I might never have done another alpine climb. However, the Smolikas trip earlier that year persuaded me that there was still enough juice left in the tank to take up her challenge to climb Mont Blanc together that same autumn. Her team included her future husband Rui Fiske de Gouveia, her chum Rose Cottam and their mutual friend Rupert Harris. To add ballast, I roped in David Seddon and Mike Binnie, an old friend and a former president of the Oxford University Mountaineering Club.

Concerns about my being fit enough were partly allayed when Aubrey Leatham invited me to join his party for a week's walking in the Valais on dates that neatly dovetailed with our proposed Mont Blanc trip. Aubrey, a fine ski mountaineer who, as a vice-president, had been a pillar of support in my efforts to achieve the Alpine Ski Club/Alpine Club merger, was an eminent heart surgeon who had once been the King of Bhutan's personal physician. His team of ten included J.H. Emlyn Jones, a distinguished mountaineer and former Alpine Club president whose principal wartime task had been to destroy Hitler's secret V3 'super gun' before it destroyed London. Emlyn was aged eighty-four, Aubrey seventy-nine and several others, including Emlyn's wife Louise, were over seventy. At sixty-five I was almost the youngest. However, any doubts that I might have had about my seniors' stamina were soon dispelled when, without missing a beat, the party surged on from hotel to hotel; breezed up the Eggishorn; inspected a length of the Aletsch Glacier and finished the week off with a thousand-metre climb to the Fründenhütte above the Oeschinensee for midday schnapps. That same evening, the Leathams insisted that I join them to play two sets of tennis before dinner.

Driving on to Saint Gervais to rendezvous with my own party, I reflected that impressive as the mountains of the Valais may be, they do not compare with the ever-lasting universe that is Mont Blanc. It was the grandeur and magnetic attraction of this mountain that had originally influenced Georgina's and my decision to buy an apartment in Saint Gervais in whose commune its summit is situate. So often, I had gazed up from our apartment's balcony to the Dome de Miage's tumbling ice cliffs and the Aiguille de Bionnassay's soaring west ridge recalling past climbs. However, on the threshold of the new adventure I would soon be sharing with Joanna and her friends, my anticipation and excitement were tempered by the lateness of the season. Now well into September, the snowline was very low and both the Tré la Tête and Conscrits huts had already closed for winter.

To get everyone fit and acclimatised, we did several long training hikes and one full day practising crampon and crevasse rescue techniques on the Tré la Tête Glacier. For the actual ascent of Mont Blanc, I chose the *Voie Royale* via the Aiguille de Gouter, the route that had repulsed Georgina and I twenty-four years before but now on our doorstep. My plan was to spend one night at the Gouter Hut and climb Mont Blanc the following day before returning by the same route to Saint Gervais. However, when both the Syndicate d'Initiative and the Guides Bureau forecast the onset of bad weather within the next forty-eight hours, I brought this programme forward by a day.

On 22 September, the 9.40 a.m. Mont Blanc cog-tramway whisked us 1,500 metres up to the 2,372-metre-high Nid d'Aigle station, thus saving a monumental hike. The train was packed with trippers and others laden with climbing gear.

After a quick squint round, all the trippers and several of the climbers caught the next tram back to Saint Gervais leaving us to follow in the tracks of the remaining few who were already trudging through deep snow to the Tête Rousse Hut. Here, most of those who had set off so confidently from the Nid d'Aigle station decided to stay put, leaving us to rope up before tackling the Aiguille de Gouter. In summer, the only objective hazard on this popular route is from the rockfalls that frequently come down the Grand Couloir. At this time, the rocks were frozen in solid but also smothered in snow, so the Aiguille looked disconcertingly steep in its winter garb. The girls stormed up it like veterans, but there was naught for our comfort at the near-deserted Gouter Hut which was refrigerator cold and manned by a grumpy warden who was reluctant to provide supper and totally unhelpful about the weather.

During the summer climbing season, Mont Blanc can resemble an ant heap and in order to secure a place at the Gouter Hut, you must book months in advance. Now at the back-end of the season, the only starters for tomorrow were ourselves, a jolly party of young Ulster climbers determined to avenge their failed attempt the previous year, and a Frenchwoman with her guide who repeatedly expressed his grave concerns about the weather. I dozed fitfully during those tense, uneasy hours before take-off, unable to rid my mind of the weather warnings and the reflection that climbing Mont Blanc with one precious daughter and her young chums was a very different proposition from when Steve Town, Graham Luker and I had done our grand traverse twenty-one years before.

The guardian's brutish 2 a.m. reveille next morning was over-zealous. The man was anxious to get back to bed and did his best to accelerate our departure by flicking the *dortoir's* lights off and on. After saddling up with harnesses and fastening on our crampons in the hut's freezing ante-room, we stepped outside to be met by a bitter wind that was blowing so strongly that I cursed myself for not previously roping-up inside. The sky was clear with a myriad of lights twinkling in the valleys below, but the cold was intense and at night, Mont Blanc can be a lonely, frightening place. With only the Ulstermen ahead, I felt vulnerable and was somehow disturbed to think that at the base of this huge mountain, millions of people were sleeping sound in warmth and comfort.

We were climbing on two ropes. Me, Joanna and David on one: Mike, Rose, Rui and Rupert on the other. Soon, the Ulstermen were pulling ahead with the lights of their head torches bouncing back off the snow before they disappeared into the darkness. I had never imagined that crossing the Dome de Gouter would give us any route-finding problems for had it been earlier in the year, dawn would almost have broken by now. But in the blackness of a moonless night, its featureless slopes seemed steeper than I remembered and the faint imprints of the Ulstermen had long since vanished. Only when I twigged, with mounting horror, that the pin pricks of light to our right must be those of Courmayeur, 4,000-metres below at the bottom of the colossal precipices that guard Mont Blanc's South Face, did I realise that we had strayed disastrously off route. Mont Blanc's magnetic granite rock had upset my compass bearings. We had a brief confab; took fresh bearings and then carried on in silence.

Reaching the Vallot Refuge at the first glimmerings of dawn, its trapdoor entrance gave access to a deep-freeze cubicle with heaps of rubbish and rock-hard faeces strewn around. The Ulstermen gave us a cheery welcome but were then on their way. I glanced at my watch. We were still within guidebook time, but my heart was racing, I was feeling sick and had a splitting headache. Judging from the general lack of animation and desultory conversation, the others felt the same. After a short rest, I went out to inspect the way ahead. A bullying wind had got up and was tearing strips of spindrift off the narrowing Grande and Petites Bosses. But what really made me blink was the view to the west. The sky had turned dark-red and the horizon was rapidly filling up with baggy, black clouds.

The climbing history of Mont Blanc is replete with tales of accident and death. The well-publicised Victorian tragedies of Dr Hamel and his three guides and of Captain Arkwright's disappearance in an avalanche are as nothing when compared with the mountain's modern death toll which can average one hundred a season. Even the most experienced alpinists can fall victim to its savage weather, and during a week-long storm in 1961 only three of the seven crack climbers, who were attempting the Central Pillar of Frêney under Walter Bonatti's leadership, survived. What I now saw on the horizon was nothing less than the bad weather that had long been forecast. We were only two hours short of the summit, but in no way was I going to take the risk.

Route finding across the Dome de Gouter is notoriously difficult in bad visibility. David and Mike agreed that a direct descent down the Bosses Glacier to Chamonix would now be the safer option. Joining up as a single rope, we took particular care when traversing beneath the threatening ice cliffs above the Grand Plateau. Once well below them, the pressure eased though being so late in the season, many of the snow-bridges over the crevasses had become too thin to cross. Spurred on by lowering clouds and the occasional snow flurry, we zigzagged repeatedly from one side of the glacier to the other and, during a momentary break, spotted the spectral figures of the Ulstermen going strongly for the summit.

It had taken us three hours to reach the Grands Mulets Hut, once the traditional staging post for climbing the mountain from Chamonix, only to find it closed. However, having got this far, I imagined that we were virtually home and dry. In fact, our trials were only just beginning for the crevasses below the hut were so enormous that to avoid them I was forced to traverse the scoured rocks above before descending to the glacier below. Here, it was sundered by chasmic depths which could only be avoided by weaving a delicate path between them and which involved some desperate leaps and frantic scramblings to reach the other side. Now reverting to two ropes, Joanna led David and Mike oblivious to a barrage of well-meant, if misdirected, veteran advice. Below the chaotic icefalls of the 'Junction', I made the mistake of going too far down and became enmeshed in another nightmare world of tottering séracs before eventually regaining the correct route. The final knee-wrenching section of that fifteen-hour descent was completed by torchlight, but at the Mont Blanc tunnel's entrance closed by a recent roof collapse, Rose managed to charm the guard to raise the taxi that took us back to St Gervais. The Ulstermen's car was no longer in the car park, so we assumed they must have made their summit. That descent down the Bosses Glacier had concertinaed a lifetime's experience of glacier travel into a single day Next morning, while breakfasting al fresco on the apartment's balcony in bright sunshine, I pondered on what might have been. But as we packed up to go home the sky darkened, thunder and lightning rolled around the valley and Mont Blanc disappeared under a dense, black cloud.

MONTE VISO TRAGEDY

When do you finally bow out? In 2001, the prospect of having to undergo a radical prostatectomy operation with its intimations of mortality concentrated my mind on one last ski tour. It had to be something special and, in the tradition of the Kackar Traverse, had to have a historic theme. I chose the ski circuit of Monte Viso for both those reasons. First, I wanted to repeat in winter the *Tour du Mont Viso* that I had already done in summer seven years before and which makes the complete circuit of one of the most striking mountains in the Alps. Secondly, I wanted to resolve in my own mind the tantalising question of where exactly Hannibal had crossed the Alps in 218 BC.

The two most famous crossings of the Alps by Roman generals – Pompey's via the Col de Montgenévre and Caesar's via the Petit St Bernard – are both clearly documented. But the site of Hannibal's much earlier and more daring passage remains the subject of speculation. The arguments rumble on, but what can be categorically stated is that both Bernard Levin's and Ian Botham's heavily publicised road-crossings over familiar Alpine passes were miles off the mark. The pass most favoured by the late Sir Gavin de Beer, an Alpine Club member, Hannibal scholar and fellow of the Royal Society, is the 2,947-metre Col de la Traversette which lies some four-kilometres north of Monte Viso. Another strong contender, promoted by Arthur Bonus, ex-Indian Civil Service, is the 2,536-metre Col de Malaure which is sixteen-kilometres north of Monte Viso and 411 metres lower than the Traversette.

Back in August 1994, Georgina and I had already made one Hannibal quest with Peter Lowes, Julian and Sarah Lush, Jean and Francoise Coubet and team-leader, Stewart Hawkins, whose house in the upper Alpes Maritimes had made a most convivial start point from which to inspect these competing claims. Both de Beer and Bonus were agreed that Hannibal must have approached the alpine watershed from France up the Guil Valley and sure enough, at its road-head car park, a plaque embedded in La Roche Ecroulée confirmed that Hannibal had indeed passed this way. From here, we tramped up to the Monte Viso Hut on the French side and the following morning crossed the Col de Traversette. The walk to the col had hardly raised sweat, but the descent down the Italian side was steep and rocky and for an army to have had managed this passage under snow would have been a remarkable achievement. The precise size of Hannibal's army is disputed, but according to one estimate only half his original 38,000 infantry and 8,000 cavalry (though most of his thirty-seven elephants) survived the crossing quite probably as a result of avalanches. Nonetheless, the fact that this pass was for many years used as a summer trade route between France and Italy after the construction of a tunnel beneath its crest in AD 1480, seemed to belie its reputation for extreme difficulty.

After spending a night at the lavishly appointed Quintino Sella Hut on the Italian side of the watershed, we completed three further stages of the *Tour du Mont Viso* before driving to Valpreveyre and walking up the Malaure Valley to the Col Malaure. This approach was easier than that to Col Traversette and just below the col, there is a glacial basin spacious enough to accommodate a small army. According to Livy (59 BC– AD 17), it was at such a place that Hannibal had addressed his assembled troops before attempting his crossing, There had been no comparable marshalling area below the Col Traversette, but peering down from the Col Malaume into the gloomy depths of the Plan della Crosenatta, that descent looked much longer and steeper than that from the Traversette as confirmed by the IGN 1:25,000 map *Mont Viso* which marks its first few hundred metres with the dotted lines that signify a 'difficult and delicate passage'. Due to lack of time, we were unable to pursue the matter further, but if Hannibal had indeed crossed the Col Malaure, it is easy to understand why he had sustained such heavy losses.

Seven years on, my proposed *Tour de Mont Viso* on ski was intended to follow broadly the same route as our 1994 summer circuit. However, instead of starting from France before crossing the Col de Traversette, we would begin the tour at Crissolo at the head of the Po Valley; spend the first night at the Sella Hut and after completing two further stages return to Italy either by the Col Malaume or by the 2,299-metre Col Lacroix which I had identified as another prospective 'Hannibal Col' as it lay roughly halfway between the Traversette and the Malaure and was appreciably lower than either. Further, it was crossed by the GR58 trekking route. Perplexingly, neither De Beer nor Bonus had referred to this col, but it met de Beer's topographical prerequisite of being easily accessible from the upper Guil Valley.

For old times' sake, I roped in two close friends who had both played critical roles on the Pyrenean High Route. Alan Wedgwood, the anchorman of its early stages, and Rupert Hoare, one of its spearheads during the latter. None of my other ski mountaineering companions were currently available and to make up a four, Rupert suggested a friend of his, Ian Steen. On meeting Ian for the first time at Gatwick on 30 March, his only comment on seeing me reading my *Daily Telegraph* was 'Good God, you must be seriously right wing!'

We flew to Turin, hired a car and drove through the undulating hills of Piedmont past the famous vineyards of Barbera and Barolo and thence up the Po Valley. At its head, the snow-white spire of Monte Viso looked as sublime as the Elijah Walton painting I proudly possess depicts. This, the most southerly of the great mountains of the Alps, holds a special place in Italian legend and history as the source of the Po. Its isolation makes it look even higher than its 3,851 metres and on a clear day its summit can be seen from the spires of Milan Cathedral.

After settling in at the welcoming hostelry of La Miera at Crissolo, I told Tristano, a local guide and son of our affable mine host Lucano Gallo, what we were planning.

'The Monte Viso circuit is an excellent choice,' said Tristano. 'What's more, you're going to be lucky with the weather which should be set for the next few days.'

'We're thinking of returning to Crissolo by either the Col de Malaume or the Col Lacroix,' I explained. 'Which pass is better?'

'No, no, no my friend,' Tristano replied, vigorously shaking his head. 'I must strongly advise you *not* to attempt the Col Malaume which is very dangerous and subject to avalanches at this time of year. On your itinerary, the only safe passage would be across the Col Lacroix.'

It was unseasonably warm for the time of year when we set off from the Plan Melze the following morning for the Quintino Sella Hut, another nine hundred metres higher. Soon enough, both Alan and I were struggling to keep up with both Rupert, recently back from a month in the Himalaya, and Ian, who had just completed a fortnight's ski touring in the Oberland. For Alan, weighing in at sixteen stone and handicapped by brand new skins that wouldn't stick properly, that climb must have been an ordeal.

The main Sella Hut, which I remembered as buzzing with trekkers and trippers in summer, was now closed. Its winter quarters had neither electricity nor heating and due to a silly misunderstanding as to who was to be responsible for food, we had to make do with AFD 'spagboll' cooked over the tiny Gaz stove that Rupert had thoughtfully packed 'just in case'. The hut was so cold that no one was minded to chat, let alone play cards or roll dice and even with six blankets, I shivered for much of the night. But what kept me awake were my worries about Alan. Though he never complained, he was patently very unfit and on arrival at the hut, had confided that he was having heart fibrillations. His skis were brand new but his old skiing breeches had split down the seams and now needed some heavy cross-stitching to keep them together. Without mentioning my concerns to the others, I asked Alan if he really wanted to carry on, knowing full well what his answer would be.

At dawn on the 1st of April, Rupert was already cosseting his Gaz stove to boil enough water for tea. Bizarrely, it occurred to me that on another April Fool's Day exactly twenty years before, our erstwhile French ski mountaineering companion, Jean-Pierre Leire, had played a particularly silly April Fool jape on Alan and his wife Janet halfway through the fifth stage of the Pyrenean High Route and the day after my night-time rescue off the mountain in a blood wagon by the French Mountain Police. Jean-Pierre had chosen this inappropriate occasion to persuade Alan, who had scarcely slept a wink over the past thirty-six hours, to join him in what turned out to be a completely bogus mountain-rescue exercise. When the joke was sprung, both Alan and Janet were justifiably furious and left for England the following day. That unhappy incident had taken place two decades ago. I was now sixty-seven and Alan sixty-three. This time round, we were going to have to rely heavily on Rupert.

After yesterday's exhausting flog, I reckoned that today's stage to the Vallanta Hut over the Passo Gallerino was bound to be a deal easier. The weather was set fair, the sky ice blue and the veil of haze that swathed the upper Po Valley gave the impression of infinite space. We left the Sella Hut at 8.15 a.m. with Rupert initially taking a higher, independent line in order to obey a call of nature. I went on ahead, followed by Alan with Ian as sweeper. The snow was iron-hard and fast running. Just right in fact, for Alan's new skis with their razor-sharp edges.

We had been going for less than ten minutes, when I led down into a shallow depression. As I started to climb out of it I heard Ian's voice, shrill with anxiety, shouting out behind me, 'Alan's injured, Alan's injured!' Swinging round, I saw Alan lying motionless in the snow with Ian and Rupert kneeling at his side. Racing back to join them, I was appalled to find Alan barely conscious, unable to speak and obviously in extreme pain. A thin trail of blood led down from a low, rocky outcrop to where he was lying with the snow around tinged red. His breeches had been severed open and blood was welling out of a deep gash between his crotch and inner thigh.

'Christ!' I thought, 'he's bleeding to death.'

Ian, a qualified first aider, was feeling Alan's pulse.

'This is bloody serious,' he muttered. 'I didn't see him fall, but heard him scream. His pulse is dropping fast.'

Rupert agreed to get back to the Sella Hut and telephone for help while Ian and I tried to ease Alan into my bivouac bag to keep him warm. We soon gave up when realised that we couldn't get his boots off without causing further excruciating pain.

'We can't possibly move him in this state,' said Ian. 'It looks as if he's broken his thigh or hip or both.'

'Okay Ian, you're best qualified to stay with him here. I'll get back to the hut to see if Rupert has managed to raise a helicopter. If not, he and I will have to ski down to Crissolo to get help.'

A helicopter was whirring its way up the valley even as I approached the hut with my lungs bursting. Landing in a flurry of snow, the mountain gendarme who leapt out had to clamber in again immediately when Rupert and I pointed our ski sticks towards the depression shouting 'That way, that way!' On rejoining Ian, we found the gendarme kneeling in the snow examining Alan.

'I can't do much to help this man,' he said grimly. 'He's already lost so much blood that he's gone into shock. He needs immediate medical attention. Keep him as warm as you can. I'm flying back to get a doctor and proper medical support.'

Within twenty minutes of taking off, the helicopter returned with a young doctor and two medical assistants. After they'd put Alan on to a morphine drip, the five of us eased him on to a stretcher and then into the helicopter. I almost retched at the sight of the swelling gout of black blood barely held back by the first-aid dressings plastered over Alan's long johns. None of us realised at the time quite how serious Alan's injuries were, nor could we have understood how a fall off a seemingly innocuous three-metre-high rock outcrop could have shattered his pelvis, ruptured his rectum, punctured his bowels and severed a main artery. Incredibly, the time lag between the accident and the helicopter's take-off with Alan inside had taken less than one and a half hours. Without Rupert's heroic dash back to the hut and the Italian Mountain Rescue team's superbly fast response, Alan would have died from loss of blood.

The young woman helicopter pilot's last words to me were, 'There's still a chance. I'm flying him direct to the hospital at Savigliano.'

Rupert, Ian and I shared out Alan's skis and equipment before skiing very cautiously down to Crissolo. Stunned by the turn of events, I simply could not believe that Alan, the indestructible strongman of so many expeditions, had been reduced to a wreck. 'God forbid,' I thought to myself, 'that I shall have to break fatal news to Janet.' Drained by the emotional strain and struggling to cope with the additional load through deep, variable snow, I found it hard to concentrate and at one point my ski path crossed with Ian's. As we collided, he burst out, 'Get that damned ice axe out of my way and into your rucksack! All the guides put their ice axes in their rucksacks. It's bad practice to do otherwise.'

Ian was right, of course, but with Alan's life hanging in the balance the last thing on my mind was bad practice and I gave a heated reply.

Down at the Plan Melze car park, now swarming with weekend skiers, the place had a holiday atmosphere with banks of crocuses swathing the lower slopes. At the hostel La Meira, Lucano Gallo had already heard of the accident and had prepared a table and food for us. We then drove to Savigliano's ultramodern hospital where a lady doctor in the Intensive Care Unit explained that Alan was in the operating theatre.

'He has lost eight litres of blood and needed a transfusion of eighteen units. His condition remains critical and his life now depends on the outcome of this operation.'

After booking into a hotel, I telephoned Georgina to explain what had happened and then returned to the hospital praying that Alan would still be alive before I telephoned Janet. Mercifully, he had come through the operation, but his condition was still critical. Janet took the news with icy calm and said that she and the family would fly out immediately. Next morning, Rupert and I drove to Turin airport to meet Alan's mother Sally and his doctor son Tom who was suffering from a very serious kidney complaint that needed immediate attention. The Savigliano Hospital carried out blood, urine, X Ray and ultra-sound tests on Tom with the same speed and efficiency as had characterised Alan's rescue and medical treatment. We then drove to Milan airport to take Janet to the hospital where Alan was still under sedation. The Wedgwood's two daughters and other family members would soon be flying in from various parts of the world, so Rupert, Ian and I returned to England the following day.

Miraculously, Alan survived, though on return to England had to have his broken pelvis reset. Recovery took many months, but he was walking again and even skiing black runs within a year. Yet the injuries sustained during that traumatic fall never fully healed and in early 2013 the damaged leg had to be amputated.

Nothing daunted, Alan then set his sights on climbing his local Cumbrian hills by wheelchair and by Christmas 2014 was ticking them off one by one. His accident marked the end of my own ski mountaineering career for I reckoned that if this could happen to Alan, it could happen to anyone and I owed it to Georgina not to be next in line. Monte Viso was also the last time I ever climbed with Rupert, a fine, all-round mountaineer with whom I had shared many adventures in the Pyrenees, Spain, Corsica and Scotland. As a geophysicist, Rupert was as much respected by his professional colleagues for his abilities and integrity as he was dearly loved by his many friends. The hills had been the inspiration that shaped his aesthetic and spiritual values and his death from pancreatic cancer in 2011 at the age of fifty-five was yet another capricious tragedy.

18

TREKS FAR AND WIDE

BHUTAN

Inevitably perhaps, as the years slipped by I became more attracted to travelling in mountains than climbing them. No doubt, this reflected my age but also a maxim of Lord Conway, the first man to traverse the Alps from end to end, that the ideal mountaineer is one who 'loves first and foremost to wander far and wide among the mountains'. A mountaineer's most vivid memories may well be of those when life has hung in the balance. Yet quite as permanent are those when you made time to stop and stare, watch the clouds pass by, paint and photograph or even ponder on the meaning of life.

No mountain lover would think his life fulfilled without visiting the Himalaya. Marriage, family responsibilities and limited holidays scuppered realistic prospects of climbing there seriously, but trekking was always an option and in 1991, Georgina and I took up Peter Mould's invitation to join his Alpine Club 'Green' expedition to Bhutan, one of the least spoilt corners in the Himalaya, thanks to the King of Bhutan's decision to preserve his country's indigenous culture and Buddhist way of life. Until 1978, no tourists had been allowed into the country and, apart from Spencer Chapman's officially sanctioned ascent of Bhutan's sacred mountain Chomolhari in 1937, no mountaineering expeditions had been permitted there until 1983, when Doug Scott climbed the virgin peak Jichu Drakye.

Peter's aim was to demonstrate that 'clean' expeditions could preserve the mountain environment. Yet 'Green' did not come cheap and the expedition eventually cost £50,000, as compared with Spencer Chapman's £40 all found.

I had never previously been to India, yet Delhi's atmosphere was reassuringly familiar reflecting, perhaps, my family's past connections with India and my own Colonial Service career in Aden which, for a hundred years until 1937, had been administered under the aegis of the governments of Bombay and India. New Delhi's wide avenues and spacious gardens; Lutyens's magnificent public buildings and the Imperial Hotel's palatial ballroom were nostalgic monuments to an empire over which the sun was never supposed to set.

Peter's expedition included both a climbing and trekking component. Georgina and I opted for the fourteen-day trek from Paro to Panaka, a source of everyday wonder the further we progressed. Bhutan's unique vernacular architecture, ranging from stone-built houses with half-timbered upper storeys decorated with intricately carved wooden ornamentation to immense fortified monasteries, or *dzongs,* has few rivals in any mountain environment. From Paro, our yak train progressed in leisurely fashion past terraced fields where women winnowed wheat and rice, before plunging into scented forests of giant oak, cedar, blue pine, ash, birch and juniper whose canopy shaded carpets of forget-me-nots, hypericum, helichrysum violets and orchids. The hillsides around were swathed in rhododendron, azalea, berberus and edelweiss while always to the north, the horizon glittered with an array of colossal snow peaks and for four days, Chomolhari, the 'Divine Queen of the Mountains', was our constant companion.

Jichu Drakye's summit cornice, surmounting a tremendous wall of fluted ice, had looked like the crest of a tsunami about to engulf our caravan as it breasted the 4,900 metre Shinche-la. The Shangri-La village of Laya, at the limits of the inhabitable world, marked the culminating point of our trek. It had its own dispensary, primary school and a monastery where twenty novitiate monks were taught by rote, though very existence depended on meagre crops grown on scanty soil ploughed by yaks and harrowed with crude wooden picks. Summer offered a short respite before long, snow-bound winters made movement outside the village virtually impossible. On our first night there, we were perched on low stools in sub-zero temperatures at the edge of the village's midden to watch the belles of Laya, dressed overall in black, sing traditional folk dirges as they slow-shuffled round a blazing log fire.

If local nightlife had been a discomfiting experience, the lives of the yak-men who journeyed up and down the high valleys, were harsher. A race apart, with each team operating within strictly defined parishes, they were compulsive gamblers and when one of them lost his entire trek earnings during an all-night session, another fingered his dagger and insisted that the wretched man carry on.

A fatal stabbing was only avoided when our dauntless cook Karma intervened. Their yaks emerged as the real stars of the trek. Dignified souls, they carry as much as horses, but are surer-footed and hardier. Though disinclined to give way on narrow paths, in deep snow they will break the trail for their masters who, when crossing icy stretches, hang on to their tails for the ride. For the last five days of the expedition both trekkers and climbers joined up to witness the architectural wonders of Bumthang's Buddhist monasteries and the grotesque demon dancing of their monks. Georgina and I had hoped that our trek through the 'Land of the Peaceful Dragon' would never end. For Peter Mould it had been a triumph, but his premature death not many years after, a tragedy. Ffald y Brenin, a complex of vernacular farm buildings in Pembrokeshire that he and his wife Phyllida had lovingly restored as a Christian retreat, remains as his memorial.

SIKKIM

The following year, Georgina and I embarked on a very different style of trek in Sikkim. In addition to John Blacker, Peter Lowes and David Seddon from the Bhutan party, we brought along our eldest daughter Emma, her future husband Sasha and her girlfriend Louisiana to add some zest. The tour was organised by *Kangchenjunga Trek and Tours* which was owned by Tenzing Norgay's widow and two of his four sons, Jamling and Dhamey. Sikkim's particular attraction for me was its proximity to Kangchenjunga, the world's third highest mountain and arguably its most beautiful. The view of it from Darjeeling is one of the world's greatest spectacles and had been imprinted on my imagination ever since the previous owner of our house on Putney Heath had bequeathed us a superb black and white full-plate photograph of it taken from Darjeeling.

It is one of the flukes of mountaineering history that Kangchenjunga was not climbed before Everest. Curzon, then viceroy of India, had suggested as much to Younghusband, for unlike Everest Kangchenjunga had the advantage of relative accessibility being only forty-miles direct from Darjeeling. Detailed information about its approaches had already been gathered by both Joseph Hooker during his botanical explorations in 1848 and 1849 and by the Pundit surveyor Namgyal Rinsing who made the mountain's first complete circuit in 1884. Moreover, in the course of Douglas Freshfield's subsequent 1899 circuit of Kangchenjunga his surveyor, Professor Edmond Garwood, had made an excellent map of the whole massif. In the event, Kangchenjunga proved a very hard mountaineering nut to crack. Unsuccessful attempts included those by the black magician Aleister Crowley in 1905 and by three subsequent German expeditions during the 1930s. When, in 1955, Brown and Band, members of Charles Evans's British Kangchenjunga expedition, made its first ascent, John Hunt described it as 'the greatest feat of mountaineering'.

Had it not been for the Indian Government's travel restrictions, the choice of treks in Sikkim might have included the Rinsing/Freshfield circuit and the approach marches taken through the country by all three British 1920s Everest expeditions and the 1955 Kangchenjunga expedition. As it was, with only a fortnight's holiday in hand, one of Sikkim's few authorised treks from Yuksum to the 4,940-metre Giuche La and back, exactly fitted our requirements. We flew in to Delhi on 24 October still recovering from a catalogue of travel incidents that began when Georgina's and my new passports got lost in the post and had our car clamped at BA's Victoria Terminal. Emma and Sasha might never left England due to Emma's being informed the previous day that she couldn't be spared as her boss was having a nervous breakdown, while Sasha managed to mislay both his passport and ticket. Luckily for them, take-off was delayed for three hours as a result of our plane being struck by lightning while still on the tarmac. Peter Lowes was always a doubtful starter after developing a hernia, but disregarded medical advice.

After three aborted attempts to land at Delhi airport, we checked in at the Imperial Hotel at 3 a.m. when David Seddon discovered that he had picked up the wrong rucksack. He raced back to the airport immediately and somehow managed to retrieve his own. Later that day, Jamling Norgay, the spitting image of his father, met us at the Imperial's bar to break the news that his mother, the company's CEO, had just died. I offered to cancel the trek, but Jamling insisted that the show must go on and it was left to Peter Lowes, a connoisseur in the workings of Indian bureaucracy, to resolve the 'problem' of our mysteriously cancelled 'confirmed OK' flight to Bagdogra. En route to the airport, David announced that he had left his wallet and passport back at the hotel, but as luck would have it, that flight too was delayed. At Bagdogra airport, Dhamey Norgay fitted everyone plus luggage into his Nissan Patrol. After barging his way through a chaos of buses, lorries, 4x4s, bicycles, tricycles, rickshaws and cattle, we hit the road to Darjeeling that shadows that miracle of Victorian engineering, the mini-gauge Himalayan railway.

Darjeeling's sprawling modern town clings limpet-like to steep, terraced hillsides overlooking cavernous drops that plunge to luxuriant forests below. This former Raj hill station had become an improbable alpine resort with its once fashionable hotels and grandiose public buildings slowly disintegrating as an older India reasserted itself. The walls of the Sinclair Hotel's teak-floored ballroom were cluttered with faded group photographs of sporting Edwardian gents and their ladies dressed for tennis. On checking in, Peter Lowes discovered that his rucksack had gone missing along with his irreplaceable size-twelve boots.

Tenzing Norgay's house, formerly a British tea-planter's villa, had been donated to the Hero of Everest by Nehru who was determined that India should have 'A thousand Tenzings'. Nehru had paid for all Tenzing's children to be educated in the USA and Dhamey, now on vacation from Greenwich University, Connecticut, regaled us with anecdotes about his father.

'He always remained a simple, unassuming man who loved gardening in his old clothes and would explain politely to inquisitive visitors that "Sherpa Tenzing is away today".'

In the house that had once entertained Nehru, Indira and Rajiv Gandhi, one room was dedicated solely to Everest memorabilia, certificates, presentations, plaques, and a collection of Everest books. There were many photos of Tenzing; one of Nehru with one arm clasped around Tenzing's shoulder and several of the Swiss guide Raymond Lambert with whom Tenzing had formed a special relationship during the 1952 Swiss attempt on Everest. Of mementoes or photographs of the British 1953 Everest expedition, Hunt or Hillary there were none. Dhamey said that the family were disappointed that they had not yet been invited to the 1993 Everest fortieth-anniversary celebrations in London.

After sipping cups of strong Darjeeling tea and sweet biscuits served by a kindly aunt with a beatific smile, we all trooped off to visit the family shrine. Built like a Buddhist temple and decorated inside with rich and elaborate fabrics, carvings and paintings, forty-nine candles were burning to mark the number of days that would elapse between Mrs Tenzing's death and nirvana. An old monk sat praying by the window. The place had an atmosphere of humility, sanctity and peace.

On 26 October, our eight Giuche La trekkers set off from Darjeeling in the Nissan Patrol into which Dhamey had somehow managed to squeeze his uncle Nima, an Indian Himalayan Institute mountain guide; Dorjay, a genial Bhutanese entrepreneur who ran a restaurant in Delhi; Karma, our ever inventive cook, and a liaison officer who wore a sign 'Police' on his rucksack and smiled politely, but never uttered a word. The roof rack was already bulging with luggage, food and camping equipment when a couple of hangers-on hitched a last-minute lift on the vehicle's tailgate. When negotiating numberless hairpin bends during the white knuckle, 2,000-metre descent into the trough of the Tista Valley, the Nissan's gear lever refused to engage reverse and on reaching the bottom the back-axle packed up. Dhamey repaired it on the spot.

At Yuksum Dhamey recruited four surly porters and three mangy yaks and here we met a Swedish trekking party just back from the Giuche La who said they had experienced nothing but rain and snow throughout. One of them cheekily offered Peter Lowes his climbing boots for US $300 and got a raspberry for his trouble. Two days out, our expedition might have got no further than Pedang when Sasha took it upon himself to climb to the top of a forestry lookout. On swinging down from a crossbeam Tarzan-style he dislocated his shoulder. I knew from experience how excruciatingly painful this can be and with Darjeeling now well out of mobile-phone range to raise a rescue helicopter, things were looking very serious. Doctor David's geriatrician's training had never previously run to replacing a dislocated shoulder and his first attempt failed. He managed it second time round. Sasha, with typical Russian stoicism, never flinched.

During the night, the temperature plunged to thirteen degrees Fahrenheit and next morning the ground was white with frost. The yaks had to be rounded up after escaping across the river and a stray dog now joined the band. As the trail wound its way over a couple of high passes, there were stupendous views of Kabru, Pandim and Kangchenjunga to the north. Once upon a time, I might have salivated at such a sight but now, with no remote prospect of climbing them, I was more than content to be sauntering along at my own pace through lush forests and rhododendron thickets scented with flowers.

There is little to choose between Bhutan and Sikkim's natural scenery, but Bhutan's vernacular architecture is incomparable and Sikkim's trekking camps little more than scruffy shacks. The venerable stone shrine on the Sameti Pass, once a staging post on this most ancient trade and pilgrimage route, had been replaced by a ghastly modern building with a rusting tin roof. Nearby, on the shore of a sacred lake luminescent with green-hued water, Georgina joined Nima to light a ceremonial Buddhist incense fire and to contemplate nirvana.

The trail continued up the broad Prekchu Valley whose floor, dotted about with black, brown, spotted and white-hued yaks, was littered with colossal erratic boulders as relics of some gigantic prehistoric glacier. That afternoon, we made our highest camp at Sameti at over 4,000 metres as a base for climbing the 4,940 metres Giuche La. But who would be on for the final assault? Georgina, who had been menaced earlier that day by an aggressive bull yak, was in no fit state to climb due to altitude sickness, conjunctivitis and an upset tummy. Others might have been discouraged by Doctor David's putting a sign outside his tent – 'Surgery Closed'. An intensely cold night followed by a 04.40 hours reveille reduced the party to Peter, John, David and me plus Dhamey, Nima and Dorjay.

The approaches to the Guiche La were a chaos of grimy glacier snouts and colossal moraines laden with trillions of tons of fallen debris. Dorjay soon dropped out and was shortly followed by Nima, only to be replaced by two young Sherpas we had never seen before carrying emergency food and kit. We climbed on very slowly, stopping frequently for breath as the bitter cold of early morning was replaced by a blisteringly hot sun. The Guiche La never seemed to get any nearer but exactly four hours after leaving camp, we breasted our objective and stared in wonder at the tremendous spectacle that had even awed J. Claude White, the autocratic British political officer who for twenty years had made Sikkim his personal fiefdom and been the first European to cross the Guiche La in 1890. From the depths of the Talung Glacier, Kangchenjunga's 3,500-metre high south face reared up in a single uninterrupted sweep. It was like some vision of blinding light, a thing of grandeur beyond expression.

On the trek back to Yuksom, the heavy hoar frost that coated the tents each morning presaged the approach of winter. The great peaks that had broken the northern horizon on the way up were now replaced by the swelling curves of forested hills that formed a green mosaic melting away into Sikkim's misty southern plains. After a week cut off from the outside world, the spell was broken at Bakkim when we bumped into the advance guard of a Himalayan Mountain Institute team that was aiming to repeat Freshfield's 1890 seven-week circuit of Kangchenjunga. Before leaving England, our daughter Victoria had lovingly photocopied and encased in a plastic cover Edmond Garwood's map of Kangchenjunga extracted from my precious copy of Freshfield's *Round Kangchenjunga*. When I presented it to one of the HMI team, he flung his arms around me in gratitude and insisted that we exchange addresses. I never heard from him again, but learned later that his team had successfully completed the circuit.

The Sikkim trip ended almost as badly as it had begun due to a succession of strikes and cancelled air flights, which left us on tenterhooks for several days.

Without Peter Lowes's negotiating skills and the taxi driver who cut an indiscriminate swathe through animals, children, carts and vehicles alike to get us to Patna airport on time, we would have missed the plane home. On arrival at Gatwick, I knelt down and kissed the tarmac.

There was also an unusual coda to our Kangchenjunga adventure. In 1872, Edward Lear had been commissioned by Henry Austin Bruce, the first Lord Aberdare and father of Charles ('Bruiser') Bruce, leader of the 1922 Everest expedition, to paint Kangchenjunga. Lear's reaction on seeing the mountain from Darjeeling was 'Wonderful ... very God-like and stupendous' and his oil painting *Kinchinjunga* has been described by the art historian Vivien Noakes as 'a supreme example of the sublime'. During the war, I had lived for a time at Aberdare with my great aunt Marie who had spent most of her married life in India. In 2001, some years after her death, I paid a nostalgic visit to what I remembered as her lovely Georgian house 'Ty Draw' overlooking the Dare Valley and also took this as an opportunity to inspect Lear's *Kinchinjunga* which the Bruce family had donated to the Aberdare local authority. Ty Draw had been desecrated by its subsequent owners and Lear's painting relegated to a dark stairwell in the Aberdare Public Library. When I pointed out to the librarian that the picture had historical importance, he must have taken some notice for it now hangs in the National Gallery of Wales at Cardiff.

CENTRAL ASIA
KYRGYZSTAN I

Long before I ever went there, the very words 'Central Asia' had struck in me subliminal chords. Echoes perhaps of Kim, John Master's Raj novels, Matthew Arnold's poem *Sohrab and Rustum* or Marco Polo's account of travels through those long-vanished kingdoms that had once become fabulously rich from the caravan trade that plied the Silk Road. Their ancient cities have long since crumbled to dust, but what imperishably remains are the mountains that form four of the world's greatest ranges – Karakorum, Tien Shan, Kuen Lun and Hindu Kush, which converge on Central Asia to form the Pamir Knot.

For much of the nineteenth century it was here, on what the Persians called the 'roof of the world', that British and Russian adventurers engaged in what the British called 'The Great Game' and the Russians 'the tournament of shadows'. This contest of exploration, surveying and intelligence gathering, played in deadly earnest between the world's two greatest empires, reached its climax in 1902 when Curzon, as viceroy of India, authorised Younghusband's invasion of Tibet. Curzon's aim was to check what he saw as Tzarist Russia's inexorable annexation of Central Asia and the threat it posed to British India, a long-held suspicion that Sir Halford Mackinder's geo-political theory – *'Who Rules the World Island commands the World'* – seemed to confirm, for Mackinder's *'World Island'* was central Asia itself.

In fact, 'The Great Game' had already been as good as won by Russia in 1868 with its capture of Samarkand which marked the end of Turkestan's debauched Khanate rule and ushered in an era of imperial Russian colonisation that was to transform these medieval lands into a recognisably modern state. The Tzar's Bolshevik successors restructured them as the Soviet Socialist Republics of Kyrgyzstan, Kazakhstan, Uzbekistan, Turkmenistan and Tajikistan after deliberately destroying their traditional nomadic way of life with a brutal programme of forced collectivisation, deportation and famine. When in 1990 Soviet Russia's central Asian empire collapsed in the aftermath of its disastrous Afghan war, these former soviet republics became independent states and though initially plunged into political and economic chaos have since regained a measure of order and prosperity.

Having witnessed at first hand the end of Britain's empire in the Middle East, I imagined that a visit to central Asia in the aftermath of Soviet Russia's precipitate disengagement would offer some interesting comparisons. But more than that, I longed to see something of its great mountains which, ever since the Russian revolution, had effectively been closed to westerners and so, when in 1998 John Ducker suggested that Georgina and I join him to visit Kyrgyzstan, we didn't hesitate. John, with whom I had served in South Arabia and been his best man, was particularly well qualified to organise this trip for his post-Arabian career with the World Bank had included a stint in Kyrgyzstan where he had set up a travel company, Dostuk Trekking, in partnership with a Russian, Nicolai Chetnikov. Nikolai had not only been the head of Kyrgyzstan's Geological Survey until replaced after independence by an indigenous Kyrgyz, but was also a distinguished mountaineer who had climbed all five of the former USSR's highest peaks thereby earning himself the coveted 'Snow Leopard' award.

At 1 a.m. on 27 May 1998, John and his wife Patricia, Bill and Christine Heber-Percy, Julian and Sarah Lush, John Shipman, Miles Gladwyn, David Waterhouse, Mandy Weatherill, Georgina and I (later to be joined by British diplomats Martin Harris and Linda Macloughlin then serving in Kiev), touched down at Almaty's airport. Here we were met by Nicolai who lost no time bundling us into a six-wheel ex-Soviet Army troop carrier that had seen active service in Afghanistan and which, over the next fortnight, transported us a thousand miles around Kyrgyzstan.

A six-hour drive across the rolling Kyrgyz steppe, ablaze with spring flowers with distant mobs of horses scattered around, led to our first camp in the lower Chellick Valley. Over the next four days, Nicolai was to lead the twelve of us through spruce and fir forests and up into the snow-covered upper reaches of the Kungey Alatan Range, supported all the way by a dozen highly disciplined Russian young men and women who humped ridiculously heavy loads without demur. Leisured lunch stops for painting, photography or lazing by lakesides with tea served from the samovar became the order of each day, while for supper we ate fresh trout caught with Christine's rod and grilled over a log fire.

Apart from one undistinguished 3,000-metre peak that John and I nipped up early one morning, only the long snow-trudge to the Sary-Bulak Pass tested lung and limb. From this belvedere, we had a grandstand view of the Tien Shan, the 'Celestial Mountains' that stretch in a thousand-mile, east to west arc that begins at the Turfan Depression and ends in the ice peaks of the Pamirs. Dimly discernible were Peak Pobeda, at 7,430 metres the highest mountain in the range, and the 6,995-metre Khan Tengri, the 'Matterhorn of Central Asia'. Seemingly at our feet, Lake Issyk-Kul's waters shimmered a dozen shades of blue.

Our day's ride down the Baskoon Gorge on sturdy Kyrgyz horses was rewarded with a horse-steak supper in a local Kyrgyz family's yurt. It was here that Nicolai, hard-eyed, moody and humourless until loosened up by vodka, drank himself insensate and before leaving our hosts next morning bribed their teenage daughter to part with her adored pet puppy. It was as well that the dog was given a more loving home with Linda Macloughlin who christened it 'Talisker', for had this Kyrgyz maiden been forewarned of Nicolai's evil intent, she might have served him with aconites rather than wild mushrooms for supper. Kyrgyz women who wish to get rid of their husbands wash their shirts in a solution of this deadly stuff to achieve the desired result, Medea fashion.

Much of the following week was spent bouncing about heavily pot-holed, dirt roads in Nicolai's troop carrier. From Tash Rabat, a former *caravanserai* set high on the ancient trade route that crosses the Tien Shan into Chinese Sinkiang, golden eagles and griffon vultures circled lazily above as we struggled through thigh-deep snow to reach the 3,752-metre Touragat Pass, only to be frustrated near the top by a vicious hail storm. The journey to Osh occupied three particularly uncomfortable days with one night spent en route at Arslanbob, an abandoned former Soviet worker's 'holiday paradise' camp whose concrete buildings were fast disintegrating and whose Olympic-size swimming pool was overgrown with brambles. Nicolai managed to get the sauna working and after supper, my rendering of Chaliapin's *Song of the Volka Boatman* encouraged the snake-eyed Valerie, who doubled as the expedition's medical officer and Nicolai's travelling companion, to insist that I partner her in a wild polonaise. The evening ended with maudlin toasts in vodka and sickly Russian champagne.

Osh, about to celebrate its 3,000th birthday, had a fruit and vegetable market that would have put Covent Garden's to shame and a public lavatory more like an Augean stable where long lines of men squatted down to do their business in open cubicles. An internal air flight spared us the three-day road journey to Kyrgyzstan's capital Bishkek whose wide, leafy avenues were laid out in the late nineteenth century when 30,000 Russians, Ukrainians and Germans came to settle here. After Kyrgyzstan's independence, many Russians left only to drift back disillusioned with modern Russian life.

Closing Bishkek's southern horizon rose the glaciated Kyrgyz Alatau range. On our penultimate day in Kyrgyzstan, John and I, accompanied by our favourite guide Sasha Miusobi, stomped up the Al Archa Gorge as far as the Ak Cau climbers' hut. Set amidst peaks and glaciers wilder than anything in the Alps, we were disappointed to find that a couple of lissom English girls had already claimed priority and, having shacked up with a sixty-year old Russian scientist, were now living with him in a tent. In the closing stages of our farewell lunch hosted by Nicolai's elegant wife Tatiana at a chic Bishkek restaurant, our Snow Leopard, now all smiles and bonhomie, gave Georgina a ring and earrings that he had made himself and presented me with a Russian ice axe as robust as a Kalashnikov. Nicolai Chetnikov exemplified that confusing Russian paradox by combining a degree of finesse with raw brutality.

KYRGYZSTAN II

Six years on from that first Kyrgyzstan trip, John Ducker suggested an altogether more ambitious fourteen-day trek from Lake Issyk-Kul to the 4,000-metre-high Khan Tengri Base Camp at the head of the Inylchek Glacier. Five of us – John, Bill Heber-Percy, Neil Macpherson, Peter Christie and me – with an average age of sixty-eight, touched down at Bishkek on 30 July 2004 and then discovered that Neil and Peter's baggage, forwarded from Edinburgh, had gone missing. Some items of equipment were easily replaced at Bishkek's 'Red Fox' climbing shop and I had to lend Neil my heavy-duty German-made trainers and spare trousers. Over a morale-boosting breakfast of brandy, coffee and chocolates in the shaded garden of the Chetnikov's dacha, Tatiana explained that Nicolai would not, after all, be available to guide this trek.

'Unfortunately, he has had go to Tajikistan with another Dostuk party. They are hoping to climb Pik Stalin'.

I wished them luck. The 7,495-metre Pik Stalin, once known as Garmo, later Kommunizma and most recently Somoni, is the highest mountain in central Asia and was reckoned a tough call even by Joe Brown when he and Malcolm Slessor were the only two Brits of John Hunt's ill-fated 1962 Anglo-Russian Pamirs expedition to make the summit. Nicolai's replacement was a much younger man, Dima. Lean, hard-faced and a chain-smoker, he conversed with John in a mixture of rudimentary Russian and English without syntax. As neither mule nor yak transport were available, six of Dostuk's Russian employees were detailed to act as porters leaving us to carry only our personal kit. To save weight, I jettisoned my sleeping mattress and spent the next fourteen days bitterly regretting it.

Apart from our ever-cheerful cook Fatima (married with several children) and a super-tough ex-paratrooper Basha, the other four were young but experienced mountaineers. Twenty-year-old Timothy, who wore heavy-duty skiing salopettes throughout, had already climbed Khan Tengri three times. Save for Dima, none of the others admitted to speaking English and, apart from the rumbustious Basha, kept a low profile. After the briefest of introductions, all twelve of us piled into Nicolai's ex-Soviet Army ten-wheeler juggernaut for a seven-hour drive to Dostuk's 'Tosor Camp'. Set on a spit of land jutting out into the 182-kilometres long Lake Issyk-Kul, our semi-permanent yurts looked out across its azure waters to a distant panorama of snow-covered peaks. The lake's semi-saline waters never freeze even at an altitude of 1,606 metres and in summer it was a popular resort with beaches packed with non-Islamic, scantily-clad bathers of both sexes and noisy, picnicking families.

Dostuk had labelled our trek '*On the Footsteps of Semenov-Tien-Shansky*' to commemorate the nineteenth century Russian scientist/explorer Pyotr Semenov who first discovered the sixty-two kilometre long Inylchek Glacier in 1856. For this feat, he was awarded the honorary suffix 'Tien Shansky' by the Imperial Geographical Society. Semenov was just one of several outstanding nineteenth Century Russian explorer/scientists who first penetrated and mapped Central Asia. Few of these men are known to the British, save perhaps General Nikolai Przhevalsky, who discovered the wild horse, the forerunner of the modern version that bears his name. His Ozymandian statue, hewn out of a colossal granite block that took five years to fashion, is a must-see in Karakol which is now a pleasant garden town, but was originally founded as an Imperial Army garrison in 1869 and named Przevalsky to honour this formidable 'great gamer' of Cossack and Polish nobility parentage who was reputedly the father of Stalin. Przevalsky led four major pioneer expeditions into Central Asia, including one that nearly succeeded in reaching the forbidden city of Lhasa. He died of typhoid at the age of forty-nine and was buried on the shores of Lake Issyk-Kul, probably the last resting place he would have chosen for he cordially detested the peoples of central Asia and had recommended to the Tzar that their lands be colonised by Cossacks.

Karakol was the last place of human habitation we saw for the next fortnight. A six-hour drive into the mountains past scattered herds of sheep, cattle and horses ended up in an alpine meadow above the Turgan Aksu Gorge where a thick mist obscured everything. The moment we arrived it began to sleet and as there was no mess tent or communal shelter, Fatima had to cook supper al fresco as she did for all other meals throughout the trip. The trek proper began the following day, 2 August, which happened to be my seventieth birthday. Its initial stages were new to Dima who had to rely on a large-scale aerial map for navigation. After spending a couple of hours investigating the way ahead while the rest of us sat it out on a sleet-swept ridge sustained by Fatima brewing up tea in her samovar, he returned glum-faced to report that the col he had first selected was impassable.

The 3,869-metre high col he chose as an alternative was hard grind for the un-acclimatised, but harder still for the porters who were staggering under colossal loads. The descent down its far side by a steep, icy couloir would have been challenging even with proper alpine equipment. All that Dima had brought with him were one ice axe, one ice screw and a thin twenty-metre long rope. It was inevitable that someone would take a tumble and it fell to Fatima to slip out of one of Dima's bucket steps before shooting off headfirst down the couloir towards an ugly band of serrated rocks. She would have been a certain casualty had not Basha, moving with astonishing speed despite his Herculean load, performed a throttle rugby tackle, which stopped her dead. That evening, stretched out on a grassy sward over supper, Dima disclosed that our crossing had been a 'first' though begged us not to mention Fatima's fall back at Bishkek. He then presented me with a magnificent gold-embroidered Kyrgyz felt hat to close a memorable first trekking day to the strains of 'happy birthday' and toasts in vodka to Russo-British solidarity.

The long, winding trail to the Khan Tengri Base Camp involved tramps across pristine alpine meadows carpeted with primulas, gentians, orchids and marigolds; thigh-deep fordings through icy streams and stiff climbs to high passes bestrewn with clumps of edelweiss. To the north, the rolling steppes of Central Asia stretched illimitably far away while always ahead, range upon range of huge snow mountains broke the southern horizon. Neil, the evergreen Highland stalker and fittest of the Brits, was first to spot the bleached horns of an *ovis poli* while Bill, always nonchalant, looked as if he were strolling across a grouse moor. Peter, who had seldom before taken a proper holiday from farming his Fife estate, marvelled at everything like an excited schoolboy while John and I stomped stolidly on. At the Sary-Djaz camp, the Russian lads tried, unsuccessfully, to snare a marmot for supper. A Kyrgyz shepherd shot one instead. It tasted like rabbit.

Despite the occasional cloudburst, the weather had held fine up to day seven and the river crossings had given us no real trouble. But that same evening, we reached the upper Tuz River to find it in spate. Dima rigged up a safety rope, but when it came my turn to wade across, the current swept me off my feet. I managed to hang on to the rope, but my precious Exakta camera got a soaking. That night, it snowed heavily for the first time and the following morning we ate a cheerless breakfast squatting in the snow. Dima now led the way up the narrowing Tuz Valley to its 4,001 metre pass from where the Tien Shan burst into view as an uninterrupted wall of rock and ice rising sheer from the trench of the Inylchek Valley. Dead ahead, the sight of the 5,697 metre Nansen Peak's glistening flanks, corniced ridges and pendulous ice cliffs was as dramatic and unexpected as the view eastwards up the sixty-four-kilometre-long Inylchek glacier. At this juncture, the glacier appeared to have split the main Tien Shan chain into two, 6,000-metre-high parallel ranges flanking either side. Fleetingly, it reminded me of New Zealand's Tasman Glacier, but this one was on an altogether vaster scale, too savage and outlandish to be beautiful. Apparently, were the Inylchek Glacier to melt, its floodwaters would inundate much of Kyrgyzstan.

Late that afternoon, we reached Kontash Camp perched atop a lateral moraine overlooking the Inylchek river. This was a critical moment, for the camp marked the start point for the three-day march up the Inylchek Glacier that was intended to take us to the Khan Tengri Base Camp. Dima had deliberately chosen this 'classic' route rather than the daily helicopter shuttle from the Maydahdyr airstrip further down the valley, for although the helicopter flight would have saved us three-days' hard graft, it would have lost the venture. From this vantage point, the glacier's dirty snout was clearly visible across the valley, but I could see no way of getting across to it for the river below, a raging, roiling flood several hundred metres wide, was tossing huge boulders about as if they were pebbles.

Dima's normally expressionless face betrayed a trace of emotion.

'This is not good,' he muttered to John. 'We have come at a very bad time. The ice dam high up has burst. The river could take days to settle.'

Throughout most of the year, the two great arms of the Inylchek Glacier are ice locked in an immense glacial lake far up the valley. However, in August, summer part-melt causes the pent-up water to break through the lake's containing walls and sweep everything before it. Dima spent the remains of the day reconnoitring an alternative route up the near-vertical flanks of our side of the valley but returned long after dark defeated.

Was this journey's end? Semenov had been the first man to discover the Inylchek Glacier, but hadn't gone further than its snout. It was another forty-six years later, in 1903, when the Austrian explorer Merzbacher forced his way up the glacier with a team of Tyrolean guides and Cossack escorts to fulfil his lifetime ambition of finding the fabulous Khan Tengri, the 'Lord of Heaven', then thought to be the highest mountain in the range. During his journey up the glacier, he discovered the twin lakes that now bear his name and the secret of the great flood.

That evening, none of us would have given odds for crossing that river, yet by 7 a.m. the following morning it had dropped three metres and the Germans who had trekked up from Maydahdyr late last night were already wading across it knee deep. We followed after a decent interval on stepping-stones and reached the top of the glacier's snout within an hour. However, any hopes of finding an easy way up the glacier were dashed the moment we took stock. Hemmed in on either side by giant ice peaks and disintegrating rock ridges, the glacier's surface was a ruptured wasteland of moraine slag heaps dissected by miniature canyons carved through the ice by fast-running melt streams. It took another three hours to reach the vestige of a track that made a precarious traverse along the steep lateral moraine on the south side of the valley. We met a yak train on its way down. Yaks don't give way. We did.

Eleven hours on, we stumbled into Zelena Poliana, an idyllic campsite surrounded by mountains with the dam of the lower Merzbacher lake faintly visible up one branch of the valley. Popular with both herdsmen and trekkers, the site's grassy swards were dotted about with grazing yaks and tents, though none were going any further up the Inylchek Glacier. Henceforth, we would be on our own grinding up its unforgiving moraines like tiny insects. Next day, for the first time in years, my artificial hip was giving me real trouble and when Bill nobly offered to carry some of my kit, I didn't refuse. On that second night, I was so tired that after tumbling into the tent I shared with Neil, I fell asleep without even noticing the sharp rocks directly under my sleeping bag. A foot of snow fell overnight; the glacier seemed endless and when the moraine gave way to bare ice, Dima was forced to make long detours to avoid gaping crevasses. Both his rope and the ice screw were now coming in handy and he reduced the intervals between rest stops from fifty to thirty minutes. At lunch, normally a long-drawn-out affair, no one had any inclination to chat so we just wolfed down raw chunks of bacon fat.

The Tien Shan Base Camp came up late on the third evening as the sun sank behind the mountains to the west. More like a village, it was packed with over a hundred climbers of every nationality living in semi-permanent tents set up on wooden platforms. None were going spare so we camped once again on the moraine. With beer going at $5 a can, our cups were full enough but when John bought an additional three bottles of vodka to celebrate safe arrival, I correctly anticipated that another $5 spent in the camp's three-compartment sauna next day would go some way to alleviate a monumental hangover.

Dominating the head of the glacier, rose the gleaming marble pyramid of Khan Tengri. At 6,995 metres high, this tremendous mountain dwarfs the Matterhorn by another 2,518 metres and like it, was for long reckoned to be inaccessible. Though first climbed from the north in 1931, the ascent of its much harder, scimitar-shaped south-west ridge which directly faced our camp had to wait until 1964. A couple of Polish climbers told me that this was now the 'normal' route thanks to 1,200 metres of fixed rope supposedly reducing its climbing grade to IV. To me, it didn't look a bit like that. The Kyrgyz call it the 'Blood Mountain' because it glows red at sunset. Climbers give it a somewhat similar name, though for different reasons. Only a few days before our arrival, a party of ten had been killed when a sérac wall collapsed. Due south, beyond the scarred surface of the main branch of the Inylchek Glacier, rose the massive bulk of Pik Pobeda. At 7,439 metres, this brute of a mountain, 2,000 kilometres north-west of Everest, is the highest in the Tien Shan and was first climbed by a Russian team in 1956. It is intensely cold at all times of the year and prone to unexpected and violent storms that usually prove fatal.

On the morning of 14 August, the twelve-strong Dostuk party was waiting anxiously on the glacier along with sixteen other hopefuls for the daily helicopter to arrive. The moment it touched down, there was an unseemly race across the ice to secure places. In the event, we needn't have bothered as neither seats nor seatbelts were provided and everyone had to squeeze up together along the plane's bare-metal fuselage. As the helicopter's engine roared and the rotor blades whirled, I was not the only one mouthing a silent prayer as it skimmed across the surface of the glacier trying to gain height. And then, instead of flying down the valley, it headed direct for the mountainside. John Ducker, no stranger to Russian air travel, gasped in horror with his hands over his face as the helicopter sheared away with barely fifty metres to spare. Further down the valley, the pilot picked up four Kyrgyz hunters and two dead ibex, but by then I had given up worrying about overloading having long passed the corpses of several helicopters that littered the upper glacier. Only later did I learn that we had been lucky. The following year, twenty-seven members of a German scientific expedition only just survived when this same helicopter crashed seconds after take off.

Safely back at Tosor Camp a day later, Nikolai joined the party for a farewell supper at which the Russian contingent at last let their hair down. To keep the British flag flying, I had brought with me copies of *Hearts of Oak, Men of Harlech* and *The Volga Boatman* in the original Chaliapin version. None of the Russians had heard of either the song or Chaliapin, but after my rendition Victor broke his silence and, after complimenting me for being 'veray cultured', reeled off a long list of the English classics he had read. He must have understood everything we had said from the outset. This was another glimpse into the enigmatic recesses of the Russian character, yet the stoicism and sheer toughness of our porters left me in no doubt why Russia had defeated both Hitler and Napoleon before him.

At Bishkek, Nicolai's last hurrah was to take the Brits to a swish restaurant where two ravishing Kyrgyz girls in traditional costume danced like Scheherazades as they sang to their own instrumental accompaniment. Flushed with champagne and brandy, Nicolai made a succession of tearful speeches before the evening closed with hugs, kisses and protestations of eternal friendship. When we got back to England, I told my son-in-law's Russian mother, a survivor of the siege of Leningrad, about our trek up the Inylchek Glacier and the Khan Tengri Base Camp.

'Oh that place!' she said, with a dismissive shrug. 'I once spent a fortnight there as a Young Stakhanovite doing ski training!'

TAJIKISTAN

For a complete change from Central Asia and as something unusual to do in Europe the year after the Tien-Shansky trek, I remembered Ronald Naar's recommendation that Bulgaria's Rila and Pirin Ranges were well worth a visit. During Bulgaria's communist regime these mountains had been popular with holidaying comrades who had been well served by a network of guarded mountain huts. By 2005, the guardians had left for more gainful employment and the huts were in bad need of repair. Nonetheless, colourful local bed and breakfast hostelries offered us warm hospitality and at Melnik, the local wines were more than just drinkable for they had been famous in Roman times. The traverse of both these ranges gave excellent trekking and peaks such as Malyovitsa, Musala (the highest in Europe between the Alps and Caucasus) and Vihren offer good rock climbing as well as enjoyable scrambling. However, with the years slipping by, I was determined to make another visit to Central Asia while I was still able and so, when the Royal Society for Asian Affairs (RSAA) advertised a 'wilderness trek' to Tajikistan in 2012, I joined it.

What is now Tajikistan only became a recognisable state after the First World War and, like those other former Soviet central Asian republics, suffered the same horrors of Bolshevik collectivisation, forced deportation, famine and mass emigration. Yet it differs in one significant respect from the others in that eighty per cent of Tajiks are of Iranian, rather than Turkic stock, and still speak a form of Farsi. They also hark back to ancient Iran as the source of their culture and heritage to the extent of renaming their highest mountain – formerly Stalin and Kommunisma – Somoni after a tenth-century Iranian ruler.

The Iranian connection certainly appealed to me, though even more was the prospect of seeing something of Tajikistan's superb mountains, which encompass most of the Pamirs.

Tajikistan was once a prosperous nodal point on the Silk Roads, but with no natural resources, save for water, it remains the poorest of all Central Asia's states and has become a conduit for Afghan heroin. Tourism, particularly in the form of mountaineering, is beginning to make some difference to the economy but in 2012, the only major British mountaineering expedition to have been there since the Russian Revolution was John Hunt's 1962 Russo-British Pamir expedition.

Things had been very different in Victorian times when the Pamirs were the principal arena of the 'great game'. For this contest, the British tended to field pundits and political officers while the Russians leavened their teams with distinguished scientists. Prominent amongst these were Alexei and Olga Fedchenko who discovered the eponymous, seventy-kilometre Fedchenko Glacier, the longest in the world outside the polar regions. Also, the botanist Grumm-Grshimailo who collected 32,000 different plant species, while outstanding Russian soldiers/explorers included the Polish aristocrat Captain Grombchevsky who explored 7,860 miles of previously unknown territory, and Colonel Yanov whose famous confrontation with Francis Younghusband on the wastes of Bozai Gumbaz might have triggered the mobilisation of Britain's Indian Army had not wiser counsel prevailed.

The RSAA team of twelve which flew into Tajikistan's capital Dushanbe on 28 June 2012 included one artist, two seventy-plus-year-old lady botanists and three judges, one of whom, Alan Pardoe, an old friend from way back, maintained the highest judicial standards by travelling throughout the trek with four pairs of Jermyn Street silk pyjamas. Some members chose to ignore their insurer's strictures about their having full helicopter rescue cover and most were light on mountaineering experience. Fortunately, tentage, fuel, food, equipment (as well as the occasional exhausted member) were carried by sturdy Kyrgyz horses.

My old South Arabian chum Stewart Hawkins had recommended Surat Toimastov as the trek's guide and Surat's programme was based on one that he and Stewart had undertaken together four years before as part of Stewart's quest to locate the stone cairn in the Garmo Valley which Russian climbers had erected as a memorial to Wilfred Noyce and Robin Smith who had perished on Garmo Peak during John Hunt's 1962 Pamirs expedition. Stewart had been taught by Noyce at Charterhouse and has since repaid that debt with his fine biography of Noyce *Far, Far The Distant Peak* published in 2014.

Surat, a passionate naturalist and photographer, adhered to the Babi sect of Islam whose principal tenet is the promotion of tolerance worldwide. His mysterious disappearances to commune with nature were disconcerting, but only he could have negotiated half-decent terms with our hard-nosed Kyrgyz horsemen escort. His sometimes wayward route along the fringes of the Peter the Great Range steered us through rolling alpine pastures dotted with the sheep, cattle, donkeys and horses and frequently led to elaborately decorated yurts of Kyrgyz families who pressed upon us lavish spreads of bread, yoghurt, cheese, butter and honey. The weather remained almost flawless throughout and the air temperature was ideal for trekking. Camps were sited against stunning mountain backdrops and were usually adjacent to lakes in which some bathed while lammergeiers, Egyptian and griffon vultures cruised lazily above.

Peak bagging was never a serious agenda item, though four of us did climb one unremarkable virgin summit overlooking the Karashura Valley for some tantalising glimpses of the many unclimbed ice peaks that throng the hidden heart of the Pamirs. Another trek highlight was the superb lakeside camp on the Tipchak Plateau where Rickmer Rickmers had based his first Pamir expedition in 1913 and from which the whole team achieved a collective 3,750-metre high-point, leaving Bill Blackburne and Surat to push on to over 4,000 metres where they spotted a snow leopard. Other excitements included some near-duckings when less agile members forded fast-flowing melt-streams on foot and horse-back and when the whole caravan had to negotiate a vertiginous landslip above the Zen i Zamin River, a glacial torrent which had previously unhorsed and almost drowned Stewart Hawkins when he had passed this same way.

If there was one disappointment it was our failure to complete the last leg from Puli Sangin to Sanjar across the Kaftar Pass, an ancient trade route followed by both Grombchevsky and Yanov a hundred years before. Our reconnaissance party did reach a high vantage point to assess conditions, but on finding the pass heavily snowed-up decided that to attempt this passage with a largely inexperienced and ill-equipped party could be disastrous if the weather turned. That decision was vindicated the following day after we had returned to the Karashura Valley, for a violent storm then broke at precisely the time we might otherwise have been crossing the Kaftar Pass.

The two-day journey back to Dushanbe, involving one white-knuckle, helter-skelter 1,850-metre descent from the Sagir Baset Pass to Kalai-Khumb by a superbly engineered 1914 Russian military road, was memorable for the drive through the Panj River's stupendous gorge. At the bottom of its sky-scraping cliffs, incised by defiles and overlooked by tottering rock buttresses, an im-probable dirt road, hewn out and blasted through the mountainside, threaded its way through billions of tons of fallen debris as it clung desperately to the banks of the mighty river. At times, Afghanistan lay barely a hundred metres across the roiling, eddying waters of this irresistible force of nature, yet it might have been a mile away. And it was fitting that our Tajik adventure should have ended on the banks of this, the main tributary of the Oxus, whose true source had once been as elusive as that of the Nile. Appropriate too, that its discoverer had been Britain's most illustrious great gamer, George Nathaniel Curzon, who had spent fifty-four days in the saddle with his back supported by a steel corset, to achieve the prize that earned him the Royal Geographical Society's gold medal. Curzon had described the Oxus as 'that great parent stream of humanity ... whose waters tell of forgotten peoples and whisper of unknown lands'. I too, was beginning to hear whispers, though pointing in another direction. The Tajikistan trek had been a particularly congenial one for companionship counts more than mere achievement. It was also the summa-tion of my trekking days and marked another crossroads with a sign that seemed to say 'Do not outlive your mountain dream'.

DISTANT
A MOUNTAINEER'S
SNOWS
ODYSSEY

BIBLIOGRAPHY

GENERAL

Band, G. (2006). *Summit: 150 Years of the Alpine Club.* London: Collins.

Douglas, E. (2011). *Mountaineers.* Dorling Kindersley with The Alpine Club & Royal Geographical Society.

Huxley, J. (1954). *From An Antique Land.* Parrish.

Longstaff, T. (1950). *This My Voyage.* London: John Murray.

Lunn, A. (1957). *A Century of Mountaineering.* New South Wales: Allen & Unwin.

Noyce, W., & McMorrin, I. (1969). *World Atlas of Mountaineering.* Nelson.

Winthrop-Young, G. (1949) *Mountaincraft.* London: Methuen.

THE ALPS

Bonus, A. (1925). *Where Hannibal Passed.* London: Methuen.

De Beer, G. (1955). *Alps & Elephants.* London: Geoffrey Bles Limited.

Evans, C. (1956). *On Climbing.* London: Museum Press.

Irving, R.L.G. (1939). *The Alps.* London: Batsford.

Kugy, J. (1934). *Alpine Pilgrimage.* London: John Murray.

Longstaff, T. (1950) *This My Voyage.* London: John Murray.

Smith, I. (2011). *In the Shadow of the Matterhorn.* Herefordshire: Carreg.

Stephen, L. (1894). *The Playground of Europe.* London: Longmans Green.

Whymper, E. (1900). *Scrambles Amongst the Alps.* London: Murray.

ANTIPODES: AUSTRALIA & NEW ZEALAND

Bowie, N. (1969). *Mike Bowie.* Auckland: Reed.

Du Faur, F. (1915). *The Conquest of Mount Cook.* New South Wales: Allen & Unwin.

Green, The Revd. W.S. (1883). *The High Alps of New Zealand.* London: Macmillan.

Harris, G. & Hasler, G. (1971). *Land Apart: The Mount Cook Alpine Region,* Auckland: Reed.

Harding, J. (1974). Antipodean Ventures I. *Alpine Journal,* vol. 78, pp. 28–33

Harding, J. (1976). Antipodean Ventures II. *Alpine Journal,* vol. 80, pp. 100–107

Harding, J. (1977). Antipodean Ventures III. *Alpine Journal,* vol. 81, pp. 55–64

Harding, J. (1990). Tasmania Overland. *Alpine Journal,* vol. 94, pp. 77–84

Harding, J. (1991). Mountaineering Eden – The Southern Alps. *Alpine Journal,* vol. 95, pp. 98–103

Moorhead, A. (1966). *The Fatal Impact.* London: Hamish Hamilton.

Wilson, J. (1968). *Aorangi.* Christchurch: Whitcombe & Tombs.

ARABIA

Botting, D. (1958). *Island of the Dragon's Blood.* London: Hodder & Stoughton.

Hamilton, R.A.B. The Master of Belhaven. (1949). *The Kingdom of Melchior.* London: John Murray.

Harding, J. (2009). *Roads to Nowhere. A South Arabian Odyssey.* London: Arabian Publishing.

CENTRAL ASIA & HIMALAYAS

Hawkins, S. (2014). *Far, Far the Distant Peak.* Curbans.

Evans, C. (1956). *Kanchenjunga.* London: Hodder & Stoughton.

Freshfield, D. (1903). *Round Kanchenjunga.* London: Arnold.

Hopkirk, P. (1990). *The Great Game.* London: John Murray.

Middleton, R., & Thomas. H. (2012). *Tajikistan.* Hong Kong: Odyssey.

White, J.C. (1992). *Sikkim & Bhutan.* India: Sagar House.

CORSICA

Carrington, D. (2008). *Granite Island.* London: Penguin.

Harding, J. (1995). Corsican Retrospective. *Alpine Journal,* vol. 99, pp. 125–130

EAST AFRICA
(MOUNT KENYA & RUWENZORI)

Benuzzi, F. (1952). *No Picnic on Mount Kenya.* London: Kimber.

Busk, D. (1957). *Fountains in the Sun.* Connecticut: Parrish.

Dutton, E.A. (1929). *Kenya Mountain.* London: Jonathan Cape.

Jeal, T. (2011). *Explorers of the Nile.* London: Faber & Faber.

Prettejohn, M. (2012). *Endless Horizons,* Old Africa Books

Shipton, E. (1943). *Upon That Mountain.* London: Hodder & Stoughton.

Tilman, H.W. (1937). *Snow On The Equator.* London: Bell.

Woolaston, N. (2003). *My Father Sandy.* London: Short Books

GREECE

Gage, N. (1983). *Eleni.* London: Panther.

Harding, J. (1987). Olympian Triad. *Alpine Journal,* vol. 91, pp. 136–147

Harding, J. (2001). In Praise of Greek Mountains. *Alpine Journal,* vol. 105, pp. 89–97

Hunt, J. (1978). *Life is Meeting.* London: Hodder & Stoughton.

Nikopoulos, I. (1957). *Mount Olympus.* Athens: Efstathiadis Group.

Sfikas, G. (1982). *The Mountains of Greece.* Athens: Efstathiadis Group.

Tsigakou, F-M. (1981). *The Rediscovery of Greece.* London: Thames & Hudson.

IRAN

Bobek, H., Dr. (1958). A Map of the Central Elburz. *Alpine Journal*, vol. 62, pp. 207–208

Busk, D. (1946). *The Delectable Mountains*. London: Hodder & Stoughton.

Curzon, G.N., Maquis of Kedleston. (1892). *Persia*. London: Longmans Green.

Harding, J. (1957). Cambridge Expedition to the Elburz Mountains, Iran. *Himalayan Journal*, vol. 61, pp. 112–121

Morier, J. (1897). *Haji Baba of Isfahan*. London: Lawrence & Bullen Ltd.

Mustoe, J. (1957). Contrasts in the Elburz. *The Geographical Magazine*, October.

Norton, W.J.E. (1957). Solomon's Snows. *Cambridge Mountaineering*, vol. X, pp. 44–47

Stevens, R. (1962). *The Land of the Great Sophy*. London: Methuen.

Stewart, J. (1989). *Envoy of the Raj: The Career of Sir Clarmont Skrine*. UK: Porpoise Books.

Stark, F. (1934). *The Valleys of the Assassins*. London: John Murray.

Wright, D. (2003). *Britain and Iran 1790–1980*. The Iran Society.

PYRENEES

Belloc, H. (1906). *The Pyrenees*. London: Methuen.

Fedden, R. (1962). *The Enchanted Mountains*. London: John Murray.

Harding, J. (2000). *Pyrenean High Route*. Wheathampstead: Tiercel Publishing.

Ollivier, R. (1978). *La Haute Route d'Hiver des Pyrenees*. France: Pau.

SCOTLAND

Murray, W.H. (1951). *Mountaineering in Scotland*. Darlington: Dent.

Murray, W.H. (1947). *Undiscovered Scotland*. Darlington: Dent.

SKI MOUNTAINEERING

Berruex, M. & Parmentier, M. (1981). *Les Grands Raids a Ski*. Paris: ACLA.

Cliff, P. (1987). *Ski Mountaineering*. New South Wales: Unwin Hyman.

Fedden, R. (1956). *Alpine Ski Tour*. G. P. Putnam's Sons.

Harding, J. (1998). Ski Mountaineering is Mountaineering. *Alpine Journal*, vol. 102, pp. 140–145

Lunn, A. (1925). *The Mountains of Youth*. Oxford: Oxford University Press.

Lunn, A. (1952). *The Story of Skiing*. London: Eyre & Spottiswode.

Naar, R. (1994). *Sneeuw Hoogten*. Utrecht: Bosch & Keuning.

Sheridan, G. (1987). *Tales of a Cross Country Skier*. Oxford: Oxford Illustrated Press.

Sheridan, G. (2006). *Taxi to the Snowline*. White Peak Publishing.

Wyatt, C. (1952). *The Call of the Mountains*. London: Thames & Hudson.

SPAIN

Harding, J. (1988). The Picos de Europa. *Alpine Journal*, vol. 92, pp. 137–140

Harding, J. (1988). Sierra de Gredos. *Alpine Journal*, vol. 92, pp. 141–145

TURKEY

Ashenden (S. Nowill). (1954). *The Mountains of my Life*. London: Blackwoods.

Ashenden (S. Nowill). (April, 1966). Hakkari – 1965, *Blackwood's Magazine*, vol. 1806, pp. 313–318.

Bean, G. (1968). *Turkey's Southern Shore*. London: Ernest Benn.

Bryce, J. (1877). *Transcaucasia and Ararat*. London: Macmillan.

Hills, C. D. (1964). *My Travels in Turkey*. New South Wales: Allen & Unwin.

Lynch, H.F.B. (1967). *Armenia*. Khayats.

McMeekin, S. (2010). *The Berlin to Baghdad Express*. London: Allen Lane.

Percy, Lord. (1901). *The Highlands of Asiatic Turkey*. London: Arnold.

Scott, D.K. (1966). *The Cilo Dag Mountains*. The Author.

Tozer, Revd. H.F. (1881). *Turkish Armenia & Eastern Asia Minor*. London: Longmans Green.

Weir, T. (1958). Peaks & Passes in Kurdistan. *Scottish Mountaineering Club Journal*, pp. 235–244

Wigram, W., & Wigram, E. (1914). *The Cradle of Mankind*. London: A & C Black Ltd.

Williams, G. (1972). *Eastern Turkey, A Guide & History*. London: Faber.

INDEX

INDEX

DISTANT
A MOUNTAINEER'S
SNOWS
ODYSSEY